Studia Fennica
Historica 9

The Finnish Literature Society was founded in 1831 and has from the very beginning engaged in publishing. It nowadays publishes literature in the fields of ethnology and folkloristics, linguistics, literary research and cultural history.

The first volym of Studia Fennica series appeared in 1933.

Since 1992 the series has been devided into three thematic subseries: Ethnologica, Folkloristica and Linguistica. Two additional subseries were formed in 2002, Historica and Litteraria.

In addition to its publishing activities the Finnish Literature Society maintains a folklore archive, a literature archive and a library.

Medieval History Writing and Crusading Ideology

Edited by Tuomas M. S. Lehtonen
and Kurt Villads Jensen
with Janne Malkki and Katja Ritari

Finnish Literature Society • Helsinki

Publication reviewed by experts
appointed by the Finnish Historical Society.

Medieval history – crusader –
historiography – Baltic Sea Region

ISBN 951-746-662-5
ISSN 1458-526X

www.finlit.fi/books

Tammer-Paino Oy
Tampere 2005

Contents

CCCM   *Corpus Christianorum Continuatio Mediaevalis.* Turnhout 1966–.

CCSL   *Corpus Christianorum Series Latina.* Turnhout 1953–.

CSEL   *Corpus Scriptorum Ecclesiasticorum Latinorum.* Vienna 1866–.

DD   *Diplomatarium Danicum.* Det Danske Sprog- og Litteraturselskab, København 1938–.

DMP   *Documentos medievais portugueses.* Academia Portuguesa da História, Lisboa 1940–.

DS   *Diplomatarium Suecanum.* Stockholm 1829–.

EC   *Epistulae et chartae ad historiam primi belli spectantes.* H. Hagenmeyer (ed.), Innsbruck 1901.

HER   *English Historical Review.*

FMU   *Finlands medeltidsurkunder*, vol. I–VIII. Helsingfors 1910–1935.

HGL   *Histoire Générale de Languedoc*, vol.1–16. C. Devic & J. Vaissete (ed.), Toulouse 1872–1892.

HSH   *Handlingar rörande Skandinaviens historia* vol.1–40, Stockholm 1816–1860.

HZ   *Historische Zeitschrift.*

JMH   *Journal of Medieval History.*

JVS   *Jómsvikinga saga.* Ó. Halldórsson (ed.), Reykjavík 1969.

KLNM   *Kulturhistorisk leksikon for nordisk middelalder*, vol 1–23 Copenhagen 1956–1978.

KS   *Kirkehistoriske Samlinger.*

LM   *Lexikon des Mittelalters*, vol.1–9. Turnhout 1977–1999.

MGH   *Monumenta Germaniae historica inde ab anno Christi quingentesimo usque ad annum millesimum et quingentesimum auspiciis societatis aperiendis fontibus rerum Germanicarum medii aevi.* G. H. Pertz et al. (ed.). Hannover 1826–.

MGH Ep.   MGH *Epistolae.*

MGH SRG   MGH *Scriptores Rerum Germanicarum.*

MGH SS   MGH *Scriptores.*

N1L   *Novgorodskaia pervaia letopis' starshego i mladshego izvo-dov*, Moskva1950.

NSEOD   *The New Shorter English Oxford Dictionary.* Oxford 1993.

PG   *Patrologiae Cursus Completus, Series Graeca*, vol. 1-161. J.-P. Migne. Paris 1857–1886

PL   *Patrologiae cursus completus... series latinae*, vol. 1–221. J. P. Migne (ed.). Paris 1844–1864.

RHC   *Recueil des historiens des croisades. Historiens occidentaux*, Académie des Inscriptions et Belles-Lettres, vol. 1–5. Paris 1844–1895.

RHG   *Recueil des historiens des Gaules et la France*, vol. 1–24. Paris 1737–1904.

Rule   *The Rule of the Templars: The French Text of the Rule of the Order of the Knights Templar.* J. M. Upton-Ward (transl.), Woodbridge 1992.

SC   *Sources Chretiénnes.* Paris 1941–.

SD   *Svenskt Diplomatarium* = DS

SM   *Scriptores Minores Historiæ Danicæ Medii Ævi*, vol. I–II. M. C. Gertz (ed.), København 1922.

SMK   *Svenska medeltidens rimkrönikor*, G. E. Klemming (ed.), Stockholm 1867–1888.

ST   *Sveriges traktater med främmande magter*, O. S. Rydberg (ed.), 1, Stockholm 1877.

SVS   *Sverris saga etter Cod. AM 327 4°.* G. Indrebø (ed.), Kristiania 1920.

VSD   *Vitae sanctorum danorum.* M. C. Gertz (ed.). København 1908–1912.

Scandinavia and the Baltic Sea Region

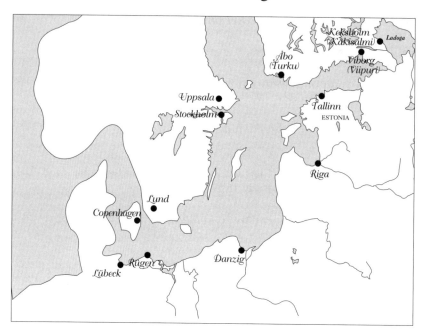

Medieval Europe and Mediterranea

TUOMAS M. S. LEHTONEN & KURT VILLADS JENSEN

Preface

The origins of this book go back to a colloquium and research workshop entitled *Medieval Historiography and the Crusades* held in Rome at the Institutum Romanum Finlandiae and the Romanum Institutum Danicum in January 2001. The imperative question was to examine how the crusading ideology was formulated in medieval historiography and how the crusading movement affected Christianity and the world beyond. The second main theme was the spread of the crusading movement to Northern Europe, especially Scandinavia and the Baltic Sea area. Northerners not only participated in the crusades in the Holy Land, but also learned and were inspired to create and take part in a new crusading movement within the Baltic Sea region itself. The relationship between the crusades to Jerusalem and those in the North must be of fundamental importance to understanding the dynamics that created history, both locally and in a general European context, but this relation itself has seldom been the object of thoroughgoing research; on the contrary, the considerable scholarship on both the North and the South has been pursued in isolation. The colloquium held in Rome was the first step towards bringing people working with these two areas together. The contributions from this meeting have now been complemented with some chapters not presented at the original colloquium.

Divided into three parts, this volume opens with the different forms of and reactions to the crusading ideology. The importance of ideology as a driving motivation for the crusaders has again been recognized in international studies since the 1970s, and its impact is also now felt in Scandinavian research environments. Arnved Nedkvitne examines how crusading ideas were received in Norway and what inspired the first Norwegian crusaders to venture into the Holy Land. The crusading ideology was not an established ideology but underwent a series of changes and transformations from the early stages up to the late Middle Ages. Janus Møller Jensen focuses on the emergence of the early crusading concepts. We also need to ask whether the Crusades were an anachronistic construct or whether they were seen as a specific category of Christian action. Samu Niskanen's analysis of the critique of the crusades by

St. Anselm is linked to these questions. Tuomas M. S. Lehtonen analyses the monumental historical work by William of Tyre and his explanations of the crusaders' initial success and later setbacks, while Ane Lise Bysted puts forward twelfth-century theological arguments for the crusading movement. The justification for crusading was also important to the early mendicant movement, especially St. Francis, who sought in different ways to resolve the contradiction between Christian charity and violent crusading. St. Francis also adapted contemporary ideas of imagination in creating a new Bethlehem and the first Christmas crib in Greccio, a small Umbrian village, as an alternative to peregrination to Jerusalem. Ritva Palmén analyses this attempt in the context of the theories of mind and imagination in twelfth-century theological mysticism. St. Francis' action during the fourth crusade is examined by Pauli Annala. Futher on, the emergence of the myth of the Three Magi, its relation to the Crusades and its spread to the North is examined by Lars Bisgaard.

The second part moves on to examine the crusading ideology and its impact upon society in a broader context – through its relation to violence, its portrayal of the enemies, and its representations in the policy and construction of the Danish crown and royal mythology. Henrik Janson analyses Adam of Bremen's historical work and its interpretation of the enemies of Christianity, while Tuomas Heikkilä scrutinizes the pogroms of the First Crusade and their ideological background. Sini Kangas considers the historical writing of the First Crusade, focusing on the representation and explanations of violence and its relation to the Salvation. The crusading movement, which also helped to adapt the new idea of knighthood in Scandinavia, is analysed by Björn Bandlien in the context of Norwegian knighthood and its relation to the Templars. Vivian Etting then analyses the Crusades, pilgrimage and royal policy in Denmark. Kurt Villads Jensen compares the two Atlantic crusading states, Portugal and Denmark, and their ideological formation in relation to the crusading movement.

The Northern Crusades in the Baltic Sea region are discussed in the third part as seen through contemporary sources and modern historical writing. This also includes dealing with some of the impacts of the Crusades in Russia and even farther east in Mongolia. The essays in this section show how the general idea of crusading was applied to the Northern areas and frequently resembles in its details the Mediterranean crusades, as well as demonstrate how Scandinavian scholars have often neglected this aspect in modern history writing. The early chronicles of the Livonian mission are discussed by Carsten Selch Jensen. In analysing the Chronicle of Henry of Livonia, Torben K. Nielsen highlights the representations of pagans and their conversion to the Christian faith. Barbara Bombi examines the activities of Pope Innocent III in promoting missionary work in Livonia, while Thomas Lindkvist turns to the late medieval Swedish chronicles and their use of crusading ideology. Modern historiography and the interpretations of the alleged Swedish crusades to the Finnish coast fall under the critical gaze of John Lind, and the Danish role in the crusades both to Livonia and to Finland is examined by Iben Fonnesberg Schmidt. Mari Isoaho turns her attention to Russia and the creation of the myth of

Alexander Nevskiy as the protector of the Eastern Church. Finally, Antti Ruotsala discusses the papal and other attempts to build an anti-Muslim alliance with the Mongols.

This volume and the research workshop at Rome in 2001 were set in motion in February 1999, when Kurt Villads Jensen and John Lind, leaders of the Danish research project on the crusading movement and its impact on the Nordic countries, landed on Finnish soil. They were met by a Finnish research project led by Tuomas M. S. Lehtonen on medieval intellectual history and historiography. The seminar at the Renvall Institute, University of Helsinki, initiated innovative Danish-Finnish co-operation which was soon expanded to other Nordic countries and international fields. The research workshop was organised in Rome to gather the researchers and PhD students within these projects and other historians at the Finnish and Danish Institutes. The structure of the colloquium and the workshop is repeated in this volume, which contains extensive research articles as well as shorter accounts of work in progress. All contributions have been refereed.

We wish to thank both the Institutum Romanum Finlandiae and its director Dr. Christian Krötzl and Romanum Institutum Danicum and its director Dr. Gunver Skytte for their warm welcome and the facilities that made the colloquium and workshop possible. We would also like to thank the Finnish Historical Society and the Finnish Literature Society for accepting and refereeing our book in their prestigious series and for all their editorial help. Last but not least, we would like to thank Janne Malkki and Katja Ritari and Roderick McConchie for their considerable skill in editing the book and revising and polishing the English.

KURT VILLADS JENSEN

Introduction

The crusades began with the famous sermon of Pope Urban II at Clermont on the 27th November 1095. His call for help for the Eastern
Christians and his promises of spiritual benefits to the participants, even
martyrdom if they fell in the battle against the infidel, was met with an
instant and overwhelming response. Much more, probably, than the pope
could ever have imagined. Preparations for the expedition began immediately and, from the early spring months of 1096, many thousands of
Western Europeans began the long march towards the Holy Land – perhaps
as many as a hundred thousand or more. After immense difficulty and
hardship, the greatly reduced army succeeded in taking Jerusalem in mid
July 1099, more than three years later.[1] It was a conquest that contemporary Christian sources described as extremely bloody and understood it in
the light of the Bible's descriptions of cleansing the holy city of evil.[2]

Medieval historiography must have begun in Jerusalem on the late
Sunday afternoon of the 17th July when fighting had ceased and the city
was completely in the control of the Christians. What had actually happened? What did it mean for the future? In spite of the long journey and
the expressed aim of conquering Jerusalem, the crusaders do not seem
to have had any clear notion of what they actually wanted to do with the
city after the conquest. Some suggested establishing a kind of theocratic
state, perhaps directly under the pope. Soon, however, the serious leaders
gathered to elect Godfrey of Bouillon as the *Advocatus Sancti Sepulchri*,
the Defender of the Holy Grave. The uncertainty about the practicalities of
organising a city government indicate that the crusade was conducted in an
intensely religious atmosphere, for some perhaps even in an apocalyptic
expectation of the immediate return of Christ to take over the liberated
city. Direct divine intervention to help the crusaders and their feeling of
doing God's will were fundamental elements in the very first histories of
the crusade, some of which were begun by eyewitnesses in the very first
months after the conquest. Their interpretation of what had happened was
summed up in the loud and spontaneous outburst that these historians put
into the mouths of those who had heard the sermon of Pope Urban: *Dieu
le vult, Dieu le vult* - God wills it.[3]

Very soon, however, other explanations were added, and God was replaced by man. This has been showed in a convincing study by Veronica Epp who compares the different versions by Fulcher of Chartres, the first of which was written shortly after the conquest, while later revisions were made into the 1120s. 'With the help of God' of the first version was replaced by formulations such as 'because of the ingenuity of Prince Baldwin.' Epp has suggested that these changes may be explained as an attempt to stress man's free will and ability to act against contemporary ideas about the unchangeable course of history. Another explanation is, however, clearly recognizable in Foulques and others of the early crusade historians, that it was as their obligation to depict the conquest as the result of the efforts of their secular masters while it was also a combined Christian enterprise involving individuals from all over the Latin world.

Most of the narratives stem from French areas, at least those that have been most widely circulated and have formed the later historiographical tradition, and it is possible to follow closely how the historians solved the paradox of presenting a joint Christian expedition as specifically French. The earliest history is probably the anonymous *Gesta Francorum,* written by a member of the contingent of the Norman ruler Bohemund before 1100. The crusade was initiated by the sermon of Pope Urban II, which immediately created a major movement in all regions of France, and the French decided to follow Christ and had crosses sewn on their shoulders. Three groups set out on different routes to Constantinople and the Holy Land – after which the terminology begins to become complicated. The *franci* in the *Gesta Francorum* first means the inhabitants of France, but it then describes how they consisted of people from France, Southern France, Flanders, and Southern Italy. *Franci* means French, but also those following the French. Since later in his narrative the author distinguished between French and Normans, he was obviously aware of the difference between these groups, so that the shift in meaning of the word *franci* in the opening chapters is deliberate. It reflects his concept of the crusade as being a French movement which was joined by Norman and Flemish princes. Other participants are not mentioned in the introduction. This is also the case with the other chroniclers who had participated in the First Crusade themselves or came immediately after the conquest, such as Fulcher of Chartres, Peter Tudebode and Raymond of Aguilers.

Albert of Aachen, who wrote shortly after the First Crusade, had a considerably broader concept of the crusade. Inspired by the sermon of Pope Urban, he tells us in the introduction to his work that the barons swore to take the holy way to Jerusalem, to the Sepulchre of the Lord. As a sign of divine approval, the earth trembled in an enormous earthquake 'which was nothing but the marching legions form different kingdoms', from France, but also from Lothringen, Germany, England, and Denmark. In his introduction, therefore, Albert stressed that the movement consisted from the outset of peoples from all over the Christian world. Later historians added more and more peoples to the list of participants and emphasised the spread of the sermon. 'Who ever heard about so many princes and dukes and nobles and foot soldiers fighting without a king, without an emperor?' wrote Baldric of Bourgeuil in 1108. Baldric clearly knows of the anonymous *Gesta Francorum*, but he has chosen a very different perspective. He explained the expedition through the inspiration of the Holy Spirit, which is now introduced as the driving force behind the crusade. He continues to describe how the word of Urban spread to all Christianity. 'It came to England and the other maritime islands separated from France by the abyss of the wave-sounding sea'; and it also came to Bretagne, Gascogne, Galicia in Spain, the cities of Venice, Genoa and Pisa which provided ships for the army. Baldric understood the crusade as having a centre in France but also as including the areas on the periphery of Europe and of Christianity. All the peoples along the shores of Western Europe.

The dynamic between centre and periphery was analysed more fully by Guibert of Nogent, also in 1108. Guibert also knew of the *Gesta Francorum* and lifted a great lot of information from it, but just as Baldric did, he also attempted to describe the crusade as both a French enterprise and a general Christian movement. *Gesta dei per Francos* is the title of Guibert's work, and the French are the real heroes of his narrative. The conquest of Jerusalem was not due to military tactic as victories were in Antiquity, but to faith and strength and to French audacity and bravery, he concluded in his work written in a Northern French monastery. Guibert had already emphasized in the opening of the work how the crusade began as a mass movement without leaders. The crusaders 'were like grasshoppers that have no king but cover the whole earth with their crowds. When it is cold they do nothing, but when they are warmed by the sun' – the sun of justice – 'they begin to swarm.' The exhortation of the pope to go on crusade came to the French people alone; but the heat of the French attracted all other peoples who swarmed towards them, tried to imitate them and to communicate with them. Then follows an often-quoted and famous passage wherein Guibert describes the people coming from the remotest confines of the Ocean. 'You would see groups of Scots coming from their damp and marshy border regions, barelegged and with filthy cloaks, wild and ferocious at home but peaceful elsewhere, carrying their ridiculous old-fashioned weapons in great quantities, but they would give help to the French by their piety and devotion.' Guibert himself had seen great numbers of men from barbarian countries who could not speak any civilised language but only lifted their hands and crossed their fingers to show that they were joining the crusade, 'but they helped with their prayers.'

Not only did Guibert depict the crusading movement as being a common Christian enterprise including the periphery of Europe while still retaining a French centre, but he also introduced a new distinction between the French, who conquered Jerusalem militarily, and the barbarians of the periphery who participated and gave spiritual help but had no decisive military function in the expedition.

Guibert's distinction was imitated by later historians. One example is William of Malmesbury, who wrote in the early 1120's: 'Not only the Mediterraneans, but also those on the most remote islands and the barbarian nations were moved by love of God and left for Jerusalem after Urban's sermon. Fields were left without farmers, houses without inhabitants. The Welsh left their poaching, the Scots their familiarity with flies, the Norwegians their gorging on fish, and the Danes their continuous drinking.' Northerners participated, but they were depicted as barbarians.

To William of Malmesbury, there was a good scientific explanation for the differences between peoples, which he put into the mouth of Urban. In the very elaborated version of the sermon in Clermont, William had the pope say that nations live under different climates. Under the burning sun in the south, people dry out and have very little blood in their bodies, but they are knowing and wise. They are not good fighters, and Urban refers to the Turkish tactic of fleeing and avoiding open battles. The success of the Turks in Spain and North Africa is caused by their cunning and their use of poisoned arrows. In the cold north, in contrast, people are remote from the warmth of the sun. Because of the cold, they are big and strong, filled with blood and mighty fighters, but they are not very clever. 'But you – and here Urban is addressing the French audience – you live in the temperate zone, you do not lack prudence, and you have enough blood to show contempt for death and wounds, you are outstanding in both knowledge and strength, you go on this glorious expedition.'[4] With William of Malmesbury, the barbarisation of the northerners is made not only a question of cultural difference, but also an unavoidable and unchangeable scientific fact. It is all due to the difference in climate, an explanation that ultimately goes back to Aristotle who, however, was convinced that the Greeks lived in the temperate climate.

The understanding of the crusades proposed by Guibert and William had a long afterlife in crusading studies. It is a misleading understanding constructed to reconcile the two opposing aims of the authors, to depict the crusades as both specifically French and generally Christian. Two results are clearly recognizable. One is that historians from the Northern periphery have accepted and believed that their countries played no role in the crusading movement, many even denying that there were any from the North participating at all. This impression was reinforced by the Scandinavian Lutheran historical tradition, which dismissed crusading as a medieval, popish, and hypocritical pretext for pursuing purely political aims. It was even more reinforced by a strong pacifist political attitude among leading historians in the early twentieth century who were simply not interested in military history or anything related to war. This does not mean to say that the crusades were primarily a phenomenon of the periphery and that the French participation was negligible, but it is an explanation of the strange fact that there has been a markedly weak tradition for crusading studies in Scandinavia in spite of the few but sufficient sources, which show that the general crusading movement in the middle ages also had a profound influence upon Scandinavia.

The second result of Guibert and William's writing is that the concept of crusading has been defined, normally without further reflection, simply as the French expedition to Jerusalem and the attempts during the following two hundred years to secure the Latin presence in the Holy Land. Only fairly recently has this definition been seriously challenged and replaced by a much broader one. We will return to this later in this introduction, but first I briefly outline some major trends in crusading historiography since the Middle Ages.

Criticism of crusades existed in the middle ages, but with very few exceptions there was no criticism of crusading. Individual crusades could be accused of being led only by the prospect of gaining wealth and land, not for the conversion of the infidels or the defence of Christians. In 1147, Bishop Henry of Mähren led a crusade against Stettin and was met by the sight of crosses hanging from the city walls, put up by the inhabitants who had by then been Christianised for a generation. They directly accused the so-called crusader of being led by land hunger more than by any obligation to defend Christianity.[5] A similar criticism was raised by Helmold of Bosau in the twelfth century against the Saxon nobles and their Danish allies for trying to proclaim their expedition against Wendic tribes a crusade, which actually impeded the conversion to Christianity.[6] Other crusades could be dismissed as not genuine because of their military failure, as seems to have been the case with the second crusade to the Middle East in 1147.[7] Saint Bernard had to write in defence that the failure was actually a success because so many participated and gained an indulgence or had become martyrs, many more than would have been the case if the crusade had actually achieved its military goal. Later, in the middle of the fourteenth century, Saint Bridget from Sweden accused the Swedish king Magnus of losing the crusade against the schismatic Russians, and ascribed it to the size of Magnus's army. If he had brought fewer peoples with him, he would certainly had been victorious, but he had gathered far too many followers and thereby shown that he trusted more in his own strength than in the Lord, and had therefore lost. But it is worth stressing that such criticisms were directed towards specific crusades, not crusading in general.[8] Crusading as such was viewed positively and deemed necessary. This is the general impression of the historical writing of the Middle Ages, and it continues into the sixteenth century both in Northern and Southern Europe.

It is only with the Enlightenment period in the eighteenth century – the gothic novel, the Middle Ages as the dark ages, criticism of all kinds of religion – that crusading as such was rejected as superstitious, frivolous and political fanaticism, as Voltaire put it. The people had been misled by ambitious and cynical so-called religious leaders, be it the pope, be it Muhammad; between the two there was no difference in the view of Voltaire. Voltaire was followed by Gibbon to whom the crusades had been 'savage fanaticism', and who wrote that 'If the ninth and tenth centuries were the times of darkness, the thirteenth and fourteenth were the age of absurdity and fable.' David Hume, in 1761, called the crusades 'the most signal and durable monument to human folly that has yet appeared in any age or nation.'

Nineteenth century Romanticism reacted against this attitude toward the crusades. This was a century that shared with the eighteenth an obsession with history's progress, but crusading was normally accorded an important role in the development of mankind. 'When the light of civilization was lit in Europe – and the crusades contributed significantly to this – the states of Europe could feel secure and soon inspired their enemies with fear', the French historian J.-F. Michaud wrote in his *History of the Crusades*, published in three volumes in 1812–1817. (It was re-edited in seven volumes in 1824–1829.) If the crusades had succeeded properly, a permanent French domination over the whole of the Mediterranean would have been established, exchange of ideas and commodities would have made Europe prosper, and all would have spoken the same language, i.e. French, Michaud wrote. This did not happen for various reasons, but the crusades were no failure for that reason. On the contrary, if they had never taken place, it would have been a catastrophe and Europe would have been invaded by the Muslims. The crusades 'A revolution of society', the work of divine providence, and they always had one and the same goal: to civilize the barbarians and to unite East and West, Michaud wrote. His positive appraisal of the crusades and their contribution to civilisation was followed by Friedrich Wilken's *Geschichte der Kreuzzüge* in seven volumes (1807-32) and Charles Mills's *History of the Crusades* (1820) in only two volumes.

Michaud wrote in the period between Napoleon's conquest of Egypt in 1798 and the French occupation of Algeria in 1830, which marked the beginning of modern French colonialism. Throughout the nineteenth and the early twentieth centuries, crusading studies were greatly influenced by contemporary political discussions about the colonies, as well as reflecting contemporary administrators' considerations about simple practical matters such as how to govern a foreign people in a foreign country. Studies of the Latin administration of the Kingdom of Jerusalem were published,[9] and sources for the legal history of the Latin East were edited in great numbers.

This necessary but also somewhat dull approach was supplemented during nineteenth century Romanticism by a popular, heroic depiction of crusaders that became very widespread. The best-known examples today are certainly still sir Walter Scott's novels *The Talisman* and *Ivanhoe*, re-edited, translated, immortalised as a movie in 1952 with Elizabeth Taylor as Rebecca. They were copied shamelessly by other authors like the Dane B. S. Ingemann in his 'Historical Novels' of the first half of the nineteenth century, which are still re-edited and widely read. Scott published *Ivanhoe* in 1819 and *The Talisman* in 1825, in the years immediately after the first modern mass military killings, the Napoleonic wars. Warfare had become industrialised, and Scott and others looked back upon the Middle Ages as the great time when the individual fighter's bravery and strength decided the outcome on the battlefield, and when justice and truth and not the sheer number of people would ultimately prevail. The literary themes of Scott were also given artistic expression in wonderful heroic paintings of the nineteenth century and in a large number of poems, songs and operas with crusading themes in most if not all European countries.[10]

The nineteenth century was also the epoch when the métier of the historian became a modern, professional and academic discipline. Fundamental in this development, at least on the continent, was modern historical source criticism, primarily formulated by the Prussian professor Leopold von Ranke. He explained his methods in a series of lectures in 1837 on the sources for the First Crusade, which inspired some of his students to take up crusading history, as for example Heinrich von Sybel, who published his *Geschichte des ersten Kreuzzugs* in 1841. This work compared the earliest crusading histories of c. 1100 and shortly after and could dismiss some of them as dependent upon others and therefore of no primary interest to modern historians. Von Sybel also tried to show general tendencies in the narratives and establish the degree of 'confidence' that historians could have in each of the authors. While some of von Sybel's conclusions are valid today, others must be considered less balanced; for example, his rejection of Albert of Aachen as untrustworthy. With Ranke and his students, however, crusading studies gained a new and firmer methodological foundation than ever before.

The general academization of historical studies also led to the founding of a great number of learned societies, new journals being published, and especially renewed editing of sources based on modern philological principles. In crusading studies, the French count Paul Riant founded the prestigious *Société de l'Orient latin* in 1875 which brought crusade historians together from all parts of Europe in spite of the political crises of the time. The society began publishing a journal and supported editions of sources. After the death of Paul Riant in 1888, it had to close down in spite of the lavish financial support from Riant's considerable family fortune, which had maintained the society for years. Many other organisations took up editing of source texts. The French Academy decided to launch an edition of crusading history sources – *Receuil des historiens des croisades* – which appeared in 12 folio volumes in 1844–1906. This collection had to be interrupted before the First World War but was resumed after the Second by a number of excellent editions in the *Documents relatifs à l'histoire des croisades* series. In one sense it was a series of editions with a truly international perspective including both Occidental and Oriental authors (Greek, Arabic and Armenian). In another sense it became – because the crusades were seen as a truly French undertaking – a very national project and part of the nineteenth century's use of history to form a national identity and parallel to editorial series such as the great *Monumenta Germaniae historica* founded in 1819 by Freiherr von Stein or the many diplomataria such as *Diplomatarium norvegicum* of 1848, *Mecklenburgisches Urkundenbuch* since 1863, etc.

Fundamental changes in crusading studies are clearly recognizable in the years between the two wars in the twentieth century. This was a time generally characterised by much stronger emphasis upon social and economic explanations in history than before, and two new understandings of the crusades were introduced. One was a social change in European society, namely, the new principle of primogeniture in the late ninth and tenth centuries so that only the oldest son could inherit the family possessions. Younger sons had to wait for their older brother to die before they could marry and become masters in their own house, and many were therefore attracted by the possibilities of creating a career outside the land of their fathers in the Middle East, and so joined the crusades. The second new understanding of the crusades was economic and stressed much more than before that the Middle East was an immensely rich area compared to Europe because of long distance luxury trade and the mining of gold, all of which attracted Europeans who believed that they could quickly acquire a fortune there much easier than at home.[11]

Social and economic approaches continued the tradition in the history of administration and could convincingly be combined with broad cultural syntheses which both appraised the crusades and criticised the crusaders. A good instance of this is the very well-written three volume *History of the Crusades* by the French Orientalist Grousset that was published in 1934–1936. The first volume is subtitled 'Muslim anarchy and French monarchy', the second 'French monarchy and Muslim monarchy', and the third 'Muslim monarchy and French anarchy.'

Social and economic history dominated, but there were alternative studies focussing more on the ideological background. The best-known and most influential throughout the nineteenth century was undisputedly Carl Erdmann's 1935 study *The Origin of the Idea of the Crusade*. This has been translated from German into English – late, only in 1977 – been reprinted several times, and has increasingly become the natural starting-point for modern crusade historians, much more than the economic and social histories of Erdmann's contemporaries.

The First and Second World Wars led to understandable criticism of warfare and a search for alternative ways of conflict resolution, which had a profound influence upon crusading studies. First of all, many historians began directly to criticise the crusades and crusaders on moral and theological grounds that were no less harsh than those of the Enlightenment period. The fanaticism of the crusades was 'a sin against the Holy Spirit', Sir Steven Runciman wrote in the conclusion of his three volume *History of the Crusades* from 1951–1954. They were barbaric and irrational, he wrote. He was followed closely by R. C. Smail who published his *Crusading Warfare* in 1956. Smail considered at length whether it was actually possible to write a military history of crusading at all, because a war driven by fanaticism could not be analysed rationally, as military historians could do with other wars throughout history. Both Runciman and Smail became standard works in university teaching in America and Europe until recently, and Runciman was especially widely read outside academia.

Criticism of contemporary warfare also led to the quest for the first tolerant European who stood up against war, and who suggested other, more pacific approaches to enemies. Most influential in this genre is the study by the American historian P. A. Throop, 1940, which argues that the thirteenth century witnessed severe criticism of crusading in general and proposed an alternative, namely, the peaceful mission to the Muslims by the Mendicants. Throop was soon followed by specialists in missionary history and historians working with the cultural transfer between Islam and

Christianity through translations on the Iberian Peninsula.[12] It was not until 1984 that Throop's ideas were seriously challenged, in the Israeli historian Benjamin Z. Kedar's *Crusade and Mission. European Approaches toward the Muslims,* which became one of the most influential crusading books in the second half of the twentieth century. Kedar showed in detail that crusade and mission were not felt to be mutually exclusive in the Middle Ages, but that the same individuals very often travelled among Muslims to preach and tried to convert by example and word, and later stood on the street corners back in their European cities and used all their rhetorical skills to persuade others to go on crusade and fight the infidel. Kedar's book completely changed the idea of widespread, medieval criticism of crusading. Forty-four years of belief among historians evaporated almost overnight. This change was due to the great work by Kedar with many different sources, but it was also somehow in the air at the time. The year after Kedar and independently of him, the English historian Elizabeth Siberry published her *Criticism of Crusading, 1095–1274,* in which she had reached the same conclusion as Kedar, but to a large extent on the basis of other sources.

A fundamental link between mission and crusading was the polemical literature written primarily by mendicants in the thirteenth and fourteenth centuries. This had been difficult to access for historians because many of the texts existed only in older and rare editions or, sometimes worse, in modern, politically correct editions of the late nineteenth and early twentieth centuries, which had suppressed and simply skipped all the defamatory epithets and insults directed at the non-Christians. Historians such as Norman Daniel and R. W. Southern had already shown an interest in this kind of literature in 1960 and 1962 – an openly critical interest, but without demurring over the more indelicate expressions. Norman Daniel's work was for patient specialists, but his monumental collection of source references and paraphrases laid the foundation for Benjamin Kedar's synthesis. Southern's little book, *Western Views of Islam,* consisted of four lectures at Harvard University. It was a well-written story and accessible to everyone and became much read.

Apart from the efforts of individual scholars, crusading studies in those years became heavily influenced by the Second Vatican Council in 1960–1962. The Catholic Church formulated a new official attitude to non-Christians characterised by a more open approach and recognition of both Judaism and Islam as valuable religious ways of thinking, and the council openly distanced itself from the persecution and intolerance of the earlier history of the Church. One result of this was that many historians in Southern Europe, often members of religious orders, became interested in the medieval Church's attitude to other religions, and a number of religious and polemical treatises were edited. It was a literature that created the images of enemies that were necessary for mobilising crusaders, and a literature that formulated the theological and legal justification for fighting religious wars. The aim of these treatises was normally to argue that Islam was a devilish invention and could not have been a revealed religion because of the immoralities of both the prophet Muhammad and of the Quran and its allegedly obvious absurdities. Many of the medieval theologians also attempted to show that the Quran, if scrutinized properly, contained confirmations of Christian truths, such as the Trinity and the divinity of Jesus, but that these truths had been suppressed and explained away by Muslim theologians. Islam was thus a deliberate heresy and neither paganism nor a new religion.[13] As concerns Judaism, the polemical literature considered twelfth and thirteenth century Judaism an aberration from classical Old Testament Judaism, a blasphemous modernity and therefore also a heresy, if not against Christianity then against the Christological understanding of the Old Testament. The polemical literature was a refutation of Islam and Judaism, but was very often also presented as an attempt to argue with Muslims and Jews and to convince them of the truth of Christianity by using arguments from their own religious books and from the new, Aristotelian logic. Whether these arguments have ever been presented to living members of the other religions has been much discussed by modern scholars, but in any case the declared missionary aim of the texts ensured that the authors could freely express themselves and discuss the new and much disputed logic in a medium that was orthodox *per se*, without being accused of attempting to supplant revelation with Aristotle. The modern editions of these texts after 1962 have sometimes had a clearly apologetic aim and attempted to show that the Church in the Middle Ages was also engaged in peaceful mission, but they have provided a firm and scholarly textual basis for crusading studies no matter how we should interpret the texts themselves. They also show clearly that a number of medieval theologians actually studied the other religions and often made the great effort of learning Hebrew and Arabic to consult the religious texts in the original language, and that they strove hard to achieve a better understanding of both Islam and Judaism.[14]

Much less studied by modern crusade historians is the knightly literature, which is equally polemical and must have played an even greater role in creating images of the enemy and mobilising crusaders. The depiction of Muslims here differs greatly from that of the theologians. Muslims were idolaters worshipping a silver statue of Muhammad, or who believed in a perverse kind of Trinity of Muhammad, Apollo and a strange figure, Tergevan. Their women were dangerously seductive, their armies consisted of uncountable hordes and black monsters, but also of a few true heroic fighters who would have been perfect knights had they only been Christian. It is a genre that invented tradition freely, made Charlemagne a proto-crusader, and postulated a century-old *reconquista* on the Iberian Peninsula, a genre with thousand of stanzas of elaborate descriptions of heroic fighting and killing which seems to have been extremely popular in the Middle Ages but which to a modern and less heroic age is felt to be repetitious and sometimes even a bit dull. It is also a genre with a taste for the grotesque. When Richard the Lionheart fell ill in Acre during the third crusade, he claimed that the only thing that could cure him was roast pork, which for good reasons was difficult to get in Muslim Palestine. His doctors then cooked a young fat Muslim boy, Richard ate and immediately became better. When he learned what he had been eating, he thought it was such a good joke that he ordered his Muslim prisoners fed with young Muslims, whom they had to eat while he was watching.[15] This is grotesque, but it is also part of a widespread dehumanisation of the Muslims characteristic of the knightly literature and much contemporary history writing.

The knightly literature has been little used by crusade historians compared to the theological. This may be because it has not been considered a good and proper source for history and has been left to those studying literature; it may also be because it is written in older vernacular languages and not in Latin. This has slowly been changing since the 1980s, probably because of a new interest in the history of mentalities. Some studies have been published on the knightly literature,[16] and general histories of the crusades often now include chapters on this topic. It is still rare, however, for mutual relations between the theological polemical literature and the knightly to be considered in more detail, which would be extremely interesting for getting a better understanding of the general dynamics of recruiting crusaders.

Since about 1970, crusading studies have reached their second 'Golden Age', comparable to the vitalism of the late nineteenth century. An international society was re-established in 1980, this time with an English name, the Society for the Study of the Crusades and the Latin East, which comprises scholars from all over the world. Every fourth year, it arranges a big international conference, and sponsors annual crusader sessions at international conferences such as the medieval conferences in Kalamazoo and Leeds. It has published an annual newsletter since its foundation, and in 2003 appeared the first volume of a new journal of the society, a clear sign that crusading studies are a growing academic field.

One feature that clearly distinguishes the new crusading history from former ones is that the moral condemnations of crusading have almost entirely disappeared. Medieval warfare and its ideologies have become topics that historians can work on without having a bad conscience. It is possible to imagine or at least try to understand the argument that violence may be necessary in a good cause. This shift in attitude probably has many explanations. One may be that many historians were educated in the post-1968 university environments in Europe where left wing students discussed for days and weeks how they could produce a socialist revolution and whether it was ideologically possible to argue that the use of violence might be necessary to this revolution. An extremely small minority actually took up weapons and joined the *Rote Armee Fraktion* in Germany and similar terrorist organisations in other countries, while thousands of university students who never practised violence got used to discussing it as an imaginable political construct. Parallel to these academic discussions, theologians in South America developed Liberation Theology, which also at least theoretically accepted a certain amount of violence in fighting evil, fighting capitalistic oppressors. For historically interested academics and theologians, it became natural to seek the roots of this kind of ideology in the Middle Ages. Another reason that the moral disapproval of warfare diminished after 1970 may have been a renewed interest in the history of mentalities combined with a growing discomfort with the idea that one's own time is always the high point of evolution. It became more interesting to attempt to understand people of another time than to judge what is true and false according to modern moral standards.

Whatever the reason might have been, a new and strong interest in the personal motivations of the individual crusaders is clearly recognizable after 1970. The earlier understanding of crusader motivation was now felt to be insufficient. The economic motive – that crusaders left to gain a fortune in the rich Middle East with its long-distance trade and its gold mines – was shown to have been highly doubtful. It was in fact extremely expensive to invest in the normal and proper equipment for a knight and to cover his own and his retinue's travel expenditures for the years a personal crusade lasted for. And after he had reached the Holy Land and fought bravely, he would normally always return home, loaded with relics and bankrupt, but not with gold. It has been shown by studies in local archive material that in economic terms it was simply bad business to go on a crusade. The sociological explanation has also been severely criticised, because the postulated introduction of primogeniture, in which only the oldest son could inherit, has been very difficult to substantiate in the medieval source material. Neither was crusading the privilege of the younger sons only. On the contrary, participating in a crusade seems to have been a very common way of ending a long and active life as warrior, often with the avowed aim of dying at or near the Holy Sepulchre. Family fathers and leaders of the great kinship groups of Europe, not sons, played the decisive role in crusading.[17]

The criticism of economic and social explanations has led to a much greater emphasis on the crusader's personal conviction and his striving to gain access to the spiritual benefits of the church. If the participants were lucky, they could hope to become martyrs and enter heaven directly, as Urban had promised at Clermont. If they did not die and returned to their own country, they would still have gained indulgence. Crusading was primarily a spiritual exercise, an act of penance, and from that perspective there was little difference between traditional pilgrims and new crusaders, and the same words were used for them both for a long time. The crusades were therefore a kind of moving monastery[18] in which the monks were crusaders. The new and different aspect of crusading was that the spiritual exercise consisted in wielding the sword, or simply that laymen could continue to do what they had been brought up to do and were best at, but that it was now a spiritually meritorious act and not a sin in itself.

The military history of the crusades has gained new momentum in two directions. One is the study of the how people were killed in the Middle Ages, the other is why. Within the first topic, there is a tendency to stress the role of the infantry more than in earlier military histories. Foot soldiers were much more common and necessary in warfare than the medieval sources indicate, because most of the narratives and poems of battles were written for the entertainment of the knightly class and had no room for common people. They were often decisive, however, in protecting the flanks and rear of the cavalry, or formed specially trained troops equipped with longbows or crossbows. After the Second World War, the medieval line of heavily armoured mounted knights was often compared to a modern tank, which no enemy could withstand. More military historians now would emphasise that the knights fought as individuals more than as a group and that there were huge problems simply with keeping the knights back and in order so that they could attack together. It is also being stressed now that most military campaigns actually attempted to avoid open battles as long as possible. Since medieval warfare consisted much more of sieges than battles, the military strongholds became extremely important not only as defensive means but also as offensive ones. Crusader castles in the Latin East have been the topic of recent studies by historians and archaeologists in Israel, which has reassessed their military role.[19]

The second aspect of the interest in warfare is the ideology behind the theological justification for crusades. The modern work on this began in 1975 with the definitive study by F. H. Russell entitled *Just War in the Middle Ages*. The medieval theories and maxims attempting to regulate war have a background in both the Old and New Testaments, Classical Greek philosophy, and Roman law, but it was only from the beginning of the twelfth century that they were systematically collected and presented in coherent form. The scattered references to warfare in Augustine were brought together in *Causa 23* of Gratian. The overall principle is that warfare is evil, but it may be necessary to tolerate one evil to prevent an even greater evil. War may be necessary to stop evildoers doing evil, or simply to defend the society from forces that threaten to destroy it. In its fully developed form, the theories often consisted of five criteria for *jus ad bellum*, five criteria to judge whether a war was just or not: *persona*, *res*, *causa*, *auctoritas*, and *intentio*. Only the right persons could participate in a war, that is, soldiers and not priests, etc., the *res* about which the war is waged should belong rightly to those fighting, e.g., Jerusalem, which belongs to the Christians; the person authorizing the war should be a legitimate prince or the pope; and the participants should fight with the intention of doing justice and restoring the status quo, not to gain money or because they got used to killing and began enjoying it. These criteria are still the fundament for modern theories about war with the appropriate adjustments regarding authorities. Islamic theories about jihad underwent similar developments in the twelfth and thirteenth centuries and eventually operated with exactly the same criteria, but which religion inspired which has not been studied sufficiently and is simply unknown as yet.[20]

With few exceptions, historians have not been able to combine the study of hard-core military history with the medieval theories of war. The military historians are often very sceptical about whether the theories had any impact on actual warfare at all, and most of them end up regarding war as entirely directed by sheer power politics and the quest for fame and honour, while the theoretical historians are often engulfed in the theories and their logical beauty and have little interest in actual warfare. A way of combining the two approaches to war would be to determine how the great medieval narratives on the wars of individual princes incorporate elements from the theories in their justification. This has been done with a few of the Spanish narratives and could be done also with texts like the Danish historian Saxo's description of the Wendic crusades in the twelfth century.

There was a marked shift in history in general about 1970 – a little later in Scandinavia – from an interest in differences to one in similarities, from stressing the uniqueness of one's own county or topic of study to assuming that one's own country is only a variation of a common theme. In crusading history, this shift is probably the reason why a whole new definition of the word 'crusade' itself has been introduced and has become increasingly common.

The traditional definition of a crusade as a military expedition to liberate and protect the Holy Sepulchre in Jerusalem has been called the exclusivist definition, excluding all other expeditions than those to Jerusalem. The new definition says that crusades were all the wars against enemies of the Church, which were authorized by the pope and which gave indulgence to the participants. This has been called the inclusivist definition, because it includes many more wars than those in Jerusalem. A stout defender of the traditional exclusivist definition is H. E. Mayer, whose *Geschichte der Kreuzzüge*, 1965, has come in new and revised editions, the most recent being the ninth edition of 2000. It has thus been one of the most influential books on crusading in the twentieth century and extremely valuable for its references to and discussions of the historiography. In a lengthy footnote, Mayer expresses hesitation as to whether it is still worthwhile to debate further with the inclusivists because 'die Fronten auf beiden Seiten dogmatisch verhärtet sind.' It is also Mayer's impression that the inclusivist approach is entirely English, with a couple of exceptions, and not shared by German, French, American, and other scholars. The latter claim is more disputable; both on the Iberian Peninsula and in Northern Europe more historians use the broad definition of the inclusivists.

On the traditional definition, crusading began in 1095/99, lasted till 1291, and was directed only against the Holy Land. With the inclusivist definition, the phenomenon of crusades is enormously expanded both geographically and chronologically. Wars against Muslims in Spain and Portugal[21] and against heathen Wends and Lithuanians in the Baltic were crusades, as were the wars against the Albigensian heretics in Provence in the early thirteenth century. The crusades then began in the latter half of the eleventh century, perhaps with the battle at Barbastro in 1064, perhaps a little earlier with papal acceptance of the Normans' war in Italy in support of the papacy. According to this definition, crusading also continued in Northern Europe till the early sixteenth century; even the Danish-Norwegian king Christian II's trial and execution of about one hundred Swedish nobles and ecclesiastics in Stockholm in 1520 would then be a kind of crusade, because they were all accused of heresy. After the Reformation, however, although there was no papal authorization, the idea of a religious and meritorious war continued for another two centuries. In Southern

Europe, crusading continued in the sixteenth and seventeenth centuries both to Africa, America, and against the Ottoman Turks.[22]

The expansion of the crusading concept has opened up new research areas. The obvious one is the later crusades, after 1291, which were a study restricted only to a few historians until about 1970, but is being studied by more scholars now. Another obvious research area is national histories from a crusading perspective, such as Scotland and the Crusades[23] or England and the Crusades[24] or even Denmark and the Crusades.[25] Other topics are an interest in the practical organisation of crusading, preaching, financing, recruitment, securing provisions on the way, the role of cities and burghers in crusading, etc. Crusading history has, like other fields of history, also been hit by the biographical fashion, which has led to more prosopographical studies of crusaders and crusader networks.

The expansion of the definition of crusading has been criticised by H. E. Mayer, based among other things upon a different evaluation of the importance of Jerusalem in the middle ages. Mayer's criticism has been supported by Christopher Tyerman in a 1998 book entitled *The Invention of the Crusades*. One part of Tyerman's criticism is an interesting example of the so-called linguistic turn and its impact upon history. Tyerman basically claims that as no fixed and commonly accepted word for crusade existed during the twelfth century, the phenomenon itself did not exist as something separate or distinguishable from other kind of religiously motivated wars – in the twelfth or preceding centuries. The success of the expedition to Jerusalem arose from it being something that people knew and could understand, Tyerman claims. Medieval lawyers and theologians had immense difficulty in defining a crusade, which indicates that it was a very uncertain category in the middle ages, and should rather be considered an invention of ambitious younger scholars since 1970 in an attempt to create for themselves a research profile and an academic career. According to Tyerman and Mayer, the inclusivist definition of crusading is also so broad and unfocussed that it loses all meaning. If one can participate in crusading not only by fighting but also by paying or by praying or simply by listening to a crusader sermon, it is not religious warfare but simply a normal penitential practice and nothing out of ordinary compared to pilgrimage and prayer.

Tyerman suggests a number of sources and assumptions about crusading that still merit much more and careful study, but he also goes too far in his criticism, ignoring those medieval sources that actually presented the crusades as something qualitatively new, a major progressive step in the history of mankind that no former age had ever achieved, as Guibert of Nogent wrote. Tyerman also ignores all the institutions that were established specifically to support the crusades such as preaching and taxation and collection of money, and which can be demonstrated to have been used both for crusades to the Holy Land and to crusades in other theatres of war. Crusading studies are not dead since the attack by Tyerman; on the contrary, they are a research area that is becoming larger both in the topic it treats and in the number of scholars engaged in it.

NOTES

1 Riley-Smith 1986; France 1997.
2 Gesta Francorum, introduction by Hill.
3 Cole 1991.
4 William, iv, 348,2; iv, 347, 8.
5 Vincent of Prag, under 1147.
6 Helmold cap. 65; cf. 84.
7 Constable 1953; cf. Taylor 2000.
8 Kedar 1984; Siberry 1985.
9 Dodu 1894.
10 Siberry 2000.
11 Cf. Anderson 1992; García-Guijarro Ramos 1997, Martínez 1997.
12 E.g. Théry 1944; Monneret de Vilard 1944; Rouillard 1941.
13 Among the latest works on this, see Blanks and Frassetto 1999; Tolan 2002.
14 Burman 1994.
15 Comfort 1940.
16 Daniel 1984; Nicholson 2001.
17 Riley-Smith 1997.
18 The expression is borrowed from Riley-Smith 1986.
19 Ellenblum 1998; Marshall 1992; France 1994, 1999.
20 Partner 1998.
21 A strong tradition among Iberian historians of distinguishing between crusade and *reconquista* is being strongly challenged at present. See O'Callaghan 2003.
22 Housley 2002.
23 Macquarrie 1984.
24 Tyerman 1988.
25 Lind et al., 2004.

BIBLIOGRAPHY

Sources

Albert of Achen, *Historia Hierosolymitana,* RHC 4.
Baldric of Bourgueil, *Historia de peregrinatione Jerosolimitana*, RHC 4.
Foulques of Chartres, *Historia Iherosolymitana ... auctore domno Fulcheri Carnotensi*, RHC 3, pp. 311–485.
Gesta francorum, *Gesta Francorum et aliorum Hierosolimitanorum. [The deeds of the Franks and the other pilgrims to Jerusalem. Ed. by Rosalind Hill].* T. Nelson (ed.), London 1962.
Guibert af Nogent, *Gesta dei per francos*, RHC 4, pp. 113–263.
Raimundus de Agiles, *Le "Liber" de Raymond d'Aguilers, publié par John Hugh et Laurita L. Hill. Introd. et notes traduites par Philippe Wolff.* P. Geuthner (ed.), Paris 1969.
Tudebodis: Peter Tudebode, *Historia de Hierosolymitano Itinere*, J. H. & L. L. Hill (ed.). Librairie Orientaliste Paul Geuthner, Paris 1977.
William of Malmesbury, *Gesta regum anglorum,* R. A. B. Mynors, R. M. Thomson & M. Winterbottom (ed. and transl.), 1–2. Oxford 1998–1999.
Vincent of Prag: *Vincentii Pragensis Annales.* Wilhelm Wattenbach (ed.). MGH SS XVII. Hannover 1861, pp. 654–684.

Secondary works

P. J. Cole 1991, *The preaching of the crusades to the Holy land, 1095–1270*. Cambridge, Mass.

G. M. Anderson et al. 1992, 'An economic interpretation of the medieval crusades', *Economic History Review* 21, pp. 339–363.

D. R. Blanks and M. Frassetto (ed.) 1999, *Western Views of Islam in Medieval and Early Modern Europe. Perceptions of Other.* New York.

T. E. Burman 1994, *Religious polemic and the intellectual history of the Mozarabs, c.1050–1200.* Leiden–New York.

W. W. Comfort 1940, 'The Literary Role of the Saracens in the French Epic', *Publications of the Modern Language Association* 55:3, pp. 628–659.

G. Constable 1953, 'The Second Crusade as seen by contemporaries.' *Traditio* 9, pp. 215–279.

N. Daniel 1960, *Islam and the West: The Making of an Image.* Edinburgh.

N. Daniel 1984. *Heroes and Saracens. An Interpretation of the Chansons de Geste.* Edinburgh.

G. Dodu 1894. *Histoire des institutions monarchiques dans le royaume latin de Jérusalem 1099–1291.* Paris.

R. Ellenblum 1998, *Frankish Rural Settlement in the Latin Kingdom of Jerusalem.* Cambridge.

V. Epp 1990, *Fulcher von Chartres : Studien zur Geschichtsschreibung des ersten Kreuzzuges.* Düsseldorf.

C. Erdmann 1935, *Die Entstehung des Kreuzzugsgedankens.* Stuttgart. English Translation, *The Origin of the Idea of Crusade.* Princeton 1977.

J. France 1994, *Victory in the East: A Military History of the First Crusade.* Cambridge.

J. France 1997, 'Patronage and the appeal of the First Crusade.' In J. Phillip (ed.), *The First Crusade. Origins and impact.* Manchester, pp. 5–20.

J. France 1999, *Western warfare in the age of the Crusades, 1000–1300.* Ithaca, N.Y.

L. García-Guijarro Ramos 1997, 'Expansión económica medieval y cruzadas', in García-Guijarro Ramos (ed.), *La primera cruzada, novecientos años después: el concilio de Clermont y los orígenes del movimiento cruzado.* Madrid, pp. 155–166.

E. Gibbon 1776, *The history of the decline and fall of the Roman Empire* 1–6. London.

R. Grousset 1934–1936, *Histoire des Croisades et du Royaume Franc de Jérusalem* 1–3. Paris.

N. Housley 2002, *Religious Warfare in Europe, 1400–1536.* Oxford.

D. Hume 1761, *The history of England from the invasion of Julius Cæsar to the accession of Henry VII.* London.

B. Z. Kedar 1984, *Crusade and mission: European approaches toward the Muslims.* Princeton.

J. Lind et al. 2004, *Danske korstog. Krig og mission i Østersøen.* København.

A. Macquarrie 1984, *Scotland and the Crusades 1095–1560.* Edinburgh.

C. Marshall 1992, *Warfare and the Latin East, 1192–1291.* Cambridge.

C. de Ayala Martínez 1997, 'Hacia una comprensión del fenómeno cruzado: las insuficiencias del reduccionismo económico', in García-Guijarro Ramos (ed) 1997, pp. 167–195.

H. E. Mayer 2000, *Geschichte der Kreuzzuge.* Stuttgart.

J.-F. Michaud 1812–1817, *Histoire des croisades.* 1–3. Paris.

C. Mills 1821, *The history of the Crusades, for the recovery and possession of the Holy Land* 1–2. London.

U. Monneret de Villard 1944, *Lo studio dell'Islam in Europa nel XII secolo.* (= *Studi e Testi;* 110) Rom.

H. Nicholson 2001, *Love, war and the Grail.* Leiden-Boston.

J. F. O'Callaghan 2003, *Reconquest and Crusade in Medieval Spain.* Philadelphia.

P. Partner 1998, *God of battles: holy wars of Christianity and Islam*. Princeton, N.J.

J. Riley-Smith 1986, *The First Crusade and the Idea of Crusading*. London.

J. Riley-Smith 1997, *The First Crusaders, 1095–1131*. Cambridge.

F.H. Russell 1975, *The Just War in the Middle Ages*. Cambridge.

C. D. Rouillard 1941, *The Turk in French history, thought and literature (1520-1660)*. Paris.

S. Runciman 1951–1954, *A History of the Crusades,* 1–3. Cambridge.

E. Siberry 1985, *Criticism of Crusading, 1095–1274*. Oxford.

E. Siberry 2000, *The new crusaders: images of the crusades in the nineteenth and early twentieth centuries*. Aldershot–Brookfield, USA

R. C. Smail 1956, *Crusading Warfare (1097–1193)*. Cambridge.

R. W. Southern 1962, *Western Views of Islam in the Middle Ages*. Cambridge, Mass.

H. von Sybel 1841, *Geschichte des ersten Kreuzzugs*. Düsseldorf.

P. Taylor 2000, 'Moral agency in crusade and colonization: Anselm of Havelberg and the Wendish crusade of 1147.' *International History Review* 22, pp. 757–784.

G. Théry 1944, *Tolède: grande ville de la Renaissance médiévale, point de jonction entre les cultures musulmane et chrétienne, le circuit de la civilisation méditerranéenne*. Oran.

P. A. Throop 1940, *Criticism of the Crusade: A Study of Public Opinion and Crusade Propaganda*. Amsterdam.

J. V. Tolan 2002, *Saracens: Islam in the medieval European imagination*. New York.

H. Trautner-Kromann 1993, *Shield and sword: Jewish polemics against Christianity and the Christians in France and Spain from 1100–1500*. Tübingen.

C. Tyerman 1988, *England and the crusades 1095–1588*. Chicago.

C. Tyerman 1998, *The Invention of the Crusades*. Oxford.

F. Wilken 1807, *Geschichte der Kreuzzüge nach morgenlandische und abendlandischen Berichten*. 1–7. Leipzig.

Part I

Ideology and Medieval Historiography

ARNVED NEDKVITNE

Why Did Medieval Norsemen Go on Crusades?[1]

In an article published in *Den jyske historiker* in June 2000, Kurt Villads Jensen has surveyed historical research on the crusades from the beginning up to the present time. He finds that the research in recent decades has been characterised by interest in the crusaders' personal motives. Concerning these motives a clear picture has emerged:

> The conclusion at the present time is that the crusades can only be explained by the participants' personal motives, and the desire to take part in the spiritual benefits promised to all crusaders. The crusades can be seen as a spiritual exercise, and many historians now emphasise the similarities between monastic life and pilgrimages. The crusades were an enormous 'rolling monastery.'[2]

This new understanding is opposed to earlier generations of historians focusing on the crusaders' secular and material motives. The main explanations in this older research were that knights and merchants sought economic profits, younger sons in knightly households without land sought a livelihood and princes sought to expand their territories and power.[3]

Kurt Villads Jensen has led a project which has created a new and positive interest in the crusades in Scandinavia. For the first time there has been a will in Scandinavia to take the crusades seriously. The project must be understood as part of the new interest in cultural history which has been evident in Scandinavian medieval research in the last two decades. This trend has created an upsurge in interest in medieval history, particularly among students and younger researchers. All medievalists should consider this a positive development, and I for one have made my contribution to it,[4] but the question should be asked whether the pendulum perhaps in some cases has swung too far in the direction of an idealistic interpretation of medieval history, and whether the new crusading history might be an example of this.

The criticism voiced in this article concerns a limited part of Danish crusading. The project has mainly focused on Danish and German military and political expansion in the Baltic and discussed the importance of religion for this process.[5] Another field of interest has been the connection between papal taxation of Denmark and crusading ideology. To my knowledge no systematic analysis has been made of the crusaders' motives. When motives are mentioned, however, the views are, explicitly or implicitly, similar to those mentioned above.[6]

The Sources

Most of the sources describing crusades were written by clerics, both in Scandinavia and elsewhere in Europe. In Denmark the language used for narratives up to the end of the fourteenth century was Latin. This means that longer narratives were almost exclusively written by clerics. Exceptionally, laymen like Svend Aggesen mastered Latin so well that they were able to write Latin narratives, but they had received a clerical education and worked in a clerical tradition. An emphasis on religious motives in narratives written by clerics is not surprising. These descriptions should not be taken at face value as representing the motives of the crusaders, since these were mainly laymen.

Before c. 1400 our understanding of the crusades in Scandinavia have come to us through clerics – with one exception. In Norway and Iceland the commonly used written language was Norse from the twelfth century, which made it much easier for laymen to master narrative composition. The Norse sagas are narratives mostly written by laymen for a secular public. They give an alternative to the ecclesiastical perspective, and should give the best impression of how laymen understood the crusades. Most of the crusaders were laymen. How then do the sagas present the crusaders' motives?

First it is necessary to identify crusades in the sagas. No particular word for 'crusade' existed in the Norse language, the term 'Jerusalem-journey' (*Jorsalaferd*) being used, but this term included any journey to Jerusalem, regardless of whether the purpose was piracy, a pilgrimage or a crusade. The Latin word *peregrinatio* had the same general meaning. Ecclesiastical as well as lay terminology failed to distinguish between pilgrimages, crusades and journeys for other purposes.

In this article, however, we need the term 'crusade' as an instrument in the analysis. How can it be defined for our purposes? 'Crusade' is defined by the Oxford Dictionary as 'a war or expedition instigated by the church for alleged religious ends.'[7] If 'instigated' is understood in the sense that the Church took the initiative to organise the expedition, that term is not useful in a Norse context, where secular princes took the initiative themselves. But if 'instigated' is understood in the sense that the Church approved the expedition, the definition is productive even in Scandinavia. From the first crusade, the Church gave indulgences to all who went to Jerusalem to 'liberate the church of God.'[8] Those who went to Jerusalem on an expedition whose purpose is alleged to be religious, had the approval of the Church and were therefore crusaders according to the definition quoted above. This definition does not exclude the expedition also having other purposes in addition to the religious ones. The Oxford Dictionary definition understood in the latter sense permits us to distinguish 'crusades' from 'pilgrimages' on the one hand, and other kinds of 'wars' on the other.

Two unquestionable crusades according to this definition are described in the sagas, one organised by the Norwegian King Sigurd in 1108–1111 and the other by the earl of Orkneys, Ragnvald Kale in 1152–1155. They were both undertaken when the crusading movement was at its peak and Jerusalem was in Christian hands. Sigurd's crusade has been discussed recently by Gary Doxey and Janus Møller Jensen, but neither of them have analysed the motives systematically.[9]

The sources describing these journeys are skaldic poems written shortly after the events, and sagas written 70–110 years later. The sagas used are *Ágrip* (c. 1190),[10] *Morkinskinna* (c. 1220),[11] *Orkneyinga saga* dated in its final version c. 1230,[12] *Heimskringla* (c. 1230) and *Fagrskinna* (c. 1230).[13] The skaldic poems express the understanding and mentalities of the crusaders themselves, while the sagas express the understanding of the later saga authors.

All the skalds and saga authors were laymen composing for a secular audience, with one exception. The saga *Ágrip* was written by a cleric at the see of Nidaros c. 1190.[14] There is a clear difference between this ecclesiastical source and the other secular sources in the understanding of the motives for these crusades.

The Religious Motive

In his description of King Sigurd's journey to Jerusalem eighty years earlier, the clerical author of *Ágrip* focuses on the benefits for the organised Church. In Jerusalem the king swore to introduce the tithe, create a Norwegian church province, introduce a fast on Saturdays. He also brought back a splinter of the Holy Cross which should protect his kingdom, and which later was preserved at the cathedral in Nidaros. All this the saga author sees as preparation for the creation of the Norwegian archbishopate forty years later in 1153. He does not mention personal piety as a motive for the king's journey, but he stresses that the undertaking gave the king great secular fame.[15] In this clerical account the motives for the crusade were the will to support the organised Church and seeking secular fame, the two being obviously connected, as might be expected.

Skaldic poems and the other sagas reflect the mentalities of the secular elite. *Morkinskinna* and *Heimskringla* both mention the promises made by King Sigurd in Jerusalem, just like *Ágrip*,[16] but the two secular saga descriptions of the crusade are far more comprehensive than in *Ágrip*.

Some additional information concerns religion. *Morkinskinna* tells us that Sigurd's motive for going was to 'earn God's mercy and a reputation for valour.' Before leaving Norway he asked the crusaders on his 60 ships to 'conduct themselves in a princely fashion so that the expedition may enhance our fame and the good of our souls.'[17] Earl Ragnvald asked the bishop of Orkney to participate in his crusade in 1153 because 'the bishop was educated in Paris, and the earl wanted him to be their interpreter. The bishop promised to follow.'[18] Nothing is said about the religious services the bishop provided for the crusaders.

Sigurd later motivated his warriors before the attack on the Muslim castle of Sintra in Portugal by saying that it would 'advance and strengthen Christendom.'[19] In a skaldic poem the slain Muslims are called 'the devil's slaves.' Time and again the authors stress that the king only attacked pagans, and killed them only if they refused to accept the Christian faith.[20] The one exception to this rule was that both Sigurd and earl Ragnvald attacked Christians once each, in Galicia. They ran out of food and solved the problem by plundering a Christian castle.[21]

The crusaders visited all the holy places in Jerusalem and the surrounding country and bathed in the river Jordan. This was done to obtain religious merit, imitate Christ's baptism in Jordan and purify themselves from sin. The crusaders of course knew this religious meaning, the skald telling us that king Sigurd 'washed in the pure water of the river Jordan.'[22] Nothing more is said in the saga about the religious benefits of the bath or the visit to the Holy places; one gets the impression that it was 'the things crusaders usually do.'[23]

The Christian elements are very few and short compared to the long and detailed descriptions of honourable secular events. Little is said about the religious aspect of the two crusades. One possible explanation is that since the listener knew that they went to Jerusalem mainly for religious reasons it was unnecessary to say it, but an alternative explanation is more likely. The religious motive was present in the minds of the saga writers, the skalds, their audience and the crusaders, but it was not the most important thing about crusades. It was not what the listeners wanted to hear about, or the main reason for undertaking such a perilous and expensive voyage.

What other motives appear in the texts describing these voyages?

The Economic Motive

Reasons of state can be ruled out. The Danish crusades in the Baltic conquered new land for the realm and strengthened the king's political power, but the Norse crusaders did not expand the frontiers of the king's and earl's realms, and did not create new political alliances.

The Norse crusaders apparently did have economic motives. The saga writers provide a similar background to both crusades. A Norwegian chieftain sailed to the Mediterranean with five ships about 1100. He himself died on the way, but his men returned, reporting that 'in Constantinople all Norwegians who wanted it could get employment as mercenaries in the emperor's army, and they were well paid.' Many asked Sigurd to lead an expedition, and he consented. He equipped 60 ships, with perhaps 2500–3000 warriors on board.[24] This makes it clear that economic motives were important from the outset. *Morkinskinna* describes in great detail how the emperor gave a generous gift to Sigurd: 'large tubs' filled with 'the reddest gold' 'to overflowing' and the emperor himself laid two large gold rings on top.[25] Sigurd left all his ships in Constantinople and went home on horseback. 'A large number of his men stayed behind in Constantinople and entered the emperor's service.'[26]

The prologue to earl Ragnvald's crusade was that the Norwegian chieftain Eindride Unge returned from Byzantium where he had served for many years in the emperor's army. He got the earl and many others interested in an expedition to *Jorsalaheim* (Jerusalem). When Ragnvald arrived in Constantinople, he received rich gifts from the emperor, and the crusaders were offered employment as mercenaries. Eindride Unge, who owned six of the crusaders' fifteen ships, stayed behind with his men and took another term in the emperor's army.[27]

Riches were also acquired through plunder. Sigurd fought eight battles in Spain, several of them yielding a rich booty, according to the skalds and saga tradition.[28] In the island of Formentera in the Balearic islands a large band of pagan raiders lived in a cave. The Norwegians lowered a small boat full of men from the cliff above the cave, and managed to kill them all. 'Here they collected more war-booty (*herfang*) than anywhere else on their journey', valuable cloth and other goods.[29] Sigurd's greatest victory was, however, the siege and capture of Sidon in a joint campaign with King Baldwin of Jerusalem. According to the sagas the soldiers were allowed to plunder it.[30] Ragnvald half a century later 'plundered widely in the pagan part of Spain, and acquired much goods. They went ashore at a village (*Porp*), but the villagers assembled ready to fight. The resistance was hard, but finally the villagers fled and many were killed.' Later they plundered a large Saracen trading ship called *dromund*.[31] It was perfectly legitimate and honourable for crusaders to accumulate riches through piracy and plunder if the victims were Muslims.

It was honourable to be rich, but it was even more so to spend one's riches lavishly. Sigurd is praised by the skald for giving his rights over the conquered Sidon generously (*af mildi*) to king Baldwin.[32] *Morkinskinna* has inserted some fairy-tale stories to show Sigurd's lavish spending in Constantinople. He entered the city riding a horse with shoes of gold, and arranged for one of the shoes to fall off so that the inhabitants could examine it for themselves. Later he invited the emperor and the empress to a lavish banquet where the cooking was done by burning walnuts, because firewood was in short supply in the city.[33] Even if these stories are just tales, they show the understanding of the saga authors c. 1230. Acquiring riches was an end in itself on these crusades, but riches were also a means of acquiring great honour by spending lavishly. Generosity on that scale, however, was only possible for the king.

Warrior Honour

Honour on a more modest scale could be acquired by all participants. The key to the most important motive for the crusaders is given in the final comment of *Morkinskinna* and *Heimskringla* on Sigurd's crusade: 'People say that no more honourable voyage (*virdingarfor*) has been undertaken from Norway than the one King Sigurd accomplished.'[34] A similar comment also concludes the description of earl Ragnvald's journey.[35] Snorri thought the crusaders gained *virding*, the most common Norse word for secular honour.[36] Secular honour to be gained at these crusades was of two kinds: warrior honour and courtly honour.

In skaldic verses and sagas most space and the greatest attention is given to the warrior skills of the crusaders. The following verses were written shortly after king Sigurd's return to Norway: 'The king maimed the heathen men who hastily fled before the army. There was horrible clamour in the cavern. Again you offered the devil's slaves death when you captured the old stronghold. The luckless people were tormented in the fire.'[37] After the capture of Sidon: 'Feeder of the wolf [=the king], powerfully you captured the pagan city and generously gave it away. Every battle was fought honourably.'[38] In 1152 Ragnvald wrote about the capture of the Saracen trading ship: 'The illustrious Erling [*skakke*], a warrior strong in battle, attacked the *dromund* with skill and was victorious. Our banners became red, we killed the courageous Saracens. People around us had to bleed. Brave men made the swords red.'[39]

Turning from the skaldic verses to saga descriptions written c. 1220–1230, they also focus on battles. Sigurd's journey to Jerusalem is structured by his eight battles in Spain and Ragnvald's by his conquest of a castle in Galicia and a Saracen trading ship. The saga authors give few or no heroic descriptions of the warrior-crusaders' bravery, however. The main emphasis is on showing how clever they were inventing stratagems to trick the enemy. In the attack on the castle in Galicia the strategy was invented by Erling Skakke, and the chieftain commanding the defenders of the castle recognised that Erling's strategy was 'wise (*vitrligt*) and harmful to us.'[40] This is the same attitude to warfare found in *Sverres saga* written in its final version c. 1210. The viewpoint is that of the commanding officers: the king, the earl and their closest advisors. While the focus in the sagas is on the warrior honour of the officers, the work of the foot soldier is not neglected, because extensive quotations of old skaldic stanzas praising the personal courage of warriors are inserted in the prose saga texts. Most space in both skaldic poems and sagas is given to the praise of the warrior honour of the crusaders. The sagas were clearly written for the king's and earl's *hird* or court where both kinds of warrior skills produced honour.

Courtly Honour

Courteousness or *hoeverska* was the ability to behave as they did at courts, preferably at prestigious foreign courts. Courtly honour was recognition by others, preferably by those who knew when a person belonged to the exquisite group of courteous people. Religion, riches and warrior honour seem to have been constant motives all through the period, but courtly honour became increasingly important from 1110 to 1230.

Secular honour for King Sigurd's crusaders c. 1110 seems to have been synonymous with warrior honour. None of the surviving skaldic poems written shortly after the events tell us that Sigurd was received well at foreign courts or by foreign princes. This might be explained by the genre, since skaldic poems were expected to praise warrior bravery and little else. But it should then be asked why this genre was so dominant in this early period. Was it not because warrior skills were considered to be the most important skill for the king and his men? The skaldic genre did change in the following decades.

The poems from Earl Ragnvald's crusade in 1152–1155 demonstrate that courtly honour now was important. In Narbonne, on the Mediterranean coast of France, the crusaders visited the court of 'Queen' Ermengard, an historical person, who reigned as *vicomtesse* of Narbonne from 1143, when her father died, to 1192. She acquired a reputation for her patronage of troubadour poets, and is mentioned in Andreas Capellanus's *The Art of Courtly Love* written in the 1170s.[41] In the saga she appears as a beautiful, unmarried young woman, and the object of the crusaders' love and admiration.

A courtly culture had developed in Southern France between the two crusades. The patrons were powerful and independent nobles like Ermengard, and cultural creativity was centred around troubadour poets. This courtly culture carried great prestige at the time, and the Norse crusaders were at pains to show they were part of it. The poems they composed to honour Ermengard were obviously not composed to impress *her*, because she would not be able to understand them, but to impress those back home. The earl wrote: 'Your hair is more beautiful than that of most fair-haired women. Her hair, yellow as silk, falls down on her shoulders. I have made the greedy eagle's foot red [bloody].'[42] Another of the skalds wrote: 'We are hardly worthy of Ermengard. The wise woman is rightly called king among women, a better destiny awaits her.' And a third skald: 'I shall never see Ermengard again, if destiny does not decide otherwise. Many have a broken heart because of the wise woman. The greatest bliss would be to sleep one night with her.'[43] These are clearly efforts to imitate the poetry of the troubadours. But the Norse skaldic tradition's praise of bloody battles is still there when the earl tries to impress Ermengard by telling her that he has given the eagle bloody corpses to eat. We must believe, however, that the crusaders impressed the audience back home by showing that they had lived up to the norms of the prestigious court in the exotic Mediterranean city of Narbonne.

The meeting of the earl and his crusaders with the courts in the two most important cities they visited was less glorious. In Jerusalem the earl and his nine ships apparently were considered as yet another group of pilgrims, while the skaldic poems fail to mention any contact with the court of the king of Jerusalem. On approaching Constantinople, Earl Ragnvald composed the following poem: 'Let us approach *Miklagardi*… let us enter the emperor's service, advance in battle, give the wolf's mouth a red colour, and act so that the emperor gets honour.'[44] The earl and his men considered themselves as potential mercenaries, not as the emperor's equals and potential guests at his court. Neither did they try to hide this fact from their public back home.

To conclude, there was an ambition for courtly honour in 1155 which does not seem to have existed half a century before. Between 1150 and

1230 the courtly culture matured and spread all over Western Europe, with its main centres in Northern and Southern France. From the 1220s chivalric romances were translated into Norse under the patronage of the Norwegian king. To introduce courtly culture in Norway became part of royal policy. The sagas written c. 1230 present the crusaders as patterns of courtly behaviour. Courtly honour had become almost as important as warrior bravery. Sigurd visited several prestigious courts, and made a splendid impression, if we are to believe the sagas.

Sigurd spent his first winter of 1108-9 in England. *Morkinskinna* is at pains to tell us how honourably he was received by king Henry I, but it is not clear from the text whether he was actually received at Henry's court. English sources indicate that he was not, the welcome probably being given him by letter or messenger.[45]

The next court Sigurd visited was that of count Roger II of Sicily. He was a prestigious person in his own right, but also because he was the great-grandfather of Frederich II who was German emperor c. 1230. The count held a banquet for King Sigurd lasting seven days, 'and every day of the feast the *hertogi* (duke) Roger stood at King Sigurd's table and served.' On the last day Sigurd conducted Roger by the hand to a throne 'and conferred on him the title of king and the right to rule Sicily in perpetuity.' The king of Sicily in 1230 was of course Emperor Fredrick II. The story is not correct, Roger became king in 1130 and the title was given him by the pope. Nothing about the visit is to be found in skaldic poetry.[46]

King Baldwin of Jerusalem followed Sigurd in person to the river Jordan, and held a great banquet for him. Baldwin had expensive carpeting spread on the road into Jerusalem to honour Sigurd. Baldwin tested the courtesy of Sigurd. If he and his crusaders rode over the carpets, this would show they were used to such honours. If they left the direct road to avoid stepping on the precious carpets, they had failed the test. Needless to say, Sigurd proved his courteousness.

King Sigurd and his crusaders showed the most splendid evidence of his courtesy in Constantinople, however. Sigurd wanted a cross-wind when sailing into the city, because then his splendid sails would show off better. He had to wait two weeks for the right wind so that he could sail gloriously up the Bosporous. Again precious fabrics had been spread out on the street, the emperor opened the gate he himself entered when he had won a great victory, and they were given quarters in the greatest hall in the royal palace. The emperor offered to organise horse-games at the hippodrome in Sigurd's honour, or give him as much in gold as the games cost. Sigurd courteously chose the games.[47] Sigurd arranged a banquet for the emperor 'according to the customs that were appropriate for powerful men', and the emperor was shown honour (*somi*) and received princely treatment (*veitir han konungliga*). The empress gave King Sigurd the certificate of being a man who 'saves nothing if it can promote his honour (*somi*).'[48]

On his way back through Germany he also met the German emperor and the Danish king, and was received by both with great reverence. The meeting with the German emperor, however, is difficult to fit into what we know from other sources about the emperor's itinerary.[49]

Sigurd's crusaders visited some of the most prestigious courts of Europe, being shown honour through kind words, magnificent entries into the cities and above all sumptuous banquets and gifts. These honours are also seen as tests for the crusaders, and they always tackled them in a manner which proved their courteousness.

The saga description of Earl Ragnvald's crusade of c. 1230 differs less from what can be read from the skaldic poems, probably because the oldest (no longer extant) version of the saga was written only forty to fifty years after the events.[50] We are told that the most prominent men in Narbonne counselled Ermengard to invite the Norse crusaders to an honourable banquet (*veizlu virdiligrar*) and that she would gain fame (*frægd*) if she received such splendid men (*göfgum mönnum*) well. That would benefit Ermengard, because the crusaders would then spread her fame further (*bera frægd hennar*). At Ermengard's banquet everything was done which could increase the earl's honour (*jarlsins somi*). Ermengard herself appeared and poured wine to the earl. To illustrate how well the earl was able to mix socially with noble ladies at prestigious courts, the saga writer tells us that he seated 'the queen' on his knee, and they talked all day.[51]

There are several ways to measure the relative importance of religion, riches, warrior honour and courtly honour as motives for the crusades. The first is to examine what is said explicitly to be the motive; secondly, to examine the space devoted to the various events and, thirdly, look at the interest, enthusiasm and joy the author shows in describing these events. As shown above, these methods show that there can be no doubt that secular honour was the main prize sought by the crusaders. At the beginning of the twelfth century, secular honour was synonymous with 'warrior honour', but 'courtly honour' became increasingly important and, by 1230, the latter seems to have been of almost equal importance.

The Social Meaning of the Crusades

Crusading was the most prestigious way for the Norse elite to show that they were on a par with the secular elite in other countries, both in warrior bravery as well as courteous behaviour. It was an occasion for the crusader to prove that he possessed personal skills which were considered important for those who should serve prince and state. These qualities were the same in Norway as in other countries.

Courage was needed to fight the pagans in open battles, and to sail in waters unknown to themselves both geographically and mentally.

Intelligence was needed in war, inventing clever stratagems to vanquish superior enemies. Intelligence was also needed when socialising with experienced courtiers like King Baldwin and the Empress of Byzantium, who time and again time put the Norwegians to the test and tried to outwit them.

Generosity was expected, like giving away the rights over a conquered city or sparing the life of a noble and defeated enemy, but above all the crusader showed his generosity by 'conspicuous consumption', spending his riches lavishly on gifts, banquets and beautiful textiles.

Charity was a related and highly valued quality. King Sigurd conquered Sintra and other pagan strongholds to help the poor Christians who were oppressed by the plundering heathens.

Even if secular honour was the highest prize sought by the crusaders, riches and religious merit was also important, as shown above. To be a courageous and intelligent warrior, courteous, generous, charitable and a religious man confident of one's own salvation, were the most appreciated personal qualities among the secular elite 1100–1350. All these qualities could be proved or acquired in a crusade.

In modern historical literature the Norwegians who visited foreign courts and were so eager to live up to foreign standards are often ridiculed as superficial. They themselves, however, and their public back home no doubt considered this a test of human qualities which were considered valuable. Courage, intelligence, generosity and charity are even today considered as such.

The crusaders no doubt felt the experience made them better men than those sitting at home. A part of the Norse crusaders' rituals in the Holy Land was to swim across the river Jordan. Several of them tied a knot on a tree, challenging a named person at home to go and loosen the knot. One of Earl Ragnvald's skalds even wrote a poem about it: 'Today I tied a knot for the big-bellied lazy man who sits at home. Our army has endured great dangers!'[52] This feeling of great merit was also a reality in the eyes of those at home, the crusaders were much admired.

In medieval Norse society, social position was less dependent on formal exams and offices, and more on social respect than in later centuries. Personal qualities were important in such a society, but it was even more important to make others understand and accept that one had these qualities. Social position, at least among the elite, depended on the personal qualities which others imagined that one possessed, that is, one's honour. The crusade was perhaps the highest and most prominent exam for members of the elite. Participation in a crusade proved that the crusader possessed the honourable qualities necessary to serve king and state.

All the prominent crusaders had competitors back home. Sigurd was co-regent with his brother, and the saga gives us to understand there was competition between them. Ragnvald had rivals in the Orkneys, and was killed three years after his homecoming. Erling Skakke and Eindride Unge, who had been on Ragnvald's crusade, both participated in the civil war in Norway on opposing sides. In 1163 Erling defeated and killed Eindride, while Erling himself was killed in 1179 by the pretender Sverre. In an unstable society, the prestige and honour acquired on a crusade was a valuable asset. Secular honour could be equally important for all the private crusaders on a smaller scale in their local societies.

A crusade originally and officially had a religious purpose. In the minds of the medieval Norse, however, it seems to have been more an occasion for social 'distinction', to use Bourdieu's terminology. In most societies there are practices which make it possible for elite people to prove that they possess personal qualities which justify their social prestige and power. In medieval society many of these practices had a religious as well as a secular dimension.

Some Methodological Considerations

Kurt Villads Jensen concludes the article mentioned in the introduction as follows:

> The first historians of the crusades c. 1100 thought that the first crusade was God's will and the result of men's efforts to do His will. Interestingly, that is where research on the crusades since 1970 has ended. The motive force behind the crusades was above all the individual crusader's desire to do penance and God's will, and historical research focuses on understanding how this was done in practice. Earlier generations' efforts to reveal other motives behind the crusades – economic, social and political – regarding crusades as a pretext for something else, has almost disappeared in international research. The crusades are taken more seriously than before, and the crusaders are understood on their own terms.[53]

If this is right, the Norse crusades must have been highly atypical. But were they really? A systematic comparison of the results of the Danish crusading project as presented in this conclusion, to the motives of the Norse crusaders as presented in this article, is beyond the scope of this article, but those who want to do it have to take some methodological questions into consideration.

First, does opposing monocausal explanations as is done in the conclusion quoted above provide a good understanding? Medieval people were able to keep more than one idea in their heads at a time, in which they were no different from modern people, who pride themselves on having a complex mind with many partly conflicting values, and one should not expect medieval people to be more simple-minded.[54] As shown above, the medieval Norse had several ideas about why they themselves and others went on a crusade.

Secondly, does limiting oneself to a dichotomy between religious motives on the one hand and material motives like profit and power on the other provide good understanding? There are modern sociological approaches which could be useful in analysing the crusades.

It has been shown that Bourdieu's theory of 'distinction' and 'cultural capital' was useful in analysing the motives of the Norse crusaders.

Thirdly, one should take into account that different social groups might have different mentalities. Even if the same complex set of motives was present in the minds of most of the crusaders, these motives were not equally important for all of them. Motives were often socially differentiated. We have seen above that clerics and the secular elite both recognised religion and secular honour as motives for going on a crusade. The clerics, however, not surprisingly, emphasised religion far more strongly. The religious motives emphasised in sources written by clerics in Denmark and other European countries do not necessarily give an accurate picture of the motives of laymen who made up the bulk of the crusaders.

Finally, it is easy to be dismissive about earlier research in introducing a new field of research like crusading history or cultural history in Scandinavia considering it to be outdated and old fashioned. In my view, however, it is more fruitful to take one's point of departure from the research of earlier generations, and regard one's own research as an addition to what has already been done. A major problem will then be to discuss how new results can be fitted into and reconciled with the knowledge and theories produced by earlier generations of historians. This is a precondition for understanding the complexities of medieval society. It is also a precondition for grasping how the complexities of medieval society are reflected in the medieval Norsemen's understanding of the crusades.

NOTES

1 The article was published in Norwegian as Nedkvitne 2002.
2 K. V. Jensen 2000, p. 19. The expression 'rolling monastery' he has borrowed from Riley Smith, but the views quoted are Jensen's own. See also op.cit., pp. 23, 25–26.
3 K. V. Jensen 2000, pp. 14–15.
4 E.g., Nedkvitne 1997.
5 K. V. Jensen 2001.
6 E.g., J. M. Jensen 2000.
7 NSEOD: 'Crusade'.
8 Bysted 2000, p. 35.
9 Doxey 1996; J. M. Jensen 2000.
10 Pulsiano (ed.) 1993: *Ágrip*.
11 *Morkinskinna*, pp. 66–67.
12 Pulsiano (ed.) 1993: *Orkneyinga saga*.
13 Pulsiano (ed.) 1993: *Heimskringla*; KLNM: *Fagrskinna*.
14 It is possible that *Orkneyinga saga* was also written by a cleric, Bjarne Kolbeinsson, the bishop of Orkneys, but this is a hypothesis only.
15 *Ágrip*, pp. 47–49.
16 *Morkinskinna*, p. 322; *Heimskringla*: *Magnussønnenes saga*, ch. 11.
17 *Morkinskinna*, pp. 313–314.
18 *Orkneyinga saga*, ch. 85.
19 *Morkinskinna*, p. 316.
20 *Morkinskinna*, p. 319.
21 *Orkneyinga saga*, ch. 86–87.
22 *Morkinskinna*, p. 322; *Heimskringla*: *Magnussønnenes saga*, ch. 10.
23 *Orkneyinga saga*, ch. 88; *Morkinskinna*, p. 321; *Heimskringla*: *Magnussønnenes saga*, ch. 10.
24 The warships in the Norwegian *leidang* fleet had 20–25 rooms, that is 40–50 rowers, see KLNM: 'Leidang'.
25 *Morkinskinna*, pp. 323–324.
26 *Heimskringla*: *Magnusssønnenes saga*, ch. 13; *Morkinskinna*, p. 325.
27 *Orkneyinga saga*, ch. 89.
28 *Morkinskinna*, p. 320; *Heimskringla*: *Magnussønnenes saga*, ch. 13.
29 *Morkinskinna*, p. 319; *Heimskringla*: *Magnussønnenes saga*, ch. 6.
30 *Morkinskinna*: p. 322; *Heimskringla*: *Magnusssønnenes saga*, ch. 11.

31 *Orkneyinga saga*: ch. 87.
32 *Heimskringla*: *Magnusssønnenes saga*, ch. 11; *Morkinskinna*, p. 322.
33 *Morkinskinna*, pp. 324–325.
34 *Morkinskinna*, p. 325; *Heimskringla*: *Magnusssønnenes saga*, ch. 13. The sentence is almost identical in both sagas.
35 *Orkneyinga saga*, ch. 89.
36 Morkinskinna and Orkneyinga saga use derivations of *frægd* meaning 'famous'.
37 *Morkinskinna*, p. 319; *Den norsk-islandske skjaldedigtning*, p. 459.
38 *Morkinskinna*, p. 322; *Den norsk-islandske skjaldedigtning*, p. 459.
39 *Den norsk-islandske skjaldedigtning*, p. 485.
40 *Orkneyinga saga*, ch. 86.
41 Bandlien 2001, p. 107.
42 *Den norsk-islandske skjaldedigtning*, p. 482.
43 *Den norsk-islandske skjaldedigtning*, pp. 510–511.
44 *Den norsk-islandske skjaldedigtning*, p. 486.
45 *Morkinskinna*, p. 314; *Fagerskinna*, p. 315.
46 *Morkinskinna*, p. 321; *Heimskringla*: *Magnusssønnenes saga*, ch. 8–9.
47 *Morkinskinna*, pp. 322–324; *Heimskringla*: *Magnusssønnenes saga*, ch. 12; *Fagerskinna*, pp. 319–320.
48 *Morkinskinna*, p. 325. This story appears in *Morkinskinna* only, not in *Heimskringla*.
49 Koht 1924, pp. 166–167.
50 Pulsiano (ed.) 1993: *Orkneyinga saga*.
51 *Orkneyinga saga*, ch. 86.
52 *Orkneyinga saga*, ch. 88.
53 K. V. Jensen 2000, pp. 25–26.
54 This is discussed as a general problem in Nedkvitne 2000 and Ferrer 2001.

BIBLIOGRAPHY

Sources

Ágrip, in B. Einarsson (ed.), *Íslenzk Fornrit*, vol. 29. Reykjavík 1985, pp. 3–54; English translation and Old Norse text in M. J. Driscoll (ed. & trans.), *Ágrip af Nóregskonungasögum*. Viking Society for Northern Research, text series vol. 10. London 1995; Norwegian translation in G. Indrebø, *Ágrip*. Oslo 1973. *Íslenzk Fornrit* and English translation have the same division in chapters. The Norwegian translation has no chapter divisions.

Fagrskinna, in B. Einarsson (ed.), *Islenzk Fornrit*, vol. 29. Reykjavik 1985, pp. 57–364.

Den norsk-islandske skjaldedigtning, series B, vol. 1. F. Jonsson (ed.), Copenhagen 1912–1915.

Heimskringla. F. Jonsson (ed.), Copenhagen 1911. English translation in L. M. Hollander, *Heimskringla: History of the Kings of Norway*. Austin 1964/1995. Numerous translations into Scandinavian languages. All editions and translations have identical chapter divisions.

Morkinskinna. English translation with an introduction by T. Andersson & K. E. Gade, Itacha–London 2000. Printed in the original language in C. R. Unger (ed.), *Morkinskinna*. Christiania 1867.

Orkneyinga saga, in F. Gudmundsson (ed.), *Islenzk Fornrit*, vol. 34. Reykjavik 1965, pp. 1–300. English translation in H. Pálsson & P. Edwards, *Orkneyinga saga: The History of the Earls of Orkney*. London 1978. Norwegian translation in A. Holtsmark, *Orknøyingenes saga*. Oslo 1970. The division in chapters is identical in all editions and translations.

Literature

B. Bandlien 2001, *Å finne den rette*. Oslo.

A. L. Bysted 2000, 'Korstogsafladens opståen og teoretiske udvikling', *Den Jyske historiker* 89, pp. 30–47.

G. B. Doxey 1996, 'Norwegian Crusaders in the Balearic Islands', *Scandinavian Studies* 2, pp. 139–160.

M. Ferrer 2001, 'Middelaldermenneskets emosjonelle atferd. Et uttrykk for en kompleks psykologi', *Historisk tidsskrift* (Norwegian) 2, pp. 147–172.

J. M. Jensen 2000, 'Danmark og den hellige krig', *Historisk tidsskrift* (Danish) 2, pp. 139–160.

K. V. Jensen 2000, 'Temaer i korstogshistorien – et historiografisk rids', *Den Jyske historiker* 89, pp. 8–29.

K. V. Jensen 2001, 'Introduction', in A. Murray (ed.), *Crusade and Conversion on the Baltic Frontier 1150–1500*. Aldershot, pp. xvii–xxv.

H. Koht 1924, 'Kong Sigurd på Jorsal-ferd', *Historisk tidsskrift* (Norwegian) 5 vol. 5, pp. 153–168.

A. Nedkvitne 1997, *Møtet med døden i norrøn middelalder*. Oslo.

A. Nedkvitne 2000, 'Beyond Historical Anthropology in the Study of Medieval Mentalities', *Scandinavian Journal of History* 25/1–2, pp. 27–51.

A. Nedkvitne 2002, 'Hvorfor dro middelalderens skandinaver på korstog?' *Den jyske historiker* 96, pp. 114–129.

P. Pulsiano (ed.) 1993, *Medieval Scandinavia*. New York–London.

JANUS MØLLER JENSEN

War, Penance and the First Crusade

Dealing with a 'Tyrannical Construct'[1]

Thirty years ago, the American historian Elizabeth A. R. Brown wrote a very influential and important article called 'The Tyranny of a Construct.'[2] The article was about feudalism, but it might as well have been the title of an article on the crusades. For the last forty years there has been much debate on how we should define or 'construct' the concept of the crusade.[3] This whole discussion stems from the fact that no parallel term is congruous with any modern definition of crusade existing in the twelfth century.[4] Historians of the twentieth century, it is possible to argue, used the legal definitions that emerged towards the end of the twelfth century to create the modern concept of crusade.[5] This has even led one historian, Christopher Tyerman, to ask whether there were any crusades in the twelfth century and then decide in the negative.[6] It is, however, obvious from the contemporary sources that people believed that something new was initiated by Urban II at the council of Clermont in 1095.[7] It is also apparent that the call to arms against the infidels made by Urban contained some sort of institutional aspect in the form of new privileges granted to people who wanted to embark upon the expedition to the Holy Land.[8] In my view therefore it is still quite convenient for historians to speak of crusade in denominating this 'new thing' to maintain a common point of reference for this particular feature of the High and Later Middle Ages. But the main conclusion we have to draw from the work of Tyerman, I think, is to keep in mind that Urban did not intend to start a crusading movement nor produce a charter for the movement he mentioned in the speech at Clermont.[9] The notion of crusade changed during the twelfth century because of the practical and ideological experiences of crusading, which contributed to forming and developing the more institutionalised features recognisable in the writings of the theologians and canon lawyers towards the end of the twelfth century and in the thirteenth century. To apply a modern definition of crusade based on these later texts as a stereotype for the sources of the twelfth century wanting this and that criteria to be fulfilled in order to speak of 'crusade' would deprive us of an understanding of the dynamics and true nature of the ideas that formed the background for what for want of a clear-cut, congruous contemporary term we call crusade. While this may seem obvious, it is in my view one of the more fundamental problems of the study of the crusades today.

A lot of very stimulating and very fine research has, of course, been done, especially in the last twenty years, which has increased our understanding of the phenomenon tremendously and which forms the basis of this brief presentation. The works of Professor Jonathan Riley-Smith and the inclusion of the charter material have increased our knowledge of the motivation and ideas of the first crusaders.[10] His observation that the rendering of Urban's speech in Clermont in the chronicles of the first crusade was greatly influenced by the experiences of the first crusaders and not least the success of the expedition, for which the chroniclers gave a theological explanation, and therefore must be used with caution when trying to extract the original message that Urban delivered, has of course been long recognised.[11] But it seems as if the full consequences of this have not been realized. If the ideas of the crusaders were formed during the march to Jerusalem under the influence of the hardships they endured and the theological explanation was accordingly interpreted with the benefit of hindsight, what was the original idea that inspired people to leave on the crusade in the first place? What was the initial message that Urban delivered that had such an impact on contemporaries? Although it might now no longer be possible to recover the actual words of the pope at the council of Clermont it is possible to identify a number of themes that most likely were very prominent. It was to the message of this sermon and the subsequent preaching to which the arms-bearers and everybody else responded. The success of the call to arms must be found here and is therefore independent of the hardships of the journey and the initial outcome. What then was the message that struck such a chord in contemporary minds and society?

However much historians disagree about how to define a crusade, they all seem to agree to the main characteristic and innovative idea behind Pope Urban's preaching of the First Crusade. The Crusade was a fusion of holy war and pilgrimage to the Holy Sepulchre. This was the brand new concept, which had such a tremendous appeal to the arms-bearing sector of Latin Christian society. This aspect has even become part of what is called the pluralist definition of crusade, whose most prominent spokesman is Riley-Smith,[12] who claims that the crusader was a pilgrim, because the vow he made before departing on crusade was always based on the vow to go on a pilgrimage.[13] Because of this one can 'safely presume' that the vow to go on a crusade stemmed from the fact that the crusade was considered a pilgrimage.[14] There can be absolutely no doubt that in order to obtain their spiritual privileges many of the first crusaders made a vow – but was it a pilgrimage vow?

Even though there are some references to vows made before people went on pilgrimage prior to 1095,[15] the development of a proper canonical theory concerning religious vows and their legal and theological implications did not take place until the latter half of the twelfth century. This is to be seen in connection with the development of canon law in general in the twelfth and thirteenth centuries. The legal implications of the pilgrimage vow were specified only during this process.[16] Although the idea of a religious vow can hardly be seen or indeed be considered as an innovation towards the end of the eleventh century, the canonical doctrine concerning the vow and the obligations that resulted from it did not exist.[17] It thus seems too hasty simply to conclude that the crusading vow in 1095 was based on the pilgrimage vow. One cannot thus easily conclude, as Riley-Smith does, that the crusade vow came into existence because the crusade was considered a pilgrimage. The first question is whether Urban believed that he was combining pilgrimage and holy war. The next question, then, is obviously whether people who heard his message believed, that the call to arms was a combination of holy war and pilgrimage. I believe this to be an important issue for the debate concerning the definition of crusade, because it has consequences for reading the sources both before and after Clermont analysing firstly the origin of the idea of crusade, and secondly the characteristics of crusading thought as it developed through the twelfth century.

Turning to the first question of whether Urban II himself believed that he was combining pilgrimage with holy war. I believe he did not. There are two main reasons for this. First of all, he did not once say that he did so. In an often-cited letter to some Spanish princes dated 1089, Urban is believed to have combined the war in Spain with the pilgrimage to Jerusalem, and this letter has thus been interpreted as a crucial step towards the crusade. The letter states that anyone who wanted to go to Jerusalem *or any other place* either as a penitent or as a devotional act should instead give support to the reconstruction of the archbishopric of Tarragona.[18] This means that either military or monetary support for this work was a substitute for penance otherwise imposed for sin. It means that the war in Spain was considered a penitential act just like a pilgrimage, but did not actually turn the war into a pilgrimage. This was precisely what the statute from the council of Clermont concerning the crusade said - all penance would be commuted by the expedition to Jerusalem.[19] Perhaps the interpretation of this letter is a result of historians trying to look for the preliminary steps towards combining pilgrimage and holy war, thus looking for the origin of their own definition.[20] I believe we have to look to Urban's other letters in order to understand the significance of this letter. Urban did actually describe the enterprise he had initiated in Clermont in his own words,[21] describing it as a military campaign that would earn the participants remission of their sins. The war itself would be a penitential act. It is important to establish the tradition that Urban II worked within in order to understand the background to the call for a penitential war to liberate Jerusalem. Is the concept of penitential warfare found in other eleventh century sources?

Now leaving the much disputed Barbastro campaign and the pontificate of Alexander II and turning directly to the pontificate of Gregory VII, there are plenty of examples of the notion of penitential war. Gregory built up a network of kings, lords and princes whose powers he called upon in return for spiritual benefits. The concept was not perhaps explicitly expressed in his letters, but there are instances in which penance is substituted for military aid to the papacy. In 1076 Gregory had been informed that Count Roger of Calabria wanted to be reconciled with Rome. Gregory then asked Bishop Arnald of Acerenza to arrange that the penance the Normans had to perform to be reconciled with the papacy should be their war against the Muslims of Sicily.[22] We catch a glimpse of how this was performed in practice during the Battle of Sorbria, in which Mathilda of Tuscany fought victoriously against the imperial forces. Before the battle Anselm of Lucca instructed Bishop Bardo to grant absolution and make it clear to the soldiers with what intent they had to fight in order to obtain remission of their sins (*remissio peccatorum*).[23] To the enemies of Gregory, these ideas were perceived to mean that fighting would bring salvation to the soldiers,[24] an idea they believed to be utterly against Christian doctrine. The reforming circles around Gregory had however developed a theological explanation for this, which is to be found precisely in the *intentio* of the soldiers.[25] True penance was dependent upon true and complete inner conversion of the penitent. It was not the actions themselves that counted as much as the true intentions of those who performed them that were important.[26] Here Urban II was building on the decretals and synodal decisions during the pontificate of Gregory VII as testified by the Council of Melfi and some of his letters.[27] In a letter to Bishop Geoffrey of Lucca he declared that he who kills an excommunicate is not guilty of the crime of murder.[28] A penance is to be imposed, however, because due to the fragility of the human mind a mean motive could be behind the killing. How then did war become a penitential act?

The answer is again, I believe, to be found within the reforming circles towards the end of the eleventh century. In his *Liber ad amicum* Bonizo of Sutri replied shortly after Gregory's death in 1085 to a friend, answering two questions. How can it be that God is deaf to the cries of the earthly Church and does not come to its aid and is it fitting for a Christian to bear arms for the true faith?[29] The answer to the first was plainly that, because Christ had suffered on Earth, we have to take up the cross and follow him. We have to endure hardships and die in Christ in order to be resurrected and rule with him.[30] Taking up the cross of Christ was one of the essential themes of preaching the crusade.[31] Bonizo explained this through the commentary of Augustine on the Sermon on the Mount. Augustine had cited Matthew: 'Blessed are those who suffer persecution for righteousness, because they shall inherit paradise.'[32] Bonizo says that in quoting this, Augustine had aligned those who punished on behalf of justice with those who were persecuted.[33] By fighting for righteousness you became blessed. Thus he could conclude on the second question put by his friend:

> Let therefore the soldiers of God fight for the truth, strive for righteousness, and fight with a true heart against the heresy that exalts itself against every so-called god or object of worship. Let them emulate in good the most excellent Countess Mathilda, a daughter of St Peter, who with a man's heart has renounced all worldly things and would rather die than break the laws of God and by all powers at her command fight the heresy that now rages within the church.[34]

The call to crusade was an expression of this line of thought.[35] It is clear from this that if one had the right intention and was willing to give up one's life for Christ, then it could be legitimate for a Christian to take up arms.[36] If a person took the cross of Christ, that is, applied the papally proclaimed motives of the war and turned them into his own motives, he could then engage on a war that was penitential. Direct emphasis was thus placed on the right intentions of the people who departed on Urban's expedition in 1095 as for example in the crusade statute of the Council of Clermont. Thus the war became a penitential act which could replace other imposed penance. Therefore, whenever talking of the crusade, Urban did not speak of a pilgrimage but of a *labor* or a military expedition, using the terms *iter* or *expeditio*, which would bring about remission of the sins of the participants.[37]

This leads directly to my second reason why Urban did not think of the crusade as a pilgrimage. The official declaration found in the statutes of the council of Clermont says the same thing, the word used to describe the 'crusade' being *iter*. In diplomas both before and after the first crusade this term could denominate a pilgrimage,[38] but its most usual sense is 'military expedition' or plain 'journey' or 'travel.'[39] This seems the most reasonable translation of the word in the statute, as Urban II himself used terms like *expeditio*, clearly in the sense of a military expedition, when talking of the crusade. The conclusion is thus that the war itself is a penitential act and the crusade was preached as such. This was Urban's notion of the crusade and not some fusion of two distinct institutions like holy war and pilgrimage.[40]

But if Urban himself did not describe the crusade as a *peregrinatio*, the participants themselves, as well as some leading ecclesiastics, did. Geoffrey, the Abbot of Vendôme, referred to the expedition as a *peregrinatio*:

> The lay people were enjoined to go to Jerusalem whereas it was prohibited to the monks by the apostolic seat. I learned this myself when I heard the words of pope Urban II when he urged the lay people to *peregrinare* to Jerusalem and at the same time prohibited this *peregrinatio* to the monks.

> Hierusalem etenim ire, sicut indictum est laicis, sic interdictum est monachis ab apostolica sede. Quod novi ego ipse … cujus aures erant ad os domini Urbani papæ, cum et eundo Hierusalem peregrinari præciperet laicis, et ipsam peregrinationem monachis prohiberet.[41]

This statement by Riley-Smith is taken to be the evidence for considering the expedition as a pilgrimage.[42] Being a trained ecclesiastic, Geoffrey most certainly should have known what Urban II was preaching. But in the same letter Geoffrey also referred to the expedition as an *iter* and it would be quite as possible simply to translate both words by 'journey.' Urban had forbidden monks to go on the crusade in his letter to the congregation in Vallombrosa and although this letter states that they could go with the permission of their abbots it was clearly understood as a prohibition both by Geoffrey of Vendôme and Anselm of Canterbury.[43] The context was that monks had no need to seek the earthly Jerusalem but should rather seek the heavenly Jerusalem that was within them.[44] In the charters of departing crusaders we often find both the words *peregrinatio* and *expeditio* used to describe the crusade at the same time.[45] In one charter from Anjou these two are used in opposition: *peregrinatio sive expeditio*.[46] Riley-Smith takes this as an indication of how interchangeable these two had become.[47] But what did *peregrinatio* mean? How do we translate it?

The word *peregrinatio* changed meaning during the twelfth century. Before the first crusade and the creation of the Latin kingdom of Jerusalem, the Latin term *peregrinus* simply meant traveller and as such had no religious connotation. If there was any, it was clear simply from the purpose of the journey. Only after 1187 did the word *peregrinus* came to mean pilgrim.[48] The classical meaning of the word was stranger or traveller. It became part of the Christian ideal of the sixth-eighth centuries to wander about aimlessly. In the ninth century it seems as if people distinguished between travellers who had a worthy objective and those who did not, which usually meant that people who travelled had to have permission to embark on a journey or show some letter of recommendation. This became part of the canonical collections of both Burchard of Worms and Ivo of Chartres in the eleventh century. Robert of Rheims wrote in his chronicle of the crusade that it was not fitting for lay people to journey – *peregrinare* – on the first crusade without permission from their priest.[49] This could also be taken to imply that people needed to be absolved by their own priest in order to get remission of sins on completing the journey. A recurrent problem concerning pilgrimages throughout the High Middle Ages was that people had to be turned away from cult sites because they had not received absolution from their parish priests.[50] In the ninth century the penitential practice of forcing people into exile seem to have developed.[51] The theological model was fratricide Cain, who was forced to wander about. During the ninth century this wandering or religious exile was described by the term *peregrinare*. During the eleventh century this sometimes aimless wandering became absorbed with a specific destination like Tours, Rome, Santiago or Jerusalem.[52] Thus when the participants in the first crusade referred to themselves as *peregrini*, I believe it to be in this sense of wandering about or being in religious exile. This would be quite fitting descriptions for the warriors in a military campaign for God which would give the participants remission of sins. I cannot argue definitely that all departing crusaders had a good and clear-cut idea of what they were embarking on when they set out for Jerusalem or that they fully comprehended all the theological explanations of the remission of sin that they could gain, but I am quite convinced that they were very conscious of the spiritual rewards and fully aware that the war was undertaken as a substitute for penance otherwise imposed on them.[53] They knew that they were in a state of religious exile about to fight for their heavenly lord in return for remission of sins. In that sense they were *peregrini*.

The historian Giles Constable argued in a study of the charters as a source for the history of the crusades that the terms used in charters to describe people going on a crusade was verbs like *pergere* and *agere*. These terms, he said, were pilgrimage terms and therefore the crusade was a pilgrimage.[54] But why are they specific pilgrimage terms? They are simply verbs that describe people who are going away on a journey.[55] In my opinion this is quite a fitting description for departing crusaders. When we have to distinguish today as historians between pilgrims and crusaders it must be done from the context and purpose of the journey. We have to look at people's actions. When people went armed to Jerusalem, or any other place for that matter, to fight the enemies of the Church, they could gain remission of sins because the war itself was a penitential act. This idea had roots in the investiture contest of the last half of the eleventh century and I believe we have to understand the message of Urban II within the context of the ideas and discussions of that day. Taking up the cross of Christ, that is, making the motives of a suffering Church your own and thereby joining a holy war, could gain you remission of sins. This idea might not have been so revolutionary in the last decade of the eleventh century, thoroughly grounded in the moral theology and canonical teachings of the day. However the events of the years preceding Clermont, as Riley-Smith believes, the hardships of the expedition, the religious experience of being so near the holiest places and the success of the expedition seemed amazing to contemporaries and only could be explained as the work of God, and placed this idea at the heart of Latin Christendom. The concept of penitential warfare was copied and used as a model for later expeditions to the Holy Land, Spain and the Baltic. I also believe it to be this idea that evolved naturally into the lay religious military confraternities of the first half of the twelfth century and eventually the military orders.

Does this mean that pilgrimage was unimportant in the formation of the crusade idea? I certainly believe not. But I think we have to make a distinction – as certainly many contemporaries did – between fighting a war as a penitential practice and visiting a holy shrine for the same reason. The religious reforms in the eleventh century certainly had a grip and were indeed promoted by lay advocates as the many pious donations and intensified pilgrimage traffic of this century testify. The response to the call to arms in 1095 is to be seen as another expression of this piety and for the same purpose, the remission of sins. To borrow a phrase from Marcus Bull going on crusade and donating land to monasteries were intimately, even organically linked just as going on pilgrimage was organically linked to the religious practices of the day.[56] It is therefore not surprising to find the experiences of crusaders described in terms that we find in donation charters and descriptions of pilgrimage practices,[57] since taking up arms on behalf of God was considered a penitential practice just like a pilgrimage. This is the idea fundamental to crusade and not the combination of holy war and pilgrimage.

NOTES

1   This paper was originally given at the Finnish Institute in Rome in January 2001. Prior to its publication here it has appeared in a different and expanded version with the consent of the editors as Møller Jensen 2003.

2   Brown 1974/1998.

3   Riley-Smith 1995; Riley-Smith 1993; Mayer 1990, pp. 312–313; Hehl 1994.

4   In the sources concerning the first crusade you will often find the words *iter, peregrinatio* or *expeditio* used to describe the expedition. The participants often referred to themselves as *cruce signati* or *peregrini*, but the term *cruce signati* only became a technical term in canon law towards the end of the twelfth century; Brundage 1966, p. 291; Markowski 1984; Constable 1985, p. 75. For a description of the words used to describe the first crusade and its participants, see Riley-Smith 1982.

5   See also Reynolds 1994/1996, esp. ch. 6.

6   Tyerman 1995; Tyerman 1998. See also in this respect, Gilchrist 1985; Gilchrist 1988.

7   Guibert of Nogent, p. 124; Fulcher of Chartres, pp. 136–137; Ralph of Caen, pp. 605–606; *Chronica Monasteri Casinensis*, p. 475. Cf. Bull 1993b, pp. 353–355; Althoff 1981.

8   PL 162, cols 170–173, 176–177. At col. 177 he cites a board of clerics calling the privileges of protection granted to soldiers departing for Jerusalem as a novelty: 'dicentes novam esse institutionem de tuitone ecclesiastica impendenda rebus militum Hierosolymam proficiscentium.' Discussed by Bull 1993a, pp. 59–61. For other examples concerning this aspect, see Brundage 1984, pp. 178–179.

9   See e.g. Atiya 1962, p. 20: '[the speech] constituted the charter of the whole movement'. It was reported most fully by Fulcher of Chartres, Atiya says, and 'presents Urban's own definition of the Crusade.' This is highly unlikely considering the works of Jonathan Riley-Smith; see below.

10 Riley-Smith 1998; Riley-Smith 1986/1997; Riley-Smith 1997; Constable 1985.

11 Riley-Smith 1986/1997, pp. 139, 135–152. Marshal W. Baldwin pointed this out in Baldwin 1941, p. 459.

12 It is not that I want to criticise professor Riley-Smith for the many ways his studies and observations has been put to use by various other historians, and Riley-Smith himself acknowledges the problems by applying a stereotyped definition of crusades to the sources; see Riley-Smith 1987/1996, pp. xxviii–xxx. For rhetorical matters I mention him as his works are the most influential, although other historians like Norman Housley seems much more 'hard-core' pluralist; see Housley 1985, p. 23. Here Housley's comment 'that an indulgence, not even a crusade indulgence, constituted a full crusade' is with direct reference to the definition of crusade given by Riley-Smith 1992, p. 78.

13 J. & L. Riley-Smith 1981, p. 1.

14 Riley-Smith 1986/1997, p. 23.

15 Brundage 1969, p. 17, n. 64.

16 Brundage 1969, pp. 17–18, 30–65. One probably has to understand the observation made by Giles Constable that the vow apparently became more important in the later crusades than in the early crusades in this respect; Constable 1985, p. 75, n. 22.

17 Brundage 1968, pp. 77–78.

18 *Documentación pontificia*, pp. 46–47, my emphasis.

19 'Quicumque pro sola devotione, non pro honoris vel pecunie adeptione, ad liberandam ecclesiam Dei Hierusalem profectus fuerit, iter illud pro omni penitentia ei reputetur,' Somerville 1972, p. 74.

20 My interpretation of the Spanish letters is contrary to Mayer 1990, pp. 29–30. Another example is H. E. J. Cowdrey's conclusion in his superb study of the Mahdia campaign on the north coast of Africa in 1087, in which he claims this expedition was a stepping-stone towards combining pilgrimage and holy war in the mind of Urban II (then Odo of Ostia); Cowdrey 1984. In my eyes however the reading of the poem

praising the victory of the Christians (mostly people from Pisa) over the heathens does not seem to indicate this. It is said that St Peter helped the Christians when he saw they bore his mark, i.e., pilgrim-badges from Rome, but that was because they had been on pilgrimage prior to the expedition and in no way are these two things combined. Cowdrey says that the crucial step has not yet been taken, but this poem to my mind does not indicate that such a step should be taken from this campaign. The poem praising the victory of the Christians, *Carmen in victoriam Pisanorum*, has been edited by Cowdrey and printed as an appendix to his article. In fact I believe the many other examples from Urban II's letters, in which fighting in Spain is considered a penitential act, to be as important as the origin of the call in 1095.

21 *Epistulæ et chartæ*, pp. 136–138; *Papsturkunden für Kirchen* , pp. 88–89; PL 151, col. 504; HGL, pp. 744–746.

22 *Das Register Gregors VII*, pp. 271–272: 'Quapropter pastorali cura hoc laboris onus tibi imponimus, immo ex parte beati Petri imperamus, ut postposita omni torporis desidia illum adeas eumque huius nostri precepti auctoritate fultus, si nobis parere sicut pollicitus est voluerit et pênitentiam, ut oportet christianum, egerit, ab omni peccatorum suorum vinculo tam illum quam etiam suos milites, qui cum eo contra paganos, ita tamen ut agant pênitentiam, pugnaturi sunt, peccatis maxime absolvas. Addimus preterea, ut eum pia admonitione admoneas, quatenus se a capitalibus criminibus custodiat et christiani nominis culturam inter paganos amplificare studeat, ut de eisdem hostibus victoriam consequi mereatur.' The penance thus has to be the fighting itself. *Ut agant penitentiam* cannot be read as a temporal clause, because *ago* is in the subjunctive. This is contrary to Gottlob 1906, p. 53.

23 *Vita Anselmis*, p. 20: 'Quia dominus noster sanctus Anselmus episcopus suam eis benedictionem per nostram direxit parvitatem, hoc in mandatis praecipue commendans nobis, ut si qui cum excommunicatis communicassent, primitus illos absolveremus, et tunc pariter omnes auctoritate apostolica et sua benediceremus, instruentes eos, quo pacto quave intentione deberent pugnare, sicque in remissionem omnium peccatorum eorum instantis belli comitteremus periculum.'

24 Weinrich of Trier, p. 296; Sigebert of Gembloux, pp. 460, 462.

25 This aspect was one of the central themes of my MA thesis, Møller Jensen 2001.

26 These ideas were also expressed towards the end of the eleventh century by some leading philosophers, including the teachers of Peter Abelard, William of Champeraux and Anselm of Laon; see Clanchy 1997/1999, pp. 80–85, 279–280. Cf. in this respect Marenbon 1997, p. 253.

27 *Das Register Gregors VII*, pp. 400–440, 472, 479–487; Somerville & Kuttner 1996, pp. 257–258, 293–294; Cowdrey 1995, pp. 78–82; Somerville 1989, pp. 44ff.

28 PL 151, col. 394.The letter was cited by Ivo of Chartres, *Decretum*, p. 706 and *Panormia*, p. 1308, and by Gratian, C. 23 q. 5. c. 47, CIC, 945. Cf. Manegold of Lautenbach, pp. 376–377: 'Quod hi qui excommunicatos non pro privata injuria, sed ecclesiam defendendo interficiunt, non ut homicidie peniteant vel puniantur.'

29 Bonizo of Sutri; Cowdrey 1985.

30 Bonizo af Sutri, pp. 571–572.

31 Riley-Smith 1997, p. 161.

32 Matthew 5:10, 'Beati, qui persecutionem patiuntur propter justitiam, quoniam ipsorum est regnum caelorum.'

33 Bonizo of Sutri, p. 619: 'Idem de sermone Dei in habito in monte, cum de beatudinibus loqueretur et venisset ad "Beati qui persecutionem paciuntur propter iustitiam" equaliter dixit beatos eos, qui persecutionem inferunt propter iustitiam, acsi qui persecutionem paciuntur propter iustitiam.' Cf. Ivo of Chartres, *Decretum*, pp. 709–710; Anselm of Lucca, p. 523; Cushing 1998, p 137.

34 Bonizo of Sutri, p. 620: 'Igitur pugnent gloriosissimi Dei milites pro veriate, certent pro iustucia, pugnent vero animo adversus heresim … Emulentur in bonum excellentissimam comitissam Matildam, filiam beati Petri, que virili animo, omnibus mundanis rebus posthabitis, mori parata est potius quam legem Dei infringere et contra heresim, que nunc sevit in ecclesia, prout vires suppetunt, omnibus modis impugnare.'

35 Cowdrey 1985, p. 49.

36 Cf. Hehl 1980, pp. 19–20.

37 Iter: *Epistulæ et chartæ*, pp. 136, 138; Somerville 1972, p. 74. Labor: *Epistulæ et chartæ*, p. 136. Expeditio Jherosolimitana: HGL, p. 745. Expeditio: *Papsturkunden für Kirchen* , pp. 88–89.

38 Petrus Tudebodus, p. 13; *Thesaurus Lingvae Latinae*, p. 539.

39 *Thesaurus Lingvae Latinae*, pp. 538–545; Niermeyer 1976, pp. 558–559. Here *iter* does not even occur in the sense of pilgrimage. Likewise Du Cange 1883–1887/1954, p. 430.

40 This was also the conclusion of Alfons Becker, but he thought that public opinion combined the two; Becker 1988, pp. 396–398.

41 PL 157, col. 162. On this testimony see Cowdrey 1995, pp. 721, 728; Becker 1988, p. 391.

42 Riley-Smith 1986/1997, p. 22. Also Cowdrey 1995, pp. 728–729.

43 *Papsturkunden für Kirchen*, pp. 88–89: 'Audiuimus quosdam uestrum cum militubus, qui Ierusalem liberandê christianitas gratia tendunt, uelle proficisci. Recta quidem oblatio, sed non recta diuisio; nos enim ad hanc expeditionem militum animos instigauimus, qui armis suis Saracenorum feritatem declinare et christianorum (ecclesias) possint libertati pristinê restituere; eos autem, qui derelicto seculo spirituali se militiê deuouerunt, nos nec arma baiulare nec iter hoc inire uolumus, immo etiam prohibemus. Porro religiosos clericos siue monachos in comitatu hoc proficisci sine episcoporum uel abbatum suorum licentia secundum disciplinam sanctorum canonum interdicimus … Volumus, ut has litteras coram conuentu monachorum et laicorum legatis atque per alia monasteria intimare curetis.' Also printed in *Papsturkunden in Florenz*, pp. 313–314. Geoffrey of Vendôme: PL 157, col. 162; Anselm of Canterbury: *S. Anselmi Opera Omnia*, vol. 4 (1949), pp 85–86. Anselm maintained this attitude to monks leaving the monastery; see *S. Anselmi Opera Omnia*, vol. 5 (1951), p. 355. A brother P. had wished to go to Jerusalem, but this desire did not derive from good and helped him therefore not to save his soul: 'Est enim contra professionem tuam, qua promiisisti stabilitatem coram deo in monasterio, in quo habitum monachi accepisti; et est contra apostolici oboedientiam, qui praecepit magna auctoritate sua, ne monachi hanc viam arripere praesumerent.' Anselm says that he was present when Urban commanded this. As he was not at Clermont, he must have heard it during his exile, during which he participated in several councils where the crusade was discussed, and spent a lot of time together with Urban. Even Bernard of Clairvaux, an eager spokesman for crusades, later took the same attitude towards the participation of monks; see PL 182, col. 612: 'It is the vocation of a monk to seek not the earthly but heavenly Jerusalem.'

44 Geoffrey cited Benedict's rule that it was not necessary for monks to go on pilgrimage, and Anselm believed that monks never should leave the peace of the monastery. Cf. also *Liber de Poenitentia*, p. 894: 'Eant milites armati, non monachi, non barbati [=fratres laici]:/ Tales domi remaneant, vota sua adimpleant' and cap. 28, 894. The anonymous author also stated that it was not necessary for a monk to visit the holy places in and around Jerusalem because these also existed in the monastery and within the monk himself; *Liber de Poenitentia*, pp. 891–893. This little work was written around the time of the third crusade.

45 E.g. HGL, p. 753: '[Raymond] qui jussu & obedientia Urbani Romani Pontificis & multorum archiepiscoporum … ad peregrinandum transierat, ut expugnaret exteras gentes & debellarat barbaras nationes.' *Recueil des charters*, vol. 5 (1894), pp. 51–53 (12th April 1096): 'in hac … expeditio christiani populi decertantis ire in Iherusalem, ad belligerandum contra paganos et Sarracenos.' Op. cit., p. 59 (c. 1096): 'in expedicione Hierosolymam' and 'in hac peregrinatione'.

46 *Cartularium monasterii*, p. 186.

47 Riley-Smith 1997, pp. 157–158.

48 Wilkinson et al. (ed.) 1988, p. 81; Birch 1998/2000, pp. 2–5.

49 Burchard of Worms, p. 648; Ivo of Chartres, *Decretum*, p. 896; Robert of Rheims, p. 729. Birch 1998/2000, pp. 70–77, esp. 74–75.

50 Cf. Sumption 1975, pp. 228–229.
51 Cf. Albert 1999, pp. 49ff. Whether or not this was a formative phase in the pilgrimage tradition of the high Middle Ages as argued by Albert will not be discussed further here; cf. the review in Rollason 2000, pp. 1257–1258.
52 Schmitz 1883, pp. 152–154.
53 I completely agree here with Bull's idea that the mutual relations between the religious institutions and the laity fostered a shared perception of religion and religious practices and their meanings, Bull 1993a. See also McLaughlin 1994.
54 Constable 1985, p. 75. According to Constable the standard terms were *adire*, *aggredere*, *ire*, *pergere*, *petere* and *proficere*.
55 In at least one instance it can be definitely shown that *pergere* did not describe going on a pilgrimage but a military campaign; see *Charters de l'abbaye de Nouaillé*, p. 252.
56 Bull 1993a, pp. 176–177.
57 Cf. McGinn 1978.

BIBLIOGRAPHY

Sources

Anselm of Lucca, *Liber contra Wibertum*. E. Bernheim (ed.), in MGH, *Libelli de lite* 1 (1891), pp. 517–528.
Bonizo of Sutri, *Liber ad amicum*, E. Dümmler (ed.) in MGH, *Libelli de lite* 1 (1891), pp. 568–620.
Burchard of Worms, *Decretum*, in PL 140, cols 437–1058.
'Cartularium monasterii beatae mariae Caritatis Andegavensis.' P. Marchegay (ed.) in *Archives d'Anjou*, 3. Angers 1854.
Chartes de l'abbaye de Nouaillé de 678 à 1200. P. de Monsabert, (ed.), Poitiers 1936.
Chronica Monasterii Casinensis, MGH SS, 34. H. Hoffmann (ed.), Hannover 1980.
Das Register Gregors VII. MGH, *Epistolae selectae*, 2/1–2. E. Caspar (ed.), Berlin 1955.
Epistulæ et chartæ ad historiam primi belli sacri spectantes quæ supersunt ævo æqvales ac genuinæ. Die Kreuzzugsbriefe aus den Jahren 1088–1100. Eine Quellensammlung zur Geschichte des ersten Kreuzzuges. H. Hagenmeyer (ed.), Innsbruck 1901.
Fulcher of Chartres, *Historia Hierosolymytana*, H. Hagenmeyer (ed.), Heidelberg, 1913.
Guibert of Nogent, *Gesta Dei per Francos*, in RHC 4, pp. 117–263.
HGL *Histoire Générale de Languedoc*, vol. 5. C. Devic & J. Vaissete (ed.). Toulouse 1875.
Ivo of Chartres, *Decretum*, in PL 161, cols 59–1023.
Ivo of Chartres, *Panormia*, in PL 161, cols 1041–1344.
La Documentación pontificia hasta Inocencio III (965–1216). D. Mansilla (ed.), Rome 1955.
Liber de Poenitentia et Tentationibus Religiosorum, in PL 213, cols 865–904.
Manegold of Lautenbach, *Ad Gebehardum Liber*. K. Francke (ed.) in MGH, *Libelli de lite* 1 (1891), pp. 300–430.
Papsturkunden für Kirchen im Heiligen Lande. R. Hiestand (ed.), Göttingen 1985.
'Papsturkunden in Florenz.' W. Wiederhold (ed.) in *Nachrichten von der Gesellschaft der Wissenschaften zu Göttingen. Philologisch-Historische Klasse* 1901, pp. 306–325.
Petrus Tudebodus, *Historia de Hierosolymitano Itinere*. J. H. Hill & L. L. Hill (ed.), Paris.
Ralph af Caen, *Gesta Tancredi in expeditione Hierosolomytana*, in RHC, vol. 3, pp. 603–716.
Recueil des chartes de l'abbaye de Cluny, 6 vols. A. Bruel (ed.), Paris 1876–1903.
Robert of Rheims, *Historia Hierosolimitana*, in RHC, vol. 3, pp. 717–882.
S. Anselmi Opera Omnia, 6 vols. F. S. Schmitt (ed.), Edinburgh 1946–1961.

Sigebert of Gembloux, *Leodicensium epistola adversus Paschalem papam*. E. Sackur (ed.) in MGH, *Libelli de Lite* 2 (1892), pp. 449–464.

Thesaurus Lingvae Latinae, vol. 7. Leipzig 1956–1979.

Vita Anselmis. R. Wilmans (ed.) in MGH SS 12, pp. 1–35.

Weinrich of Trier, *Epistola Hilthebrando papae*. K. Francke (ed.) in MGH, *Libelli de lite* 1 (1891), pp. 280–299.

Literature

B.-S. Albert 1999, *Le pèlerinage à l'époque carolingienne*. Bruxelles.

G. Althoff 1981, 'Nunc fiant Christi milites, qui dudum exstiterunt raptores. Zur Entstehung von Rittertum und Ritterethos', *Saeculum* 32, pp. 317–333.

A. S. Atiya 1962, *Crusade, Commerce and Culture*. Bloomington.

M. W. Baldwin 1941, 'Some recent Interpretations of Pope Urban II's Eastern Policy', *Catholic Historical Review* 26, pp. 459–466.

A. Becker 1988, *Papst Urban II. (1088–1099), Schriften der MGH*, 19/2. Stuttgart.

D. J. Birch 1998/2000, *Pilgrimage to Rome in the Middle Ages*. Woodbridge.

E. A. R. Brown 1974/1998, 'The Tyranny of a Construct: Feudalism and Historians of Medieval Europe', in L. K. Little & B. H. Rosenwein (ed.), *Debating the Middle Ages. Issues and Readings*. Oxford, pp. 148–169.

J. A. Brundage 1966, 'Cruce signari: The Rite for taking the Cross in England', *Traditio* 22, pp. 289–310.

J. A. Brundage 1968, 'The Votive Obligations of Crusaders: The Development of a Canonistic Doctrine', *Traditio* 24, pp. 77–118.

J. A. Brundage 1969, *Medieval Canon Law and the Crusader*, Wisconsin.

J. A. Brundage 1984, 'St Anselm, Ivo of Chartres and the Ideology of the First Crusade', in *Les mutations socio-culturelles au tournant des XIe–XIIe siècles*, Études Anselmiennes, IVe session. Paris, pp. 175–187.

M. Bull 1993a, *Knightly Piety and Lay Response to the First Crusade. The Limousin and Gascony, c.970-c.1130*. Oxford.

M. Bull 1993b, 'The Roots of Lay Enthusiasm for the First Crusade', *History* 78, pp. 353–372.

M. T. Clanchy 1997/1999, *Abelard. A Medieval Life*. Oxford.

G. Constable 1985, 'Medieval Charters as a Source for the History of the Crusades', in Edbury 1985, pp. 73–89.

H. E. J. Cowdrey 1984, 'The Mahdia Campaign', in H. E. J. Cowdrey, *Popes, Monks and Crusaders*. London, nr. XII.

H. E. J. Cowdrey 1985, 'Martyrdom and the First Crusade', in Edbury 1985, pp. 47–56.

H. E. J. Cowdrey 1995, 'Pope Urban II and the Idea of Crusade', *Studi Medievali*, 3rd series, 36, pp. 721–742.

H. E. J. Cowdrey 1997, 'The Reform Papacy and the Origin of the Crusades', in *Le Concile de Clermont de 1095 et l'Appel à la*. Rome, pp. 65–83.

K. G. Cushing 1998, *Papacy and Law in the Gregorian Revolution. The Canonistic Work of Anselm of Lucca*. Oxford.

Du Cange 1883–1887/1954, *Glossarium Mediae et Infimae Latinitatis*, vol. 4. Graz.

P. W. Edbury (ed.) 1985, *Crusade and Settlement: Papers read at the First Conference of the Society for the Study of the Crusades and the Latin East and Presented to R. C. Smail*. Cardiff.

J. Gilchrist 1985, 'The Erdmann Thesis and Canon Law, 1083–1141', in Edbury 1985, pp. 37–45.

J. Gilchrist 1988, 'The Papacy and War against the "Saracens", 795–1216', *The International History Review* 10, pp. 174–197.

A. Gottlob 1906, *Kreuzablass und Almosenablass. Eine Studie über die Frühzeit des Ablasswesens*. Stuttgart.

E.-D. Hehl 1980, *Kirche und Krieg im 12. Jahrhundert. Studien zu Kanonischem Recht und Politischer Wirklichkeit*. Stuttgart.

E.-D. Hehl 1994, 'Was ist eigentlich ein Kreuzzug?', *HZ* 259, pp. 297–336.

N. Housley 1985, 'Crusades Against Christians: their Origins and Early Development, *c*.1000–1216', in Edbury 1985, pp. 17–36.

J. Marenbon 1997, *The Philosophy of Peter Abelard*. Cambridge.

M. Markowski 1984, 'Crucesignatus: its origin and early usage', *JMH* 10, pp. 157–165.

H. E. Mayer 1990, *The Crusades*, 2nd ed. Oxford.

B. McGinn 1978, '*Iter Sancti Sepulchri*: The Piety of the first Crusaders', in B. K. Lackner & K. R. Philp (ed.), *Essays on Medieval Civilisation*. Austin, pp. 33–71.

M. McLaughlin 1994, *Consorting with Saints. Prayer for the Dead in Early Medieval France*. Ithaca.

J. Møller Jensen 2001, *For hengivenhed alene. Bod, fred og korstog i det 10.-12. århundrede*. MA-thesis, University of Copenhagen.

J. Møller Jensen 2003, 'Peregrinatio sive expedition: Why the First Crusade was not a Pilgrimage', *Al-Masâq* 15, pp. 119–137.

J. F. Niermeyer 1976, *Mediae Latinitatis Lexicon Minus*. Leiden.

S. Reynolds 1994/1996, *Fiefs and Vassals. The Medieval Evidence Reinterpreted*. Oxford.

J. Riley-Smith 1982, 'The First Crusade and St Peter', in B. Z. Kedar et al. (ed.), *Outremer. Studies in the History of the Crusading Kingdom of Jerusalem*. Jerusalem, pp. 41–63.

J. Riley-Smith 1986/1997, *The First Crusade and the Idea of Crusading*. London.

J. Riley-Smith 1987/1996, *The Crusades. A Short History*. London.

J. Riley-Smith 1992, *What Were the Crusades?* 2nd ed. London.

J. Riley-Smith 1993, 'History, the Crusades and the Latin East, 1095–1204. A Personal View', in M. Shatzmiller (ed.), *Crusaders and Muslims in Twelfth-Century Syria*, The Medieval Mediterranean. Peoples, Economies and Cultures, 400–1453, 1. Leiden, pp. 1–17.

J. Riley-Smith 1995, 'The Crusading Movement and Historians', in J. Riley-Smith (ed.), *The Oxford Illustrated History of the Crusades*. Oxford, pp. 1–12.

J. Riley-Smith 1997, 'The Idea of Crusading in the Charters of early Crusaders, 1095–1102', in *Le Concile de Clermont de 1095 et l'Appel à la Croisade*. Rome, pp. 155–166.

J. Riley-Smith 1998, *The First Crusaders, 1095-1131*. Cambridge.

J. & L. Riley-Smith 1981, *The Crusades. Idea and Reality, 1095–1274*. London.

D. Rollason 2000, 'Review of B.-S. Albert, Le pèlerinage à l'époque carolingienne', *EHR* 115, pp. 1257–1258

H. J. Schmitz 1883, *Die Bussbücher und die Bussdisciplin der Kirche. Nach handschriftlichen Quellen dargestellt*. Mainz.

R. Somerville 1972, *The Councils of Urban II, vol. I, Decreta Claromontensia*. Amsterdam.

R. Somerville 1989, 'The Councils of Gregory VII', *Studi Gregoriani* 13, pp. 33–52.

R. Somerville & S. Kuttner 1996, *Pope Urban II, the Collectio Britannica and the Council of Melfi (1089)*. Oxford.

J. Sumption 1975, *Pilgrimage. An Image of Mediaeval Religion*. London.

C. Tyerman 1995, 'Were There Any Crusades in the Twelfth Century?', *EHR* 110, pp. 553–577.

C. Tyerman 1998, *The Invention of the Crusades*. London.

J. Wilkinson & J. Hill & W. F. Ryan (ed.) 1988, *Jerusalem Pilgrimage 1099–1185*. London.

63

SAMU NISKANEN

St Anselm's Views on Crusade

Anselm of Canterbury (c. 1033–1109) was one of the most prominent figures of his age.[1] He entered the monastery of Bec in Normandy in 1059, became a monk a year later, and was made prior in 1063. Finally, he was elected abbot in 1079. He reached the peak of his career with his election to the See of Canterbury in 1093. Anselm had espoused the ideals of the reform papacy, whereas King William Rufus II held very strongly to the regal rights of the Norman kings. In the schism between Urban II and the antipope, Clement III, supported by the emperor and more conservative churchmen, Anselm had already opted for Urban, who represented the reformers. William Rufus first tried to exploit the situation to the maximum by not recognising either of them and thus entered into a violent conflict with his archbishop, who adamantly refused to abandon the party of Urban II. Although William did finally decide to recognise Urban, he was never able to make peace with his reformist archbishop. The conflict culminated in 1097 when Anselm was sent into exile. As an obedient servant of the pope, he went to consult Urban. There was, however, nothing to be done; both William and Anselm maintained their positions.

On William's untimely death in 1100, the English throne was taken by his younger brother, Henry. As a politician he was much more skilful than William. Since he was also in need of ecclesiastical support against his elder brother, Duke Robert, a renowned crusader, he called Anselm back to England. New problems arose immediately. On his return, Anselm set out to proclaim the doctrine of the exclusive right of the Church to appoint prelates; in other words, he brought the investiture contest to England. This was to be the cause of his second exile from 1103 until 1107. In 1103, he again personally consulted the pope in Rome.

After returning to England, Anselm continued his campaign for church reform on English soil. He attacked the sins of simony (commerce in ecclesiastical offices) and nicolaitism (marriage of priests), two issues which had been central on the agenda of the reform papacy.

It is fair to say that Anselm was a zealous papal reformer and an obedient servant of the pope. However, Anselm's relation to the papal reform moment was not completely harmonious, there being some discrepancies between Anselm's policies and the reform papacy. The most important problems arose from the recognition of the rights of papal legates. Anselm was very unwilling to admit any higher ecclesiastical power than that of Archbishop and Primate, except the papal power. This topic has been discussed extensively by historians such as Sir Richard Southern and Sally N. Vaughn.[2] Anselm's lack of crusading enthusiasm has attracted less interest, mainly due to a lack of sources since Anselm's writings include only nine passages referring to crusade directly or indirectly.

At Clermont in 1095, Pope Urban II called upon Christians to take up arms against the enemies of the Christ. Although Clermont opened a new phase of Christian, and more specifically papal, violence, the issue was not unheard of. The reconquest of Spain had already begun under the auspices of the papacy,[3] and Gregory VII had planned a campaign under his own command in order to help the Christians of the East.[4] The papal reform movement was characterised by an increased use of violence.

Anselm must have heard of the first crusade from a special representative of his quite soon after the council of Clermont.[5] He also personally knew several leaders of the first crusade, such as Duke Robert of Normandy, Count Robert of Flanders, Count Eustace of Boulogne and his two sons, Godfrey and Baldwin of Bouillon; later he met Prince Bohemund of Taranto.[6] There are no documents indicating that Anselm would have been interested in sending English knights to the Outremer. Indeed, English participation in the first crusade was poor, as it was in Southern Italy and Germany where hardly anybody had heard of Urban's call before the crusades entered those lands. The pope had obliged bishops to preach the crusade; the task was fulfilled in France, since the vast majority of the episcopal attendants of the council of Clermont were French.[7] If Anselm was informed of the preaching duty, as could be expected, his lack of action is worth noting and is contrary to his general obedience in matters of papal policy. During the Investiture Contest he observed and followed the pope's command punctiliously, although he may not have been convinced of the soundness of the papal point of view. Anselm probably thought that he did not have to follow Urban's order to preach the crusade as he had not heard it himself but from a messenger.[8]

He was, however, ready to follow Urban's instructions not to let any monk participate in the crusade. In 1096 he wrote to Bishop Osmund of Salisbury that no monk in his diocese was permitted to go to Jerusalem. In this letter, Anselm disapproved strongly of the Abbot of Cerne for inciting his monks to go to Jerusalem. The abbot had already sent a young oblate, was himself prepared to go to the East, and was pawning the goods of the Church. According to the letter, the participation of the abbot or his monks in the crusade would lead to 'confusion and damnation.' The abbot was accused of other vices too: he wandered from door to door like a *levis iuvenis* and played dice 'even with women.' The picture Anselm drew of the clerical crusader was absolutely negative. Osmund of Salisbury was also to inform the bishops of Exeter, Bath and Worcester on behalf of the King and Anselm that going to the East was forbidden *sub obtentu anathematis*.[9]

The success of the crusade did not change Anselm's attitude to the participation of monks. In c. 1107, he forbade a monk of St Martin of Séez to go to Jerusalem. The monk's desire did 'not come from a good quarter, nor [was] it good for the salvation of [his] soul.' Going to Jerusalem was against the *stabilitas loci* pronounced in his vows, the pope's command and his abbot's wish. The duty of the clergy was to control the Church and teach the people, not to fight the infidels in the Holy Land.[10]

Indeed, well before the crusade Anselm had at least once been opposed to even an ordinary pilgrimage to Jerusalem. In 1086, as Abbot of Bec, he instructed William, a young nobleman, not to go to the East to help his brother. Instead, he advised that William should come to Bec and become a monk, a true *miles* of Christ. For 'the [earthly] Jerusalem is now not a vision of peace but of tribulation … The heavenly Jerusalem … is a vision of peace, where you will find treasures which you can only receive by despising those [worldly treasures].' The heavenly Jerusalem was, of course, a cloister. It seems that for Anselm the earthly Jerusalem was nothing more than a city in the East with no special spiritual importance, just like any other city. Moreover, Anselm seems to have had an utterly sceptical idea of the noble pilgrims, worrying that they were interested in pillaging the treasures.[11]

Nevertheless, Anselm's letters to the first Christian King of Jerusalem, Baldwin I, whose family Anselm knew well, seem to hint that he held Jerusalem in special esteem. He thanks God for having raised Baldwin 'to the dignity of king in the country where our lord Jesus Christ himself, after having sown the seeds of Christianity, has planted his church anew, so that it might be spread from there throughout the world.'[12] He also wrote that God had chosen Jerusalem *'quasi propriam* before the coming of the Lord and at his coming.'[13] However, it is easy to misinterpret these words, for Anselm's intention was not only to congratulate Baldwin, but also to advise him: 'You should strive to reign not so much for yourself as for God.'[14] Anselm also warned Baldwin against the example of the bad kings who thought 'that the church of God has been given to [them] as if to a master whom she should serve; but they have been entrusted with her, as her advocates and defenders.'[15] Instead, Baldwin should 'govern [his] own person and all his subjects according to the law and the will of God, so that, by [his] life, [he] may set a bright example to all the kings of the earth.'[16] The edifying words on Jerusalem must be interpreted against the background of these admonitions: Anselm's primary aim was not to praise Jerusalem, but to advise the king. Indeed, the king of Jerusalem did not possess anything special in comparison with the other kings as he was bound by the same laws as they were. It is also worth noting that Anselm did not mention the circumstances under which the Christian kingdom of Jerusalem had been created, i.e., the first crusade.[17]

In a different context, another text, of somewhat dubious attribution but probably written by Anselm well before the crusade, expresses the idea behind the distinction between the two Jerusalems. Benedictine monks having taken a vow of pilgrimage to Rome or Jerusalem *in saeculo*, before entering the order, have completed their duty by entering the order.[18] The same idea is expressed in a letter written to a monk who had vowed to go to St Giles under such circumstances. Anselm wrote: 'You must be certain that when you vowed yourself totally to God and gave yourself [to Him] through monastic profession you dissolved all lesser vows of whatever action which you had earlier made *sine iureiurando et fidei alligatione*.'[19]

Against the background of the preaching of the first crusade, Anselm's explicit distinction between the two Jerusalems is most interesting. The preachers often blurred the features of the earthly and the heavenly Jerusalem, so much so that it has been assumed, quite convincingly, that the hearers of those crusade sermons had no clear idea whether they were to conquer the earthly or the heavenly city.[20]

It is doubtful whether Urban referred to Jerusalem explicitly in the sermon delivered at Clermont, since the oldest report of the sermon, the one written by Fulcher of Chartres, does not mention the city.[21] The versions of the later reporters, however, did refer to Jerusalem explicitly and mixed earthly and heavenly elements. According to Robert of Rheims, Urban said that 'Jerusalem is the hub of the world and like paradise.'[22] The version of Baldric of Dol explains that the Hebrews, who left Egypt, conquered, '*instar*', the heavenly and earthly Jerusalem. In contrast with Anselm, who equated the knightly pilgrims with robbers, Baldric reported that the sermon suggested that the Hebrews prefigured the crusaders.[23] The belief in the co-existence of the heavenly and the earthly city was by no means rare amongst the clergy. In order to encourage the crusaders who were to attack Jerusalem, Baldric of Bourgueil preached that 'the Jerusalem which you see … and in presence of which you stand … represents the heavenly city.' Moreover the crusaders risked their entrance to the heavenly city, if they were incapable of reclaiming it from the hands of their enemies.[24]

Anselm's distinction between the earthly and the heavenly Jerusalem was important, considering that the English churchman, Ralph Niger, who was perhaps the most important critic of the crusades in the twelfth century, used the same allegory in his *De re militari et triplici via peregrinationis ierosolimitane*. However, it is uncertain whether he had actually read Anselm's text.[25]

Nevertheless, Anselm recognised the crusade and pilgrimage to Jerusalem as a valuable act of piety for the laity. He gave his approval to the plans of his brother-in-law, Burgundius, who wanted to go to Jerusalem c. 1100. Anselm was, however, quite sceptical about Burgundius's chances of coming back alive. He advised Burgundius to confess his sins, provide for his wife and children, and dispose of all his possessions, 'just as [if he] knew [he] was about to die.'[26] Anselm's letter to his sister conveys very much the same tone. A similar scepticism may be discerned in Anselm's letter to his friend Hugh, Archbishop of Lyons, who had actually returned from Jerusalem.[27]

Anselm had a lukewarm attitude to the Spanish reconquest as well. The bishop of Santiago de Compostela had sent Anselm a letter, unfortunately not preserved, asking him to send some of his soldiers to fight the Saracens. Politely, but explicitly Anselm denied the bishop's request because 'the kingdom of the English is terrorised almost daily by the reports of wars rising up against her on all sides… While taking care to protect *propria*, one is less able to care for *communia*.'[28] It is interesting to see that Anselm was prepared to use violence when defending *propria* of his own church.

Of course, Anselm's opposition to the crusade did not arise from a generally negative attitude to war. He certainly did not neglect his military responsibilities. For instance, in 1095 Anselm maintained that he did not dare leave Canterbury, the king having appointed him head of the troops guarding the city, despite the explicit request of a papal legate to meet him. It has been argued by James Brundage that Anselm did not consider 'the use of military force entirely appropriate for spiritual purposes.'[29] This argument is plausible, but does not reveal the ultimate reason for Anselm's lack of enthusiasm.

Anselm was a true papal reformer, fighting nicolaitism, simony and lay investiture as fervently as any reformer of his age. In the fundamental questions of faith, he was, however, of more conservative stock than his Roman comrades. When it came to the salvation of the soul, Anselm adhered to Benedictine traditions: God was to be served in a cloister, not in the world. The world was too dangerous a place in which to live. The best path to salvation was to leave the world and become a monk. This was infinitely preferable to taking the cross.

NOTES

1 For the chronology of Anselm's life, see Southern 1990, pp. xxvii–xxix.
2 Southern 1963, pp. 130–132; Vaughn 1987, pp. 187–193, 199, 227–229, 236–237.
3 Erdmann 1935, pp. 124–127, 267–270.
4 Cowdrey 1982.
5 Southern 1963, p. 202; Brundage 1984, p. 177.
6 Brundage 1984, p. 177.
7 Mayer 1988, p. 39.
8 Vaughn 1987, p. 215.
9 *Epistola Anselmi*, 195.
10 *Epistola Anselmi*, 410: '… non est hoc desiderum tuum ex bona parte neque ad salutem animae tuae'.
11 *Epistola Anselmi*, 117: 'Moneo, consulo, precor, obsecro, praecipio ut dilectissimo, ut dimittas illam Ierusalem, quae nunc non est visio pacis sed tribulationis, et thesauros Constantinopolitanos et Babylonios cruentatis manibus diripiendos; et incipe ciad ad caelestam Ierusalem, quae est visio pacis, ubi invenes thesauros non nisi istos contemnentibus suscipiendos.' On Jerusalem see Siberry 1985, pp. 37–38, esp. note 71.
12 *Epistola Anselmi*, 235: '… ad regis dignitatem … in illa terra exaltavit, in qua ipse dominus noster Iesus Christus, per se ipsum principatum Christianitatis seminans, ecclesiam suam, ut inde per totum orbem propagaretur, novam plantavit.'
13 *Epistola Anselmi*, 324: '… civitatem Ierusalem et ante adventum domini et in ipso eius adventu eius adventu elegit deus quasi propriam sibi.'
14 *Epistola Anselmi*, 235: '… non tam vobis quam deo regnare studeatis desidero.'

15 *Epistola Anselmi*, 235: 'Ne putetis vobis, sicut multi mali reges faciunt, ecclesiam dei quasi domino ad serviendum esse datam, sed sicut advocato et defensori esse commendatam.'

16 *Epistola Anselmi*, 324: '… vestram personam et omnes vobis subditos sic regere secundum legem et voluntatem dei studeatis, ut lucidum exemplum omnibus regibus terrae in vita vestra praebeatis'.

17 Brundage 1984, p. 178.

18 *Epistola Anselmi*, 95b. See Siberry 1985, p. 36.

19 *Epistola Anselmi*, 188. Written before October 1097. 'Certus enim esse debes quia, cum te ipsum deo totum vovisti et reddidisti per monachicam professionem, solvisti omnia minora vota quarumlibet actionum, quae prius sine iureiurando et fidei alligatione promisisti.'

20 Riley-Smith 1993, p. 147.

21 Fulcherius, pp. 323–324. Considering the fact that Urban saw the Spanish reconquest as the equivalent of a crusade, it is more convincing to assume that he did not see Jerusalem as a heavenly city. See Housley 1992, pp. 32–33; Mayer 1988, p. 28.

22 Robertus, p. 729: 'Iherusalem umbiculus est terrae … quasi alter Paradisus.'

23 Baldricus, p. 14: 'Filii Israel ab Aegyptis educti … vos praefiguraverunt … et instar Jerusalem coelestis, Jerusalem terrenam incoluerunt.'

24 Baldricus, p. 101: '… Jerusalem, quam videtis, cui advenistis, cui adestis, illam civitatem coelestam et preafigurat et praetendit. … Pro certo timendum est ut civitas illa coelestis nobis claudatur, nobis auferatur, si nobis desidiosis a malignis hosbitibus nostra domus abdicabitur.'

25 Radulfus Niger, p. 93; (on the tradition of *Ierosolima = visio pacis,* see note 15).

26 *Epistola Anselmi*, 264.

27 *Epistola Anselmi*, 261; Hugh's letter to Anselm: *Epistola Anselmi*: 260.

28 *Epistola Anselmi*, 263: 'Sed noverit sanctitatis vestra quia regnum Anglorum bellorum contra se undique consurgentium nuntio fere cotidiano commovetur. … Nam dum quisque curat tueri propria, minus potest curare communia.'

29 Brundage 1984, p. 183.

BIBLIOGRAPHY

Sources

Baldricus, *Baldrici episcopi Dolonensis Historia Ierosolimitana*, in *RHC* iv, pp. 1–111.
Epistola Anselmi, in F. Schmitt (ed.), *S. Anselmi Canturariensis archiepiscopi opera omnia*, vol iii–v. Edinburgi mdcccxlvi–mdccccli.
Fulcherius, *Historia Iherosolymitana gesta Francorum Iherusalem peregrinantium ab anno domini MXCV usque ad annum MCXXVII auctore domno Fulcherio Carnotensi*, in *RHC* iii, pp. 311–585.
Radulfus Niger, *De re militari et triplici via peregrinationis Ierosolimitane*, L. Schmugge (Einl. & Ed.), Beiträge zur Geschichte und Quellenkunde des Mittelalters, 6. Berlin 1977.
Robertus, *Roberti Monachi Historia Iherosolimitana*, RHC iii, pp. 717–882.

Literature

J. A. Brundage 1984, 'St Anselm, Ivo of Chartres and the Crusade', *Spicilegium Beccense* 2, pp. 175–187.
H. E. J. Cowdrey 1982, 'Pope Gregory VII's "crusading" plans of 1074', in B. Z. Kedar & H. E. Mayer & R. C. Smail (ed.), *Outremer. Studies in the history of the crusading kingdom of Jerusalem presented to Joshua Prawer*. Jerusalem.

C. Erdmann 1935, *Die Entstehung des Kreuzzugsgedankens*. Stuttgart.

N. Housley 1992, 'Jerusalem and the development of the crusade idea, 1099–1128', in B. Z. Kedar (ed.), *The Hours of Hattin: Proceedings of the Second Conference of the Society for the Study of the Crusades and the Latin East*. Jerusalem.

H. E. Mayer 1988, *The Crusades*. Second Edition. Oxford.

J. Riley-Smith 1993, *The First Crusade and the Idea of Crusading*. London.

E. Siberry 1985, *Criticism of Crusading 1095–1274*. Oxford.

R. Southern 1963, *St Anselm and his Biographer. A Study of Monastic Life and Thought 1059–c. 1130*. Cambridge.

R. Southern 1990, *Saint Anselm: a Portrait in a Landscape*. Cambridge.

S. N. Vaughn 1987, *Anselm of Bec and Robert of Melulan. The Innocence of the Dove and the Wisdom of the Serpent*. Berkeley–Los Angeles–London.

TUOMAS M. S. LEHTONEN

By the Help of God, Because of Our Sins, and by Chance

William of Tyre Explains the Crusades

Why Did the Enemy Become More Powerful Against the Christians?

Libet paulisper ab historie textu, non evagandi inutiliter gratia sed ut inferatur aliquid non absque fructu, discedere. Solet queri, et vere merito querendum videtur, quid cause sit quod patres nostri in numero pauciore maiores hostium copias in conflictu sepe sustinuerunt fortius et frequentius, propicia divinitate, in manu modica maiores eorum cuneos et innumeram plerumque multidinem contriverunt, ita etiam quod ipsum nomen christianum gentibus deum ignorantibus esset formidini et in operibus patrum nostrorum glorificaretur dominus, nostri autem temporis homines versa vice et a paucioribus sepius devicti et cum pluribus nonnunquam adverus pauciores frustra aliquid temptasse et subcubuisse aliquotiens reperiuntur.[1]

At this point I must digress somewhat from the course of my story, not to wander about aimlessly, but to bring out something of value. The question is often asked, and quite justly, why it was that our fathers, though less in number, so often bravely withstood in battle the far larger forces of the enemy and that often by divine grace a small force destroyed the multitudes of enemy, with the result that the very name of Christian became a terror to nations ignorant of God, and thus the Lord was glorified in the works of our fathers. In contrast of this, the men of our times too often have been conquered by inferior forces; in fact, when with superior numbers they have attempted to exploit against adversaries less strong, their efforts have been fruitless and they have usually been forced to succumb.[2]

William, Archbishop of Tyre, wrote this in the 1180s, a few years before his own death,[3] thus initiating an analysis of 'why the enemy became more powerful against the Christians' ('assignantur cause quare contingat quod super populum nostrum solito amplius hostes invalescent').[4] William gives three reasons, and expands on them with further explanations. 'The first reason that presents itself, as we carefully and thoughtfully study this condition of our times, looking for aid to God, the author of all things, is that our forefathers were religious men and feared God. Now in their places a wicked generation has grown up, sinful sons, falsifiers

71

of the Christian faith, who run the course of all unlawful things without discrimination [...]. From such, because of their sins, the Lord justly withdraws His favour, as if provoked to wrath.' ('Considerantibus ergo nobis et statum nostrum diligenter discuentibus prima occurrit causa, in deum auctorem omnium respiciens, quod pro patribus nostris, qui fuerunt viri religiosi et timentes deum, nati sunt filii perditissimi, filii scelerati, fidei christiane prevaricatores, [...]. Quibus merito, peccatis exigentibus, gratiam subtrahat dominus tanquam ad iracundiam provocatus.')[5] Here William explains history in the traditional biblical, or should we say the old-testament way: God is the Lord of history and everything happens as he wills it to happen. God is not only present as Providence but as a willing and active actor in human history. William, however, did not usually favour this explanation, usually preferring mundane explanations. As modern historians from Heinrich Sybel up to recent times have emphasised, William, 'despite his belief in the divine ordering of the affairs of men, could adopt an essentially human-centred approach.'[6]

The second reason given by William is that 'those first revered men who came to the lands of the East led by divine zeal and aflame with spiritual enthusiasm for their faith were accustomed to military discipline; they were trained in battle and familiar with the use of weapons. The people of the East, on the contrary, through long-continued peace, had become enervated; they were unused to the art of war, unfamiliar with the rules of battle, and gloried in their state of inactivity.' ('cum illi viri venerabiles zelo ducti divino, ardore fidei interius succensi primum ad Orientales partes descenderunt, erant bellicis assueti disciplinis, preliis exercitati, usum habentes armorum familiarem, populus vero Orientalis econtrario longa pace dissolutus, rei militaris expers, inexercitatus legibus preliorum vacatione gaudebat.')[7] Here, William moves from the divine to the human sphere. The first crusaders were stronger in their faith and better in martial arts, while the people of the East had become accustomed to a long peace. William's explanation is hierarchical: God rules history, but human skills and decisions are relevant in conducting the course of secular history. He continues with the human element. The Easterners had been weak because they had not been united under the command of one man, but things had changed. Saladin, 'a man of humble antecedents and lowly station, now holds under his control all these kingdoms, for fortune has smiled too graciously upon him.' ('vir genere quidem humilis, extreme conditionis homo, secunda nimis arridente fortuna possidet.')[8] William brings in the third reason, fortune or chance, a new element in explaining changing situations.

In what follows, my argument is that William did not attribute causes either exclusively to God or to men, but he used an explanatory hierarchy current in twelfth-century schools. Further, I wish to demonstrate more generally that medieval historical works cannot be understood either separately or simply in comparison with other historical writings. I argue that historiography has to be placed in its wider intellectual context, which, in the case of William, is that of twelfth-century learning and schools in Northern France and Italy.

William, Archbishop of Tyre, and his History of Deeds Done beyond the Sea

William of Tyre was born in Jerusalem around 1130. His parents were probably non-nobles originating from Italy. William received a good education. From 1146 to 1165 he studied in Northern France and Italy. In an autobiographical chapter he talks about his studies, first in Paris and Orléans, where he spent a total of sixteen years reading liberal arts and theology, and then in Bologna, where he studied canon law.[9] In this respect William belongs to the same group of twelfth-century historians as Otto, Bishop of Freising, and John of Salisbury, Bishop of Chartres,[10] both of whom had also studied in the cathedral schools of Northern France. This fact is of some importance when considering William's theology of history and his explanations of crusading history, especially because scholastic education did not encourage historical writing.[11]

William was also a prolific writer. He composed a history of oriental princes, now unfortunately lost, and the acts of the Third Lateran Council, in which he participated.[12] He is of course most widely known for his vast *Chronicon* or *Historia rerum in partibus transmarinis gestarum* or *Historia Ierosolymitana*. Its English translation is entitled *History of Deeds Done Beyond the Sea*.[13] He seems to have taken a long time in writing this work, completing it in 1184, two years before his death in 1186.[14]

The *Historia* covers the foundation and history of the Latin kingdom from the preaching of the First Crusade until the year 1184.[15] Peter W. Edbury and John Gordon Rowe, the authors of a recent monograph on William of Tyre and his historiography, write of his *Historia*: 'It is a long work: in the most recent edition William's Latin text fills just under a thousand pages. Its very size makes it difficult to view as a whole, and for this reason scholars have been far more ready to use it as a quarry for historical information than to try to assess its strengths and weaknesses as an example of twelfth-century historiography or to seek to examine the presuppositions of its author.'[16] While Edbury and Rowe's study is well documented and thorough, I will suggest some amendments to their analysis concerning William's relation to the twelfth-century theory of causation.

His English translators, E. A. Babcock and A. C. Krey, have praised William's historical writing as exceptionally objective, which might be an overstatement.[17] Nevertheless, more important from my point of view is that William gives complex explanations for historical events. He does not give a simple, straightforward account of the Crusades, as does the anonymous chronicler of the First Crusade in the *Gesta Francorum*, or Odo of Deuil, a monk from the monastery of St Denis, who participated in the Second Crusade with the French king Louis VII.[18] Nor does William attribute the success of the First Crusade only to divine providence as did, for example, Guibert of Nogent in his *Gesta Dei per Francos*. William tries to analyse the causes of the events, and is interested in why some strategies succeeded while others did not. He comments on how well or poorly the Christian leaders prepared their military expeditions, thus emphasising the human role not only from a theological or moral point of view but also giving strategic and other explanations.[19]

Another interesting feature is that William does not articulate theology of history in his work. As Edbury and Rowe have pointed out, he rarely refers to Christian eschatology and, when he does, he does not seem to relate his historical account to an eschatological interpretation of the human past. However, this does not mean that he did not have a theology of history or that he would not have used divine intervention as part of his explanatory arsenal.[20]

By the Help of God

The basis of the crusading ideology was the conviction that the movement was willed by God: 'Deus lo volt!' as the crowds are said to have shouted after the famous sermon of Pope Urban II at Clermont in 1095.[21] Several chroniclers saw the Crusades as part of a divine plan, even as part of the eschatological events. This of course is the ideological background for William's question, quoted at the beginning: 'Why did the enemy become more powerful against the Christians?'

Despite the lack of any explicit theology of history in the fashion of some twelfth-century historians such as Anselm of Havelberg, Gerhoh of Reichersberg or Otto of Freising, William did nevertheless see God as an active participant in the course of history,[22] thus following the common interpretation among the twelfth-century historians which had its roots in Orosius's *Historiae adversum paganos*.[23] Orosius deviated from the theology of his teacher, St Augustine, in seeing God's providential plan as coinciding with the history of earthly empires.[24] Among others, Otto of Freising did not see the fundamental difference between the two, entitling his work *De duabus civitatibus* in the fashion of Augustine's *De civitate Dei*, although his theology of history was more or less written under the influence of Orosius.[25]

In William's work there are several different kinds of divine intervention. The most rare are direct interventions in the form of miracles. Much more often God acts through natural events such as storms, earthquakes, etc. Several times God's action is mediated by men, God guiding men's minds to finally choose the right path. It should be noted, however, that not all natural phenomena or good and wise decisions are attributed to God.[26] In this way William is closer to the Augustinian vision of earthly history than most of his learned contemporary writers.

Because of Our Sins

Peter Edbury and John Gordon Rowe thoroughly analyse the various instances where human sinfulness and God's anger are interpreted as the final causes of setbacks which Christians encountered on their expeditions.[27] In some cases they tend to think that William was following convention rather than genuinely blaming the crusaders for their supposed sins. According to Edbury and Rowe, this is especially obvious in the case of the failure of the Second Crusade,[28] when William repeats the phrase 'by hidden though just judgement of God' ('ex occulto, iusto tamen, iudicio sprevit [...] dominus').[29]

In applying the general explanation that setbacks and adversities are caused by the human postlapsarian condition and original sin, he is, again, close to St Augustine, for whom *civitas terrena* and its secular history was a recurrent story of human sinfulness. Because men had free will they could also choose evil, and because of original sin, this was the primary tendency. Thus secular history was more or less repeating itself as an endless story of human miseries caused by sin.[30] William of Tyre, however, deviated from the Augustinian view by claiming that men were fulfilling divine orders on earth by waging a holy war against the Saracens. At the same time, his history of the crusading principalities was becoming more similar to a history of any ordinary Christian kingdom.

As Edbury and Rowe point out 'he was not writing universal history; nor was he writing the history of a nation or *gens*. Rather, the *Historia* conforms to the definition by Isidore of Seville: it is a *narratio rei gestae*, an account of past events, which in this instance are the events of the First Crusade and the doings of its leaders and their successors. ... There is no hint anywhere in the *Historia* that William subscribed to an apocalyptic view of history.'[31]

Individual men were sometimes, even if rarely, already punished by God during their earthly lives. However, William understood well enough that God's reward and punishment do not apply to earthly life: even the good and blameless suffer here.[32]

By Chance

William did not always attribute prosperous or adverse turns of events to God or human sinfulness. He often spoke about chance and good and bad luck or fortune. However, this gets no attention from Edbury and Rowe. *Casus* or chance and *fortuna* or fortune are repeatedly mentioned by William as explanations for lucky or unlucky events. I have not counted all the cases of one or the other being used to explain a sudden turn of events, but they occur throughout the *Historia* perhaps even more often than divine providence or human sin. *Casus* and *fortuna* are sometimes related to God, but on several occasions they are mentioned independently.[33]

I quote William:

> Nostri autem sive ex industria sive casu divisi sunt abinvicem et variis ceperunt partibus incedere, [...] quam prior exercitus observaverat, disciplinam omnino contemptentes. Suscitatus est ergo eis, exigentibus meritis, potens adversarius et dati sunt in manus hostium, ita quod ex eis una die in ore gladii promiscui sexus ceciderunt plus quam quinquaginta milia. Quibus autem concessum est divinitus hostium manus effugere, hii nudi vacuique amissis sarcinis et omnimoda suppellectile perdita salutem quocumque modo invenerunt tan-

demque casu magis quam industria in Ciliciam pervenientes, apud Tarsum, eiusdem provincie metropolim, dominum Hugonem Magnum fatali sublatum necessitate amiserunt; [...]

Ubi de consilio domini Raimundi comitis Tolosani civitatem impugnantes, quoniam eis expugnabilis videbatur, auctore domino infra paucos dies violenter occupaverunt, civibus eius aut peremptis gladio aut perpetue mancipitatis servituti.[34]

But the Christians, either purposely or by chance, separated from one another and advanced different routes; [...]. Moreover, they utterly scorned the military discipline which the earlier army had observed. Hence, a powerful adversary was raised up against them, as they deserved, and they were given into the enemy's hand. For in one day, while on the march, more than fifty thousand of both sexes fell by the edge of the sword.

Those whom divine providence permitted to escape the hand of the enemy lost their baggage and equipment of every kind. Naked and empty handed, they sought safety as they could, and it was by chance rather than by their own efforts that they finally reached Cilicia. At Tarsus, the capital of that province, they lost Hugh the Great, who was carried away by inevitable fate. [...]

By the advice of Raymond, count of Toulouse, they attacked this city, since it seemed possible to win it, and, with the help of God, within a few days they took it by force. The inhabitants were either slain or consigned to perpetual slavery.[35]

In this quotation, William speaks of chance (*casus*) and human purposes as alternative explanations, although he often praised or blamed Christian leaders because of their decisions without any mention of chance, and clearly evaluated and explained their deeds according to their rational consideration and decisions. Nor does good or bad luck always follow good or bad decisions, luck in human enterprises, and especially in warfare, being an unpredictable and unreliable force. But it is definitely present and needed when historical events are to be explained. God's will and human choice, whether sinful or rational, are not sufficient when events ought to be explained, and then chance enters the stage.[36]

William seemed to link fortune and chance similarly to the classical authors like Lucan and Sallust (with whom he might have been familiar).[37] They also play a central role in the work of Boethius, one of the most favoured authors in twelfth-century schools.[38] Chance or fortune is something that follows from intended human action when it unintentionally crosses someone else's intentions and some unexpected things occur.[39] There is no way to avoid these changes in luck.

William goes on to give further explanations. Human intention or chance is the first cause of the adversities of the crusaders. However, divine providence gives some crusaders an opportunity to escape from the hands of the enemy. Curiously enough, divine providence (*divinitas*) is followed by chance: '...and it was by chance rather than by their own efforts that they finally reached Cilicia...' ('...intervenerunt tandemque casu magis quam industria in Ciliciam pervenientes...'). After this, 'inevitable fate' (*fatali necessitate*) carries Hugh the Great away. Then again, it is divine help (*aucore domino*) that makes the crusaders successful. William seems to use these different types of explanation without any clear logic or hierarchy of causes. One is tempted to think that chance, providence, inevitable fate, and divine help are all rhetorical devices with no further theological or philosophical significance. Nevertheless, a closer look at the ideas of his contemporary thinkers suggests that his use of different explanations is not simply rhetorical or random but closely knit with the explanatory models current in the mid- and late twelfth century.

The Fourfold Explanatory Model

William of Tyre studied in the schools of Northern France and Northern Italy from 1146 to 1165. Since he lists Bernard of Moëllan, Petrus Helias, Ivo of Chartres, Peter Lombard, Gilbert of Poitiers, and several others among his teachers,[40] it seems reasonable to compare William's thought to his scholarly background.

In the mid-twelfth century, several school teachers and philosophers distinguished between things made or events caused directly by God or the Creator, and those made or caused indirectly by lower instances such as nature, human beings, or chance or fortune. Chance and fortune were closely bound to the concept of free will.[41] Basically, there was an Augustinian distinction between divinely originated and man-made things.[42] Furthermore, authors like William of Conches and Hugh of St Victor discussed a three-tier hierarchy of *opera Dei*, *opera naturae* and *opera artificis imitantis naturam*.[43] A fourth level that caused by chance (*casus*) or fortune (*fortuna*) was added later. This four-level hierarchy of instances was articulated by Ralph of Longchamps, a Cistercian monk active in Narbonne, in his thirteenth-century commentary on his master Alan of Lille's long allegorical poem *Anticlaudianus*:

> Materia huius libri sunt quattuor artifices et quattuor artificium opera. Est enim artifex Deus, artifex natura, artifex fortuna, artifex culpa. Deus autem specialiter dicitur artifex eorum, quae facit de nihilo, ut sunt spiritus et animae; unde Deus dicitur proprie creare et eius operatio dicitur creatio. Natura autem proprie dicitur artifex eorum, quae sunt ex praeiacente materia, quia natura est potentia naturaliter rebus sive causis inferioribus insita, similia ex similibus procreans, ut hominem de homine, bovem de bove. Unde dicitur procreare, quasi procul creare, id est aliunde creare, scilicet ex praeiacente materia. Fortuna sive casus, quia pro eodem hic accipitur, est artifex eorum, quae casualiter fiunt vel eveniunt, ut si rusticus fodiens agrum inveniat thesaurum. Est autem fortuna sive casus inopinatus rei eventus ex causis confluentibus, uti patet in praemisso exemplo. Inventio enim thesauri est inopinatus rei eventus. Causae confluentes sunt ea, quae ad hoc concurrunt, ut accessus rustici ad thesaurum, terrae fossio et similia. Huius artificis opera sunt libertas, servitus, divitiae, adversitas, prosperitas. Artifex culpa malus artifex est, cuius opera sunt diversa vitiorum genera.[44]

The matter of these books is four artificers and their works. The artificers are God, nature, fortune and sin. God is especially said to be the artificer of those things, which are made of nothing, like the spirits and souls. For this reason God is said to create in the proper sense and his work is called creation. Nature, then, is said properly to be the artificer of those things which are made of pre-existent matter because nature is a power which naturally combines lower things or causes and procreates similar from similar, as human from human or bovine from bovine. For this reason it is said to procreate, to create proximately, that is, to create from something else as it creates from pre-existent matter. Fortune or chance (because here these two are the same) is the artificer of those things which come into being or happen randomly as when a rustic tilling his field finds a treasure. Fortune or chance is thus an unexpected event which is a consequence of confluent causes as one can see from the preceding example. The discovery of treasure is an unexpected event. The confluent causes are those which concur with each other here, such as the access of the rustic to treasure, tilling of land and similar things. The works of this artificer are freedom, slavery, wealth, adversity and prosperity. Sin is the artificer of evil, and its works are diverse genres of vices.(Translation by Tuomas Lehtonen.)

This could be read as a comment on William's work. What is relevant is that in twelfth-century thought, fortune and chance were taken as concepts useful in describing earthly history. Things attributed to fortune were also a subject matter of history writing.[45] Furthermore, William closely follows the model used by Ralph of Longchamp. God, chance or fortune and sin do occur frequently in his work but nature as inevitable fate is also referred to a couple of times. Fate conceptualises inevitable natural processes and William uses it when he describes somebody's natural death.[46] Hence William is indeed writing his history with philosophical concepts that he probably learned at Chartres, Paris and Orléans in the mid-twelfth century.

History Writing and Crusading Ideology

William of Tyre certainly considered crusading as a just war. Despite this, he does not seem to share the point of view of Guibert of Nogent and others, who took the Christian warriors in the Holy Land as the fulfillers of a divine plan.[47] Furthermore, as I have tried to show, William used his contemporary philosophical explanatory model, which could be used to describe any principality. This clearly shows that his attitude toward the crusading ideology was more or less 'disenchanted', that is, the holy cause had lost at least part of its original spell. The Crusades were no different from any other just wars that Christian kings fought on their lands to maintain peace and order (as Louis IV the Fat and Louis VII in Abbot Suger's biographies, for example).[48] Secular events have no function in the salvation history in William's work.[49] This, indeed, differentiates him from Otto of Freising, another pupil of mid-twelfth-century French cathedral schools.

As such, twelfth-century crusade historiography (from the anonymous writers up to William) seems to put forward three interpretations. The first is in the form of a story told by a participant who simply records the events and does not give them any further theological or philosophical signification. Nor does he give any complex explanations. Those who fall into this category include the anonymous writer of *Gesta Francorum*, who chronicled the First Crusade, and Odo of Deuil, a monk of St Denis, who participated in the Second Crusade.[50] The second type of interpretation is heavily ideological and theological, Guibert of Nogent's *Gesta Dei per Francos* being the most famous example of this.[51] The third category is William's view of crusading history, according to which the Crusades were initially an act of God carried out by men, but their successes and adversities require the same explanations as the histories of any Christian – and perhaps even non-Christian – kingdoms: divine intervention, human volition and sin, and chance.

At the very end of his work, William wrote a preface for the 23rd book, in which he reflected on his own history-writing:

> Iam enim ad ea tempora, quibus nec nostra vicia nec eorum remedia pati possumus, perventum est: unde nostris id merentibus peccatis, facti sunt hostes in capite, et qui de inimicis triumphantes palmam frequentius solebamus referre cum gloria, nunc in omni pene conflictu, divina destituti gratia, deteriorem calculum reportamus ideoque silendum erat consultiusque videbatur nostris defectibus noctem inducere quam solem inferre pudentis. Sed quibus cordi est ut in eo, quod semel cepimus, nos continuemus proposito quique orant instantius ut regni Ierosolimorum status omnis, tam prosper quam adversus, posteritati nostra significetur opera, stimulos addunt, proponentes historiographorum disertissimos, Titum videlicet Romanorum non solum prospera, sed etiam adversa mandasse litteris, Iosephum quoque non solum que a Iudeis egregie gesta sunt, verum et que eis sunt ignominiose illata longis tractatibus publicasse. Habundant et aliis exemplis qui ad hoc nos nituntur impellere eoque facilius persuadent, quia plane liquet rerum gestarum scriptoribus utramque sortem pari esse ratione propositam, ut sicut gestorum feliciter narratione posteros ad quandam animositatem erigunt, sic infortunium subiectorum exemplo eosdem reddant in similibus cautiores. Annalium enim conscriptores non qualia optant ipsi, sed qualia ministrant tempora mandare solent litteris ex officio, rerum autem, et bellorum maxime, varius esse solet eventus et non uniformis, in quo nec prosperitas continua nec casus oppositus sine lucidis intervallis. Vincimut ergo et que subsequentia ministrabunt tempora, sicut cepimus, utinam fausta feliciaque, auctor domino, vita comite, scripto mandare curabimus diligenter, a secundo proposito revocati.[52]

It is therefore time to hold our peace; for it seems more fitting to draw the shades of night over our failures than to turn the light of the sun upon our disgrace. There are some, however, who desire us to continue the task once undertaken, who earnestly entreat that every phase of the kingdom of Jerusalem, adverse as well as prosperous, be recorded in this work for posterity. For our encouragement, they cite the example of the most distinguished historians, namely Titus Livius, who recorded in his history not only successes of the Romans, but also their reverses, and Josephus, who made known in his comprehensive works not only the brilliant deeds of the Jews, but also those shameful things which were done to them.

In their efforts to persuade us to continue this work, they offer many other examples also. We are the more readily influenced to acquiesce in this request, since it is indeed evident that chroniclers of past events have recorded without partiality adverse as well auspicious happenings. For, by narrating successful achievements, they hope to inspire posterity with courage, while by furnishing examples of misfortunes patiently endured they may render later generations more cautious under similar conditions.

The writer of annals, by virtue of his office, must commit to the letters not such events as he himself might desire, but such as the times afford. The outcome of worldly affairs, especially of wars, is ever variable and uncertain; prosperity is never continuous, nor is adversity wholly without brighter intervals.[53]

For William, the subject matter of history writing, is 'worldly affairs, variable, and uncertain' ('tempora [...] rerum autem [...] varius esse solet eventus et non uniformis'), which he depicted, as did his contemporaries, as chance and fortune, and as a constant cycle of prosperity and adversity. William's history writing was closer to classical models and the idea of *historia magistra vitae* than to any theology of history.

NOTES

1 William of Tyre, *Chronicon* 21.7, p. 969.
2 William of Tyre, *History* XXI.7, p. 406.
3 Huygens 1962, pp. 811–829; Huygens 1986, pp. 1–3; Edbury & Rowe 1988, pp.13–22.
4 William of Tyre, *History* XXI.7, p. 406; William of Tyre, *Chronicon* 21.2, p. 969.
5 *Ibidem.*
6 Edbury & Rowe 1988, 6; Rödig 1990, pp. 9–12.
7 William of Tyre, *History* XXI.7, pp. 406–407; William of Tyre, *Chronicon* 21.7, pp. 969–970.
8 William of Tyre, *History* XXI.7, p. 408; William of Tyre, *Chronicon* 21.7, p. 971.
9 William of Tyre, *Chronicon* 19.12, pp. 879–882; Edbury & Rowe 1988, p.15; see also Huygens 1962.
10 Edbury & Rowe compare him to twelfth-century ecclesiastical careerists such as Peter of Blois, Thomas Becket, Reinald of Dassel and Robert Pullen, all of whom, except Rainald, were of humble origin and reached high positions in the ecclesiastical hierarchy. The list might be continued with Abbot Suger of Saint Denis and Maurice of Sully and many other leading twelfth-century ecclesiastical figures. The latter was among William's masters. On the other hand, it is especially interesting to compare William to bishops and historians who studied at the same schools and reported on the scholarly world of the mid-twelfth century, such as Otto of Freising and John of Salisbury. Cf. Otto of Freising, *Gesta Friderici* I.48–55, pp. 67–80; John of Salisbury, *Metalogicon* I.5, pp. 20–22; II.10, pp. 70-73. See also Huygens 1962, pp. 814–815; Ward 2000, pp. 72–100; see also Jeaunaeu 2000.
11 Goetz 1985, pp. 165–213; see also Boehm 1965; Guenée 1980, pp. 25–38.
12 Edbury & Rowe 1988, pp. 13–22; Huygens 1962; Huygens 1986, pp. 1–3.
13 Babcock & Krey 1943.
14 Huygens 1986, pp. 1–2; William of Tyre, *Chronicon Prol.* 86, p. 100.
15 Edbury & Rowe 1988, p. 1.
16 Edbury & Rowe 1988, p.1; other important monographs on William of Tyre are Schwinges 1977 and Rödig 1990.
17 Babcock & Krey 1943, pp. 3–49.
18 *Gesta Francorum*; Odonis de Deoilo, *De profectione.*
19 Eg. William of Tyre, *Chronicon* 18.13, p. 829; see also 5.15, p. 291; 13.9, p. 596; 14.8, p. 640; 17.5, p. 766.
20 Edbury & Rowe 1988, pp. 41–42, 153–155, 165–170.

21 Schwinges 1977, pp. 1–2; Flori 2001, p. 299 ff.; see also Kangas 2005.

22 On Anselm of Havelberg, Gerhoh of Reichersberg and Otto of Fresing see Classen 1991, pp. 404–411; Goetz 1984; Lehtonen 2000; Roversi Monaco 2000.

23 Marrou 1970; Goetz 1980.

24 Orosius himself did not seem to think this way; see *Historiae adversum paganos* I prol. pp. 6–10; Mommsen 1959, pp. 299–348; Marrou 1970, pp.76–81; Lacroix 1965; Goetz 1980; on Augustine see Markus 1970; Fredriksen 1992.

25 Otto of Freising, *Historia de duabus ciuitatibus*; Goetz 1984; Lehtonen 2000.

26 Eg. William of Tyre, *Chronicon* 1.9, p. 77; 8.16, pp. 407–408; 8.22, p. 415; 11.23, pp. 529–530; 17.27, p. 798; 20.18, pp. 934–936.

27 Edbury & Rowe 1988, p. 155ff.

28 Edbury & Rowe 1988, pp. 158–159.

29 William of Tyre, *Chronicon* 16.19, lines 55–61, p. 743; William of Tyre, *History* XVI.19, p. 167.

30 Augustinus, *De ciuitate Dei*; Orosius, *Historiae adversum paganos* I. prol. pp. 6–10; see also Mommsen 1959; Lacroix 1965; Marrou 1970; Markus 1970; Goetz 1980.

31 Edbury & Rowe 1988, p. 40.

32 William of Tyre, *Chronicon* 16.25, pp. 751–752; 21.29, pp. 1003–1004.

33 William of Tyre, *Chronicon* 2.18, p. 185; 3.18, p. 219; 3.20, pp. 221–222; 3.21, p. 224; 4.17, p. 257; 5.16, p. 291; 6.14, p. 325; 7.4, p. 347; 7.25, p. 378; 10.12, p. 467; 11.9, p. 508; 12.20, p. 570; 12.23, pp. 574–575; 13.9, p. 596; 13.27, p. 624; 14.24, p. 662; 15.17, p. 699; 15.27, pp. 710–711; 16.26, pp. 752–753; 16.27, p. 755; 16.29, p. 757; 17.11, p. 775; 17.12, p. 775; 17.28, pp. 799–800; 19.9, p. 875; 19.11, p. 879; 19.29, pp. 905–906; 20.6, p. 918; 20.9, p. 922; 20.17, pp. 933–934; 20.25–26, pp. 947–949; 20.30, p. 955; 21.21–23, pp. 990–994; 21.26, p. 999; 21.29, p. 1003; 22.17, p. 1032; 22. praef., p. 1061–1062.

34 William of Tyre, *Chronicon* 10.12 (13), lines 12–25, 37–40, p. 467–468.

35 William of Tyre, *History* X.13,9 pp. 432–433.

36 Eg. William of Tyre, *Chronicon* 2.12, p. 185; 5.16, p. 291; 5.22, p. 301; 7.4, pp. 347–348; 10.25, p. 485; 11.9, p. 508; 11.24, p. 532; 12.17, p. 567; 12.20, p. 570; 12.23, pp. 574–575; 13.9, p. 596; 13.27, p. 624; 14.24, p. 662; 15.6, pp. 683–684; 15.17, p. 699; 15.27, pp. 710–711; 16.25, pp. 750–752; 16.26, p. 752; 17.11–12, p. 775; 17.28, pp. 799–800; 19.9, pp. 874–875; 19.11, p. 879; 19.23, p. 895; 19.25, p. 900; 19.29, pp. 905–906; 20.6, p. 918; 20.9, p. 922; 20.12, p. 926; 20.17, pp. 933–934; 20.25–26, pp. 947–949; 20.29–30, pp. 953–955; 21.6, p. 968; 21.11, p. 977; 21.21–23, pp. 990–991; 21.26, p. 999; 21.29, p. 1003; 22.7, p. 1015; 22.11, p. 1020; 22.16, p. 1028; 22.17, p. 1032; 22.19, p. 1036; 22.24, p. 1043; 22. praef., pp. 1061–1062.

37 Schwinges 1977, pp. 286–290; Edbury & Rowe 1988, pp. 33–34; see also Frakes 1988; Chesnut 1976/1986.

38 Chenu 1957, pp. 142–158; Courcelle 1967; Troncarelli 1987; eg. Thierry of Chartres on Boethius's theological treatises in Häring (ed.) 1971; and William of Conches on *Consolatio Philosophiae* in *Guillelmi de Conchis Glosae super Boethium. Fortuna* and *casus* also occur in other works by twelfth-century masters, cf. Lehtonen 1995; Lehtonen 2000.

39 Boethius, *Consolatio Philosophiae* V.1.11–19, p. 89; see also Bernard Silvestris, *Commentum in Martium* 8.600–615, p. 193; William of Conches, *Glosae super Boethium* Vpr1, pp. 288–293; Alan of Lille, *Anticlaudianus* VII.405–480, pp. 169–171; cf. Lehtonen 1995; Lehtonen 2000.

40 William of Tyre, *Chronicon* 19.12, p. 880. William lists seventeen teachers of whom thirteen were masters in the schools of Northern France and four from Bologna. Most of the teachers are also listed by John of Salisbury in *Metalogicon* I.5, pp. 20–22; II.10, pp. 70–73 and in a poem entitled *Metamorphosis Goliae*. Some of them are also mentioned by Otto of Freising in his reports on theological and philosophical quarrels about the teachings of Peter Abelard in *Gesta Friderici* I.48–55, pp. 67–80. See also Huygens 1962, pp. 825–829; Edbury & Rowe 1988, pp. 14–15.

41 See e.g. William of Conches, *Glosae super Boetium*, "Accessus ad Consolationem",
    p. 5; see also Lehtonen 1995, p. 76 ff.; Lehtonen 2000.
42 Augustinus, *De ciuitate Dei* passim; see also Calcidius, *Timaeus a Calcidio*.
43 William of Conches, *Glosae super Boetium*, III m. 9, pp. 150–152; Hugh of St Victor,
    Didascalicon I.ix. The idea may be tracked down to Plato's *Timaeus*. See also Cal-
    cidius, *Timaeus a Calcidio translatus commentarioque instructus* 23–25, pp.73–76;
    Bernard of Chartres, *Glosae super Platonem* 4, p. 158. See also Stock 1972, pp. 78,
    86, 91–92, 148, 157, 254–255, 265, 268–269.
44 Radulphus de Longo Campo, *In Anticlaudianum Alani commentum* V.lxiii, p. 166.
45 Lehtonen 2000.
46 William of Tyre, *Chronicon* 10.12, p. 467; 11.22, p. 528.
47 Edbury & Rowe 1988, pp. 151–166.
48 Suger of St Denis, *Vita Ludovici grossi regis*, passim; Suger of St Denis, *De glorioso
    rege Ludovico* I, pp. 156–157.
49 Edbury & Rowe 1988, pp. 154–156.
50 *Gesta Francorum*; *Odonis de Deoilo de profectione*.
51 Guibert of Nogent, *Gesta Dei per Francos*.
52 William of Tyre, *Chronicon* 22. praef., pp. 1061–1062.
53 Babcock & Krey 1943, pp. 506–507.

BIBLIOGRAPHY

Sources

Alan of Lille, *Anticlaudianus de Antirufino*. R. Bossuat (ed.), Paris 1955.
Augustinus, *De ciuitate Dei contra paganos libri viginti duo*. Oevres de Saint Augustin
    33–37. Texte de la 4ᵉ édition de B. Dombart & A. Kalb, introduction et notes par G.
    Bardy, traduction française de G. Combès. Paris 1959–1960.
Bernard of Chartres, *Glosae super Platonem*. P. E. Dutton (ed.), Toronto 1991.
Bernard Silvestris, *Commentum in Martianum*. H. J. Westra (ed.), Toronto 1980.
Boethius, *Philosophiae consolatio*. Ed. L. Bieler. *Anicii Manlii Severini Boethii Opera
    Pars I*. CCSL 94. Turnholti 1962.
Calcidius, *Timaeus a Calcidio translatus commentarioque instructus*. J. H. Waszink (ed.).
    Plato latinus. R. Klibansky (ed.), Londoniae–Leidae 1972.
Gesta Francorum et aliorum Hierosolimitarum. Histoire anonyme de la première croisade.
    L. Bréhier (ed.), Paris 1924.
Guibert of Nogent, *Historia quae inscribitur 'Dei Gesta per Francos' quiqunque ac-
    cendentibus*. R. B. C. Huygens (ed.), Turnhout 1996.
Guillelmi de Conchis Glosae super Boethium. L. Nauta (ed.), Turnhout 1999.
Hugh of St Victor, *Didascalicon: de studio legendi*. C. H. Buttimer (ed.), Washington,
    D. C. 1939.
N. M. Häring (ed.) 1971, *Commentaries on Boethius by Thierry of Chartres and His
    School*. Toronto.
John of Salisbury, *Metalogicon*. J. B. Hall & K. S. B. Keats-Rohan (ed.), Turnhout 1991.
Odonis de Deoilo, *de profectione Ludovici VII in Orientem*. Eudes de Deuil, *La croisade
    de Louis VII roi de France*. Publiée par Henri Waquet. Documents relatifs à l'histoire
    des croisades 19:3. Paris 1949.
Orosius, *Historiae adversum paganos*. T. I–III. Ed._M.-P. Arnaud-Lindet, Paris 1990–
    1991.
Otto of Freising, *chronica sive Historia de duabus ciuitatibus*. MGH Scriptores rerum
    Germanicim in usom scholarum separatim editi 46. Ed. G. Waitz. Hannover 1912/
    1978.
Otto of Freising, *Ottonis et Rahewinis gesta Friderici I imperatoris*. In MGH, Scriptores
    46. G. Waitz (ed.), Hannover 1912/1978.

Radulphus de Longo Campo, *In Anticlaudianum Alani commentum*. J. Sulowski (ed.), Warszava 1972.

Suger of St Denis, *Vita Ludovici grossi regis. La vie de Louis le Gros*. H. Waquet (ed. & trad.), Paris 1929.

Suger of St Denis, *De glorioso rege Ludovici, Ludovici filio. Histoire de Louis VII*. In *Oeuvres* I. Ed. F. Gasparri (ed.), Paris 1996, pp. 156–177.

William of Conches, *Glosae super Boethium*. Ed. L. Nauta, *Guillemus de Conchis Opera omnia. Tomus II*. CCCM 158. Turnhout 1999.

William of Tyre, *Chonicon*. Ed. R. B. C. Huygens. Identification des sources historiques et détermination des dates pr H. E. Mayer & G. Rösch.CCCM 63. Turnholti 1986.

William of Tyre, *A History of Deeds Done Beyond the Sea*. Trans. E. A. Babcock & A. C. Krey, 1943.

Literature

E. A. Babcock & A. C. Krey 1943, 'Introduction' in William of Tyre, *A History of Deeds Done Beyond the Sea*, pp. 3-49.

L. Boehm 1965, 'Der wissenschaftstheoretische Ort der historia im Mittelalter Die Geschichte auf dem Wege zur "Geschichtswissenscahaft"' in C. Bauer & L. Boehm & M. Müller (ed.), *Speculum historiale. Geschichte im Spiegel von Geschichtsschreibung und Geschichtsdeutung*. München, pp. 663–693.

M.-D. Chenu 1957, *La théologie au douzième siècle*. Paris.

G. F. Chesnut 1976/1986, *The First Christian Histories. Eusebius, Sozomen, Socrates and Evagrius*. 2ⁿᵈ ed. Macon, GA.

P. Classen 1991, '*Res Gestae*, Universal History, Apocalypse. Visions of Past and Future' in R. L. Benson, G. Constable with C. D. Lanham (ed.), *Renaissance and Renewal in the Twelfth Century*. Medieval Academy Reprints for Teaching 26.Toronto, Buffalo, London 1982/1991, pp. 387-417.

P. Courcelle 1967, *La Consolation de philosophie dans la tradition littéraire*. Paris.

P. W. Edbury & J. G. Rowe 1988, *William of Tyre. Historian of the Latin East*. Cambridge.

J. Flori 2001, *La guerre sainte: la formation de l'idée de croisade dans l'Occident chrétien*. Paris.

J. C. Frakes 1988, *The Fate of Fortune in the Early Middle Ages. The Boethian Tradition*. Leiden–Köbenhavn–Köln.

P. Fredriks/Fredriksson 1992, 'Tyconius and Augustine on the Apacalypse', in *The Apocalypse in the Middle Ages*. R. K. Emmerson & B. McGinn (ed.), Ithaca–London, pp. 20–37.

H.-W. Goetz 1980, *Die Geschichtstheologie des Orosius*. Darmstadt.

H.-W. Goetz 1984, *Das Geschichtsbild Ottos von Freising. Ein Beitrag zur historischen Vorstellungswelt und zur Geschichte des 12. Jahrhunderts*. Köln–Wien.

H.-W. Goetz 1985, 'Die "Geschichte" im Wissenschaftsystem des Mittelalters', in Schmale 1985, pp. 165–213.

B. Guenée 1980, *Histoire et culture historique dans l'Occident medieval*. Paris.

R. B. C. Huygens 1962, 'Guillaume de Tyr étudiant. Un chapitre (XIX, 12) de son "Histoire" retrouvé', *Latomus* 21, pp. 811–829.

R. B. C. Huygens 1986, 'Introduction' in William of Tyre, *Chonicon*. R. B. C. Huygens (ed.). Identification des sources historiques et détermination des dates pr H. E. Mayer & G. Rösch.CCCM 63. Turnholti.

É. Jeauneau 2000, *L'age d'or des écoles de Chartres*. Chartres.

S. Kangas 2005, 'Deus le volt—Violence and Suffering as a Means of Salvation during the First Crusade (1095–1099)', in K. Villads Jensen & T. M. S. Lehtonen with J. Malkki and K. Ritari (ed.), *Medieval Historiography and Crusading Ideology*. Helsinki, pp. 163–174.

B. Lacroix 1965, *Orose et ses idées*. Montréal–Paris.

T. M. S. Lehtonen 1995, *Fortuna, Money, and the Sublunar World. Twelfth-century Ethical Poetics and the Satirical Poetry of the Carmina Burana*. Helsinki.

T. M. S. Lehtonen 2000, 'History, Tragedy and Fortune in Twelfth-Century Historiography, with special reference to Otto of Freising's Chronica', in T. M. S. Lehtonen & P. Mehtonen (ed.), *Historia. The Concept and Genres in the Middle Ages*. Helsinki, pp. 29–49.

R. A. Markus 1970, *Saeculum: History and Society in the Theology of St. Augustine*. Cambridge.

H.-I. Marrou 1970, 'Saint-Augustin, Orose et l'augustinisme historique', in *La Storiografia Altomedievale*, Settimana di studio del Centro Italiano di Studi sull'alto medioevo XVII, 10-16 aprile 1969, tomo primo, Spoleto, pp. 59-87.

T. E. Mommsen 1959, *Medieval and Renaissance Studies*. E. F. Rice Jr. (ed.), Ithaca–New York.

T. Rödig 1990, *Zur politischen Ideenwelt Wilhelms von Tyrus*. Frankfurt a. M.–Bern–New York–Paris.

F. Roversi Monaco 2000, '"Gesta hominum e gesta Dei": Ottone di Frisinga e Gerhoh di Reichersberg', in *Sentimento del tempo e periodizzazzione della storia nel medioevo. Atti del XXXVI concegno storico internazzionale. Todi, 10–12 ottobre 1999*. Spoleto, pp. 257–281.

R. C. Schwinges 1977, *Kreuzzuggsideologie und Toleranz. Studien zu Wilhelm von Tyrus*. Stuttgart.

B. Stock 1972, *Myth and Science in the Twelfth Century. A Study of Bernard Silvester*. Princeton.

F. Troncarelli 1987, *Boethiana aetas. Modelli grafici e fortuna manoscritta della 'Consolatio Philosophiae' tra IX e XII secolo*. Alessandria.

J. O. Ward 2000, 'The Monastic Historiographical Impulse c. 1000–1260. A Re-assessment', in T. M. S. Lehtonen & P. Mehtonen (ed.), Historia. *The Concept and Genres in the Middle Ages*. Helsinki, pp. 71–100.

ANE LISE BYSTED

Indulgences, Satisfaction, and the Heart's Contrition in Twelfth-century Crusading Theology[1]

In his book on the Sacraments, the Paris theologian William of Auvergne, who became bishop of Paris in 1228, explained the crusade indulgences by comparing the way the Church conscripted crusaders to the way a king organised his wars.[2] When a king was preparing for war, he told his officers to recruit troops and give them proper wages. In the same way, Christ had authorized and commissioned his officers, the bishops, to recruit and reward troops for his wars, the crusades.[3] Christ waged wars on the enemies of the Church, the heathens, the Saracens and the heretics, and the payment he offered his soldiers was the indulgences granted by bishops. This payment was both a promise of an eternal reward in Heaven, and a remission in this life of the penance imposed because, as William explained, just as a temporal prince had to free his soldiers of the duties that impeded them from going to war, so the prelates had to free the crusaders from fasting and other penance which was not consistent with life in the field.

Using this comparison William was able to state both the authority of the bishops to grant the indulgences, and the reasons for employing them. The authority came from God and was an effect of the apostolic power to bind and to loose. The reason for granting indulgences was that they were very popular, and would attract a great number of crusaders. This objective justified the use of indulgences for participation in the crusades.

This article will examine some of the theological difficulties of the crusade indulgences, and how the theologians of the latter part of the twelfth century and the beginning of the thirteenth tried to resolve these difficulties in order to explain how and why the indulgences 'worked'. By the time William wrote about indulgences (c. 1225), they had been practised for about 200 years – but no theologian had yet seemed to have found a really satisfactory explanation for them. This was only to be provided by the middle of the thirteenth century with the theory of the 'treasury of merit' and the works of the great scholastics, St Thomas Aquinas and St Bonaventure being among the most important.

Ever since the proclamation of the first crusade in 1095, crusaders had been granted indulgences in some form. The participants in the first crusade were promised that their penance would be remitted and their sins forgiven if they undertook the journey to Jerusalem with the pious intention of liberating the Church of God.[4] Every later call for a crusade was accompanied by a grant of indulgences.

Sometimes all the participants would receive a plenary indulgence, but sometimes they were meted out according to the effort or offer made by the participant. Those who died on crusade would always be sure to have gained a plenary indulgence, but those who survived would only be granted an indulgence of one or two years on some crusades. For example, Alexander III proclaimed in 1169 that those who fought in defence of the Holy Land for two years would gain remission of all their penance, and those who fought for a year would gain remission of half their penance.[5] A couple of years later, in 1171 or 1172, he laid down that those who fought against the Estonians would gain a plenary indulgence if they died, and one of a year if they survived.[6]

The reason for granting indulgences to crusaders was of course to attract people to go on crusade – it was a means of recruiting arms, and presumably an effective one. On the whole, indulgences were employed as a means of directing the pious works of the faithful into causes found beneficial to the Church. The institution had emerged at the beginning of the eleventh century (in the 1030s) as a privilege in connection with construction of churches.[7] For example, those who contributed to the building of a particular church would gain remission of part of their penance.

When Pope Urban II employed it for the first crusade, the meaning was accordingly to direct the efforts and pious intentions of the knightly class into the 'defence' of the Church. However, it also had a deeper, religious and theological meaning. The indulgences were also a way to declare that this war, the crusade, was going to be a particular kind of warfare, a holy war, and that those who fought in it would gain spiritual merit. The knight who fought in the crusade would not lose his soul when killing the enemies – on the contrary, he would gain spiritual merit and hopefully be saved as well.

The particular question of what Urban had in mind when he proclaimed the first crusade has been much debated among crusade-historians.[8] It has been asked what his perception of the promised spiritual reward was; what kind of reward he actually intended for the crusaders. It seems probable that his conception of the reward derived from the traditions of attributing merit to pilgrims and martyrs, and that he thought of the crusade as a combination of pilgrimage and holy war. The exact nature of the merit he intended for the crusaders however is still a matter of dispute, as is the nature of all the crusade-indulgences of the twelfth century. It has been maintained that the earlier ones were not supposed to have a so-called transcendental effect; that is, they were merely intended as remission of the penance imposed by the Church, and not a promise of God's forgiveness of temporal punishments – not, in other words, a promise of a shorter time in Purgatory.[9]

The question is much obscured by the fact that the early crusade-indulgences – as indulgences for other purposes – were expressed in varying ways. They appear in the sources as *absolutio, relaxatio, remissio peccato-*

rum or *indulgentia*, and some of these terms could even be used to signify other institutions. There was no fixed vocabulary for indulgences yet, and no general council had yet laid down guidelines for their administration. The granting of indulgences had emerged as a practice in connection with the administration of penance, and the bishops who granted them have left no explanation of how they thought they worked. They simply stated in the documents that those who performed a certain deed could be let off some of their penance. They did not explain what happened to these people's guilt for sin, or how or if the sins of these people were forgiven by God. Furthermore, since the theologians do not seem to have become interested in this subject before the latter part of the twelfth century, we cannot turn to them for explanations either.

In trying to determine the nature of the early indulgences and whether they were supposed to have a transcendental effect, one thus has to take into careful consideration the administration of penance in this period, as well as the state of theology – something which has not been duly regarded in modern crusade-historiography. The formation of the scholastic theology had just begun, and had not yet provided clear distinctions and explanations about sin and justification. Actually, the whole matter of penance, sin, and justification was very much discussed in the twelfth century.

However, the fundamental principle underlying the penitential system was that sin had to be atoned for if the sinner was to be justified and made worthy of going to Heaven – a point very much emphasized by the penitential handbooks circulating in the early Middle Ages.[10] According to these manuals, there was a certain amount of penance to be done for every sin. What happened when the Church cancelled the penance in an indulgence? How could sins be forgiven if they were not atoned for? How could one be sure that God agreed to the cancellation? Were the apostolic keys to bind and to loose powerful enough to guarantee that God did in fact agree? These questions all relate to the problem of the transcendental effect; they were precisely among the questions that the theologians of the latter part of the twelfth century tried to resolve.

Early Scholastic Theologians on Indulgences

The first theologian who had commented on the indulgences was Peter Abelard in his *Ethica* of about 1130. Abelard did not like the practice of granting indulgences, however. He thought that the bishops who granted them were being unscrupulous and bad shepherds of their flocks, precisely because the remission of penance in this life would only mean that people would have to suffer a much longer punishment after they had died. Abelard did not think that the bishop's apostolic keys to bind and to loose meant that he could absolve people of their punishments. In fact he denied that every bishop was invested with the power to bind and to loose in penance just because of his consecration – only morally good bishops had this power.[11]

Neither Peter Lombard nor Gratian treated the indulgences in their reference works of about the middle of the twelfth century, and the first theologians to address the subject after Peter Abelard appear to have been Simon of Tournai, Peter of Poitiers, and Peter the Chanter in the 1160s and 1170s – but then it seems that all the great theologians suddenly had something to say about it, and that indulgences became a frequent topic in theological *summae* and in commentaries on Lombard and Gratian.

These theologians did not go as far as to deny that the bishops had the power of the keys, but did express some concern about what this power meant, and how forgiveness in the eyes of God was guaranteed. Many of them thought that it would always be safer for a person to do his penance, even if he had obtained an indulgence.[12] Apparently, these theologians did not actually deny that the indulgences worked, their problem was rather that indulgences did not really fit in with two of their most profound beliefs. First, they thought that penance was essential to the process of justification, because sins had to be atoned for and because some kind of satisfaction for every sin had to be provided in order to set the balance right. Second, they thought that penance was also essential because it furthered the process of inner conversion and repentance in the sinner that brought him back to loving God in the right way. Penance was regarded as a kind of medicine for the soul – a medicine that might be bitter, but which taught the sinner to feel the contrition and remorse which was believed to be necessary for his justification. The indulgences seemed compatible with neither the need for satisfaction, nor that strand of twelfth century theology that stressed inner conversion and the heart's contrition.

The theologians of the latter part of the twelfth century and early part of the thirteenth then saw it as their task to provide an explanation of how indulgences were, after all, compatible with satisfaction and contrition, and how indulgences worked.

Their arguments can be divided into three main lines of argument. The first way of accounting for the indulgences was to regard them as a kind of commutation of penance, and explain how the satisfactory works were replaced by some other good works; this could be the giving of alms or building a church – or going on crusade. According to some theologians, like William of Auxerre and Giraldus of Cambrai, some of this substitution of penance could also be accounted for by the contrition felt by the person who received the indulgence. The contrition or repentance was thus regarded as a kind of interior penance that could replace the usual penance.[13]

The second main argument was based on the principle of vicarious satisfaction: that a sinner did not have to perform all of the satisfaction himself. The Church was perceived as a community in which the members were able to help each other and take each other's penances on themselves. A sinner could be helped by the good works and intercessory prayers (*suffragia*) of his fellow Christians, and of the priests and bishops – which would be even more effective. A share of the good works performed by a saint could also be counted in his favour.

The third line of argument had to do with the authority of the Church and of the issuer of the indulgences. A basic prerequisite for the issuer was the possession of the keys to bind and to loose, i.e., the power to impose penance and grant absolution, but the views on his other qualifications underwent some changes. It appears that some of the earlier theologians thought that indulgences could also be granted by priests, but increasingly theologians emphasized that the issuer had to be a bishop, because he had the authority over his diocese and the penitents living in it.[14] The Fourth Lateran Council (1215–1216) saw the first legislation on the administration of indulgences, in which it was laid down that bishops could normally grant indulgences of forty days, and only on the occasion of the dedication of a church could they grant indulgences of a year.[15] There were no restrictions on the ability of the pope to grant indulgences, who could thus grant larger and even plenary indulgences. This tendency towards centralizing the power of granting indulgences is also reflected by the theologians. James of Vitry, a Paris theologian who was commisioned by Pope Innocent III to preach the crusades, said that the issuer of indulgences had to have not only the power of the keys to bind and to loose but also the authority to commit the *suffragia* of the Church to the benefit of those who received the indulgences. The pope therefore was able to grant larger indulgences than an archbishop, because he presided over the whole Church and could direct the prayers and vicarious satisfaction of the whole Church to this end.[16]

According to this argument then, what the pope or bishop was doing when granting an indulgence was applying or directing the vicarious good works of one member of his flock to another member. Every bishop presided over the surplus of good works performed in his diocese, and the pope presided over the surplus across the whole Church.

The Problem of the Crusade Indulgences and the Solution of the High Scholastic Theologians

The crusade indulgences put this explanation to the test, because this was a very large indulgence requiring a very large amount of replacement good deeds of the Church if it was to account for a whole army of crusaders. At this time and until the Roman jubilees were instituted in 1300, plenary indulgences were granted exclusively for the crusades.[17] For this reason the crusade indulgence became the test case for the theologians, and this is reflected by a recurring question in the theological *summae*.

The question asked was whether a man who had taken the vow to go on crusade, but died before the crusade departed and thus never went into battle, would then still get the plenary indulgence. Since he had taken the cross, and the papal bull stated that whoever took the cross would get the plenary indulgence, was the papal promise valid when the man had not done anything himself? Was his intention to go enough to ensure him the redeeming effect? And was the stock of merit in the Church large enough to pay for those who did not perform very much themselves?

Another Paris theologian, William of Auxerre, considered this question about 1222–1225.[18] His answer was that only if the man's contrition was strong enough could he be sure of the plenary indulgence. If he had been sincerely determined to risk his life for Christ, this would have led him to true repentence for his sins in his heart, and would account for the missing part of the penance. The fact that he had intended to go on crusade meant that the grant by the pope would ensure that he would still get a share of the substitute *suffragia* of the Church. Not even the pope, however, could contrive that a person could go to Heaven without his sins having been atoned for one way or the other, said William. It seems that the reason for his reservations was that he was not sure that the stock of merit in the Church was large enough.[19]

The problem of the possibility of draining the stock of merit was solved in the 1230s by the teaching of the 'treasury of merit' of the later cardinal Hugh of St Cher. The Church is in possession of a treasure made up by the merits and good deeds of Christ and the saints. It is a chest which contains the blood of the just that was spilled unjustly. Just as the merits of Christ are infinite, so the treasure is inexhaustible. The Church has the keys to this treasury, can distribute the merits to its members, and can do so authoritatively and validly.[20] Obviously, this notion of the treasury was also a way to emphasize the notion of the keys to bind and to loose – it was a new interpretation that stressed their power and effect. Moreover, it was an interpretation that emphasized the power of the papacy, because the pope was said to be the holder of the keys to the treasury, just as he had the plenitude of power in the Church.[21] Thus the theological considerations concerning the crusade indulgences also played a part in the history of papal authority, and vice versa.

Thomas Aquinas answered the problem of the dead crusader in his *Questiones quodlibetales* from around 1270,[22] but in a way that stressed the authority of the pope much more strongly than William of Auxerre. Aquinas claimed that an indulgence was valid and effective if three conditions were fulfilled:

1) It had to serve a worthy cause, one pertaining to the honour of God, or the needs of the Church. A crusade met this condition.
2) The issuer of the indulgence had to have the authority to actually do so – this meant that he had to be the pope or a person to whom the pope had delegated this authority. In the case we are considering this condition was also met, because the crusade was proclaimed by the pope.
3) The person who received the indulgence had to be in the state of grace. That meant that he had to be repentant, and to have confessed his sins.

Accordingly, if the man who died before he got to fight in the crusade had repented and confessed his sins, he would get the plenary indulgence, just as stated in the bull. If the conditions of the papal bull were met, the papal grant was surely effective.

Aquinas was thus very certain that the pope did have the authority to grant remissions of penance, and no matter of what size. To him, the warrant of the effect was not based on the performance of good works or remorse by the recipient. The recipient still had to be repentant in order to be worthy of receiving an indulgence, but the effect of the indulgence rested on the authority to distribute them from the stock of merit possessed by the Church. In Aquinas's terminology the *causa efficiens* of the indulgence was the authority of the Church while the disposition of the recipient was only the *causa motiva*. The teachings on the treasury of merit and Thomas Aquinas created a shift of emphasis in the factors that secured the effect of the indulgence – less emphasis on the performance of the penitent, and more on the authority of the Church. The opinion of Aquinas was not uncontested among his contemporaries, however, and most of them, including Bonaventure and Albert the Great, maintained that the works of the recipient still had an effect on the value of the indulgence and that there had to be a certain proportion between the works and the remission, so that, for example, a person who lived far from a place of pilgrimage would get a larger remission when he visited it than a person who lived near by.[23]

The developed concept of the crusade indulgences, moreover, allowed theologians finally to explain how the crusaders won their spiritual merit. Participation in the crusades had always been believed to be meritorious and to further the salvation of the crusader – but now the theologians were able to understand and explain how it worked. The discussion of the crusade indulgences shows us that the theologians and the church hierarcy took this problem of the salvation of the crusaders very seriously. It was after all a matter of pastoral care for them. They saw the crusades as a religious undertaking and wanted to ensure that the people who took part obtained their spiritual benefits.

NOTES

1   This article is based on a paper I presented at the International Medieval Congress in Leeds, July 2000.
2   Guilielmi Alverni, pp. 551–552. Cf. also Paulus 1922 I, p. 238.
3   Guilielmi Alverni, p. 551, 'Si rex vel princeps bellum habeat, dat potestatem ducibus suis perquirendi & conducendi bellatores dignisque stipendijs remuneradi. Quia ergo rex regum & dominus dominantium Christus bellum habuit a tempore, quo caepit ecclesia bellum inquam non solum spirituale, sed etiam literale, seu corporale, sive materiale contra haereticos & alios Christianae religionis inimicos, videlicet paganos & a tempore Machometi, sarracenos, necessario dedit potestatem ducibus suis, id est, praelatis, perquirendi bellatores materiales & conducendi eos & congruis stipendiis remunerandi.'
4   Mansi (ed.) 1902, vol. 20, col. 816. Letters of Urban II to Flanders and Bologna in Hagenmeyer 1973, pp. 136–138.
5   PL 200, col. 1296.
6   PL 200, col. 861.
7   Paulus 1922 I, pp. 132–147.
8   E.g., Mayer 1965/2000; Blake 1970, pp. 11–31; Flori 1990, pp. 617–649; Hehl 1994, pp. 297–336; Riley-Smith 1997; Cowdrey 1997.
9   Gottlob 1906, pp. 91–139; Mayer 1965/2000, pp. 30–40; Riley-Smith 1977, pp. 58–61.

10 On penance see Anciaux 1949; Vorgrimler 1978; McNeill & Gamer (ed.) 1990.

11 Peter Abelard, pp. 108, 118–122. A statement on the power of the keys was among the propositions Abelard was condemned for in 1140, cf. Denzinger & Umberg 1937, p. 180.

12 E.g., Stephen Langton, ed. in Gillmann 1913, pp. 365–376, 371–375; Guilielmi Alverni, p. 550.

13 Guillermo Altissiodorensi, fo. 283 r; Paulus 1922, I, p. 228.

14 E.g., Stephen Langton, see Hödl 1960, p. 353.

15 Fourth Lateran Council, canon 62, ed. Alberigo 1962, pp. 239-240.

16 Iacobi de Vitriaco, p. 418. James of Vitry also mentioned the indulgences in his crusade sermons, which have appeared in a new ed. by Maier 2000, pp. 82–127.

17 A single example of a plenary indulgence for other purposes before 1300 is the Portiuncula indulgence, supposedly granted by Honorius III in 1216, but this appears to be forged, Paulus 1923 II, pp. 312–322.

18 Guillermo Altissiodorensi, fo. 282–283.

19 Cf. Poschmann 1948, pp. 78–80.

20 Poschmann 1948, p. 82.

21 Thomas Aquinas, *Summa*, p. 140; Thomas Aquinas, *Quaestiones*, p. 37.

22 Thomas Aquinas, *Quaestiones*, pp. 36–38. See also Cessario 1992, pp. 2, 74–96; Schaffern 1996, pp. 237–247.

23 Poschmann 1948, p. 94; Paulus 1922, I, pp. 274, 285f.

BIBLIOGRAPHY

Sources

Peter Abelard, *Ethics*, ed. D. E. Luscombe. Oxford 1971.

Guilielmi Alverni, *Opera omnia*. Aureliae 1674.

Guillermo Altissiodorensi, *Summa aurea*, Paris 1500, repr. Frankfurt am Main 1964. (I regret that I have not been able to make use of the newer ed. by J. Ribailler 1980–1987, *Spicilegium Bonaventurianum* vol. 16–20. Paris–Grottaferrata.)

Thomas Aquinas, *Quaestiones quodlibetales*, ed. Raymundi Spiazzi. Torino 1956.

Thomas Aquinas, *Summa Theologica. Vollständige, ungekürzte deutsch-lateinische Ausgabe*, vol. 32. Graz 1985.

Iacobi de Vitriaco, *Sermones in Epistolas & Evangelia Dominicalia totius anni*. Antwerpen 1575.

Literature

J. Alberigo (ed.) 1962, *Consiliorum oecumenicorum decreta*. Basel.

P. Anciaux 1949, *La Théologie du Sacrement de Pénitence au XIIe siècle*. Louvain.

E. O. Blake 1970, 'The formation of the "Crusade idea"', *Journal of Ecclesiastical History* 21, pp. 11–31.

R. Cessario 1992, 'St. Thomas on Satisfaction, Indulgences, and Crusades', *Medieval Philosophy & Theology* 2, pp. 74–96.

H. E. J. Cowdrey 1997, 'The reform papacy and the origin of the crusades', in *Le concile de Clermont et l'appel à la croisade,* Collection de l'ecole française de Rome 236. Rome, pp. 65–83.

H. Denzinger & I. B. S. J. Umberg 1937, *Enchiridion symbolorum definitionum et declarationum de rebus fidei et morum*. Freiburg im Breisgau 1937.

J. Flori, 1990, 'Guerre sainte et retributions spirituelles dans la 2e moitié du XIe siecle', *Revue d'histoire ecclesiastique* 85, pp. 617–649.

F. Gillmann 1913, 'Zur Ablasslehre der Frühscholastik' *Der Katholik* 1, pp. 365–376.

A. Gottlob 1906, *Kreuzablass und Almosenablass.* Stuttgart.

H. Hagenmeyer 1973, *Epistulae et chartae ad historiam primi belli sacri spectantes.* Hildesheim.

E. D. Hehl, 1994, 'Was ist eigentlich ein Kreuzzug?', *Historischer Zeitschrift* 259, pp. 297–336.

L. Hödl 1960, *Die Geschichte der scholastischen Literatur und der Theologie der Schlüsselgewalt*, vol. 1. Münster.

C. Maier 2000, *Crusade Propaganda and Ideology. Model sermons for the preaching of the cross.* Cambridge.

J. D. Mansi (ed.) 1902, *Sacrorum conciliorum nova et amplissima collectio*, vol. 20. Paris.

H. E. Mayer 1965/2000, *Geschichte der Kreuzzüge.* Stuttgart.

J. T. McNeill & H. M. Gamer (ed.) 1990, *Medieval handbooks of penance.* New York.

N. Paulus 1922–1923, *Geschichte des Ablasses im Mittelalter*, vol. 1–3. Paderborn. (References are to this ed. and not the second ed. Darmstadt 2000).

B. Poschmann 1948, *Der Ablass im Licht der Bussgeschichte.* Bonn.

J. Riley-Smith 1977, *What were the crusades?* London.

J. Riley-Smith 1997, *The first crusaders 1095–1131.* Cambridge.

R. W. Schaffern 1996, 'Images, jurisdiction, and the treasury of merit', *Journal of Medieval History*, 22/3, pp. 237–247.

H. Vorgrimler 1978, *Busse und Krankensalbung.* Handbuch der Dogmengeschichte, Bd. IV, Fasz 3. Freiburg.

RITVA PALMÉN

Peregrinatio Imaginaris
Twelfth Century Mystical Theology and Crusading Ideology

Introduction

In this essay, I will examine some of the fundamental features of medieval philosophy of mind, or in other words, medieval anthropology,[1]
concentrating particularly on the concept of the imagination. First, the
concept of the imagination has changed its semantic content dramatically
in the course of history. The modern idea of imagination is quite different
from the medieval one.[2] Still, it is interesting to recognise some common
characteristics between these two ideas. Second, a clearer idea of the human mental powers during the Middle Ages will help to achieve a better
understanding of some ideological changes in crusade ideology. In this
paper I want to provide some explanation of certain acts by Francis of
Assisi. This new understanding will also clarify the presuppositions and
ideology of the crusades.

Imagination in the context of the human mental powers

However, we will start with the medieval concept of imagination.[3] The
human being seems to possess an almost limitless natural capacity of producing different kinds of mental images and fantasies. This imagining does
not necessitate that there be real-life equivalents to these mental images
since man is able to construct an infinite number of elaborate figures of
mind by combining, differentiating, diminishing and enlarging any object
of choice. The source of this all is the imagination. Let me give you a
standard example of the function of the imagination which was widely
used during the Middle Ages. We can take the idea of a mountain and
some other idea, such as gold. It is possible to combine these two ideas
into one distinctive idea and imagine a golden mountain, which seemingly
does not exist in the real world. For instance, Thierry of Chartres (1156)
describes how the soul is able to attain various corporeal objects without
direct sense perception. The imagination is at work for instance when
we envision a nearly bald Caesar who is trying to conceal this by comb-

ing his few hairs on to his forehead.[4] Furthermore, the imagination was commonly attached to the epistemological process of apprehension and medical theories of man.[5] According to Aristotle's well-known account, the imagination lies between sense perception and rational activities, joining these together. As Aristotle puts it in his De anima: 'Imagination, in fact, is something different from both perception and thought, and is never found itself apart from perception any more than is belief apart from imagination.'[6] Here the focus of interest is on the orderly course of the cognitive process, from perception to concept formation.

What has happened over the centuries is then that the notion of the imagination has gradually changed to symbolise human creativity, which is distant from the limited perspective of the imagination in the Middle Ages or Antiquity.[7] In other words, the complex concept of the imagination as a faculty or potency of the soul has been replaced by the thinner modern notion of the imagination as the power of artistic creativity.

Let us take a closer look at the medieval theory of imagination. We may start by stating that there is no consistent theory of the imagination among medieval theologians and philosophers. The imagination was usually related to mimetic activity and could therefore only imitate sensible experiences derived from the material world. What mimesis meant in practice in the Middle Ages, then, is that the imagination is unable to establish the truth about itself as it can only refer to something else, some original reality of divine object. Imagination could not produce anything out of itself; it was not creative.

There are two different approaches to the imagination as a power: (1) anatomical (where is it located), and (2) functional (what its proper function is). The most common popular theories of the imagination are to be found in the so-called faculty psychologies, which assigned a proper cell in the human brain for each intellectual power according to its proper function. Generally, the underlying idea was to follow an orderly process of cognition from the very first sensation to the concept.

Nemesius of Emesa, who worked as a bishop in Syria at the end of the fourth century, provided a convenient summary of the medieval scheme of mental powers. His short book concerning the nature of man was translated into Latin 1050 as well as 1165 and was known as *premnon physikon* or *De natura hominis*.[8] It was widely used, both Thomas Aquinas and Albert the Great making use of it in their theories of mind.[9]

A common notion of many of these faculty psychologists was that there are three internal powers residing in three cavities of the brain. In the front cell/ventricle there is imagination or fantasy, which is the meeting place for separate sensations, thus constituting a common sense and forming the mental images necessary for thought. The image produced in the first cell is handed over to the powers located in the central cell, usually called *vis cogitativa*, *intellectus* or *ratio*, which is the rational faculty of the human mind. The *ratio* or reason is often seen specifically as the highest part of the soul. The simple imagination is usually only a relic of sensation, in a way a memory of impressions. The idea formed in the reason is then given into the custody of a power residing in the back of the head, the *vis memorativa*, which is thus the storehouse of ideas rather than images.[10] In Albertus Magnus (1280) one finds probably the most comprehensive psychology of the imagination. Under the term *vis imaginativa* he comprehends all functions ordinarily attributed to fantasy: presentative, retentive, schematic, productive and rational (*excogitativa*), a capacity which makes it the most noble of the apprehensive powers, a kind of reason.[11]

However, in the Middle Ages the limits of the imagination were far more restricted than they are today, since imagination was often related to medical theories and models of human anatomy. This does not mean however that there are no other important functions left for this faculty of the mind. Such theologians of the twelfth century as Hugo and Richard of St Victor as well as Isaac of Stella, who were developing their theories of the human mind in the area of Christian spirituality were original in their speculations concerning the imagination.[12]

Imagination, Transcending the Limits of Time, Space and Matter

Transcending Place

One of the interesting features of the imagination is its capacity to transcend distances between various places and hence the limits of locality. At this very moment, for instance, it is possible to imagine travelling from one place to another, but is it feasible for a man to imagine towns and cities which we have never visited before? Seemingly we may picture at least some vague representations of these places before our inner eye. For example, if one has has never visited Jerusalem, one can still be assured by the fact that Jerusalem really exists in some discernible place and time in the Near East and envision some representation of it.

According to medieval theologians too we may well imagine objects with which we are unfamiliar, but of whose existence there can be no doubt. Augustine's standard example here is imagining Alexandria, which he has never seen, in contrast to Carthage, which he knows. There can be no question of one's picture or image of Alexandria corresponding specifically to the reality, even if elements of that image may be derived from, say, a description one has heard or read, or a depiction one has seen. The overall picture is none the less 'as we imagine it.'[13]

What are these images of these particular places and how real are they, how great is the difference between the actual sense perception of the place and the imagined vision of it? The status of an imagined Alexandria or Jerusalem is thus that of an object, similar objects to which we have perceived, and of which we have received verbal or pictorial descriptions. Hence the actual status of the imagined Alexandria and the perceptible image of the 'real' Alexandria is in fact the same, in the sense in which the power of the imagination preserves some of the components of matter.[14]

Further, the assistance of the imagination is not limited to existent cities and places according to Augustine. He also describes a slightly different class of imagination namely, the capacity to imagine historical or fictional figures, or mythical places, or hypothetical cosmic models.[15]

Transcending the Time, Moving in Time

In the eleventh book of his Confessions, Augustine presents his famous arguments concerning the paradoxical nature of time. Since the human understanding of time is not an absolute and measurable entity, which runs constantly from the past to the future, the apparent non-existence of past and future is an unavoidable paradox. No past exists, because it has passed away. The future is also an illusion, since it has not come yet. All we have is now, present time. Augustine states that it is possible to manipulate images in the past and anticipate future events accordingly:

> From the same abundance I can myself join to past experiences various new likenesses of things either experienced or believed on the strength of things experienced; and from these I can, furthermore, think about future actions and events and hopes as if they were present. 'I shall do this and that,' I say to myself in the huge recesses of my mind, filled with so great a quantity of images of so many things: and this and that follows.[16]

According to Augustine, time is thus an extension of the mind which can be measured on the basis of our mental capacity for memory, attention and expectation.

This notion of the subjectivity of time was widely discussed in the Middle Ages by linking it to the debate over various human mental powers. Both memory and imagination were needed for constructing the necessary perception of time. Since past events are stored in the memory, we can say that the past exists in the memory. On the other hand, imagination predicts or anticipates the future events, and we can therefore at least imagine the future. Imagination was thus one of the essential tools for the human understanding of time. It is no wonder, then, that some theologians considered imagination as a necessary means for the flow or change of time within the human mind.

The connection between memory and imagination was particularly emphasised in medieval writings. Robert Kilwardby (1279) states that there can be no imagination without memory, since imagination is the contemplation of the image of an absent sensible thing which is represented in the memory.[17] Richard of St Victor (1173) finds imagination necessary for anticipating the future, maintaining that the imagination is able to form various representations of future things in each person's mind from that person's own judgement.[18] Richard highlights a quite practical purpose for the working of the imagination: the soul is able to control illicit thoughts and restrain from the sin by producing terrible images of hell or the joys of the heaven.[19]

Imagination and Symbolism

Previously we have seen how the imagination is able to transcend time and place, enabling the human mind to wander in places, cities and worlds where it has never been before. It is also possible to move in time and memorise past events in the present. There is also a third significant area, where the imagination is crucially active. I am now referring to the sphere of symbols and signs. In the Middle Ages many theologians eagerly debated symbolic representations and their interpretation, the Victorines and Cistercians of the twelfth century being specially involved. We might say that an object is symbolic if it makes reference to an underlying system of values, whether historical or ideal. Theologians of the Middle Ages all shared the conviction that all natural or historical realities possessed a meaning which transcends their ordinary explanation. These realities have a symbolic function in regard to that spiritual realm, which is accessible to man's mind only.[20]

Let me quote a well-known regular canon Hugh of St Victor, a leading master in Paris by the 1120s, who states that 'Symbol is juxtaposition, that is, a caption of visible forms brought forth to demonstrate some invisible matter.'[21] Various categories of symbolism could make use of both natural objects and historical events. It is possible for the literary, figural and ideological procedures to employ symbols. The range of symbolic representations is in fact as broad as the whole visible world. Hugh of St Victor continues: 'The entire sense-perceptible world is like a sort of book written by the finger of God.'[22] All these symbolic letters were meant to refer to the invisible realities.

The term *speculum*, mirror, was used to designate the world and its elements. Vincent of Beauvais would later compose his *Speculum naturale* and *Speculum historiale*. Traditionally, the term used for things that occurred at one time and referred to other things occurring later is *figura*; the generic term for things that refer to other things existing at the same time is *similitudo*, so that we may speak about horizontal series of figures and vertical series of *similitudines*.[23] In the Victorine account also, education meant in fact learning by visualisation.[24]

This symbolic structure of the medieval context had strong implications in sacramental theology. Sacraments had their reference to the past, which they commemorated, to the present that they vivified, and to the future, which they foreshadowed. Augustine supplied medieval men with material and methods for a symbolism which could express time – Christian time. Events bound up with the past, present and future have many significations in the Old Testament, the New Testament and the final kingdom. The conquest of Canaan was the entry into the Promised Land; Jerusalem was the figure of the Church, while the Church in turn prefigured the heavenly Jerusalem. History had a spiritual sense, since it could be sacramentalised just like any material object.[25]

Imagination and Symbolism Combined

There is a material and an immaterial aspect of the symbol, as there is in the human being possessing a body and a soul. The symbol is disclosed with the help of the imagination, which is capable of exceeding the limits of visible and invisible, material and immaterial and also revealing the spiritual content of the symbol. As Richard of St Victor puts it: 'We are accustomed to rise by means of visible things to invisible things, and to rise up to knowledge of them by means of the guiding hand of imagination.'[26] It is self-evident for Richard that no one should be ignorant of the fact that the imagination is the first gate for all those who enter into contemplation of invisible things. Without imagination capable of assembling, disassembling and reassembling images of corporeal things received from the corporeal senses, reasoning cannot rise to the understanding of incorporeal things. In this way the human soul may attain the important indications which are needed for meaningful knowledge of the invisible world.

Why are these symbols and their implications so important? It is because the sign or symbol conveys knowledge. It might be secret or mysterious, but its intent is to make something visible. Since it is impossible to represent invisible things except by means of those which are visible, all theology must of necessity have recourse to visible representations in order to make the invisible known.

Francis of Assisi (1181–1226), Bethlehem and Jerusalem

I will try to apply the medieval theory of symbolism and mental powers in practice, for which purpose I have chosen to analyse some of the events which happened in Italy during and after the Fifth Crusade of 1217–1221. In this third and last part of my essay we will follow Francis of Assisi's journey or pilgrimage to the Holy Land during this well-known crusade, which was directed primarily at Egypt.

Francis travelled with the young friar called Brother Illuminato. They must have been well aware that they were working in the military service of Christ, *militia Christi*, but this fundamentally meant *imitatio Christi*, imitation of Christ, for them.[27] The deeds and words of Francis demonstrate that he questioned the crusading ideology. This meant in fact that the true Christian can not own Jerusalem or any other holy places either in time or in some actual place, but has to seek the heavenly Jerusalem spiritually.[28] John Cassian (435) had already distinguished four senses which were applicable to the idea of Jerusalem. Only one of these senses was literal or historical, the others being spiritual; he gave an example which became classic in the Middle Ages: Jerusalem, in the historical or literal sense is the city of the Jews; in the allegorical sense it is the Church of the Christ; in the anagogical sense it is the heavenly city of God and in the tropological sense it is the soul of man.[29]

There was no doubt for Francis that the Heavenly Jerusalem *Ierusalem coelestis* is to be found within the inner spiritual life of man. However, the real or material and visible Holy Land was not altogether unfamiliar to Francis either, since he had visited Jerusalem and Bethlehem in 1219–1220. Both these cities have vast symbolic significance even today.

We take the status and inner symbolic implications of the city of Bethlehem as an example. As is well known, Bethlehem was one of the leading pilgrimage sites, others being Jerusalem and Santiago de Compostella. According to Francis, in order to approach Bethlehem, it is not necessary to travel with great difficulty to the Near East, since a small village in Italy is quite appropriate for this purpose. How is this possible? A few days before Christmas in 1223 Francis was making unusual preparations for the Christmas feast in a little town called Greccio, which is situated some 45 miles from Assisi. As Thomas Celano remarks, 'what St. Francis did on the birthday of our Lord Jesus Christ near the little town called Greccio in the third year before his glorious death should especially be noted and recalled with reverent memory.'[30]

Thomas Celano continues his small Franciscan narrative:

> Some days before the Christmas St. Francis sent for his dear friend and said to him: If you want us to celebrate the present feast of our Lord at Greccio, go with haste and diligently prepare what I tell you. For I wish to do something that will recall to memory the little child who was born in Bethlehem and set before our bodily eyes in some way the inconveniences of his infant needs, how he lay in manger, how with an ox and ass standing by, he lay upon the hay were he had been placed. The brothers obeyed St. Francis and the preparations required were finished without any delay.[31]

Francis's instructions were to construct new Bethlehem in Greccio, where the unique events of the first Christmas were represented and lived through again. Thomas Celano describes this process vividly, with great sensitivity. 'The manger was prepared, the hay had been brought, the ox and ass were led in. Their simplicity was honoured, poverty was exhaled, humility was commended and Greccio was made, as it were, a new Bethlehem. The woods rang with the voices of the crowd and the rocks made answer to their jubilation. The solemnities of the Mass were celebrated over the manger and the priest experienced a new consolation.'[32]

As is apparent in this little legend, Francis was an original and spontaneous person whose thinking has been described by scholars as an imaginative and visual one. Ideas appeared to him as images, and the enacted parable, mime or symbol were the natural medium which he employed in conveying his ideas to the friars.[33] The originality of the Greccio narrative lies in its transcending time and place. When it became obvious to Francis and other friars that the gates of the Holy Bethlehem were closed, he found no difficulty in reconstructing the same place in Greccio. The historical event could be lived through again; the place was localised and universalised simultaneously. Christ was born again, and the inaccessible Bethlehem rebuilt in Italy, after which this could be done at any place and any time.

The example of Greccio-Bethlehem was not alone. Francis reconstructed various sites from the Holy Land in different parts of Italy by demonstrating the biblical events, which once happened in Galilee in the countryside of Umbria as well as in the valley of Spoleto. Umbria replaced Galilee, the lake of Trasimeno was the lake of Gennesaret, and the mountain of Fonte Colombo acted as the Mount Sinai.[34]

The city of Jerusalem as well as the city of Bethlehem and the historical events tied to them are all symbols which can be approached via the imagination and projected again without the limits of time and space. The core of the symbol is always invisible, but it can be made visible and accessible to the human mind by material presentation. It is no wonder that the inscription on the front of the gates of Assisi declares: *Assisi La città gemellata con Betlehem* (Assisi the twin town of Bethlehem).

Heavenly Jerusalem

If we forget for a while the religious ethos of symbolism, we may ask what the link is between the image and the so-called real life. There is no doubt that certain images can considerably effect a person's emotions and motivation. Paul Alphandery and Alphonse Dupront have shown in their studies that it was precisely an image of Jerusalem with which the crusaders were obsessed.[35]

One element of West European society that undoubtedly influenced the formation of the ideal of crusades was excitement and speculation about the Second Coming of Christ, or millenarianism. Scholars argue over the importance of this factor, but it seems likely that at least some people believed that Jerusalem must be held by Christians before Christ would return, and some people (particularly among the lower classes) had a vague mental picture of 'Jerusalem' which conflated the earthly city in Palestine and the Heavenly Jerusalem.[36] Bad as it might be for unbelievers to govern the earthly city, it would be much worse for them to rule the heavenly one.

Richard of St Victor interrelates imagination and the Heavenly Jerusalem in an interesting way. He writes that:

> When we read about a land of flowing with milk and honey or Heavenly Jerusalem having walls of precious stones, gates of pearl and streets of gold, what person of sane sense would interpret these things according to literal (i.e. historical) sense? Therefore immediately he has recourse to spiritual understanding, and he seeks what is contained there mystically.[37]

This image of a land flowing with milk and honey does not correspond to anything in sense experience. Richard goes on to say how the imagination raises a fictive image of things and leads the human soul to true understanding. Richard gives a quite practical purpose for the human imagination and mental pictures of Jerusalem. A soul may comfort itself when it needs relief from distress with the help of these pleasing images of the future joys in heavenly Jerusalem. On the other hand, the soul may also punish itself by producing images of hell with this same mental power of imagination.[38]

In conclusion, the Heavenly Jerusalem could be built in front of the inner eyes of the soul. Why travel all the way to the Holy Land and experience only the shell of the symbol? Hence the entire inner content of the symbol could be envisioned at any time and place.

One could anticipate that this previously described symbolic mentality and its implications created some difficulty for the motivation of the crusades, at least among the intellectual circles in the Middle Ages. It seems to be that the successful and gifted preacher Eudes of Châteauroux (1273) faced the challenge of the symbolism as well as replacement of the Holy sites, and tried to give a valid answer to this problem. In one of his sermons he clearly states, that one should leave one's own country without hesitation and join the crusade. He admits that God could in principle give his blessing and a plenary remission of sin in a person's own country. Nevertheless, He wants people to leave their country in order to liberate them from the fire of demons, desire, indulgence and envy,[39] justifying this statement by quoting the Bible passage in which God commands Abraham to leave his country and family.

Furthermore, the crusading ideology was also attacked in a more practical way related to the Franciscan movement. According to the legendary testimony of James Coppoli, Pope Honorius III had granted plenary indulgences to the small, insignificant woodland chapel of Portiuncula after hearing of the private revelation received by the saint. Since about 1270 the Portiuncula had been one of the major Marian shrines of Europe owing to the fame of the 'Pardon of Assisi', a plenary indulgence without offerings, obtainable by pilgrims yearly on the 2nd of August.[40]

Crusaders were often offered an indulgence in return for participation in the hardships of a crusade. The indulgence assumed that if an individual were penitent, he might obtain remission or forgiveness of the temporal penalties for those sins by performing some arduous, virtuous or unpleasant task to compensate for them. Most medieval people were deeply interested in their fate in the next world, and the indulgence was a powerful incentive to participate in crusades.

By the end of the thirteenth century the plenary indulgences of Portiuncula were widely known and recorded in various documents. The indulgences of this kind were previously granted only to the crusaders and pilgrimages directed to the Holy Land. These examples of the small Portiuncula chapel show how the Holy sites could be replaced by others and consequently transcend the direct request for locality. It is no wonder that these indulgences provoked strong opposition among some people since it undermined one of the main arguments used in crusade sermons.

NOTES

1 For a general introduction to the concept of the soul in the medieval thought, see Kemp 1996; Kemp 1990; McGinn 1977; Michaud-Quantin 1949; Reypens 1936, pp. 433–469. For a collection of medieval psychological texts, see Lottin 1948–1960. See also Lagerlund & Yrjönsuuri (ed.) 2002.

2 Kearney 1991; Chenu 1946.

3 For the medieval concept of the imagination, see Bundy 1927, pp. 177–224.

4 Theodoricus Carnotensis, *Commentaries on Boethius by Thierry of Chartres and his school*, Glosa II, pp. 4–5 (Häring 269). Thierry quotes Suetonius, *De vita Caesarum*.

5 Harvey 1975, pp. 44–45.

6 Summers 1987, pp. 60–62.

7 Kearney 1991.

8 There is a very useful commentary and translation of Nemesius's work; see Telfer 1955.

9 The influence of the Arabic medical sources upon the Latin writers is also apparent. Many of the theologians of the twelfth and thirteenth century were deeply influenced by Avicenna (1037) and Averroes. Avicenna's philosophical anthropology was very influential. His philosophical encyclopaedia al-Shifa was partly translated into Latin by Dominicus Gundissalinus (1181) and came to be known as *De anima*, On the soul. See Harvey 1975, pp. 39–47; Jolivet 1988, pp. 113–148. For Avicenna's exceptional speculations concerning imagination, see Davidson 1992, pp. 93, 95–102, 109–110.

10 Kemp 1990, pp. 54–58; Bundy 1927, p. 179.

11 The power of imagination enables man to visualise a man with two heads, or a being with a human body, the head of a lion, and a tail of a horse. See notes in Summers 1987, pp. 207, 226–227; Bundy 1927, p. 266.

12 For anthropology in twelfth century, see McGinn 1977; Michaud-Quantin 1949; Reypens 1936, pp. 433-469.

13 Augustinus, *De Trinitate*, ch. 9.VI.ii. 'Item cum arcum pulchre ac aequabiliter intortum, quem vidi, verbi gratia, Carthagine, animo revolvo, res quaedam menti nuntiata per oculos, memoriaeque transfusa, imaginarium conspectum facit… Ista vero aut praesentia sensu corporis tangimus, aut imagines absentium fixas in memoria recordamur, aut ex earum similitudine talia fingimus, qualia nos ipsi, si vellemus atque possemus, etiam opere moliremur: aliter figurantes animo imagines corporum, aut per corpus corpora videntes; aliter autem rationes artemque ineffabiliter pulchram talium figurarum super aciem mentis simplici intelligentia capientes.' Augustinus, *Contra Faustum*, 20.7. 'Proinde cum tantum intersit inter cogitationem qua cogito terram luminis vestram quae omnino nusquam est, et cogitationem qua cogito Alexandriam quam nunquam vidi, sed tamen est; rursusque tantum intersit inter istam qua cogito Alexandriam incognitam, et eam qua cogito Carthaginem cognitam…' See also *De Trinitate*, 8.9; 9.10; Augustinus, *De genesi ad litteram*, 12.6.15; 12.23.49; O´Daly 1987, p. 109.

14 However, Augustine distinguishes such an imagined object from others which we cannot imagine for lack of any antecedently related perpetual experience. For instance, the various colours or light are unimaginable for a person who has been born blind. Augustinus, *Contra Faustum*, 25, 1; O´Daly 1987, p. 109.

15 O´Daly 1987, p. 110.

16 Augustinus, *De Trinitate*, 10.8.14. 'ibi mihi et ipse occurro, meque recolo, quid, quando et ubi egerim quoque modo, cum agerem, affectus fuerim. ibi sunt omnia, quae sive experta a me sive credita memini. ex eadem copia etiam similitudines rerum vel expertarum vel ex eis, quas expertus sum, creditarum alias atque alias et ipse contexo praeteritis; atque ex his etiam futuras actiones et eventa et spes, et haec omnia rursus quasi praesentia meditor. faciam hoc et illud dico apud me in ipso ingenti sinu animi mei pleno tot et tantarum rerum imaginibus, et hoc aut illud sequitur. o si esset hoc

aut illud! avertat deus hoc aut illud!: dico apud me ista, et cum dico, praesto sunt imagines omnium quae dico ex eodem thesauro memoriae, nec omnino aliquid eorum dicerem, si defuissent.'

17 Kilwardby, *De spiritu Fantastico*, pp. 207–208. 'Ymaginatio autem sine memoria esse non potest, quia ymaginatio est rei absentis ymaginis intra per memoriam representate contemplatio. Et ex hiis patet non solum quid memoria et quid ymaginacio set eciam quis sit ordo memorie ad ymaginacionem et ad contemplacionem que fit in ymaginando.'

18 Richardus de sancto Victore, *Benjamin Minor*, cap. XVI, p. 132. 'Nusquam hic sola bona, nusquam hic sola mala, sed permixta simul et bona et mala, et quamvis in utroque genere sint multa, nunquam tamen inveniuntur sola. ...ex eorum imaginatione quaedam futurorum imago figuratur, talis utique imaginatio rationalis esse facile conuincitur...'

19 Richardus de sancto Victore, *Benjamin Minor*, cap. XXI, p. 146. 'Sed ad Dan [imaginatio rationalis] pertinet exurgens malum, statim cum per cogitationem pulsat in iudicium adducere, diligenter discutere, deprehensum damnare, et deceptoriam cogitationem ex alia consideratione percutere, et temptantia mala ex tormentorum recordatione extinguere.' *Benjamin Minor*, cap. XXXIII, p. 180.. 'Hinc ergo Dan [imaginatio rationalis] minatur, illinc Neptalim [imaginatio intelligentiae permixta] blanditur. Dan terret minis, Neptalim fouet promissis. Ille punit malos, iste remunerat bonos.'

20 Chydenius 1961, pp. 10, 24–26; Zinn 1979, p. 167; Chenu 1968, p. 102.

21 Hugo de Sancto Victore, *Expositio in Hierarchiam Coelestem S. Dionysii*, PL 175, 960D. 'Supra jam diximus quid sit symbolum, collatio videlicet, id est coaptatio visibilium formarum ad demonstrationem rei invisibilis propositarum.'

22 Hugo de Sancto Victore, *De tribus diebus*. PL 176, col. 814B. 'Universus enim mundus iste sensibilis quasi quidam liber est scriptus digito Dei...'

23 Den Bok 1996, p. 113; de Lubac 1950.

24 Sicard 1991, pp. 155–192. Richard visualised Ezekiel's temple and certainly could have visualised his ark of Benjamin Major. See Cahn 1994, pp. 33–68.

25 Chenu 1968, pp. 118, 126–145.

26 Richardus de sancto Victore, *Benjamin Major* I, cap. XI, p.20. '... solemus per visibila ad invisibilia ascendere et ad eorum cognitionem imaginationis manuductione assurgere.'

27 The concepts of *militia Christi* and *imitatio Christi* in the crusading context are analysed by Powell 1986, p. 52.

28 Bonaventura states accordingly 'intrando in seipsam, intrat in supernam Jerusalem. Itinerarium' cap. IV, 4.

29 Smalley 1952/1964, p. 28; Lubac 1959 II, pp. 645–650.

30 Fr. Thomae de Celano, *Vita I S. Francisci*, I cap. XXX, 84, p. 63. The text was most probably written in 1228.

31 Ibid.

32 Fr. Thomae de Celano, *Vita I S. Francisci*, I cap. XXX, 85–86, pp. 63–64.

33 Lambert 1961, pp. 32–38.

34 See Di Pietri (ed.) 1980.

35 Alpahandéry & Dupront 1954, pp. 29, 74, 109, 178, 198, 279–282.

36 Alpahandéry & Dupront 1954, p. 71.

37 Richardus de sancto Victore, *Benjamin Minor*, cap. XVIII, p.138. 'Sed cum terram lacte et melle manantem, coelestis Ierusalem muros ex lapidibus pretiosis, portas ex margaritis, plateas ex auro legerit, quis sani sensus homo haec iuxta litteram accipere velit? Unde statim ad spiritualem intelligentiam recurrit, et quid ibi misticum contineatur exquirit.'

38 Richardus de sancto Victore, *Benjamin Minor*, cap. XXI, p.146. 'Sed ad Dan pertinet exurgens malum, statim cum per cogitationem pulsat in iudicium adducere, diligenter discutere, deprehensum damnare, et deceptoriam cogitationem ex alia consideratione percutere, et temptantia mala ex tormentorum recordatione extinguere.' *Benjamin*

Minor, cap. XXXIII, p.180. 'Hinc ergo Dan minatur, illinc Neptalim blanditur. Dan terret minis, Neptalim fouet promissis. Ille punit malos, iste remunerat bonos.'

39   Eudes of Chateauroux Sermo I (Maier 2000, p. 18): 'Olim dicebat dominus [Gen. xii]: *Egredere de terra et de cognatione tua*, sed non dicebat: Veni in terram quam monstravero tibi. Olim hortabatur homines ut mundum relinquent, sed modo hortatur ut veniant in terram quam ipse monstrabit eis et iam monstravit. Sed posset quis dicere: Ad quid eduxit Dominus Abraham de terra sua? Nonne in terra sua poterat ei benedicere? Certe ita, tamen causa innuitur cum dicitur quod eduxit eos de Ur Caldeorum, ut irent in terram Chanaam. Sic Dominus si vellet, in patria nostra posset nobis benedictionem suam dare et plenariam peccatorum remissionem, sed ideo vult ut patriam vestram dere linquatis ut vos liberet de igne demonum, cupiditas, luxurie, invidie.' On the model sermons for the preaching of the cross, see Maier 2000.

40   See Fratris Francisci Bartholi de Assisio, *Tractatus*. Concerning the Portiuncula Indulgence, see Huber 1944, pp. 38–41.

BIBLIOGRAPHY

Sources

Augustinus, *Confessiones*. PL 32, cols 659–868. CCSL 27.

Augustinus, *Contra Faustum*. PL 42, cols 207–518. CSEL 25, 1.

Augustinus, *De genesi ad litteram libri duodecim*. PL 34, cols 245–486. CSEL 28, 1.

Augustinus, *De Trinitate*. PL 42, CCSL 50-50A.

Avicenna, *Liber de Anima*, 2 vols. S. van Riet (ed.), Louvain–Leiden 1968–1972.

Bonaventura, *Itinerarium Mentis in Deum. Opera Omnia*. P. P. Collegii & A. S. Bonaventura (ed.), Florence, 1882–1892.

Fratris Francisci Bartholi de Assisio, *Tractatus de Indulgentia S. Mariae de Portiuncula*. Sabatier (ed.), Paris, 1900.

Hugo de Sancto Victore, *De tribus diebus*. PL 177, cols 285–289.

Hugo de Sancto Victore, *De unione corporis et spiritus*. PL 176, cols 811–838. A. M. Piazzoni (ed.), 'Il "De unione spiritus et corporis" di Ugo de San Vittore', *Studi Medievali*, III ser. 23, 1980, pp. 861–888.

Hugo de Sancto Victore, *Expositio in Hierarchiam Coelestam S. Dionysii*. PL 175, cols 923–1154.

R. O. P. Kilwardby, *De Tempore. De Spiritu Phantastico*. P. Osmund Lewry O. P. (ed.), Auctores Britannici Medii Aevi 9:1. Oxford 1987.

Nemesius Emesenus, *De natura hominis, traduction de Burgundio Pise*. G. Verbeke & J. R. Moncho (ed.), Leiden 1975.

Richardus de Sancto Victore, *Contemplatio: Philosophisce Studium zum Traktat Benjamin Maior des Richard von St.Victor*, Mit einer verbesserten Edition des Textes. Fuldaer Studien 6. M.-A. Aris (ed.), Frankfurt am Main 1996.

Richard de Saint-Victor, *Les douze patriarches ou Benjamin Minor*. Sources Chrétiennes 419. J. Châtillon & M. Duchet-Suchaux (ed.), Paris 1997.

Theodoricus Carnotensis, *Commentaries on Boethius by Thierry of Chartres and his school*. Pontifical Institute of Mediaeval Studies 20. N. M. Häring (ed.), Toronto 1971.

Thomae de Celano, *Vita Prima et secunda S. Francisci*. Analecta Franciscana. Tomus X. Ad Claras aquas, Florentiae 1926–1941.

St. Francis of Assisi, *Writings and Early Biographies. English omnibus of sources for the life of St. Francis*, 3rd ed. M. A. Habig (ed.), London 1973/1979.

Literature

P. Alphandéry & A. Dupront 1954, *La chrétienté et l'idée de Croisade*. Paris.

M. W. Bundy 1927, *The Theory of Imagination in Classical and Medieval Thought*. University of Illinois Studies in Language and Literarature, vol XII. Illinois.

Cahn 1994, 'Architecture and exegesis: Richard of St. Victor's Ezekiel commentary and its illustrations', *Art Bulletin* 76, 1, pp. 33–68.

M.-D. Chenu 1946, 'Imaginatio: note de lexicographie philosophique médiévale. Miscellanea Giovanni Mercati. II', Citta del Vaticano. *Studi e testi* 122, pp. 593–602.

M.-D. Chenu 1968, *Nature, Man and Society in the Twelfth Century*. Chicago.

J. Chydenius 1961, 'The Theory of Medieval Symbolism', *Commentationes Humanarum Litterarum* XXVII/2, pp. 1–42.

Davidson 1992, *Alfarabi, Avicenna, and Averroes on Intellect. Their cosmologies, theories of the active intellect, and theories of human intellect*. New York–Oxford.

N. Den Bok 1996, *Communicating the most High. A systematic study of person and trinity in the theology of Richard St. Victor (1173)*. Paris–Turnhout.

F. M. Di Pietri (ed.) 1980, *In the Footsteps of St. Francis in the Territory of Rieti. A Guide to the sanctuaries of the Holy Valley*. Terni.

E. R. Harvey 1975, *The Inward Wits. Psychological theory in the middle ages and the renaissance*. London.

R. Huber 1944, *A Documented History of the Franciscan Order 1182–1517*. Washington.

J. Jolivet 1988, 'The Arabic Inheritance'. In P. Dronke (ed.), *A History of Twelfth-Century Western Philosophy*. Cambridge, pp. 113–148.

R. Kearney 1991, *The Wake of Imagination: ideas of creativity in Western culture*. London.

S. Kemp 1990, *Medieval Psychology*. London.

S. Kemp 1996, *The Cognitive Psychology in the Middle Ages*. London.

H. Lagerlund & M. Yrjönsuuri (ed.) 2002, *Emotions and choice from Boethius to Descartes*. Kluwer.

M. D. Lambert 1961, *Franciscan Poverty. The Doctrine of the Absolute Poverty of Christ and the Apostles in the Franciscan Order 1210–1323*. London.

O. Lottin 1948–1954, *Psychologie et morale aux XIIe et XIIIe siècle*, 1–6 vol. Louvain.

H. de Lubac 1959, *Exegégèse Médiévale. Les quatre sens de l'ecriture*. Paris.

C. T. Maier 2000, *Crusade Propaganda and Ideology. Model Sermons for the Preaching the Cross*. Cambridge.

B. McGinn 1977, *Three Treatises on Man. A Cistercian Anthropology*. Kalamazoo.

Michaud-Quantin 1949, 'La classification des puissances de l'ame au XIIe siècle', *Revue du Moyen Age Latin* 5, pp. 15–34.

G. O'Daly 1987, *Augustine´s Philosophy of Mind*. London.

J. M. Powell 1986, *Anatomy of a Crusade 1213–1221*. Philadelphia.

L. Reypens 1937, 'Ame, (son fond, ses puissances, et sa structure d'après les mystiques)'. In *Dictionnaire de spiritualite*, Paris. Vol I, pp. 441–446.

P. Sicard 1993, *Diagrammes médiévaux et exégèse visuelle le libellus de formatione arche de Hughues de Saint-Victor*. Bibliotheca Victorina IV. Paris-Turnhout.

B. Smalley 1952/1964, *The Study of the Bible in the Middle Ages*. Indiana.

D. Summers 1987, *The Judgment of Sense. Renaissance Naturalism and the Rise of Aesthetics*. Cambridge.

W. Telfer 1955, *Cyril of Jerusalem and Nemesius of Emesa*. Philadelphia.

G. Zinn 1973, 'Book and Word. The Background of Bonaventure's use of symbols'. In, *S. Bonaventura 1274–1974* vol II. Grottaferrata. Rome, pp.143-169

PAULI ANNALA

Brother Francis and the Fifth Crusade

Introduction

'This humble man of peace had journeyed across the Mediterranean to end the crusade by converting the sultan to Christianity.' This is how Thomas F. Madden assesses St Francis and his activity during the so-called Fifth Crusade.[1] In addition to the idea of converting the sultan, in the general histories of the crusades we find another reference which indicates how successful the thirteenth century *Ordenspropaganda* actually was.[2] Drawing on the *Legenda Major* of St Bonaventure (ch. IX, 8) Steven Runciman refers to 'an ordeal by fire' when describing the meeting of the saint with the sultan of Egypt.[3] No matter how fruitful this kind of hagiographical material might be for another kind of study, a good historian cannot base his or her research on a source which so openly represents the ecclesiastical position.

It is precisely this that forces Francis de Beer 'to painfully eliminate some traditional testimonies, both inside as well as outside the Order.'[4] In order to see Brother Francis 'as he really is,' de Beer urges the historian to exclude from his or her sources 'all the witnesses of witnesses.' Consequently de Beer excludes such writers as St Bonaventure, Fra Salimbene and Thomas of Eccleston, 'since none of their writings refer us to the testimony of a contemporary of Francis.' But even this is not sufficient for de Beer. He is ready to eliminate the sources that emerged outside the Order as well, including the sermons of Philip the Chancellor, Cardinal Eudes of Châteauroux, Burchard of Ursberg, and many others.[5]

After having read the first two chapters of de Beer's study, the chapters that list all the necessary eliminations a historian should make in order to find a solid ground for a pertinent study, the reader is forced to ask the following question. Is there a single source on which a historian could build his or her historical reconstruction of St Francis and his visit to the Middle East? Fortunately such sources exist, and so the third chapter of the study is dedicated to a careful analysis of the primary witness of James of Vitry, especially his sixth letter and chapter 32 of his *Historia Occidentalis*.[6] But before we proceed to look more closely at which Francis the bishop of Acre really saw,[7] it is worth making clear in what circumstances the famous meeting between Francis and al-Kamil took place.

Historical Context of the Visit

James Powell begins his book *Anatomy of a Crusade 1213–1221* with these words:[8]

> The Fifth Crusade had its beginning in 1213, when Pope Innocent III announced his intention to summon a council of the church to meet in 1215 to discuss reform of the church and the promotion of the crusade. It ended in Egypt in 1221 on the Nile road between Damiette and al-Mansurah with the surrender of a major part of the crusader army to the forces of the sultan, al-Kamil.

The date 1213 is that of the three papal bulls, *Vineam Domini, Quia maior,* and *Pium et Sanctum,* which were sent all over the Europe to campaign for a new crusade. After four years' preparation, the first crusading fleets landed at Acre in the fall of 1217. The crusaders spent the winter of 1217–1218 in Palestine, conducting small-scale operations against the Muslims. In spring 1218, however, the crusading vessels turned their bows to the Nile Delta, to the city of Damiette, which, because of its strategic position at the mouth of the Nile, was called 'the key of Egypt'.

In May 1218 the crusaders established a bridgehead on an island west of Damiette. Their first objective was the chain tower that stood on its wooden foundation in the middle of the river and whose function was to support the iron chain stretched from one tower in the north-west wall of the city across the Nile to another. Since the whole construction served to control traffic in times of peace and to bar the passing of enemy ships in time of war, anyone who wanted to conquer the city itself had first to take over the chain tower. During the summer months of 1218 the crusaders intermittently attacked the tower without success but, finally, on 25th August the garrison with its nearly three hundred men surrendered to the crusaders. The capture of the chain tower began the stalemate that lasted more than a year and which ended with the conquest of Damiette on 5th November 1219. Without going further into the details of the war, the three months before the final conquest of Damiette are crucial from our standpoint, since it was within these months, from the latter part of August to the beginning of November 1219, when Francis and his brothers stayed in the crusader camp.[9]

Letter VI of James of Vitry

The sixth letter, addressed to Pope Honorius III, was written by James of Vitry in March at Damiette, some four months after the conquest of the city. The motive for composing the letter becomes apparent from the opening words: since the crusade was a papal enterprise, it was understandable that the bishop of Acre was responsible for reporting all events worth reporting to the papal curia, and the capture of the city was surely one. Accordingly, the major part of the letter (comprising ten pages in Huygens's edition) deals with the occupation of Damietta. But at the end of the letter his report turns to a subject that is worth quoting. Our bishop writes:

> Rainier, prior of St. Michael [in Acre], has just entered the religion of the Friars Minor. This religion has increased considerably throughout the entire world because the brothers expressly imitate the pattern of the primitive church and of the apostles. This religion is, nevertheless, in great peril because it sends brothers two by two throughout the world - not the experienced but young men without any formation, who should be constrained and tested by conventual discipline.
>
> The master of these brothers, and founder of this Order is called Francis. He is loved by God and venerated by everyone. Having reached our camp, burning with zeal for the faith, he moved on to the Saracen's camp. He stayed here a few days preaching the word of God and enjoyed minor success. The sultan, king of Egypt, even begged him to beseech the Lord so that through divine inspiration he might adhere to the religion which would be the most pleasing to God.
>
> Colin, one of our English clerics, as well as two other of our companions, Master Michael and Dom Matthew, to whom I had entrusted the church of the Holy Cross, also entered this Order. And I can scarcely hold back the cantor Henri and many others.[10]

Why did the Bishop of Acre regard the order of the Friar Minor as a perilous one? Wouldn't it have been more likely to suppose that the man who followed with sympathy the rise of the new lay movements of his era had greeted with satisfaction the engagement of some of his subordinates with a new, emerging brotherhood? The way the brothers imitated the primitive Church and the life of the apostles must have been something which made our bishop be wary of the entire movement. If we ask what this something might have been, there are good reasons to presume that it had something to do with the crusade ideology. Many scholars, James Powell among others, emphasise that Francis had not come into the crusader camp 'to cheer on the discouraged Christian army or to fight the heathen, but on a mission of peace.'[11] Reading the quotation in this light it is easy to understand why the bishop of Acre was worried. As a bishop, James of Vitry was responsible for keeping up the morale of the crusader troops, and it was merely consistent that he could not but warn of any sort of behaviour that would undermine the moral foundation of the crusade. The more the members of the traditional religious orders would have made the same decision as the four clerics mentioned by name in the letter, the more it would have sapped the fighting spirit of the crusader army. In short, the Franciscan mission of peace called the crusade ideology into question, and our bishop could not but exhort his subordinates to remain loyal to their original vocation.

Chapter 32 of James of Vitry's History of the Orient

The discourse of the two testimonies of the bishop of Acre are clearly different. Whereas the letter is more spontaneous and free in its style, the narration in the *Historia Occidentalis* is more official.[12] Hence the extensive chapter 32 'on the Order and the Preaching of the Friars Minor' (*de Religione et Predicatione Fratrum Minorum*) turns out to be a deliberate presentation of the Franciscan Order, its principles and the way of life of the early brothers. The following extract is taken from the latter part of the chapter that in its entirety comprises six modern pages:

> We saw the very first founder and great master of this Order, whom all the others obey as their sovereign prior: a very simple man, unlettered, beloved by God and everyone; the famous brother Francis. Because of his excessive inner inebriation and enthusiasm of spirit, he was so beside himself that having reached the army of crusaders at Damiette, he continued on to the camp of the sultan of Egypt, never wavering, having no other protection than the buckler of faith. The Saracens captured him on the way. 'I am a Christian', he told them. 'Lead me to your master.' They led him before the sultan. This cruel beast looked at him and was so overwhelmed by the countenance of this man of God that he was filled with tenderness. For many days, he listened most attentively while he preached to him and to his own men the faith of Christ. The sultan feared, however, that some of the men of his army would be converted to the Lord by the efficacy of his words and would join the army of Christians. So with every mark of honor and proper safeguard he ordered that Francis be led back to our own camp. When leaving him, he said: 'Pray for me! May the Lord reveal to me which law and which faith is most pleasing to him.'[13]

There are many interesting points in this passage. In what follows, we shall confine ourselves only to one, the answer Francis gave the guards who arrested him: 'I am a Christian. Lead me to your master.' I am surely not the first scholar who hears Francis saying: 'I am not a crusader, but a Christian.' 'In danger of being put to death, Francis, at all costs, wants his executioners to consider him not as a crusader, but indeed as a Christian who "confesses the Christ," like the apostle Philip before the eunuch of Queen Candace of Ethiopia,' writes de Beer.[14] Moreover, it is expected that the scholar who has given his study the title *Francis and Islam* has something profound to say about the subject, and this is how Jan Hoeberichts comments on the passage:

> When the Saracens arrested him on his way, Francis replied to their question about his identity: 'I am a Christian.' In other words, he was not a crusader, or someone sent by them, as the Saracens might have expected since he came from the camp of the crusaders. By his answer, Francis may at that moment unwittingly have touched a sensitive chord in the hearts of the Saracens, who subsequently heeded his request and took him to the sultan. For the Koran says: 'And you shall certainly experience that those who say: We are Christians, are nearest to us in love' (5:85).[15]

However intentional Francis's answer might have been, he won the confidence of the Saracens. The sentries did what they were asked and led Francis to the sultan. The first encounter with the Moslems and how things then developed, gives us the best testimony of the fact that the answer was sincere and wise. A historian can only guess the consequences of another alternative. Had Francis answered 'I am a crusader,' he would have hardly won the Moslems' confidence. On this basis de Beer, for instance, argues that 'the impetuous impulse which drives Francis to risk all, in order to encounter the enemy as a Christian, leads to a completely unforeseeable receptivity. The sultan is conquered; he takes Francis seriously.'[16]

The Testimony of the Chronicle of Ernoul

According to the well-known French Islam scholar, Louis Massignon, Sultan al-Kamil took a sympathetic view of Francis because he considered him 'a Christian Sufi.'[17] This statement is interesting in at least two respects. First, it urges us to consider more closely the relation between al-Kamil and this major Islamic mystical tradition. Secondly, it provides us with a hermeneutical key to interpret the Chronicle of Ernoul[18] and especially chapter 37, which offers us a detailed description of the dialogue taking place in Fariskur, a village lying about ten kilometres from Damiette upstream of the Nile, and where al-Kamil had retreated with his troops at the beginning of 1219.[19]

The chapter, bearing the heading 'On the two clerics who went to preach to the sultan,'[20] begins with the description of how Francis approached the papal legate Pelagius to request permission to cross over to the Moslem camp. At first Pelagius refused, because he did not want deliberately to send the brothers to death. But finally he consented by saying that 'if you go there, behold that your hearts and thoughts are always turned unto the Lord.'

When Francis and Illuminato[21] were approaching the village of Fariskur, the sentries thought that the strangers had come as messengers or to embrace Islam. The brothers were arrested and led to the sultan's tent. After having greeted the brothers, the sultan repeated the same questions as the guards had already done, to which Francis answered:

> they have no intention of becoming Moslems, but have come in the name of the Lord in order to deliver his soul over to God.' And they carried on by saying that, 'if you, sire, are willing to believe in what we say, we shall hand over your soul to God, for if you really die under the law which you now profess, God will never get your soul. It is for this reason that we have come. But if you want to listen to us and understand what we are saying, we shall demonstrate to you in front of the learned men of your country that your law is of no value.

Since the conversation took a polemic tone on the outset, al-Kamil had to call up his legal advisers. Having got acquainted with the case the lawyers had no other alternative but to tell their master what the law prescribes:

Sire, you are the sword of the law, and it is your duty to guard and defend it. Hence, we ask you in the name of God and of Muhammad, who have given us the law, to decapitate them without delay. We are not going to listen to a word of what these men are saying, and we also advise you not to listen to them, because the law prohibits lending an ear to the preachers of another religion. Whoever wants with his sermon or speech call our law into question, with such an action he will himself seal his fate. For this reason we command you to behead them at once, as it is prescribed.

Having said this, the lawyers went away, and the sultan was left alone with the two clerics. The account of the chronicle goes on as follows:

And the sultan said to them: 'Dear sires, my lawyers asked me, in the name of God and our law, to decapitate you, as the law prescribes. But for now I am going to act against the law and not to condemn you to death. For a sentence of death would be a wicked reward to you, who have deliberately endangered yourselves in order to hand my soul over to the Lord God.[22]

The narrative of the Chronicle of Ernoul raises at least two questions. First, why the sultan did not follow the lawyers' directions and why he did not comply with the law? Secondly, does a careful rereading of the text permit us to derive from the narrative some information which helps us to understand better what really happened in the sultan's tent?

In chapter 16 of the First Rule *(Regula non bullata)* we read that those who go among the Saracens and other unbelievers

can conduct themselves spiritually among the unbelievers in two ways. One way is not to quarrel or dispute, but *to be subject to every creature for God's sake* (1 Pt 2, 13) and to acknowledge that they themselves are Christians. Another way is to proclaim the word of God when they see it pleases God in order that the unbelievers might believe in God the almighty Father and the Son and the Holy Spirit.[23]

On the origin of these two counsels and on how they were inserted into the First Rule, it is worth looking at what Jan Hoeberichts has to say about the matter. In elaborating the First Rule, the brothers 'let themselves be guided by questions which arose from their contact with reality. In other words, Francis and his brothers approached their problems *a posteriori,* on the basis of their own experience.'[24] Setting the Chronicle in the light of chapter 16 of the First Rule, its testimony seems to be in glaring contrast with the first counsel of the Rule. The narrative of the chronicle gives the impression that the dialogue was polemic from the very start, while the counsel of the Rule clearly prohibits the brothers 'to engage in arguments or dispute.' Which testimony are we to prefer? As Franciscan historians, we are to give priority to the testimony that derives from Francis himself.[25]

Although the narrative of the chronicle is in this respect a fiction, this does not give us the right to scrap it. If it holds good with the history that al-Kamil called his lawyers to his tent, but after having heard them, refused to handle the case according to their directions, as the Chronicle gives us to understand, we must seek the motives of his behaviour at some deeper level. Was his relation to the Sufism of his time more intimate than has been usually considered?

Mysticism is a universal phenomenon that wells forth from deep personal experience and is independent of any prevailing religion. The majority of the scholars who have dedicated themselves to the study of mysticism are ready to accept this concise definition of mysticism. Be it a Christian or a Moslem mystic, he or she tries to enrich his or her religion by his or her own experience and thus to extend the religion towards a broader, say, cosmological dimension. Having received a special dispensation to taste the sweetness of the presence of God, the mystic has a philanthropic need to share his or her experience with others. This ardent desire for sharing is no neutral or passive state of mind, and at the same time it has within itself a protest against the power structures of the prevailing religion. Since the mystics have always challenged the integrity of the institutionalised religious community, its ministers have always reacted with some reservation to them. The history of Sufism offers many illustrating examples of this, the best known being the case of al-Hallaj, whom the authorities executed in 922.[26] One of the most famous theologians of Islam, al-Ghazali (d. 1111) had much work to do in order to gain widespread acceptance for Sufism.

What has all this to do with the encounter between al-Kamil and Francis? On the one hand it offers us a more complex picture of Islam, which is too often considered a monolithic religion. On the other hand, it is not at all unhistorical to suppose that al-Kamil, who surely knew some of the Sufi mystics of his time, was sincerely interested in knowing what 'a Christian sufi' might think about the situation into which his people has been driven. Since he was well aware of the hostile attitude of his lawyers, he had to get rid of them in some tactful manner. Hence, after having done what the procedure required, he sent the lawyers away, providing in this way a good setting for a confidential conversation.

Hagiographical Material as a Source of Historical Research

The purpose of this final section is to show how hagiographical material can be used as a source for historical study. As the material basis for this demonstration, I have chosen chapter 30 in Thomas of Celano's *Second Life of St. Francis*. Since nearly every hagiographical narrative is based on some historical event by which the fictitious description is driven, a historian should be aware of such historical backgrounds of legendary narratives. The historical frame of reference of chapter 30 in Celano's *Second Life* is related to the massive assault taking place on August 29, 1219 when the crusaders tried to put an end to the prolonged siege of Damiette and finally to take over the entire city. The narrative by Thomas of Celano reads as follows:

> At the time when the Christian army was besieging Damiette the holy man of God was present with some companions, for they had crossed the sea in a

desire for martyrdom. When therefore our soldiers were preparing to go into the fight on the day of the battle, hearing about it, the saint was deeply grieved. He said to his companion: 'The Lord has shown me that if the battle takes place on such a day, it will not go well with the Christians. But if I tell them this, I will be considered a fool; if I am silent, I will not escape my conscience. What therefore seems best to you?' His companion answered saying: 'Consider it as nothing to be judged by men, for it is not only now that you will begin to be thought a fool. Keep your conscience free from blame and fear God rather than men.' The holy man therefore arose and approached the Christians with salutary warnings, forbidding the war, denouncing the reason for it. But truth was turned to ridicule, and they hardened their hearts and refused to be guided. They went, they joined battle, they fought, and our army was pressed hard by the enemy. In the very time of the battle, the holy man, in great suspense, made his companion go and watch the battle; and when he saw nothing the first or second time, he made him look a third time. And behold, the whole Christian army was turned to flight, and the battle ended in shame, not triumph.[27]

In this way Thomas of Celano depicts a saint who has prophetic skills to foretell the future. This is the main message that a master of hagiographical literature is serving his medieval audience. A well-versed historian takes Celano's 'negative', enters his studio with it, and removes all the components that are typical of hagiographical historiography. From this elaborated negative he or she develops a new photograph and returns to daylight. What does the photo look like?

The picture of the Saint equipped with supernatural powers has turned into a picture of Brother Francis who is wandering about in the crusader camp and persuading the Christians to refrain from the battle.[28] Brother Thomas is surely right in saying that 'the holy man arose and approached the Christians with salutary warnings, forbidding the war.' But it is an inordinate request for a man who was so deeply involved in the crusade ideology that he had recognised why Francis urged the crusaders to renounce violence. Although Thomas was a gifted hagiographer, who was able fluently to utilise the biblical narratives in his production, he was in this case unable to interpret the course of events in the light of the advice Jesus gave to the man who had smitten off the high priest's ear: 'Put your sword back in its place, for whoever takes the sword shall perish by the sword' (Matt. 26:52).

Like James of Vitry, Thomas of Celano was also so deeply devoted to the execution of papal policy himself that he could not understand what Francis's mission of peace was all about. If we should find something positive to say about chapter 30 of Celano's *Second Life,* it would be that, fortunately from the standpoint of the history of salvation, there was at least one person who foresaw that 'so great was the number of soldiers lost in the disaster that six thousand were among the dead and captured.'[29] The hagiographical literature keeps up the tradition of *Heilsgeschichte* by telling about the great deeds which God does in the history of salvation. Hence, in writing the *Heilsgeschichte,* the vocation of a hagiographer is to explain why the history requires sacrifices.[30]

At the beginning of his account Celano brings up his belief that Francis had 'crossed the sea in a desire for martyrdom.' On the basis of our analysis we have good reason to argue that a desire for martyrdom was hardly Francis's main motive to do so. On the contrary, Francis and his brothers were motivated by a wish 'to establish peace between Christians and Saracens without violence and weapons, even without the weapon of the word,' as Hoeberichts argues.[31] Powell's argument goes along the same lines:

> Francis's preaching to the crusaders and his visit to the Moslem camp, viewed together suggest that his message of conversation as an alternative to war was offered not merely to the Moslems but to the Christians as well. Under these circumstances, the prophetic nature of his approach takes on a broader meaning, one that reflects some currents of contemporary criticism of the crusade and that reaffirms the pre-eminence of conversion as the resolution of conflict.[32]

Conclusions

Having completed our analysis of the four medieval texts concerning Francis's journey to the Middle East, it is now time to draw some general conclusion. Two of the texts, namely the sixth letter of James of Vitry and chapter 32 of his *History of the Orient,* have eyewitness status; the third, chapter 37 of the Chronicle of Ernoul, represents standard contemporary historiographical literature, and the fourth text, chapter 30 of Celano's *Second Life of St. Francis,* is hagiographical in its tone. When we crystallise the contribution of each writer to one thesis, we can summarise the results of our study in three hypotheses:

1. The eyewitness testimonies of James of Vitry offer a historian much material to reconstruct a reliable picture of what has really happened. Although the bishop of Acre 'devoted himself zealously to the execution of the tasks which had been entrusted to him by the ecclesiastical authorities,'[33] this does not disturb us, since he expresses his commitment to the crusade ideology so openly. For a historian it is easier to deal with material that is identifiable than with the texts that contain many unrecognisable elements. The same man who was able to write with sympathy on Francis was nevertheless unable to make the simple observation that 'the very first founder and great master of this Order' did not subscribe to the crusade ideology at all. On the contrary, the early Franciscan brothers were themselves engaged in carrying on their own mission of peace, for which the Franciscan greeting of peace, '*pax et bonum*' provides us the best known example. They wished to embrace both Christians and Moslems within this divine peace. But this was precisely the blind spot in the eye of James of Vitry.[34]

2. The Chronicle of Ernoul gives us a good opportunity to elaborate Louis Massignon's original idea that Sufism played an important role in the encounter of Francis and al-Kamil further. The sultan knew very well, without advisers in Islamic law, what kind of 'sword of the law' he himself was. By refusing to decapitate the brothers he showed that he sincerely wanted to understand the faith of a Christian Sufi better. It is

quite apparent that as a private person al-Kamil agreed with Francis that 'the religion which pleases God most' cannot be based on violence. As chief of the Moslem army waging a defensive war against foreign invaders, however, he could not act like Pilate, who 'washed his hands in front of the crowd' (Matt. 27: 24). In the Moslem camp there was simply no other person to whom he could have delegated the supreme military command. Moreover, when it turned out in the course of the conversation that the brothers were not official messengers sent by the crusader army, but were acting in their own name, there were only two alternatives from which to choose left: either ask the brothers to stay, or to send them back to the crusader camp. Al-Kamil chose the latter and, after offering them gifts and food, he asked his sentries to guide them safely back to the place where they had arrested them.

3. Thomas of Celano did not receive the request to write another *Vita* of the Saint from the pope, but from the Franciscan Order itself.[35] What does it tell us about the self-awarness of the young Order that Celano's *Second Life* does not contain a single story that would shed light on the life actually lived by the early brothers. In other words, Thomas of Celano cannot give up the ecclesiastical position in his *Second Life* and widen his horizon to recognise what was really happening within the Order. In order to be able to use Celano's work as a historical source, a historian must first eliminate this ecclesiastical bias. Having done this, chapter 30 of *The Second Life* turns out to be an account that gives support to the main thesis of this study: by his words and deeds Francis tried to persuade both parties to find a peaceful resolution to the conflict. In his account Celano gives us to understand that before the battle of August 29, Francis was worried that if he went to his fellow Christians and asked them to refrain from the battle, he would have been considered a fool, but it is precisely this that recent research tries to get around and free itself from.[36]

The more deeply one is involved in the ecclesiastical position, the more difficult it is for to see the reality. This is the lesson we learn from the case of Brother Francis when we study it in the light of the sources written or compiled by the ecclesiastical historiographers and hagiographers. Brother Francis was, however, a man who emerged from below; he and his brothers were 'idiotae et subditi omnibus,' as Francis himself puts it in his Testament. This explains his fair and unbiased attitude towards those people and events he encountered both in the crusaders' camp and in al-Kamil's residence. This explains why he could look at reality with an unideological eye, and this is the essence of my contribution to this collection of articles.

NOTES

1   Madden 1999, p. 150.
2   In the medieval culture there were at least two powerful means of exercising this kind of propaganda; the first was literal, i.e., the hagiographical literature, and the second was visual. We get a good impression of the former by getting acquainted with the numerous legends of the Saint and his deeds; the famous Giotto cycle in the upper church of the Assisi Basilica gives us an imposing view of the latter type of propaganda. These twenty-eight scenes of the life of the Saint that offer us the best example of how these two forms of the *Ordenspropaganda* work hand in hand; the frescoes are for the most part based on the *Legenda Major* of St Bonaventure. For more on this see Blume 1983 especially.
3   Runciman 1985, p. 160. See also Donovan 1950, pp. 60–61, where we find a similar reference to 'a test of the true faith in an ordeal of fire which Francis proposed.'
4   De Beer 1983, p. 2.
5   De Beer 1983, pp. 4–7.
6   There is a critical edition of both of them: for the former, see James of Vitry, *Lettres*, pp. 131–133, and for the latter, James of Vitry, *Historia Occidentalis*, pp. 158–161. Both texts were also translated into English in De Beer 1983, pp. 121–135; P. Oligny in *English Omnibus*, pp. 1609–1613.
7   In James of Vitry, *Historia Occidentalis*, p. 161 he says expressly that 'vidimus fratrem Franciscum.'
8   Powell 1986, p. 1.
9   Detailed description of the events that led to the final conquest of Damiette is given by Van Cleve 1969, pp. 413–418; Mayer 1988, pp. 222–225; Powell 1986, pp. 157–162.
10 Translation in De Beer 1983, pp. 122–123; original text in James of Vitry, *Lettres*, pp. 131–133.
11 Powell 1986, p. 158. See also Powell 1983.
12 Cf. De Beer 1983, p. 22.
13 Translation in De Beer 1983, pp. 131–132; original Latin text in James of Vitry, *Historia Occidentalis*, pp. 161–162.
14 De Beer 1983, p. 34.
15 Hoeberichts 1997, p. 80.
16 De Beer 1983, p. 34.
17 See Massignon 1969. In this respect, see also Roncaglia 1953, p. 101; Powell 1983, p. 76, where he states that 'il Sultano vide Francesco come un *sufi,* un uomo santo, rimanendo pertanto impressionato da quello che egli diceva.'
18 On the Chronicle of Ernoul, its author, date and composition, see Morgan 1973.
19 The reader is asked to look at the maps in Powell 1986, p. 139; Hoeberichts 1997, p. xxiii.
20 In medieval French, in which the Chronicle is written, the heading reads, 'De II. clers qui alerent preeschier au Soudain.' The original text of chapter 37 is easily found in *Biblioteca Bio-Bibliografica*, pp. 12–13.
21 It is commonly assumed that these 'two clerics' were Francis and Illuminato; see, e.g., Roncaglia 1953, p. 100.
22 All the three quotations above are translated from the French original found in *Biblioteca Bio-Bibliografica*, pp. 12–13.
23 I am following here the wording of David Flood; see Flood & Matura 1975, p. 87. On the Latin orginal see *Opuscula Sancti Patris*, pp. 268–269.
24 Hoeberichts 1997, p. 44. David Flood's comment on the origin of the First Rule is worth quoting here; he writes that 'they [the early brothers] put their agreement in writing, both the purpose and the stage of its realization, and they kept the text up to date. They added to it as events instructed them... Given this function, the text had to hue close to reality.' Flood 1989, p. 3.

25 The two counsels of the Rule belong closely together, as is shown by Hoeberichts: 'The motivation which is explicitly mentioned in the continuation of verse 6, namely that the brothers must be subject to every human creature "for God's sake," is thus presupposed here too. It was "for God's sake" that the brothers must not engage in arguments and disputes with the Saracens. For God is, according to a very personal expression of Francis, "humility" (PrGod 4; LetOrder 28) and God wants the brothers to imitate this humility in their lives.' Hoeberichts 1997, pp. 72–73.

26 See *al-Hallaj* on his teaching.

27 Translated by P. Hermann in *English Omnibus*, p. 388. The Latin original is found in *Analecta Franciscana*, p. 149.

28 According to Powell, 'the sermon preached by Francis in this situation, was not directed only to this particular battle, but… against the crusade itself.' Powell 1983, p. 74.

29 Thomas of Celano, *The Second Life,* ch. 30 in *English Omnibus*, p. 389.

30 On this subject, see Alexander 1968.

31 Hoeberichts 1997, p. 133.

32 Powell 1986, p. 159. Cf. Hoeberichts 1997, pp. 59, 82, 86.

33 Hoeberichts 1997, p. 41.

34 See a more detailed description of James of Vitry's attitude towards crusades and Islam, in Hoeberichts 1997, pp. 36–41.

35 On the background of Celano's *Second Life*, see the 'Introduction' by P. Hermann in *English Omnibus*, pp. 186–191.

36 By 'recent research' I mean the Franciscan scholarship that has emerged since the publication of *Die Regula non bullata der Minderbrüder* by David Flood in 1967.

BIBLIOGRAPHY

Sources

Analecta Franciscana, Tom. X. Quaracchi 1941.

Biblioteca Bio-Bibliografica della Terra Santa e dell'Oriente Francescano, vol. I. G. Golubovich (ed.), Quaracchi 1906.

English Omnibus of the Sources for the Life of St. Francis. M. Habig (ed.), London 1973.

al-Hallah, in N. Sells (ed. & trans.), *Early Islamic Mysticism*. New York 1996, pp. 266–280.

James of Vitry, *The Historia Occidentalis of James of Vitry. A Critical Edition.* J. F. Hinnebusch (ed.), Fribourg 1972.

James of Vitry, *Lettres de James of Vitry. Edition Critique.* R. B. C. Huygens (ed.), Leiden 1960.

Opuscula Sancti Patris Francisci Assisiensis, XII. C. Esser (ed.), Grottaferrata 1978.

Literature

P. Alexander 1968, 'Medieval Apocalypses as Historical Sources', *American Historical Review* 73, pp. 997–1018.

F. de Beer 1983, *We Saw Brother Francis*. Chicago.

D. Blume 1983, *Wandmalerei als Ordenspropaganda: Bildprogramme im Chorbereich franziskanischer Konvente Italiens bis zur Mitte des 14. Jahrhunderts*. Worms.

T. Van Cleve 1969, 'The Fifth Crusade', in R.Wolff & H.Hazzard (ed.), *A History of the Crusades*. Madison–London, pp. 377–428.

J. Donovan 1950, *Pelagius and the Fifth Crusade*. Philadelphia.

D. Flood 1967, *Die Regula non bullata der Minderbrüder*. Werl.

D. Flood 1989, *Francis of Assisi and the Franciscan Movement*. Quezon City.

D. Flood & T. Matura 1975, *The Birth of a Movement: A Study of the First Rule of St. Francis*. Chicago.

J. Hoeberichts 1997, *Francis and Islam*. Quincy.

T. F. Madden 1999, *A Concise History of the Crusades,* Lanham.

L. Massignon 1969, 'Muslim and Christian Mysticism', in L. Massignon, *Opera Minora,* II. Paris, pp. 482–830.

H. Mayer 1988, *The Crusades*. Oxford.

M. Morgan 1973, *The Chronicle of Ernoul and the Continuations of William of Tyre.* Oxford.

J. Powell 1983, 'Francesco d'Assisi e la Quinta Crociata: Una Missione di Pace', *Schede medievali* 4, pp. 68–77.

J. Powell 1986, *Anatomy of a Crusade 1213–1221*. Philadelphia.

M. Roncaglia 1953, 'San Francesco d'Assisi in Oriente', *Studi Francescani* 50, pp. 97–106.

S. Runciman 1985, *A History of the Crusades, Vol. III: The Kingdom of Acre*. London.

LARS BISGAARD

A Black Mystery
The Hagiography of the Three Magi

Hagiographic literature has a bad reputation, probably a legacy of the Middle Ages itself. In the twelfth century, popes and cardinals became increasingly suspicious of the many fantastic miracles that happened in the dioceses of the west and demanded, among other things, names of witnesses to be stated in each case. In this and other ways the Holy See intensified its grip on the process of canonisation, though this had only little effect on the actual reports of miracles and, quite undisturbed, people continued to celebrate local holy places and personage. The cautious and careful handling of miracles, first apparent in Rome, was further strengthened in the fifteenth century by humanists, who criticised miracles and many of the devotional habits of the laity. These were described as expressions of superstition, thus forming the arguments for the coming Reformation, which saw the demolition of medieval sainthood in the North of Europe. Protestant priests and church historians completed the condemnation by arguing that the whole hagiographic tradition had been instituted by the pope to relieve the innocent laity of money. Ironically, even the scientific movement of positivism added some understanding of the medieval mind and its way of conceiving reality. The Danish historian Kr. Erslev thus wrote that one was not to blame the Middle Ages for believing in miracles. It was an attitude of its time.[1] In general, however, positivism furthered the scepticism over hagiographic literature.

This attitude did not change until the later part of the twentieth century. Scholars like Peter Brown and André Vauchez showed new ways for historians to approach this branch of medieval historical writing.[2] The repetitive and standardised character of hagiography became not only a way of tracing ways of thinking which differed from modernity, but also an indicator of decisive shifts within the Church, telling a story of ideological changes.

Hagiography and its twin sister, iconography, thus have a story to tell about the crusades as well, or at least about the impact that the crusades had upon devotional patterns within the Christian cult. To be more specific, I have chosen the representation of the Magi or holy kings for

120

Ill. 1. The Magi bringing offerings to the Infant Jesus. Severa Epitaph, third century, the Lateran Museum in Rome. From Wienand (ed.) 1974, p. 77.

further investigation. In the west some noticeable changes can be seen in the twelfth and thirteenth centuries. The bones of the three Magi were found in 1158 and eventually transferred to the cathedral in Cologne, where a new cult to the Western Church quickly arose. At the same time the seeds for a new iconography for the three Magi were sown. In other words, a major transformation of a central Christian devotional theme seems to have taken place, which resulted in one of the Magi becoming black. The following is an investigation into the circumstances of this alteration.

The Early History of the Three Magi

The Adoration of the Magi is among the vivid and poetic stories of the Bible. It appears in the gospel of St Matthew and later on in the Apocrypha as well.[3] None of the stories say exactly how many Magi there were. Different traditions were soon established, but the most consistent number was three.[4] On the other hand, it is worth remembering that the Christians in Armenia and Syria have always believed that the right number was twelve.

Another and more serious problem was the placement of their feast in the Calendar. The obvious choice was the same day as Christ was born. In the first centuries the birth was celebrated at Epiphany, the 6th of January. Epiphany was the day of the light, a day where the divine nature of Christ was revealed and therefore commemorated. This had happened on several occasions in the life of Christ, major manifestations of this was thought to be his Birth and Baptism, the Miracle in Kana, and the Adoration of the Magi, which were all remembered on this day.[5] In the fourth century, when the dispute about the nature of Christ became intense, this clustering was abandoned. The spiritual birth of Christ, meaning his baptism and physical birth, was divided into two feasts, and the celebration of the nativity moved to 25th December. Both the Greek and Latin Church agreed upon this, but differed about the Magi. In the eastern part of the Mediterranean the wise men of the Orient followed the child faithfully, but in the west they remained loyal to Epiphany. This produced some difficulty for the learned in explaining why the Magi did not come on time.

Ill. 2. Adoration of the Magi, who wear Phrygian caps. Mosaic in St Maria Maggiore in Rome, 432–440. From Budde (ed.) 1982, p. 30.

Many considerations are met. Were they delayed by going to Jerusalem first, or did the Magi see the star on Christ's birthday but miscalculate the time for travel? Some added that although dromedaries were speedy animals, the road was simply too long. Happily neither Mary nor Joseph had moved from the stall when at last they found it.[6] On the other hand it is worth remembering that the adoration of the Magi was only one part of the celebration of Epiphany, and it did not become dominant before the High Middle Ages.[7]

The separation of the feast of the Magi in the west was furthered by a growing tendency to describe them as kings. The Latin word *magus* is derived from Greek *magoi*, which has several possible meanings. The most probable is a member of the priestly class in ancient Persia involved in astrology and astronomy. The old theological interpretation was that they were the first heathens to have worshipped Christ. This was supported by Psalm 72, which speaks about how the Gentiles were to submit to the Messiah. 'The kings of Tarshish and the isles shall offer gifts, the kings of Arabia and Sheba shall bring tribute. All kings shall pay Him homage, all nations shall serve him.'[8] However, the logical consequence of using this passage was that the Magi had been kings.[9] Kings did not become common in writings before the sixth century (Caesarius of Arles), and it happened without abandoning the use of the word Magi. In Western iconography uncertainty about their status is exhibited quite clearly. The garments of the Magi were depicted to underline their origin in the orient, their headgear especially often being a so-called Phrygian cap. It was only later, I would say in the tenth and eleventh century, that crowns began to appear on their heads.[10]

Apart from the old theme of *the Adoration of the Three Magi*, which was actually strongly influenced by church plays now being performed, whole sequence of their story began to be portrayed. *The Travelling of the Magi* and *the Dream of the Magi* thus appeared as new ways of representing the story. Representations of the Magi riding on horses became especially popular. The horse was associated with noblemen and royalty, and thus helped the transformation of the Magi into kings.

Ill. 3. Two steps from the story of the Magi: the appearance of the star and their adoration. o. 980, Codex Egberti fol. 17r, Stadtbibliothek Trier. From Wienand (ed.) 1974, p. 85.

Ill. 4. The Adoration of the Magi. The Limburger Evangelary. The Reichenau School 1000–1010. The Cathedral Library in Cologne. From Budde (ed.) 1982, p. 148.

Ill. 5 The Dream of the Magi: capital in St Lazare, Autun, 1125–1135. From Wienand (ed.) 1974, p. 87.

Ill. 6 The Journey of the Three Magi. Folkungapsalter 1170. From The Royal Library in Copenhagen 1999.

It was forgotten that some of the old apocryphal texts had claimed that the Magi travelled on dromedaries. The visualisation of the Magi also relied on the tradition of plays in their honour performed at Epiphany. Early plays are mentioned in Spain, France, Austria and Hungary in the eleventh century.[11]

Such was the situation about 1100. The three Magi were part of the cult both in the Greek and Western Churches, but had come to play a different role. In the east the Magi were mainly remembered as the first heathens to have realised the true nature of Christ, and were celebrated at Christmas. In the west their feast happened at Epiphany. In this respect more room was left to develop their own feast. Their royal nature was being increasingly stressed, but the specific features of a Western cult and iconography were only about to assume a definite form. Relics were still missing.

Relics

The right place to find the Magi was naturally somewhere in the east, and one may blame the crusaders for not carrying out this task. In the end they had to be satisfied with the Holy Lance miraculously found outside Antioch during a raid in 1118.[12] Scholars have noticed the fact that times of unrest and tension often produced relics in the High Middle Ages. At such times help from above was needed, and afterwards, when doubts of credibility normally arose, nobody would really know what had happened, no one could be held responsible, and in the end the relics would be a question of belief or not.

The discovery of the three Magi fits this pattern well. Their bones appeared during the wars between Frederick Barbarossa and the North Italian cities in the 1150s and 1160s. Our main source is a chronicle written by the abbot of the French monastery Mount St Michel, Robert Torigni, who states that in 1158, when Emperor Frederick visited Milan to put pressure on the city, the bones of the three Magi were found in a church outside Milan and brought to safety within the city walls.[13] In the following year the controversies between Milan and the Emperor broke out, and in 1161 Frederick began a siege which ended with the fall and sack of Milan in 1162. As spoils he took the best-known relics of the city, including those of the three Magi, and distributed them among his loyal men. His *Reichskansler* was the prominent bishop of Cologne, Reinald of Dassel, who received the bones of the three kings for his innumerable services on the condition that the bishop himself bring the precious gift from Milan to Cologne.[14] This happened in the summer of 1164, and on 23rd July the bones were translated to Cologne cathedral.

Hans Hofmann, who has studied the case thoroughly, argues that Milan had no cult of the holy kings before 1158. He rejects the local tradition that the bones were a gift from the Empress Helena in Constantinople in the fourth century to Saint Eustorgius, who brought them to Milan. Eustorgius was buried in a chapel in Milan that later was given his name. The bones of the Magi were found in this chapel outside the city in 1158. Hofmann is able to show that this tradition dates from after the translation of the bones to Cologne, and the story was probably part of creating a legend that would add the weight of history to the new treasures of the cathedral.[15] This interpretation is supported by the fact that the first complaint heard from Milan over the loss of the relics of the Magi dates as late as 1288,[16] at which time the cult in Cologne was flourishing and Milan envied it. This resulted in a competing cult in Milan in the fourteenth century, where things, deliberately it seems, were done in other ways than in Cologne.

The cult in Cologne was closely associated with the Holy Roman Empire from the beginning.[17] Reinald of Dassel, the bishop of Cologne, was one of the architects of the revived controversy with the papacy during the reign of Frederick I. It has been argued that Reinald compared the fate of the three kings with the situation of Frederick.[18] In the story of the Magi Christ directly confirmed their royalty when they had brought him gifts.

Thus, Reinald thought, no intermediary was needed between a king and God, such as a pope. Frederick's empire descended from Charlemagne, and at the time the relics of the three kings were brought to Cologne, a push for his canonisation was going on in Aachen. Since at this time a bishop could canonise a saint if the pope did not agree on the matter, Charlemagne was bestowed with this honour in 1165.[19]

The close relationship between the three kings in Cologne and the Holy Roman Empire was manifested again in 1198, when Otto IV was crowned king in Aachen. At that very moment, according to the many miracles reported by Caesarius of Heisterbach, a bright star appeared in the sky right over the cathedral in Cologne.[20] Otto IV knew how to acknowledge this divine intervention, showing acceptance of his crown (it was actually in considerable dispute). In 1200 he gave a most precious gift to the holy kings in Cologne, three crowns of pure gold and a quarter of a new shrine for their bones built entirely in gold and decorated with large diamonds.[21]

Those three crowns might later have inspired Nordic kings to bring either a similar gift, which Valdemar IV did in 1364, or use three crowns in their coat of arms, as did Magnus Ladulås of Sweden (1275) and the Danish Eric Menved (1287).[22]

Thus the three kings became *Reichsheiligen*. The immediate impact on their cult was that the Magi definitively turned into kings. Kings corresponded much more with Western daily life than Magi did and appealed much better to the mind of the faithful. In fact since the faithful happened to be kings and noblemen, as studies have shown, the transformation was a successful one.[23] However, other changes in the cult are also noticeable. This becomes clear if one turns to iconography.

The New Interest in the East Shown in Cologne

As a result of the acquisition of the soon famous relics, canons and other learned persons in Cologne showed a renewed interest in the east. The interest in tracing back the bones from Milan to Byzantium is one example, while another is the continued commitment to the idea of crusades to the Holy Land and later on the Baltic. A central figure in that respect is the scholastic Oliver, canon in Cologne and later bishop of Paderborn and cardinal-bishop of Sabina.[24]

Oliver participated in the fourth Lateran Council on behalf of Cologne in 1215 and was at that time a well-known preacher for crusading. He preached emotionally in Friesland and North-Western Germany before the crusade to Damiette 1217–1221, and on one occasion luminous crosses are supposed to have appeared in the sky during his sermon.[25] He was also a historian, writing the book *Historia Damiatina* on his participation in the crusade to Damiette. Recently, Anna-Dorothee von den Brincken has studied this piece of work. She regards his history-writing as an expression of a renewed Latin interest in the Christians of the east, although she admits that Oliver conceived crusades very traditionally.[26] Oliver was primarily concerned with strategic considerations. With this aim in view, he relied on what he saw and was told and combined this with what had been written about Christians in the east. The Copts in Egypt, the Maronites in Lebanon, the Nestorians in Antioch, the Georgians and the Armenians to the north, the Jacobites in Persia, and finally the Christians in Nubia and Ethiopia to the south are mentioned and described. Here Oliver shows an interest in the old story of the priest-king Prester John, who was said to have lived somewhere beyond Jerusalem.[27] His status in the Middle Ages has been described as 'a figure who always seemed contemporary, who was separated from Christian Europe in space but not in time.'[28] Oliver identifies Prester John's descendants in Ethiopia in Africa, where a long-reigning king, Lalibalá, was on the throne at the time.[29] Oliver knew from writings that Prester John had a son named David, who had become king over parts of India. Later on his Christian kingdom should have conquered parts of Persia as well and recently, according to James of Vitry, his descendants had attacked the Mongols of Chinggis Khan. With the Latin Church to the west the Arabs had enemies in all directions.

Oliver had no difficulty in explaining why so many different Christian people lived in the area around the Holy Land. Naturally, they were the descendants of the three kings who were now resting peacefully in Cologne. According to legend, St Thomas had baptised them on his way to India, a motive that was later painted in Cologne Cathedral.

In the middle of the twelfth century, Otto of Freising had pointed out that Prester John was 'a lineal descendant of the Magi...' and that, 'ruling the same people which they governed, he enjoys such great glory and wealth.'[30] Oliver now made Prester John's realm an African reality, consisting of Nubia and Ethiopia and thereby making his Empire a link with Muslim Egypt.[31] This had at least two consequences. Firstly, the identification of Nubia and Ethiopia with Prester John's reign combined with Otto of Freising's piece of information would implicitly mean that one of the three Magi had been black. Secondly and more importantly, the old idea from antiquity that the Magi represented the first heathens to worship Christ had to disappear, the kings being remembered as truly Christian, building truly Christian empires (Prester John).

The fifth crusade to Damiette failed, and Oliver went back to Paderborn, where he was appointed bishop and began to support the German order in the Baltic. He died in 1227. Today his name is primarily associated with the fifth crusade. However, I think Oliver ought to be associated with the study of iconography as well. There is reason to believe that his *Historia Damiatina* influenced the representation of the three kings in later generations.

John of Hildesheim

In Cologne the interest in the east was unchanged, and Oliver's writings became part of the knowledge to be found in the library of the cathedral. This was eventually supplemented by the writings of traveller and mis-

Ill. 7 The Adoration of the Kings and the transportation of the dead kings from Milan to Cologne. Two illustrations from John of Hildesheim's Historia Trium Regum. From Wienand (ed.) 1974, p. 65.

sionary Johannes de Plano Carpini (1241 head of the Franciscan province of Cologne), who preached against the Mongols. At the beginning of the fourteenth century some Franciscans from Cologne are reported to have been in the area and to have gone as far as Beijing in China.[32]

However, the most prominent piece of writing on the Near East is the so-called '*Orientbericht*', which appeared in the vernacular in 1355. The author is unknown, but he was presumably a merchant, who had visited the area. He was also a proud local citizen, and his account elaborates freely on what he already knew about the three kings.[33] His account was later extensively used by the prior of the Carmelites in Kassel, John of Hildesheim, when he wrote *Historia Trium Regum*.[34] The story was dedicated to the bishop of Münster, who at that time was canon in Cologne as well. We do not know exactly when the legend was written, but it has been suggested that the occasion was the 200th anniversary of the translation of the Magi's bones to Cologne in 1364.[35] In 1389 the first German translation appeared, and the first in English at the beginning of the fifteenth century. In other words, John of Hildesheim's work had a lasting influence on the Later Middle Ages. Unfortunately the scribes in the vernacular did not always stick to John's manuscript and several added new stories freely, as is the case with the surviving manuscripts in English.[36]

The names of the three kings had long been established as Caspar, Melchior and Balthasar, and several authors had stated that one of them was young, the second middle aged and the third old. John of Hildesheim, relying on the unknown author of the *Orientbericht*, now added a difference in the continental affiliation.[37] Pseudo-Bede, a presumably Irish compiler from the ninth century,[38] had already written the following about the skin of the three kings:

> The first was called Melchior; He was an old man with white hair and a long beard... He offered gold to the Lord, as to a king. The second, Caspar by name, young, beardless, of ruddy hue … offered his gift of incense, the homage due to Divinity. The third, black-skinned and heavily bearded, was named Balthasar; … the myrrh he held in his hand prefigured the death of the Son of Man.[39]

Since the *Orientbericht* 1355 was not a clerical work, the symbolic meaning of the gifts of the Magi was of no interest. The author of the *Orientbericht* was fascinated by the fact that the kings he knew so well from Cologne once had lived in the area that he was now visiting. More or less as a tourist guide, he points out places important to the lives of the Magi. In other words, all the legendary tales about the holy kings known from his years in Cologne are transferred to places the author has seen or heard of during his stay in the Arabic world.

The kings had been true Christians, he writes, and several references are made to St Thomas, because according to legend he was the one, who had baptised them.[40] The town of Sowa is stated to have been the centre of Prester John's mighty realm, consisting of Nubia, Ethiopia and now Tharsis plus 37 other kingdoms. That would make his realm fit the description in Psalm 72. According to the *Orientbericht* Sowa was situated close to India and it seems that the author never went that far. The real interest in Sowa was otherwise, because in Cologne they celebrated it as the first burial place for the three kings, who they somehow knew had all died in AD 54.[41]

According to the *Orientbericht*, Melchior had reigned in Nubia, Caspar in Tharsis and Balthasar in one of the other kingdoms. The anonymous author writes that he does not know which, because it was lost soon after the death of Prester John. John of Hildesheim is more precise in claiming that Balthasar reigned over Sheba.[42] Tharsis is usually regarded as the medieval name of Mongolia, but nonetheless the author states, that all their inhabitants are black as moors.[43] The author could not have been well informed about Tharsis, but he seems to have known that Caspar was a black man. Again the probable explanation is that this was part of his common knowledge acquired in Cologne. One of his sources might have been the *Dreikönigsspiele* performed there. Few manuscripts of these church plays survive from the Middle Ages, and certainly none from Cologne, but in later centuries Caspar was portrayed in the town as black, and he played '*eine lustige Rolle*.'[44] Caspar was often addressed Kasperle, meaning the smaller or younger of the kings.[45] A more probable explanation is that the anonymous author of the *Orientbericht* relied on other travel accounts from the beginning of the fourteenth century, according to which Tharsis was inhabited by blacks.[46] This tradition differed from the early one established by Pseudo-Bede, who had described Balthasar as the dark Magus.

No such thing appeared in the widespread Golden Legend, a clerical work compiled between 1263 and 1272 by Jacobus of Varazze (Voragine).[47] Those who adored Christ were just kings from the east; either their kingdoms were of no particular interest to the author, or he did not know about them. But in Cologne they knew. At least since the arrival of the relics of the kings in 1164 much speculation on their lives and realms had been made. Thanks to canon Oliver a written account on the possible alliances with old Christian empires beyond the Muslim areas had been produced in the thirteenth century. These empires were linked to descendants of the Magi and although Oliver did not explicitly state that one of the Kings was

Ill. 8 The coat of arms of the diocese of Cologne, the town and the three holy kings. Woodcut 1492. From Budde (ed.) 1982, p. 105.

black, the basis for such a conclusion was present in his work. St Elisabeth (1207–1231) had addressed the patron of the monastery in Schönau by saying: 'Rex Baltazar, qui niger', showing that more than one tradition about the colours and origins of the Magi had circulated.[48] In the growing cult of the Magi various ideas were present, competing with each other for authority. The need for clarity became more and more obvious. The 200th anniversary of the translation of the relics to Cologne offered a splendid opportunity and neither was it wasted. John of Hildesheim completed the task, although his contribution was nothing more that the compilation of known facts in the living hagiographic tradition of the holy kings.

The Iconography of the Three Holy Kings

The path from written text to image is a complicated one. Luckily, Paul H. D. Kaplan has written a brilliant study showing the transformation as an ongoing process. The first known, possible representations of a black king date from 1347, but not until Hans Mulscher's altarpiece in Wurzach of 1437 is a wholly original Adoration with a black Magus found.[49]

This late appearance was previously explained by the general aversion to the colour black in the High Middle Ages.[50] However, according to Kaplan several reasons may be given. Some have already been discussed here, the notion of a black Prester John, the work of John of Hildesheim, as

Ill. 9 The coat of arms of the three holy kings. The book of the herald Gelre with coats of arms, o. 1370. From Budde (ed.) 1982, p. 104.

well as the attention devoted to black figures in art and literature produced in the court of Emperor Charles IV (1346–1378). In particular, one finds that the skin of St Maurice becomes black in the same period.[51]

As a general explanation I should like to add the role of Cologne as promoter of the Magis' relics. Even St Maurice fits this pattern. His martyrdom (fourth century) took place in no other town, of course, than Cologne, and for a long time he was only venerated here. In this city it is even possible to find a black St Maurice in stained glass as early as 1320.[52] Looking more closely at the role of Emperor Charles IV, we find that his coronation in Italy took place on the day of the Epiphany 1355 with the Archbishop of Cologne present. During his lifetime the emperor four times represented himself as one of the holy kings, an entirely new arrangement. One of them is found in his castle of Karlstein and seems to be his own innovation. Politically he supported the archbishop against the city of Cologne and extended his privileges.[53]

Although the archbishops of Cologne did what was possible to enlarge the cult of their famous relics, they did not necessarily agree upon all the speculation about the nature and colour of the three kings. While the work of John of Hildesheim was supported by one of the canons in Cologne, some reluctance towards a black king is still perceptible. In the 1430s the well-known artist Stefan Lochner built a now famous altar-piece for the Cathedral, usually called *Dombild*. Significantly, he did not portray any king as black. However, examining the painting more closely it is

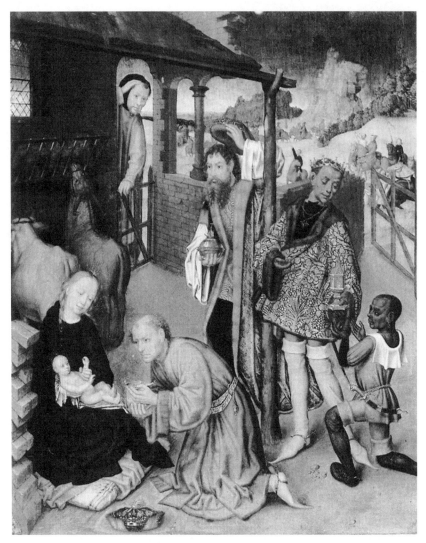

Ill. 10. The Adoration of the Kings. The School of Hugo van der Goes 1450–1500, 102x84 cm. Private property, Switzerland.

possible to find both a black herald on the banner of one of the attendants of the kings and a black servant as well.

During the later half of the fifteenth century general acceptance was won for the fact that one of the kings had been a black African.[54] The main basis of this claim is iconography. German, Dutch, Flemish and Italian altarpieces and graphic prints developed the idea of a black Magus. Nor it is unusual to see the black king with a servant at his side. Sometimes he is kneeling instead of the black king.[55] The first reference to a black king in church plays appears in 1441, from the Netherlands and indicating a diffusion of the idea at lower levels in the cult of the three kings.[56]

The kings are no longer lined up in a row as in earlier representations but pose differently and are portrayed individually. Kaplan notices that

Ill. 11. The Adoration of the Kings. The master of St Severin, o 1485–1515, 57x50,5 cm. The Wallraf-Richartz Museum in Cologne. Both from Budde (ed.) 1982, pp. 196,

the black king is given African features. Interestingly, the kings no longer have to wear crowns. Probably this reflects a growing awareness that foreign kings did not use the same crown as European princes, because their garments and whole appearance are regal indeed. This impression is even more dominant in the printed version of the story of the childhood of Christ.[57]

One of the problems with iconography is whether the observers saw the same meaning in a picture as those who had produced it intended. In areas where plays devoted to the three kings and altarpieces supported each other, this was probably the case, but altarpieces were also produced on a large scale, and sold to distant areas, where one cannot expect such a coincidence. In this context, Denmark was a periphery and surviving representations of the three kings here are often works imported from the Netherlands.[58]

Ill. 12. The adoration of the kings. Altar-panel from the church of Hagested in Zealand, now in the National Museum in Copenhagen.

The open interpretation was even more obvious in the case of prints which easily were so disseminated. This results in a new and more precise symbolic meaning becoming apparent. Not only did the kings represent different ages; they also come from different continents, Asia, Africa and Europe. Thus the whole world adored the Christ child.

Conclusion

Neither hagiography nor iconography were static and unchanging genres in the Middle Ages. Both incorporated new elements over the centuries and were open to political and ideological change. In the case of the three Magi the discovery of their bones began a series of reinterpretations of the meaning of their story. In the first place this was associated with the political intentions of the Holy Roman Empire, and no doubt was shown whether they were kings or not. Later, when the power of the emperor diminished and the cult enjoyed broader support and approval, Cologne was free to elaborate on the story once more. Thus one of the Magi turned out to be black, a process in which the crusade preacher Oliver played a minor role. At first this was a purely German tradition, but the popularity of the cult in the Later Middle Ages was so great that the idea was exported to a large part of Northern Europe. It furthered the interpretation that the adoration of the Magi was a symbol of the whole world's submission to Christ. In fact, this was a much more sophisticated way of promulgating crusading ideology than that expressed in the High Middle Ages.

In the twelfth century, eastern features had been wiped out of the story, and the Magi were represented as kings with crowns riding on proud horses. This marked a century characterised by contrasts between east and west. However, in the long run a fascination with the east prevailed. The idea of the riches of the east was transferred to the motive, and both ordinary man and the elite of the west seem to have enjoyed lavish expressions of eastern extravagance. This is even truer of the Renaissance period that was to follow.

NOTES

1   Erslev 1901, pp. 663f.
2   Brown 1982; Vauchez 1988.
3   Matthew 2:1–12; KLNM V, p. 390; LM *Drei Könige*.
4   First mentioned by Origenes of Alexandria († 252). Uncertainty about their numbers reigned for centuries. The early depiction at the cemetery of St Peter and St Marcellianus in Rome shows only two Magi, the one of St Domitilla four. Deckers 1982, p. 27.
5   The literature on the Epiphany is quite large. See Kehrer 1908–1909 I, p. 22–28; Dassmann 1982.
6   St Jerome's speculations about these particularly fast dromedaries was intensified in the Middle Ages in the West, after the discovery of their bodies in 1158. See *Legenda Aurea*, p. 105. In Danish sermons they were repeated by Christiern Pedersen; see *Christiern Pedersens Jærtegns-Postil* I, p. 152. In *Jesu Barndoms Bog,* printed in Copenhagen 1508, a whole page is devoted to various explanations. For instance, it is stated that fog in Jerusalem caused delay. Op. cit., p. 50.
7   Thus in the Latin Church the celebration of baptism tended to become a story about the appearance of the holy trinity, and the consecration of the water that originally took place on this day was moved and placed in the Easter period.
8   Psalm 72:10–11. At that time Psalm 71, 'Reges tharsis et insulae munera offerent; Reges Arabum et Saba dona adducent; Et adorabunt eum omnes reges terrae, Omnes gentes servient ei.' See also Isaiah 60:3, 'Et ambulant gentes in lumine tuo, Et reges in splendore ortus tui.' A prophecy about the gifts was found in Isaiah 60:10, 'Caravans of camels shall fill you, dromedaries from Median and Ephrah; all from Sheba shall come bearing gold and frankinsence, and proclaiming the praises of the Lord.'
9   Hofmann 1975, p. 74. With reference to Tertullian (d. after 222)
10 Kehrer 1908–1909 II, pp. 109–128. Kehrer's many illustrations from the 9–12th centuries in the West clearly show an iconography of many traditions.
11 Hofmann 1975, pp. 153f. Kehrer devotes two chapters to the theme arguing that it was a special French tradition. However he does not have many examples from Spain in his material. Kehrer 1908–1909 II, pp. 129ff.
12 Mayer 1965, pp. 62f.
13 Hofmann 1975, p. 76, 'Eodem anno inventa sunt corpora Trium Magorum, qui salvatorem nostrum infantem adoraverunt in Betleem, in quadam veteri capella iuxta urbem Mediolanum, et pro timore Frederici imperatoris Alemannorum, qui eandem urbem obsidere veniebat, levata et in civitate posita.'
14 Op. cit., pp. 96f.
15 Op. cit. pp. 77ff. Patrick J. Geary takes the argument even further and finds no evidence of an early Milanese cult at all. It was simply the invention of Reinald of Dassel. Geary 1994, p. 247.
16 Hofmann 1975, p. 220.
17 Torsy 1964, pp. 26–34.
18 Hofmann 1975, pp. 202ff; Engels 1982, pp. 33–36.
19 Hofmann 1975, p. 304.
20 Op. cit., p. 305, n. 16.
21 A summary interpretation is given by Torsy 1964, pp. 28–30. The major work on this is Bänsch 1984.

22 Hofmann 1975, p. 134, n. 141, 144; Stehkämper 1982, p. 44.

23 Hofmann 1975, pp. 201ff.

24 In the following I rely on Von den Brincken 1985.

25 Richard 1999, p. 288.

26 Von den Brincken 1985, pp. 86, 90, 92.

27 The interest in Africa and the story of Prester John was already noticeable in the chronicle of Richard of Cluny of 1172. He used Otto of Freising, who in 1145 had written about 'Prester John', 'a certain John, a king and priest' living in the remote East along with all his people, a Christian, albeit a Nestorian. Kaplan 1985, p. 45.

28 Kaplan 1985, p. 43. A book on his legend was published in Copenhagen in 1508. At that time he was a contemporary and his realm the mightiest on earth. *Historien om Jon Præst.*

29 Von den Brincken 1985, p. 97.

30 Kaplan 1985, p. 59.

31 Von den Brincken 1985, p. 97.

32 *Orientbericht*, p. 2.

33 Ibid., p. 4.

34 For the various editions see *Orientbericht*, p. 7; Budde (ed.) 1982 no. 151–152, 180–183. Three fingers were kept in Hildesheim, one from each king. The relics were donated by Reinald of Dassel right after the translation in 1164.

35 Christern 1964, p. 180.

36 John of Hildesheim, *The Three Kings of Cologne*: introduction, pp. v–xii.

37 John of Hildesheim, *The Three Kings of Cologne*, ch. 9–12 in the Latin version. The English versions added that they also differed in size. Melchior was the smallest, Balthasar average and Caspar the tallest. Ch. 21 in the English version.

38 Kaplan 1985, p. 26.

39 'primus fuisse dicitur Melchior, senex et canus, barba prolixa et capillus … aurum obtulit regi Domino. Secundus nomine Caspar, juvenis imberbis, rubicundus … thure quasi Deo oblatione digna, Deum honorabat. Tertius fuscus, integre barbatus, Balthasar nomine … per myrrham Filium hominis moriturum professus est', in Venerabilis Bedæ, *Collectanea et flores*, PL 94, col. 541C–D. It is worth noting that the word used is *fuscus* and not *niger*.

40 *Orientbericht*, pp. 9, 10, 12. St Thomas had also sent their dead bodies to Empress Helena. Ibid., p. 14. The kings' baptismal plays a major role in John of Hildesheim, *The Three Kings of Cologne*, ch. 30–33.

41 *Orientberich*, p. 10. A calendar printed in Cologne reads, 'Having undergone many trials and fatigues for the Gospel, the three wise men met at Sewa in A.D. 54 to celebrate the feast of Christmas. Thereupon, after the celebration of Mass, they died: St. Melchior on Jan. 1, aged 116, St. Balthasar on Jan. 6, aged 112 and St. Caspar on Jan. 11, aged 109.' The exact age was taken from John of Hildesheim, *The Three Kings of Cologne*, ch. 32, but the mention of Sowa by the *Orientbericht* shows that the legendary material was already present years before.

42 John of Hildesheim, *The Three Kings of Cologne*, ch. X.

43 'Vort dat lant van tharsi, da Jaspar konink was, da is ouch here over prieser Johann, ind die lude sint as swartze as Moir.' *Orientbericht*, p. 13. For a discussion of Tharsis as the third India, see Kaplan 1985, pp. 63–65.

44 Hofmann 1975, p. 156.

45 Kaplan has studied medieval drama manuscripts from Munich, Orléans, Limoges and Vienna, and found no black king mentioned. Kaplan 1985, pp. 34–37.

46 Ibid., pp. 52–58, especially p. 56.

47 *Legenda Aurea*, pp. 102–111.

48 Kehrer 1908–1909, p. 223.

49 Kaplan 1985, p. 85. Plenty of paintings formerly regarded as among the oldest with a black king, have been rejected as examples of later insertions with black.

50 Kehrer 1908–1909, pp. 223–225.

51 Kaplan 1985, pp. 75–78, 86.

52 Ibid., Fig. 37.
53 Von den Brincken 1978, p. 254.
54 Kaplan 1985, pp. 103ff.
55 This probably refers to the story, known from later church plays on the Magi, that the black king, because of prudence and ignorance, did not wish to kneel himself and asked his servant to do so instead.
56 Kaplan 1985, p. 100.
57 *Jesu barndoms bog* 1508, pp. 51f.
58 On the other hand Magi plays also might have been an integrated part of the religious landscape here. In songs known from the time after the Reformation it is obvious that one of the kings was a black man. Celander 1950, p. 67.

BIBLIOGRAPHY

Sources

Christiern Pedersens Jærtegns-Postil, I–II. C. J. Brandt & T. Fenger (ed.), Copenhagen 1850.
Historien om Jon Præst. A. Fjelstrup (ed.), København 1910.
Jesu Barndoms Bog, in *Danske Folkebøger fra 16. og 17. Aarhundrede I.* J. P. Jacobsen et al. (ed.), vol. 1–14, København 1915–1936. Vol. 1, pp. 27–105.
Legenda Aurea des Jacobus de Voragine. 9. Auflage. Heidelberg 1979.
'(Orientbericht) Ein niederrheinischer Bericht über den Orient', in R. Röhricht & H. Meisner (ed.), *Zeitschrift für Deutsche Philologie* 19 (1887), pp. 1–86.
John of Hildesheim, *The Three Kings of Cologne. An Early English Translation of the "Historia Trium Regum" by John of Hildesheim, ed. from the Mss., together with the Latin Text.* C. Horstmann (ed. & trans.), London 1886; reprinted New York 1975.
'Venerabilis Bedæ: Excerptiones Patrum, Collectanea, Flores ex diversis Quæstiones et Parabolæ (*Collectanea et flores*)', in PL 94. Venerabilis Bedæ, Anglo-saxonis presbyteri, Opera Omnia. Paris 1841–1864.

Literature

A.-D. von den Brincken 1978, 'Privilegien Karls IV. Für die Stadt Köln', in *Blätter für deutsche Landesgeschichte (BDLG)* 114, pp. 243–264.
A.-D. von den Brincken 1985, 'Islam und Oriens Christianus in der Schriften des Kölner Domscholasters Oliver († 1227)', in *Miscellanea Mediaevalia* 17: *Orientalische Kultur und Europäisches Mittelalter.* Berlin, pp. 86–111.
P. Brown 1982, *Society and the holy in late Antiquity.* Berkeley.
R. Budde (ed.) 1982, *Die heilige Drei Könige – Darstellung und Verehrung, Ausstellungskatalog des Wallraf-Richartz-Museum.* Köln.
B. Bänsch 1984, *Kölner Goldschmiedekunst um 1200 – Muster und Modelle.* Münster.
H. Celander 1950, *Stjärngosserna.* Stockholm.
E. Christern 1964, 'Dje Hystori oder Legend von den Heilligen Dryen Koeningen', *Kölner Domblatt* 23–24, pp. 180–204.
E. Dassmann 1982, 'Ephiphanie und die Heiligen Drei Könige', in Budde (ed.), pp. 16–20.
J. G. Deckers 1982, 'Die Huldigung der Magier in der Kunst der Spätantike', in Budde (ed.), pp. 20–32.
O. Engels 1982, 'Die Reliquien der Heiligen Drei Könige in der Reichpolitik der Staufer', in Budde (ed.), pp. 33–36.
K. Erslev 1901, *Den senere Middelalder.* København (= *Danmarks Riges Historie II.*)

P. J. Geary 1994, 'The Magi and Milan', in P. J. Geary (ed.), *Living with the Dead in the Middle Ages*. New York, pp. 243–256.

H. Hofmann 1975, *Die Heiligen drei Könige. Zur Heiligenverehrung im kirchlichen, gesellschaftlichen und politischen Leben des Mittelalters*. Bonn.

P. H. D. Kaplan 1985, *The Rise of the Black Magus in Western Art*. Ann Arbor.

H. Kehrer 1908–1909, Hugo: *Die Heiligen drei Könige in Literatur und Kunst I–II*. Leipzig.

KLNM 'Hellig tre konger', in *Kulturhistorisk Leksikon for nordisk Middelalder* V, pp. 390–394.

LM 'Drei Könige', in *Lexikon des Mittelalters*, pp. 1383–1389.

H. E. Mayer 1965, *Geschichte der Kreuzzüge*. Stuttgart.

J. Richard 1999, *The Crusades c. 1071–c. 1291*. Cambridge.

H. Stehkämper 1982, 'Könige und heilige Drei Könige', in Budde (ed.), pp. 37–50.

J. Torsy 1964, 'Achthundert Jahre Dreikönigenverehrung in Köln', *Kölner Domblatt* 23–24, pp. 15–162.

A. Vauchez 1988, *La Sainteté en Occident aux derniers siècles du Moyen Age*, 2nd edition. Rome.

A. Wienand (ed.) 1974, *Die Heiligen Drei Könige: Heilsgeschichtlich: Kunsthistorisch: Das religiöse Brauchtum*. Köln.

Part II

Royal Policies and Violence

HENRIK JANSON

Making Enemies

Aspects on the Formation of Conflicting Identities in the Southern Baltics around the Year 1000

When Leopold von Ranke characterised the achievements of the Wendic crusade in his *Weltgeschichte*, he said that it led to the fulfilment of work already initiated by the Saxon emperors in the tenth century. What Henry I had begun by attacking the Slavs across the Elbe in the 920s, and what Otto the Great had continued by establishing the Archbishopric of Magdeburg in 968 was completed by the Germans of the twelfth century.[1]

Thus, in Ranke's, view the Wendish crusade formed part of an ancient struggle. Long before the twelfth century, the Germans had received the historical mission to wipe out paganism and incorporate the barbarian 'Slavic' lands between the Elbe and the Oder into the civilised world. Pagan Slavs, driven by a powerful instinct of backwardness, confronted the civilised Christian race of Germans. Bravely carrying the torch of world history, the institutions of the Roman Church and Empire, the Germans confronted and conquered tribal society and inflicted the instruments of civilisation upon the western Slavs.

Today it is easy to see that this view answered the needs of the nationalistic and colonialist nineteenth century all too well. However, the idea of a conflict between Christian Germans and pagan Slavs has been very persistent over the years. The concepts of 'Christian' and 'pagan' and even 'Germanic' and 'Slavic' are still fundamental components in works on the relations on the Elbe in the early and high Middle Ages.

An important reason is of course that this is the perspective of the source material itself. Something of the *Heiliges römisches Reich deutscher Nation* into which Ranke was born is already present in two of the most important chronicles in this connection, those of Adam of Bremen, from the 1070s, and Helmold of Bosau from the 1170s. But who were in fact the enemies of these tendentious chroniclers and their lords? What was the nature of their own Christianity and how are we to understand the paganism of their enemies? To what extent is our picture of the early medieval societies across the Elbe still biased by the perspective that legitimised the aggression of the Saxon nobility in the twelfth century?

Adam and the imperium christianum

In 1935, the brilliant German scholar Carl Erdmann pointed out that the question of religion was of little importance in the political relations on the Elbe before the twelfth century.[2] In the eleventh century emperors and princes were still allying themselves with groups that German chronicles defined as pagans, even against internal enemies within the Empire. It made no difference in these conflicts whether the enemies were called Christians or pagans. They got the same treatment in any case. The political relations on the Elbe before the twelfth century were not determined by religion but, as Erdmann put it, by *'Zugehörigkeit zum Reich.'*[3]

With this in mind it is interesting to consider a statement made of Otto the Great. On establishing the Archbishopric of Magdeburg in 968, Otto proclaimed that 'We believe that the status and welfare of our empire lie in extending the divine cult.'[4] Seen in the light of the crusading era this expression may easily be interpreted to mean that Otto had already begun the work of the crusaders. However, what did the new emperor really mean by 'extending the divine cult'?

A fundamental problem here is which cult Otto considered divine and which not. We may leave aside the liturgical changes that took place in Otto's era. It is enough to state here that it is highly unlikely that a cult that had not accepted Otto's empire would have been considered divine whatever its nature, and it would be quite impossible if in times of conflict the cult had intentions directly hostile to the emperor. We can be fairly certain that the 'divine cult' for Otto was one that impressed the subjugation under his own power. By 'extending the divine cult' he understood the extension of his own sphere of influence.

An interesting example in this connection is found in Otto's relation to the Redarians, the most powerful group across the Elbe that had been subjected to the Saxons about 930. According to Adam of Bremen they had, together with 'the other peoples of the Slavs,' promised the king tribute and God *christianitas* after Henry I's triumphs around 930.[5] Later he declares that they hereafter worshipped *christianitas* for more than seventy years, and this should be understood as a relatively exact number because he also uses the designation *omni tempore Ottonum.* Accordingly, in Adam's view the Redarians were subjected to *christianitas* between c. 930 and 1002. Thereafter they broke away as he says 'from the body of Christ and the church to which they previously had been linked.'[6]

There are two problems with this. First, other contemporary sources say nothing about paganism and conversion in connection with the subjugation of the Redarians about 930. According to Widukind of Corvey, writing a century before Adam, Henry I had forced the neighbouring peoples in the east to pay tribute, but the Redarians soon revolted. The question of religion is not even mentioned. In Widukind's version the episode consists of three steps: a) the Slavs were made tributary, b) a peace agreement was established and c) the Redarians *defecerunt a fide.*[7] This makes it quite evident that the *fides* in question has little to do with Christan 'belief' in a narrow sense, but concerns the 'fidelity' to the Saxon nobility which was acknowledged by the paying of tribute.[8]

The Redarian conflict continued during the following decades and, once subjugated, the Redarians soon rebelled again. In the 950s they declared themselves prepared to pay tribute as long as they were allowed to retain their freedom and the power over their region [*domnatio regionis*].[9] The Saxons seem to have been pleased with this, but Otto had other plans. In 968, as he was about to finish making Magdeburg an archbishopric over this area, he strictly forbade the Saxon princes to make peace with the Redarians. Pointing to the fact that they had often broken their fidelity, he now ordered that the matter had to be resolved by the total destruction of Redarian society. He was even ready to finish this affair himself if necessary.[10] An interesting fact, already pointed out by Erdmann, is that Otto does not say a word about paganism or conversion in this connection.[11]

We do not know what happened to the Redarians afterwards, but later in 968 the archbishopric of Magdeburg was established. The Redarians as well as the other inhabitants across the Elbe could now rejoice in the fruits of Otto's ambition to amplify the glory of his empire by 'extending the divine cult.' The centre of this divine imperial cult was Magdeburg, where the reforming spirit of the tenth century acquired a new base. In this refulgent ecclesiastical metropolis two young relatives were brought up, sons of the same illustrious Saxon nobility from which the Ottonian emperors themselves descended. The names of these youngsters were Bruno and Thietmar, later known as Bruno of Querfurt and Thietmar of Merseburg. These two were to write the most frequently consulted sources for the conditions among the 'Slavs' at the turn of the first millennium.[12]

Thietmar, writing in the second decade of the eleventh century, explains that at some point the *gentes* across the Elbe had bound themselves to pay tribute and serve the kings and emperors by accepting *christianitas*.[13] Thus Thietmar understood that *christianitas* was intimately related to subjugation under *das Reich*, and gave these groups a certain political status. To accept *christianitas* was to accept Saxon superiority for the inhabitants in the land across the Elbe. It is with this line of argument that Adam can state that the Redarians had been converted to Christianity around 930, because both Widukind and Thietmar reported that Henry I made them tributaries. However Widukind does not mention anything about Christianisation and, in fact, when Thietmar mentions Henry's subjugation of the 'these districts', he too only mentions political subjugation.[14]

We must consequently ask when the Redarians first accepted the Christianity that they relapsed from in the late tenth century, and we have a very good source to answer this question. According to Alcuin, it was Charlemagne who made the inhabitants of this area accept the *fides Christi* in 789.[15] The first major chronicle writer to explicitly make the triumph of Henry I around 930 the grand entry of the western Slavs into Christendom is Adam of Bremen.[16]

What we see here is an aspect of the development of *christianitas* as an *imperium christianum* led by the East-Frankish ruler. Saracens, Hungarians, and Northmen had gradually filled influential parts of Western Europe with the feeling of belonging together. This feeling was strengthened by the religious revival initiated by the monastic reform movement. During the tenth century, Western society evolved an increasing feeling of being one single community.

The concept *imperium christianum* had been transmitted from the Carolingian era as a name for the society that had taken over from the Roman Empire of Antiquity. At the end of the tenth century it could still designate the whole of Christianity as a spiritual community without any common political head. However, Otto the Great's victory over the Hungarians in 955 earned him the status of prime protector against the pagans in the West. His subsequent coronation as emperor in Rome 962 made him widely known as the hegemonic head of the *imperium christianum*.[17]

A few years later, two of his neighbours, Miesco of Poland and Harold of Denmark, were subjected to him. In both cases the written sources later identified this subjugation with conversion to Christianity. Indeed, on the famous runestone in Jelling Harold himself declared that he was the one who had made the Danes Christian.

However clear this statement may seem, we know from other sources that the conversion of the Danes was a matter of definition. When Harold's contemporary, Widukind of Corvey, wrote about the conversion of Harold a few years later, he felt forced to admit that the Danes 'had been *Christiani* since ancient times, but none the less,' he explains, 'they served idols in a gentile way.'[18] Thietmar supports Widukind by explaining that the conversion of Harold and the Danes was a matter of reviving the *christianitas* of their ancestors, from which they had diverged.[19] It is characteristic of Adam to have a much more clear-cut version. 'Harold was subjected to Otto,' he writes, 'and received the kingdom from him, promising to establish *christianitas* in Denmark.'[20]

In the passage cited above, Adam declared that 'the Slavs' broke away 'from the body of Christ and the Church' after more than seventy years. What Otto and Harold had done was to incorporate Denmark into 'the body of Christ and the Church.' Interestingly enough, Harold himself had the same idea, and we seem in fact through the Jelling stone to come close to the conception of Otto the great himself.

What can we learn from this? Probably that Adam's conception of Christianisation was somewhat different from ours. It was closely connected to the idea of *christianitas* as the *imperium christianum* of the East-Frankish king and emperor. This was the *christianitas* into which the Redarians as well as Harold Gormsson were incorporated in the tenth century.

Adam and the imperium romanum

There is however another problem with Adam's statement that *christianitas* was worshipped continuously by the 'Slavs' during *omni tempore Ottonum*, that is, until 1002. There were, as we have seen, continuous struggles in the decades after 930. Finally, a famous revolt broke out in 983, followed by almost two decades of warfare along the Elbe, which forcibly swept away *christianitas* and Saxon influence in this area.[21] Adam ought to have known at least about the revolt of 983. Why then did he corrupt this chronology in such a fundamental way? The answer to this question is related to another concept that underwent important changes in the Ottonian-Salian era, the *imperium romanum*.

When Otto the Great became emperor in 962, it was rather unclear what he was emperor over. From an ideological point of view, however, it soon became clear that he was the hegemonic head of the *imperium christianum*. From a legal perspective however, the question was much more complicated. Here the military and political strength of the Franks encountered the ancient right of the Romans to designate the emperor. But Otto did not consider his empire to be Roman. In the middle of the tenth century *romani* was still a despised name north of the Alps.[22]

However, through the influence of the literature transmitted by the Carolingian Renaissance, the ancient world of the Romans had become more and more familiar to the intelligentsia of Western Europe. Otto the Great himself was compared to the ancient emperors by the Saxon nun and poet Hrotsvitha of Gandersheim. She was also the first and only to call Otto emperor over 'the Roman world' (*orbis Romanus*).[23]

The *imperium christianum* was now beginning to intermingle with the concept of *imperium romanum*, but it was not yet clear what kind of relation there was between them. It had long been thought that the old Roman Empire had ended with the Gothic invasions, but around 950 an extremely influential work was written in the West-Frankish kingdom. The author was a monk named Adso, later abbot of Montier-en-Der, and the theme of his text was nothing less than Antichrist. The work was dedicated to the West-Frankish Queen Gerberga, and it soon became widely read. Adso here articulated a new theory of the Roman Empire: the empire still existed, maintained by the kings of the Franks, but more important than this idea was the eschatological role ascribed to the empire. The author had deduced from the Bible that Antichrist would not come into the world before the Roman Empire had come to an end, but before that, one of the Frankish kings would hold the whole Empire in one hand. This would be the end and fulfilment of the *imperium romanorum et christianorum*. When all the kingdoms that had previously been subjected to the Empire had decayed, the time of Antichrist would come.[24]

When Adso's work was delivered to Queen Gerberga, her brother, Otto the Great, was not yet emperor. However, on his accession in 962 it appeared to his contemporaries that a new age was dawning. To all those who had read or heard Adso's work, Otto's career must have fitted the predictions much too well to be coincidental. Otto's reestablishment of the Empire was widely understood as an important step towards the fulfilment of history and the end of the world. The reform movement supported this idea, probably because the threat of the coming of Antichrist made the reform work much easier. In any case, the Ottonian Empire became the head of the world to the reform movement, and the Ottonian emperors became the principal defenders of *christianitas*. However, this

145

christianitas was not just the *imperium christianum*. It was now also the ancient *imperium romanum* continuously moving toward the end of the world.[25]

Carl Erdmann outlined this development in one of the last works he was able to finish[26] before he was dragged away by the Third *Reich* and tragically ended his life in the last minutes of the war on 7th May 1945. He also drew attention to another important problem that arose in this connection. If the Roman Empire was coming alive again at the end of the tenth century, what was the condition of Rome itself?

Rome was also experiencing a revival in these years. First however, this revival did not involve the contemporary town by this name. Rome was an abstraction from the classical sources. From here it was projected onto the government of the Empire, and especially the emperor himself. Rome was where the emperor was and, since the emperor was a Saxon, it seemed clear to the Saxons that they were now the most important inhabitants of Rome.[27]

This Rome was indeed a marvellous place. It was called 'golden Rome,' 'the head of the world' and Otto III stated that this capital of the world was 'pulling the reins of the earth'. As he begun his famous *renovatio imperii Romanorum*, he also set his sights on contemporary Rome. It is significant that when he picked the learned Gerbert of Aurillac, Archbishop of Rheims, to be his future pope in 997 Gerbert enthusiastically replied that 'ours, ours is the Roman Empire.' Together they began to drive the piles of the lofty heights of Rome down into the soil and ruins of the contemporary town. Rome, not Magdeburg, was to become the capital of the Christian Empire of the Ottonians. The Saxons never forgave them.[28]

At the same time Hungary and Poland were elevated to kingdoms in the service of the Empire. In the case of Poland this was later seen by the Germans as a terrible mistake, complicating politics in the east for centuries. In the case of Hungary the question was easier. The coronation of Stephen of Hungary was later identified with the conversion of the Hungarians, just as the subjugation of Harold had been with the conversion of the Danes. Yet Stephen was already Christian, as his father had also been. Even the Hungarian commander who was hanged after Otto the Great's famous victory in 955 is known in Byzantine sources to have been a Christian with the rank of *patricius* in the Byzantine Empire. The only sense in which the Hungarians were Christianised about the year 1000 is in their institutionalised subjugation to *das Reich*.[29]

However, let us return to Rome. Otto III's *renovatio* was hindered abruptly in 1001 by a rebellion of the Romans. The young emperor died in 1002 while preparing to crush them. His great project collapsed. An important people, the Romans, had relapsed from *imperium romanum christianorumque*. Was the new millennium the beginning of the end? Would Antichrist now come? The questions remained open, and the answers varied.[30]

Conrad II, the first emperor of the Salian family, tried to re-establish the Roman Empire of Otto III. After his elevation to emperor in Rome in 1027 – in the presence of Canute the Great, amongst others – Conrad began to use the same phrases about Rome as Otto had used. On his seal the core of his ideology could now be read as 'Golden Rome' and 'Rome, capital of the world, steers the reins of the orb.' However, the Rome of Conrad was not so much identified with the contemporary town, but rather his own court, the head of the sacred Roman Empire, and in a narrower understanding probably himself. Only now was the East-Frankish kingdom in a legal sense becoming a Roman Empire. Conrad is the first ruler of the Frankish realm to use the phrase *imperium Romanum* in his documents.[31]

However, the *Heiliges Römisches Reich Deutscher Nation* did not yet exist. One important link was still missing. The empire was already in some respects sacred; it was Roman and it was a *Reich*, but there was no clear political concept of a German nation.[32] But this was on its way. About 1075 we meet a sacred Roman Empire of German nation for the first time. Interestingly enough, Adam of Bremen is first to articulate this idea.[33] To Adam as to Conrad II, Rome was the beautiful, lofty heights of the German court.[34] He states that in his days the peak of the Roman Empire and the reverence for the divine cult was growing and flowering within the *populus Teutonum*, i.e., not in the hand of the modern Romans in the cities of Rome or Constantinople.[35]

We are now approaching an answer to the question why of Adam distorted the chronology of the conversion of the inhabitants across the Elbe. In fact his chronological rearrangement proves that he paid attention both to the position of the modern Romans and to the millenarian problem. Having given his entirely corrupt picture of the tenth century as a peaceful time across the Elbe, he begins his description of the Slavic revolt of 983 by saying: 'Meanwhile the millennial year after the Lord's incarnation was successfully filled.'[36] He continues by explaining that this happy ending was the beginning of a period of disruptions, his example being the Slavic revolt.

Adam thus presents the revolt of 983 in the light of the millenarian crisis at the end of the happy days of *tempus Ottonum*. In his eyes this was all a part of the process that had made the German court the centre of the world. The chronological rearrangement concerning the Slavic conversion and revolt play an important role in this perspective. With the erroneous figure of seventy years of *christianitas*, and the just as incorrect *omni tempore Ottonum* still ringing in the ears, Adam cries:

> O, indeed, concealed are God's judgements over mankind; he is 'merciful to whomever he wants, and whomever he wants he makes hard.' Admiring his omnipotence we see them fall back into paganism, who were first to believe, but those who seemed to be the last are converted to Christ.[37]

The editor Bernhard Schmeidler felt called upon to put in two footnotes here, explaining that Adam meant that Norwegians and Swedes had been converted around the year 1000, while the Slavs had relapsed. But Adam had pressed his material so far to make a rhetorical point with a much broader historical significance.

What he said about the Slavs was not quite true. It was true, however, that those who were first to believe, the Romans, had relapsed from the Roman empire of Otto III around the year 1000, and instead new believers had been incorporated into 'the body of Christ and the Church.' Adam's point was that the Roman Empire was no longer in the hands of the Romans of contemporary Rome. The 'peak of the Roman Empire' as well as the 'reverence for the divine cult' was now in the hands of the Germans. The Germans had the legitimate power in the 'Golden Rome.'[38]

This might also have been understood as an important step towards the eschatological end of the world. One of the peoples, the Romans, that had previously been under the empire, had relapsed. Later they were reincorporated, but under the guidance of Hildebrand/Gregory VII they were about to relapse again in Adam's time. In the German court it was believed that this 'dangerous man', who was trying to take control over the 'golden Rome' and the sacred Roman Empire of the Germans through the Church, might indeed be Antichrist himself.[39]

Adam and the Enemies of Christianity

I will now briefly turn to the enemies of Adam's Christianity. They can be divided into two categories: individuals and groups. Let me begin by mentioning some of the chief individual enemies in Adam's text. I set the limits at the eleventh century, because Adam is not a very good witness for earlier times. In the eleventh century the most important enemies are Sven Forkbeard, Harald the Hardruler, Emund of Sweden and his Bishop Osmund, Duke Magnus Billung of Saxony and his ancestors.[40] Thus the most important individual enemies are Christian princes. However strong paganism may seem in Adam's text, individual pagans do not seem to threaten his Christianity.

This is also true for Thietmar of Merseburg. Only in one case does an individual appear in Thietmar's description of the rebellion of 983. This individual is a certain Mistvi who ravaged Hamburg. He is called *duke of the Obodrits*, and we know from a runestone that he was the father-in-law of Harold Bluetooth. It is quite astonishing to read that a chaplain called Avico followed this man when he devastated Hamburg, information which comes to us only by chance. Thietmar refers to Avico as the witness of a miracle, and declares that Avico later became his own spiritual brother.[41] Had it not been for this, we would probably not have heard anything about Mistvi as an individual, and most certainly not that he was a Christian. Thietmar does not even say this explicitly, even in the present text. In that case we most certainly would have read that Hamburg had been ravaged by pagans, which is the impression that Adam gives of Mistvi. The Slavs under Mistvi had becom *relapsi in paganitatem*,[42] and he says that Mistvi did not leave any trace of *christianitas* across the Elbe.[43]

No, to find the threatening pagans we must leave the individual level and go to our second category, the groups. The two major pagan groups in Adam's text are the Slavs and the Swedes. According to Adam, both

Swedes and Slavs had recently been Christians – the Swedes, in fact, for most of the eleventh century, and the Slavs again, for some decades in the middle of the century. The new apostasy of the Slavs coincided with the princely revolt that drove Archbishop Adalbert of Bremen away from the royal court in 1066.[44]

In Adam's text both Redarians and Swedes constitute a religious community, and both have a central temple and a common cult. The Swedes have Uppsala, and the Redarians have a temple that Adam calls Rethra.[45] While in neither case is there archaeological support, in both cases there is conflicting material that strongly indicates Christianity in these regions. In the years after Adalbert's fall from power in 1066, we hear of major triumphs for *christianitas* in the land of the Slavs. Adalbert's enemies at the royal court were now converting pagans and destroying shrines. One of them, Bishop Burchard of Halberstadt, had even taken control of Rethra. Adam does not say a word about these successes for *christianitas*, and in fact this picture is exactly the reverse of his. The sources are plainly incompatible.[46] In the case of Uppsala we have, among other things, an abundance of Christian runestones strongly indicating that a Christian elite dominated this area. This also seems incompatible with Adam's description of the horrible cult at Uppsala.[47]

Put together, the contradictions in the sources are indeed very problematic for Adam's credibility. Might it be that his concept of paganism corresponds to the very narrow definition of *christianitas* that had dominated the German Empire since the days of Otto the Great? Might it be that his descriptions of the pagan cult are not to be taken literally?

This is the solution I chose in my doctoral thesis about Adam.[48] Both Rethra and Uppsala lie in areas over which Hamburg-Bremen was fighting for ecclesiastical supremacy. At the same time the ruler of the sacred empire, Henry IV, was fighting for political supremacy over these regions. The Redarians had a competing ecclesiastical centre in Magdeburg, and Henry IV had a political competitor in the duke of Saxony. For more than a century there was a symbolic struggle between emperor and duke about the right to sleep in the imperial bed in Magdeburg. In Adam's Rethra we find the pagan god sleeping in a bed of purple, the imperial colour.[49]

In Sweden there was a competing ecclesiastical centre in Rome, and Henry IV had a political competitor in Gregory VII. Adam's Uppsala is a temple of gold recalling the 'Golden Rome' of the Ottonian and Salian Empire. Almost every detail in the description corresponds to the criticism of Gregory VII in the Imperial Church.[50]

Epilogue

What I would like to stress is that we should be a bit reluctant to talk about pagans and Christians in Northern Europe during the Early and High Middle Ages. The sources may not say what we read. Since the nineteenth century scholars have been eager to find old Germanic and old Slavic gods and the spirit of the original religion. This has all been a part of the creation of modern Europe along nationalistic lines.

Just take the famous god Svantevit on Rügen as an example. Scholars have enthusiastically fitted him into the old Slavic pantheon, but what do the sources say? Both Helmold of Bosau and Saxo Grammaticus mention Svantevit. They agree that the cult of Svantevit in the beginning had been a cult of Sanctus Vitus, the patron of Corvey. The problem was that the people of Rügen had cut the ties with the Empire, driven away the Frankish priests, and kept the tax revenues on the island. This story, told by the only sources we have, is supported by the fact that Corvey was making claims on Rügen.[51]

Svantevit, accordingly, is only pagan in a very narrow sense. If I am right about Adam's Rethra, only one major description of pagan religion among the western Slavs remains. This was written by Thiemar of Merseburg in his despair over the fact that Henry II, after two decades of constant war, had allied with the Redarians against Boleslav of Poland.[52]

I have already discussed Thietmar's conception of Christianity and paganism. This is not the place to go into further detail about this problem.[53] It may be enough to point out that Thietmar himself declares that his description should be read in the light of the writings of Athanasius. As far as I know, this has not yet been done, at least not in modern times. Only one scholar, in an article from the early seventies, has examined the description, not by asking what the details meant to the Slavs in their religion, but what they meant to Thietmar. He immediately found hecatombs of Christian symbols.[54] Let us hope that someone soon takes up this problem again. I am convinced that Thietmar will also prove to be a poor source for pagan religion.

Finally, was Ranke right or wrong? Was there a continuous struggle for Christianity between the Germans and the Slavs across the Elbe from the time of the first Ottonians to the Wendic crusade? I would answer no. Paganism in our sense had nothing to do with this question. There was nonetheless continuity in the struggles. They were always about whether or not the Saxon nobility would get its taxes. Bernard of Clairvaux only supplied it with an ideological apparatus that opened up new, fantastic possibilities.[55]

NOTES

1   von Ranke 1887, p. 374.
2   Erdmann, 1935, pp. 91–98.
3   Op. cit., p. 93.
4   *Die Urkunden*, nr 366: 'augmentum divini cultus salutem et statum esse regni vel imperii nostri credimus.'
5   Adam of Bremen, I 56.
6   Adam of Bremen, II 44: 'Omnes igitur Sclavi, qui inter Albiam et Oddaram habitant, per annos LXX et amplius christianitatem coluerunt, omni tempore Ottonum, talique modo se absciderunt a corpore Christi et ecclesiae, qui antea coniuncti fuerant.'
7   Widukind of Corvey, I 36.

8 Only in connection with events in the 960s does Widukind begin to talk about *pagani*; see Widukind of Corvey, III 68, 69. On the *fideles regis* as identical with *fideles Dei* in Carolingian times, see Beumann 1962, p. 547.

9 Widukind of Corvey, III 53.

10 Widukind of Corvey, III 70; *Die Urkunden*, nr 355.

11 Erdmann 1935, p. 92.

12 Cf. Kahl 1955; Kahl 1978, pp. 52 ff.; Wenskus 1956, pp. 143–153.

13 Thietmar of Merseburg, III 17: 'Gentes, quae suscepta christianitate regibus et inperatoribus tributarie serviebant.'

14 Widukind of Corvey, I 36; Thietmar of Merseburg, I 10.

15 In 789 Charlemagne had crossed the Elbe and made these lands tributaries. According to a letter written by Alcuin to Bishop Willehad of Bremen in 789, Charlemagne had brought the *Wilti vel Vionudi* – which must have included the later Redarians – to accept *fides Christi*; see *Epistolae*, nr 6. It is important to point out, however, that religion does not seem to play any part in other reports, either from this or the subsequent interaction between the Carolingians and this region in these years; cf. Brüske 1983, pp. 15 f. Alcuin's letter of 789 is in this respect an interesting, telling, and important exception, reflecting an influential perspective in the Carolingian court.

16 In the annals, however, a similar interpretation of Henry's victory over the Danes and the Obodrits in 931 might be traced back to an almost contemporary notice in the 'Reichenauer Annalen', *Annales Augienses*, ad a. 931: 'Henricus rex reges Abodritorum et Nordmannorum effecit christianos, et profectus est in Galliam.' This Christianisation might not however have been quite such a decisive historical turning-point as these words lead us to think. According to Adam of Bremen, I 59, the effect was that Archbishop Unni could appoint priests in 'every single church in the kingdom of the Danes' (*Ordinatis itaque in regno Danorum per singulas ecclesias sacerdotibus sanctus Dei multitudinem credentium commendasse fertur Haroldo.*) This means that at least according to Adam, there already was an abundance of churches among the Danes before this conversion and these churches seem in fact to have been there half a century earlier, since the biographer of Unnis's predecessor, Archbishop Rimbert of Bremen, states at the end of the ninth century that Rimbert had constantly sent out priests to preach in the churches in the North, on the other side of the sea; *Vita Rimberti*, ch. 16, 'semper autem constitutos habens presbiteros … ad ecclesias inter ipsos paganos constitutas longe ab ecclesia sedis suae, quodque gravissimum erat, marinis discriminibus adeundas.' It is also important to point out that writing in 966–967 St Adalbert, who became archbishop of Magdeburg in 968 and was close to Archbishop Adaldag of Bremen, without hesitation takes up the notice from the *Reichenauer Annalen*, stating that in 931 'Heiricus rex regem Abotridorum et regem Danorum effecit christianos'; Regino of Prüm, ad a. 931. However, his contemporary, the more secular Bishop Liutprand of Cremona, did not look upon this event as a major shift in religion but as political subjugation, *Antapododosis* III 21, 'Hic [i.e. Heinricus rex] etiam Sclavorum gentem innumeram subiugavit sibique tributariam fecit; primus etiam hic Danos subiugavit sibique servire coegit; ac per hoc nomen suum multis nationibus celebre fecit'; and further, *Antapodosis* III 48, '…cuius [i.e. Heinricus rex] ex hoc apud Italos nomen maxime tunc clarebat, quod Danos, nulli ante subiectos, solus ipse debellaret ac tributarios faceret.'

17 Erdmann 1943, pp. 426–433; Cf. Beumann 1962.

18 Widukind of Corvey, III 65, 'Dani antiquitus erant Christiani, sed nichilominus idolis ritu gentili servientes.' From what Widukind says hereafter it is suggested that there was a problem with the perception of the Trinity and the lack of *fides catholica*. It is important however that despite this problem the Danes could be called *Christiani* before the conversion of Harold. And indeed, they had been *Christiani* 'since ancient times'.

19 Thietmar of Merseburg, II 14. Thietmar uses interesting formulations in this connection: 'Apud Danos regnante tunc Haroldo contempta christianitas sic per Popponem renovata est presbyterium. Contempta christianitas becomes renovata!' According to

Thietmar, Poppo had blamed the king and the people because when 'antecessorum cultura suorum deviantem' the gates were opened up for 'diis et demonibus', assuring them that there was 'unum … in tribus personis Deum.' This account also suggests that the real problem was the understanding of the Trinity.

20 Adam of Bremen, II 3, '…Haroldus Ottoni subicitur, et ab eo regnum suscipiens christianitatem in Dania recipere spopondit.'

21 See Brüske 1983, pp. 39–54.

22 Cf. Liutprand of Cremona's reflection on the *romani* in his *Relationes* from c. 970, ch. 12: '…Quos nos – Langobardi scilicet, Saxones, Franci, Lotharingi, Bagoarii, Suevi, Burgundiones – tanto dedignamur ut inimicos nostros commoti nil aliud contumeliarum nisi "Romane!" dicamus, hoc solo, id est Romanorum nomine, quicquid ignobilitatis, quicquid timiditatis, quicquid avaritiae, quicquid luxuria, quicquid mendacii, immo quicquid vitiorum est, comprehendentes.'

23 Erdmann 1943, pp. 421 ff.

24 Adso, p. 110. See Erdmann 1943, pp. 426–433; Rauh 1973, pp. 153–164; McGinn 1994, pp. 100 ff.

25 Erdmann 1943, pp. 427 ff., 433 ff. In certain leading circles in the West there seems to have been some anxiety before the middle of tenth century over the apocalyptic ending of the first millennium; see Brandes 2000, pp. 456 ff.

26 Erdmann 1943.

27 Generally on this topic Schramm 1929, to whom Erdmann 1943 adds important perspectives, but also Beumann 1950; Beumann 1958; Beumann 1962.

28 Cf. Wenskus 1956, especially pp. 171–186.

29 Moravcsik 1947, pp. 134 ff; Angenendt 1984, pp. 305 ff.

30 On the literature of millenarianism, see Brandes 2000, p. 426 note 4.

31 Schramm 1929, pp. 227 f.

32 Müller-Mertens 1970.

33 Thomas 1991, p. 265.

34 See Janson 1998, p. 52.

35 Adam of Bremen, I 10.

36 Adam of Bremen, II 42, 'Interea millesimus ab incarnatione Domini annus feliciter impletus est.'

37 Adam of Bremen, II 44, 'O vere oculta super homines Dei iudicia, qui "miseretur, qui vult, et quem vult indurat!" Cuius omnipotentiam mirantes videmus eos ad paganismum esse relapsos, qui primi crediderunt, illis autem conversis ad Christum, qui primi crediderunt.'

38 It is not a coincidence that Adam of Bremen makes an allusion to chapter 9 of St Paul's letter to the Romans, which is about the rejection of the Jews and the choice of the pagans, in the passage cited.

39 Schneider 1972, pp. 146 ff.

40 For the role of these prices in Adam's text, see Janson 1998.

41 Thietmar of Merseburg, III 18.

42 Adam of Bremen, III 19.

43 Adam of Bremen, II 42; cf. II 43 and Schol. 30.

44 Janson 1998, pp. 196 ff.

45 Adam of Bremen, II 21.

46 Janson 1998, pp. 201 ff. Helmold of Bosau, I 22–27 also describes the situation along the Elbe after 1066 as if there were a clear front between Christians and pagans, Saxons and Slavs, but contemporary sources makes it clear that Henry IV and the Saxons competed in winning the Slavs to their side; see Janson 1998, pp. 293 f.

47 Janson 1998, pp. 21 ff.

48 Janson 1998, pp. 269. ff.

49 Janson 1998, pp. 190 ff., 262 ff., 291 ff.

50 Janson 1998, pp. 265–291. A 1997 paper discussing this in English is now available as Janson 2000.

51 Janson 1998, pp. 17 ff.

52 Wenskus 1956, pp. 186–197 with note 196.
53 Cf. Kahl 1955; Kahl 1978, pp. 52 ff.; Wenskus 1956, pp. 143–153.
54 Schmidt 1974.
55 Since this article was written in 2001, a few other studies on related subjects has been produced, see Janson 2003; ibid. 2004a and b; ibid. forthcoming.

BIBLIOGRAPHY

Sources

Adam of Bremen, *Gesta Hammaburgensis ecclesiae pontificum*. MGH SRG. B. Schmeidler (ed.), Hannover – Leipzig 1917.

Adso, 'Epistola Adonis ad Gerbergam reginam de ortu et tempore Antichristi', in E. Sackur (ed.), *Sibyllinische Texte und Forschungen*. Halle 1898, pp. 97–113.

Annales Augienses. MGH SS, Bd. 1. I. von Arx (ed.), Hannover 1826, pp.67–69.

Epistolae karolini aevi, 2nd ed. MGH Ep., IV. E. Dümmler (ed.), Berlin 1895.

Helmold of Bosau, *Cronica slavorum*. MGH SRG. Bernard Schmeidler (ed.) Hannover – Leipzig 1909.

Liutprand of Cremona, 'Antapodosis', in *Liutprandi Cremonensis opera omnia*. CCCM 156. P. Chiesa (ed.), Turnhout 1998, pp. 1–150.

Liutprand of Cremona, 'Relatio de legatione Constantinopolitana', in *Liutprandi Cremonensis opera omnia*. CCCM 156. P. Chiesa (ed.), Turnhout 1998, pp. 185-218.

Regino of Prüm, *Chronicon cum continuatione Treverensi*. MGH SRG. Hannover 1890.

Thietmar of Merseburg, *Chronicon*. MGH SRG, n.s. 9. R. Holtzmann (ed.), Berlin 1935.

Die Urkunden Konrad I Henrik I und Otto I. Die Urkunden der deutschen Könige und Kaiser, 1. MGH Diplomatum regum et imperatorum, I. T. Sickel (ed.), Hannoverae 1879–1884.

'Vita Rimberti', G. Weits (ed.) in *Vita Ansgarii auctore Rimberto*. MGH SRG. Hannover 1884, pp. 80–100.

Widukind of Corvey, *Rerum gestarum Saxonicarum libri tres*. MGH SRG. G. Waitz & K. A. Kehr (ed.), Hannover – Leipzig 1904.

Literature

A. Angenedt 1984, *Kaiserherrschaft und Königstaufe*. Arbeiten zur Frühmittelalterforschung 15. Berlin – New York.

H. Beumann 1950, 'Das imperiale Königtum im 10. Jahrhundert', *Welt als Geschichte* 10, pp. 117–130.

H. Beumann 1958, 'Nomen imperatoris: Studien zur Kaiseridee Karls des Grossen', *Historische Zeitschrift* 185, pp. 515–549.

H. Beumann 1962, 'Das Keisertum Ottos des grossen: Ein Rückblick nach tausend Jahren', *HZ* 195, pp. 529–573.

W Brandes 2000, 'Liutprand von Cremona (Legatio cap. 39–41) und eine bisher unbeachtete west–östliche Korrespondenz über die Bedeutung des Jahres 1000 A. D.', *Byzantinische Zeitschrift* 93, pp. 435–463.

W. Brüske 1983, *Untersuchungen zur Geschichte des Lutizenbundes: Deutsch-wendische Beziiehungen des 10.–12 Jahrhunderts*. Mitteldeutsche Forschungen 3. Köln and Wien.

C. Erdmann 1935, *Die Entstehung des Kreuzzugsgedankes*. Forschungen zur Kirchen- und Geistesgeschichte 6. Stuttgart.

C. Erdmann 1943, 'Das ottonische Reich als Imperium Romanum', *Deutsches Archiv* 6, pp. 412–441.

H. Janson 1998, *Templum nobilissimum: Adam av Bremen, Uppsalatemplet och kon-fliktlinjerna i Europa kring år 1075*. Avhandlingar från Historiska institutionen i Göteborg 21. Göteborg.

H. Janson 2000, 'Adam of Bremen and the conversion of Scandinavia', in G. Armstrong & I. Wood (ed.), *Christianising Peoples and Converting individuals*. International Medieval Research 7. Turnhout, pp. 83–88.

H. Janson 2003, 'What made the pagans pagans', in R. Simek & J. Meurer (ed.), *Scandinavia and Christian Europe in the Middle Ages*. Papers of the 12th International Saga Conference Bonn/Germany, 28th–2nd August 2003. Bonn, pp. 250–256.

H. Janson 2004a, 'Danmarks 1100-tal och andra perspektiv. Reflektioner kring gammal forskning och nya problem', in P. Carelli, L. Hermanson & H. Sanders (ed.) *Ett annat 1100-tal. Individ, kollektiv och kulturella mönster i medeltidens Danmark*. Göteborg – Stockholm, pp. 340-367.

H. Janson 2004b, 'Konfliktlinjer i tidig nordeuropeisk kyrkoorganisation', in N. Lund (ed.), *Kristendomen i Danmark før 1050. Ett symposium i Roskilde den 5-7 februar 2003*. Roskilde, pp. 215-252.

H. Janson forthcoming, 'Pagani and Christiani. Cultural Identity and Exclusion around the Baltic in the Early Middle Ages', in a publication by the project 'Culture Clash or Compromise', *Acta Visbyesia* 12.

H.-D. Kahl 1955, '*Compellere intrare*. Die Wendenpolitik Bruns von Querfurt im Lichte hochmittelalterlichen Missions- und Völkerrechts', *Zeitschrift für Ostforschung* 4, pp. 161–193, 360–401.

H.-D. Kahl 1978, 'Die ersten Jahrhunderte des missionsgeschichtlichen Mittelalters: Bausteine für eine Phänomenologie bis ca. 1050', in K. SchSferdiek (ed.), *Kirchengeschichte als Missionsgeschichte* II/1. München, pp. 11-76.

B. McGinn 1994, *Antichrist: Two thousand years of the human fascination with evil*. San Francisco.

Moravcsik 1947, 'The Role of the Byzantine Church in Medieval Hungary', *American Slavic and East European Review* 6, pp. 134-151.

E. Müller-Mertens 1970, *Regnum teutonicum: Aufkommen und Verbreitung der deutschen Reichs- und Königsaffassung im früheren Mittelalter*. Wien etc.

L. von Ranke 1887, *Weltgeschichte*, vol. 8. Leipzig.

H. D. Rauh 1973, *Das bild des Antichrist im Mittelalter: von Tyconius zum deutschen Symbolismus*. Beiträge zur Geschichte der Philosophie und Theologie des Mittelalters n.F. 9. Münster.

R. Schmidt 1974, 'Rethra: Das Heiligtum der Lutizen als Heiden-Metropole', H. Beumann (ed.), *Festschrift für Walter Schlesinger*, 2. Mitteldeutsche Forschungen 74/II. Köln – Wien, pp. 366–394.

C. Schneider 1972, *Prophetisches sacerdotium und heilsgeschichliches regnum im Dialog 1073–1077*. Münstersche Mittelalter-Schriften 9. München.

Schramm 1929, *Kaiser, Rom und Renovatio. Studien und texte zur Geschichte des Römischen Erneuerungsgedankens vom Ende des karolingischen Reiches zum Investiturstreit* 1-2, Studien der Bibliothek Warburg XVII. Leipzig – Berlin.

H. Thomas 1991, 'Julius Caesar und die Deutschen: Zu Ursprung und Gestalt eines deutschen Geschichtbewusstseins in der Zeit Gregor VII. und Heinrich IV', in S. Weinfurter (ed.), *Die Salier und das Reich* 3. Sigmaringen, pp. 245-277.

R. Wenskus 1956, *Studien zur historisch-politischen Gedankenwelt Bruns von Querfurt*. Mitteldeutsche forschungen 5. Münster – Köln.

TUOMAS HEIKKILÄ

Pogroms of the First Crusade in Medieval Local Historiography
The Death of Archbishop Eberhard of Trier and the Legitimation of the Pogroms

S ecular and ecclesiastical leaders had encouraged Jewish migration to
Germany during the tenth and eleventh centuries, believing that they
would enhance the economic prestige of their cities. To entice the Jewish
immigrants, lords and bishops often offered benefits such as a considerable
degree of self-rule. These privileges ignited the jealousy of the Christian
burghers, their financial competitors in the communities. The economic
envy of the burghers was undoubtedly augmented by the inflammatory
rhetoric of the anti-Jewish crusading bands. Consequently, the combination of economic competition between the Jews and the Christians and
the religious zeal of the Crusades resulted in large-scale pogroms in 1096.
This new development in the previously reasonably-harmonious relations
between the Christian majority and Jewish minority was reflected in the
contemporary historiography in an interesting way.

In this article I shall deal with one widely overlooked aspect of the
medieval historiography of the Crusades – the reaction of local writers to
the pogroms of Jews of *Ashkenaz* during the First Crusade (1096–1099).
I shall tackle this problem by providing an insight into one case: the pogroms of Trier, Germany, in 1096 and the reaction of local historiography,
both Christian and Jewish, a generation later.

For medieval Christian historiography the paramount significance of
the Crusades as a topic goes without saying. High medieval Christendom
can be described as a result of several antagonisms with its neighbours,
Muslims, Jews and pagans. During the first Crusade, Christendom was
on the offensive on a large scale for the first time in its history. In spite
of the earlier heroic deeds of the missionaries in winning new areas
for the faith or the successes of monarchs like Charlemagne or Otto
the Great in securing the boundaries of the Christendom, the Crusades
represented a completely new phase in Christian history. This was clear
to the high medieval history writers who consequently stressed this
aspect of the Crusades. For them the pogroms were but a minor detail.
For Jewish historiography, however, the account of the First Crusade
concentrated understandably on the pogroms and the martyrdom of the
Jews. The comparative aspect of the Christian and Jewish historiography

of the Crusades has received relatively little attention from scholars up to recent years.[1]

The beginning of the Crusade in 1096 marked the first widespread and organised persecution of Western European Jewish communities by Christians. In addition to the traditional antagonism between the Jews and the Christians, the pogroms were closely linked with the crusading ideology. During the summer of 1096, when hordes of crusaders moved crossing Europe towards the Holy Land, the religious fervour was at its peak, and the partially anti-Jewish crusading propaganda fresh in the minds of the crusaders. One has to bear in mind this atmosphere of fanaticism when considering the importance of the First Crusade as a watershed in the relations between the Jews and the Christians. Indeed, both Christian and Jewish sources tell us unanimously that the relation between both groups had been a correct one prior to the Crusade. And, what is more, the pogroms of 1096 came as a surprise to the Jews.

Seen against this background one can understand the significance of one aspect of the crusading historiography that has in my opinion been widely overlooked – the legitimation of the pogroms. It seems to me that this aspect was emphasised in the local historiography of the High Middle Ages that was written to meet the needs of a lay public. However, legitimising crusaders' actions was a primary concern in crusading propaganda, starting with the sermon of Pope Urban II in Clermont in 1095. We shall see later how local Christian historiography dealt with legitimating pogroms in a very inventive and interesting way. The problem of legitimating these actions was necessarily closely related to another important problem of Christian writers giving an account of the Crusades: how should the brave martyrdom of the Jews during the persecutions be dealt with? Until the late eleventh century martyrs had been something of a private property of the Christian Church. Thus, the Crusades made the historians think their methods over, which led to an important contribution to Christian historiography as a whole.

These two aspects played a major part in the local historiography of Trier at the beginning of the twelfth century. It is probable that the Jewish community of Trier had its origins in the tenth century. According to the sources on the First Crusade the local Jewish community had their own synagogue and rabbi, which leads us to the conclusion that the Jewish population of the town was relatively numerous and well organised,[2] apparently one of the largest of the *regnum Teutonicum*.[3] Trier was one of the cities of the Rhineland that witnessed spontaneous and widespread outbreaks of violence against Jewish communities during the First Crusade. In comparison with cities like Mainz, Worms or Metz, however, the Jews of Trier came off well. Whereas, according to the sources, a thousand Jews died in Mainz and another eight hundred in Worms,[4] fewer than ten Jews were murdered or committed suicide in Trier. Nevertheless, the events of 1096 seem to have left an awkward memory in the mind of the local Christian community. The importance of legitimising the pogrom was stressed by the fact that the persecutors were not – as in most other cities – foreign crusaders but locals.

There are three separate major sources written in Hebrew on the pogroms of the First Crusade, all of which were written a generation later than the actual incidents.[5] The events in Trier are known from two separate sources: one Jewish, the other Christian. Let us first take a look at the Jewish source on the pogroms of Trier, the Chronicle of Solomon ben Simson, written either in Trier or Worms some decades after the First Crusade.[6] According to Solomon's account, the first wave of crusaders under the leadership of Peter the Hermit arrived in Trier at the beginning of April 1096. Interestingly, Peter had a letter from French Jews that advised the local Jewish community to finance and provision the band of crusaders in order to be left alone. The Jews of Trier acted accordingly and the crusaders left the town without doing any harm. Solomon ben Simson underlines the fact that until the departure of Peter and the crusaders there had been no friction whatsoever between the local Jews and the Christians. Having seen, however, the amount of money the Jewish community had given the crusaders, local Christians grew envious and greedy. In order to avoid the pogroms that had already taken place in many neighbouring towns, the Jews tried to bribe local Christians and to appeal to the archbishop of Trier for their safety. That only gained them some time, and finally the Jews had to choose between death and conversion to the Christian faith. According to Solomon ben Simson, some Jews accepted baptism, whereas many preferred to commit suicide.[7]

Even keeping in mind the fact that the Jewish chronicle was written a generation after the events and, taking into consideration the clearly biased attitude of its writer, there is in my opinion still a great deal of trustworthiness in the story of Solomon ben Simson. In fact, his account on the First Crusade in Trier is strikingly similar to the other – this time Christian – chronicles of Ekkehard of Aura or Albert of Aachen describing the events of 1096 in Cologne and Mainz.[8] The actions of the Jews and crusaders follow a pattern known to us from several historical sources. At first there were no problems between the two groups and the difficulties only arose when the actual crusaders had left the town. It was then that the local burghers, who had been living together with the Jews all of their lives, saw their chance to take their share of the supposed wealth of the Jews.

The most important Christian source on the pogroms in Trier is the *continuatio* of the famous history of the town, the anonymous *Gesta Treverorum*, written around 1132. Whereas the pogroms were an essential topic in the Jewish chronicle of Solomon ben Simson, they were only tangential subject in *Gesta Treverorum* and its continuation, both of which aimed to show the glorious past and present of Trier and its inhabitants. According to most scholars, *Gesta Treverorum* was an early literary product of the forming identity of the well-off inhabitants of the town and an indication of an early feeling of community of the social group in question. Consequently, its intended public was thoroughly Christian and interested in seeing its own history represented as positively as possible.

Whereas its forerunner, the actual *Gesta Treverorum*,[9] written very shortly after the First Crusade, did not even mention the Crusade, not to mention the persecutions of Jews, the *continuatio* contains a detailed description of the events of 1096. In the text Jews are shown in three different, but equally important contexts that are linked with another. Firstly, they appear in 1066 as the murderers of Eberhard, the archbishop of Trier.[10] Secondly, in the context mentioned above, i.e., during the First Crusade, some of them agree to convert to Christianity, even though almost all of the newly converted abandoned their new faith within a year. Finally, the *continuatio* tells a story of a Jewish doctor, who converted voluntarily and became a good Christian in the 1120s. Thus the author of the *continuatio* of the *Gesta Treverorum* created a perfect narrative pattern with its gloomy beginning and glorious end that marked the victory of the Christendom over the Jews – just as Christendom would conquer the Muslim lands in the east in the end. It is striking, how these three scenes, separated by a generation from each other, form a whole that exemplifies an optimistic view of potential conversions of Jews. Still, it is to be noted that the overall attitude of the *continuator* is favourable to Jews.[11]

All of these scenes were of importance in the intention of the writer of the *continuatio* to legitimise the fate of local Jews in 1096. In order to legitimise the death of local Jews convincingly, the writer of the *continuatio* had to present something more than just the traditional need to convert all peoples to Christianity.[12] Since local Jews were afraid of being forced to accept baptism by the crusaders, they sought refuge in the episcopal palace. This episode, again, is very similar to those known from other German towns. The Archbishop, however, was not able – if even willing – to protect them by any other means than converting them. In fact, he succeeded in converting some of the local Jews to Christianity, whereas some chose to commit suicide rather than accept baptism.[13] In short, in a clear contrast to the Jewish source, the Chronicle of Solomon ben Simson, the *continuatio* of the *Gesta Treverorum* absolves local Christians from bearing the blame for the Jews' death. It shows the Jews as having committed suicide to avoid eventual aggression by foreign crusaders. This, however, was not enough for the author of the *continuatio*.

Reading all three passages concerning the Jews in the *continuatio* carefully it soon becomes clear that, in addition to the second scene of spring 1096, the first was the most important when it came to the legitimating the actions of the Trier inhabitants. Conversion by force was not only prohibited by canon law, but the general opinion towards it was also clearly unfavourable.[14] Eagerness to convert the Jews was thus not an acceptable reason to massacre them. Accordingly, the writer of the *continuatio* made up an entirely fictitious story according to which the Jews had murdered the local archbishop, Eberhard, in 1066. Eberhard had in fact died on *sabbato sancto*, during mass, which had naturally been quite horrifying for his contemporaries. While the actual *Gesta Treverorum* and other contemporary sources had only mentioned the untimely death of the archbishop,[15] the *continuator* added many new details to the story. This new version insists that the archbishop had ordered local Jews to convert to Christianity or to leave the town by the Saturday before Easter. He was thus acting according to the canon law and pursuing the aims of the actual crusade at the same time. The Jews, however, did not appreciate any of the alternatives offered them. According to the *continuator*, they shaped a small image out of wax and bribed a priest to baptise it as Eberhard. On Easter Saturday 1066 they burned it, which led to the instant and painful death of the archbishop.[16]

What we have here is an instance of the black magic in use ever since antiquity.[17] Sticking pins into, burning, or otherwise mutilating an image of an enemy was believed to cause him to experience the effects of such actions in his own body. Similar stories of Jews using black magic to avenge their misfortunes on the Christians are also known earlier in Western Christendom.[18] The real background of the story was probably the Jewish tradition of burning an image symbolising Haman, their mythical enemy during the festivities of the Purim.[19]

Jewish historiography stressed the martyrdom of local Jews in giving an account of the events of 1096. Since these events could not just be glossed over, the Eberhard story might have been produced as a Christian counterpart to the Jewish accounts of the martyrs of 1096. In the *continuatio* of the *Gesta Treverorum* the connection between this act of black magic and the events of 1096 is made clear. The *continuator* insists on the Jews having actually started the hostilities in Trier in this way a generation before the First Crusade, thus giving the Christians of the town a natural and legitimate reason to persecute local Jews. In addition to this, the text had another aim to pursue. By making Archbishop Eberhard a martyr, it drew attention away from an awkward event of the Trier church history, the murder of the *electus* Cuno by some Trier knights in opposition to him, which also took place in 1066. The murder of Cuno had been the result of local intrigues and had raised broad disapproval among the prelacy of Germany.[20] Accordingly, there were two extremely embarrassing moments in the recent history of Trier by the time of writing the *continuatio*. Its author had the healing of both of these wounds as his aim.

At first sight the invented story of the local Jews murdering the Archbishop might be interpreted as an example of increasing anti-Jewish feeling during the first half of the twelfth century. However, the relations between Jews and Christians in Trier had become normalised to the degree that no pogroms or incidents whatsoever occurred in Trier during the Second Crusade (1147–1149). Thus, the story version of the *continuatio* of the *Gesta Treverorum* of the Jews murdering the local Archbishop does not seem to have echoed broader antipathy towards the Jewish minority. It is also conceivable that, in the light of the harmonious relations between Trier Jews and Christians in the mid-twelfth century, the events of 1096 would have seemed incomprehensible to contemporaries, so as to necessitate an elaborate reconstruction of causes and effects. In fact, violence would only resume a hundred years later.

The version of the *continuator* proved to be a success. The story of the Jews murdering Archbishop Eberhard lived on for at least 600 years in local Christian historiography and belief. It was added to a late edition of *Annales Hirsaugienses* by the famous abbot of Spanheim, Johannes Trithemius; interestingly enough, it is not in the original manuscript of his annals.[21]

159

Later on, the seventeenth-century historians of Trier added more details to the story depicting Jews as murderers of the Archbishop.[22] Even as late as the eighteenth century a local historian gave the death of archbishop Eberhard as a reason for medieval pogroms against the Jews.[23]

Since even the earliest history and historiography of the Crusades must be understood as a vital part of the contemporary and ongoing propaganda for the crusading movement,[24] the historical or explanatory purposes and the contemporary concerns of the history writers overlapped frequently. Almost all the historians and chroniclers of the expeditions that were later called the First Crusade considered them a response to the Muslim threats to Christian holy places and peoples in the east. This contributed to the view of the expeditions as a form of self-defence, a just war, *bellum iustum*. The anti-Jewish attitude, in turn, seems to have been an important element in the ideology of crusading from the outset.[25] When the call was made for a crusade to free the Holy Land from Muslim rule, some Christians wondered why they should not rid Europe of unbelievers before trekking east. After all, it was Jews who murdered Christ in the popular opinion of Western Christians of the late eleventh century. Guibert of Nogent, for instance, who thought it to have been illogical not to punish the Jews as well as other enemies of the faith, defended this attitude.[26]

It seems that by the 1140s – i.e., the time when both of our major sources were written – the positive part of the crusading experiences of previous generations had become an important part of the collective memory of Western Christendom.[27] During the process of the romanticisation of the First Crusade, the actual events turned into one part of the collective imagination rather than historical reality in that the later accounts reflected the view of the First Crusade as it should have been, rather than as it actually was. This was not only the case in the great and important historiographical and/or propagandistic works, but locally as well. For medieval Christian history writers of Trier the need to legitimise the actions of local fellow Christians seems to have been urgent. It is interesting, however, that this reaction only came a generation after the First Crusade, when the appearance of the events of 1096 had been romanticised. Consequently, even the awkward episodes of the Rhineland and its neighbouring areas were to be harmonised. In this context historiography proved out to be an excellent tool.

NOTES

1   For a good introduction to the historiography of the Crusades, see Constable 2001. On Jews and the Crusades specifically see, Eidelberg 1977.
2   A. Haverkamp 1996, p. 478.
3   A. Haverkamp 1991, p. 172.
4   According to Friedrich Lotter, as many as 5000 Jews lost their lives in the Empire of Henry IV. About 3000 of them were killed in the Germanic region. See Lotter 1999, pp. 107–152, esp. p. 115.
5   Cohen 1999, p. 18.
6   Chazan 1987, p. 42. According to Eva Haverkamp the writer probably came from Trier and the chronicle was written in the 1140s. See E. Haverkamp 1999, pp. 36, 41, 53–68.

7   *Chronicle of Solomon ben Simson*, pp. 287–293.

8   *Ekkehardi Chronicon Uraugiensis*; Alberti, *Historia*.

9   *Gesta Treverorum, continuatio*, pp. 175–200.

10 On this *passus*, see Heikkilä 2003.

11 See, for example, *Gesta Treverorum, continuatio*, pp. 195.

12 In general, see Riley-Smith 1986, p. 53 notes 106 & 107, with several sources. Concerning the First Crusade especially, see Lotter 1999.

13 *Gesta Treverorum, continuatio*, p. 190.

14 For example, Hugo of Flavigny, *Chronicon*; Lotter 1999, p. 114; Hiestand 1999, p. 162, with more sources.

15 *Gesta Treverorum*, p. 174: 'Eberhardus episcopus ... Sabbato sancto paschae post expletum divinum officium in sacrario, sicut paratus erat, obiit.' Cf. *Lamperti annales*, p. 102; *Continuatio Chronici Herimanni Contracti*, p. 732; *Annales Weissenburgenses*, p. 71; *Annales Augustani*, p. 128; *Annalium Laubiensium continuatio*, p. 20; *Annales S. Eucharii Treverensis*, p. 10; *Bertholdi annales*, pp. 272–273; *Bernoldi Chronicon*, p. 428.

16 *Gesta Treverorum, continuatio*, p. 182.

17 Müller-Bergström 1936, pp. 459–462.

18 One example is the case from Le Mans in 992, when the Jews were believed to have tried to harm the local count by a 'voodoo doll'. For further examples see Chazan 1973, p. 12; Fichtenau 1984, p. 422; Trachtenberg 1945, p. 122.

19 See Bible, Book of Esther: 8–9.

20 It was also mentioned by most of the German contemporary sources – cf. footnote – unlike the supposed murder of Eberhard.

21 Città del Vaticano, Biblioteca Apostolica Vaticana, Ms. Pal. lat. 929.

22 Brower & Masen 1670, p. 539.

23 Calmet 1728, p. 1132.

24 Powell 1997, pp. 127–41.

25 Cohen 1999, p. 20; Chazan 1987, pp. 99–136.

26 Guibertus, *De vita sua* II, 5, p. 903.

27 Riley-Smith 1997, p. 102.

BIBLIOGRAPHY

Original Sources

Città del Vaticano, Biblioteca Apostolica Vaticana, Ms. Pal. lat. 929.

Edited Sources

[Alberti Aquensis] *Historia Hierosolymitanae expeditionis seu Chronicon Hierosolymitanum de bello sacro*. PL 166.
Annales Augustani. MGH, Scriptores III.
Annales S. Eucharii Treverensis. MGH, Scriptores V.
Annales Weissenburgenses. MGH, Scriptores III.
Annalium Laubiensium continuatio. MGH, Scriptores IV.
Bernoldi Chronicon. MGH, Scriptores V.
Bertholdi Annales. MGH, Scriptores V.
Chronicle of Solomon ben Simson. R. Chazan (ed.) in Chazan 1987, pp. 243–297.
Continuatio Chronici Herimanni Contracti. MGH, Scriptores XIII.
Ekkehardi Chronicon Uraugiensis. MGH, Scriptores VI.
Gesta Treverorum. MGH, Scriptores VIII.
Gesta Treverorum, continuatio. MGH, Scriptores VIII.
Guibert of Nogent, *De vita sua*. PL 156.
Hugo of Flavigny, *Chronicon*. MGH, Scriptores VIII.

Lamperti annales. Lamperti monachi Hersfeldensis opera. Recognovit Oswaldus Holder-Egger. MGH, Scriptores rerum Germanicarum in usum scholarum.

Literature

C. Brower & J. Masen 1670, *Antiquitatum et annalium Treverensium libri XXV duobus tomis comprehensi.* Leodii.

A. Calmet 1728, *Histoire ecclesiastique et civile de Lorraine*, Tome I. Nancy.

R. Chazan 1973, *Medieval Jewry in Northern France.* The Johns Hopkins University Studies in Historical and Political Science. Ninety-first Series, 2. Baltimore.

R. Chazan 1987, *European Jewry and the First Crusade.* Berkeley–Los Angeles–London.

J. Cohen 1999, 'The Hebrew Crusade Chronicles in Their Christian Cultural Context', in A. Haverkamp (ed.), *Juden und Christen zur Zeit der Kreuzzüge.* Vorträge und Forschungen, XLVII. Sigmaringen, pp. 17–34.

G. Constable 2001, 'The Historiography of the Crusades', in A. E. Laiou & R. P. Mottahedeh (ed.), *The Crusades from the Perspective of Byzantium and the Muslim World.* Dumbarton Oaks Papers. Washington, D.C. [http://www.doaks.org/Crusades/CR01.pdf] (9 Feb 2004).

S. Eidelberg (ed. and transl.) 1977, *The Jews and the Crusaders: The Hebrew Chronicles of the First and Second Crusades.* Madison, Wisc.

H. Fichtenau 1984, *Lebensordnungen des 10. Jahrhunderts. Studien über Denkart und Existenz im einstigen Karolingerreich.* Monographien zur Geschichte des Mittelalters, 30: I–II. Stuttgart.

A. Haverkamp 1991, 'Die Städte Trier, Metz, Toul und Verdun. Religiöse Gemeinschaften im Zentralitätsgefüge einer Städtelandschaft zur Zeit der Salier', in S. Weinfurter (ed.), *Die Salier und das Reich. Band 3. Gesellschaftlicher und ideengeschichtlicher Wandel im Reich der Salier.* Sigmaringen, pp. 165–190.

A. Haverkamp 1996, 'Die Juden inmitten der Stadt', in H. H. Anton (ed.), *2000 Jahre Trier. Band 2. Trier im Mittelalter.* Trier, pp. 477–499.

A. Haverkamp (ed.) 1999, *Juden und Christen zur Zeit der Kreuzzüge.* Vorträge und Forschungen, Band XLVII. Sigmaringen.

E. Haverkamp 1999, ''Persecutio' und 'G^{e}zerah' in Trier während des Ersten Kreuzzugs', in A. Haverkamp (ed.), *Juden und Christen zur Zeit der Kreuzzüge.* Vorträge und Forschungen. Band XLVII. Sigmaringen, pp. 35–71.

T. Heikkilä 2003, 'Juutalaiset ja musta magia sydänkeskiajalla: Trierin arkkipiispa Eberhardin salaperäinen kuolema vuonna 1066', in M. Heinonen & J. Tunturi (ed.), *Pahan tiedon puu. Väärä tieto ja väärin tietäminen sydänkeskiajalta valistukseen.* Helsinki, pp. 38–60.

R. Hiestand 1999, 'Juden und Christen in der Kreuzzugspropaganda und bei den Kreuzzugspredigern', in A. Haverkamp (ed.), *Juden und Christen zur Zeit der Kreuzzüge.* Vorträge und Forschungen, XLVII. Sigmaringen, pp. 153–208.

F. Lotter 1999, 'Tod oder Taufe. Das Problem des Zwangstaufen während des Ersten Kreuzzugs', in A. Haverkamp (ed.), *Juden und Christen zur Zeit der Kreuzzüge.* Vorträge und Forschungen, XLVII. Sigmaringen, pp. 107–152.

W. Müller-Bergström 1936: 'Rachepuppe', in *Handwörterbuch des deutschen Aberglaubens*, VII. Berlin–Leipzig, pp. 459–462.

J. M. Powell 1997, 'Myth, Legend, Propaganda, History: The First Crusade, 1140–ca. 1300', in M. Balard (ed.) *Autour de la Première Croisade. Actes du Colloque de la Society for the Study of the Crusades and the Latin East (Clermont-Ferrand, 22–25 juin 1995).* Paris, pp. 127–41.

J. Riley-Smith 1986, *The First Crusade and the Idea of Crusading.* London.

J. Riley-Smith 1997, *The First Crusaders, 1095–1131.* Cambridge.

J. Trachtenberg 1945, *The Devil and the Jews. The Medieval Conception of the Jew and its Relation to Modern Antisemitism.* New Haven–London.

SINI KANGAS

Deus Vult

Violence and Suffering as a Means of Salvation during the First Crusade

The words 'religion' and 'salvation' have traditionally been associated with positive images, such as peace, serenity and eternal life. Acts of violence refer to the opposite, the powers of chaos and war. If faith and salvation form a contextual whole, how can violence serve as a bridge to redemption? In this article the subject will be approached from the standpoint of a medieval pilgrim and crusader. How did he (or in some cases she) experience the matching of religious fervour with extreme violence in the situations of military encounters? What were the balancing mechanisms between religious ideals and the actual bloodshed like, and how were they created and maintained?

The article will be based on three ideas: 1) Grace was earned by ultimate penance. 2) Crusaders believed that God was testing their faith by requiring them to engage in especially difficult and disgusting tasks. 3) It was the outcome of violence that proved the primary motive either pious or sinful.

Contemporary chroniclers do not directly reveal the kind of emotion violence aroused in crusaders with the exception of Raymond of Aguilers, who openly enjoys the physical suffering of the enemy.[1] Neither do sources analyse or classify violence. Having been written as a winner's history, they accept the violent treatment of those, who were officially pronounced outsiders and enemies of Christendom. The themes that the sources mainly have in common treat the vital need to combat infidel expansion and the terrible consequences of sinning.

In his thorough treatise on high medieval warfare, John France wrote that 'In the European heartlands war was about possession of land and rulership over its people, and as few wished to rule deserts, they did not try to remove or slaughter the population.'[2] It is clear that this rule cannot be extended to the crusader warfare in the Holy Land in 1098–1099, and more precisely to the climaxes of the expedition, the conquests of Antioch and Jerusalem. The siege and following battles of Antioch seem to be a decisive turning point of the First Crusade, during which violent resentment towards the enemy fully emerged. From then on assaults follow one another, culminating in the fall of Jerusalem on 15th July 1099. Whatever the bloody path from Antioch to Jerusalem was, the sources do not hint at any plans made in advance for the slaughter of the town population. Whether the outcome of the fall of the holy city was a spontaneous or a planned expression of violence remains obscure.

Generally speaking, it can be concluded that warfare in the East during the First Crusade was no more brutal than it would have been in the West and that the Western code of war was also broadly applied to the series of campaigns that form the First Crusade.[3] Nevertheless, there are features that distinguish the conquest of Jerusalem and Antioch from the taking of other important cities.

Surprisingly, the conquest of Jerusalem receives much less space and attention in the sources as compared with the siege and fall of Antioch. This seems to be quite a peculiar development, since Jerusalem was, throughout the whole expedition and preceding series of events, the main objective of the campaign.

Besides, the reaction to the capture of Jerusalem appears uncontrolled and hysterical. The conventional procedure of a prolonged siege included looting and killing, but the descriptions of men in floods of tears of joy, loudly singing in the streets is strikingly unusual.[4] Furthermore, the descriptions contain exceptionally detailed information about the outcome of violence. Lastly and most notably, one of the sources hints that there was something extraordinary in the nature of the violence. We shall return to this point later.

By declaring a crusade against the infidels on 18th November 1095 at the council of Clermont, Pope Urban II connected warfare with spirituality in a way previously unheard of. To the ancient pacifistic tradition of pilgrimage was now added an opportunity to join a violent conflict against the enemies of God and Christendom. It is no wonder that this novel institution was seen as a new way to salvation by contemporaries, as Guibert of Nogent puts it.[5] A clearly military task for warriors, the leading class of the Western society, was a natural way of doing penance and gaining spiritual rewards. The response to the papal urging was overwhelming.

From around 1000 a new wave of spirituality had been provoking religious guilt among the sinners of Western Christendom.[6] The Augustinian idea of a *peregrinus*, a lonely wanderer seeking escape from the hostile world, also found special favour within the crusading ideology. By accepting the role of an exiled pilgrim, crusaders shut themselves away in a closed mental condition locked to outsiders.[7]

Increasing intimacy between man and Christ produced a strong tradition of *imitatio Christi*, in which the pilgrim struggled towards merging into the compassionate love of Jesus. This was achieved by contemplative practices and physically imitating the earthly life of the saviour. One essential element of *imitatio Christi* was the experience of suffering.[8] This is at least a partial explanation for the considerable space given to descriptions of suffering in the primary sources of the First Crusade. Within the framework of imitation, suffering was indeed one of the basic aims of the Crusade, an objective in itself. Someone had to bleed and die so that divine imitation would become true and resurrection possible.

164

This becomes especially clear in a comparison between the conquest of Jerusalem and the events of Easter.[9]

Another very important term required to understand the mental condition of a crusader is *miles Christi*, based on an early Christian conception of the believer as a soldier of God in a constant struggle against the powers of evil. Originally, the idea of the *miles Christi* was associated with mental struggle only.[10] In the primary sources of the First Crusade the concept is treated quite otherwise. The image of a warrior for God is here entirely physical. When crusaders suffer, they suffer physically from hunger, thirst, disease or painful wounds. When they sin, they commit physical crimes. Finally, their faith is shown in a concrete way by walking in procession, fasting or giving alms.[11] Apparently, tangibly performed public worship was a more important definition of a crusading *miles Christi* than the spiritual and private forms of devotion. The emphasis of the whole relationship to God was on physical deeds.

The practices of religion and violence have a strong integral bond in this context. Of course, participating in a crusade did not sanctify violence as such. Holy violence had to be sanctified and incited beforehand by formal, collective rituals to which deep feelings of guilt and self-pity were intimately related. Forms of mass devotion including fasting, processions, prayers, and communion regularly preceded battles.[12] The supplementary unrest provoked by violence was, for its part, discharged afterwards in religious hysteria.

> Anyone who loves his father or mother more than me is not worthy of me; anyone who loves his son or daughter more than me is not worthy of me; and anyone who does not take his cross and follow me is not worthy of me.[13]

The themes of a perfect sacrifice and perfect imitation come up repeatedly in the sources. By citing Matthew in Clermont the Pope challenged the crusaders to prove their commitment. As a demonstration of their love of God the crusaders were required to express their readiness to give an extreme contribution; that is, eventually die and cause death on behalf of God. For crusaders, participation in killing was on the insistence of God claiming personal proof of their submission to his will and indeed essential for earning eternal life. Only totality could be sufficient before God.

According to the high medieval ideals of pilgrimage, a pious pilgrim was able to experience a personal relation with the saint through relics in which the saint was believed to be present. As Jesus did not leave behind primary relics, the entire city of Jerusalem, a city located some 4,000 kilometres away from Clermont, had gradually come to represent the relic of the life and death of the Saviour.[14] Among the great Catholic pilgrimage centres, Jerusalem was the most important. Against this background it is only natural that the Holy City was chosen as the primary objective for the novel movement in the process of its consolidation.

The choice of Jerusalem gave the expedition respectability and stressed its religious nature. In the sources, the earthly city is confused with the Holy, Divine Jerusalem, the capital of the thousand-year rule of peace. As belief in the miraculous atmosphere of the city was strong, it is not improbable that many among the rank-and-file pilgrims had some vague idea of entering an earthly paradise by passing through the gates of the Holy City.[15]

Through the crusade sermon in Clermont, the Pope gave sinners an opportunity to die for Christ in the very same place that He had died on behalf of the sins of mankind.[16] An utterly reconciling counter-sacrifice of this kind clearly raised itself above conventional penance and was felt to some extent to redeem personal debt to God. The message of the Pope can be reduced to Paul's letter to the Romans (8,17): 'Now if we are children, then we are heirs – heirs of God and co-heirs with Christ, if indeed we share in his sufferings in order that we may also share in his glory.'[17]

The number of Muslims in the late eleventh century was very low in the Catholic heartlands; a rank-and-file crusader hardly had any previous experience of his enemy and victim.[18] As a group generally unknown to the public, Muslims formed a safe target for an attempt to channel violence outside the familiar group, Christendom. The Pope's reference to the struggle between Jerusalem and Babylon[19] was probably a carefully planned detail. The audience knew the Augustinian allegory of psychomachia in the human soul, and could be persuaded to imagine that by defeating diabolical Muslim powers with the Prince of Babylon (Antichrist) at their head, they would also be able to defeat mortal sin in their own minds.[20] For crusaders, it was mentally a great relief to have a legitimately designated enemy on which to project their feelings of guilt and hatred. They had no reason to question the message of the Pope.

In the East, this attitude towards Muslims did not change. The idea of being a *peregrinus* fundamentally prevented the pilgrims from making much effort aimed at cultural interplay. As Roland had boldly stated, for a warrior of God the infidels were wrong and Christians right.[21] The two groups had neither a common language nor much curiosity about learning from one another.

The demonic nature of the enemy constituted a severe threat to the whole existence of Christianity. The surviving versions of the sermon of Clermont present violence without exception as an injustice suffered only by Christians. Pointing out their sacred mission to save the defenceless Eastern Christians – the sources of the sermon do not, for once, mention the Eastern emperor or his army – the Pope drew a vivid picture of a bestial enemy attacking women and children. Being both inhuman and beyond salvation, the enemy lacked the very core of human dignity. Psalm 79, quoted by Baldric of Dol, sums up the crimes of the enemy:[22]

> O God, the nations have invaded your inheritance; they have defiled your holy temple, they have reduced Jerusalem to rubble. They have given the dead bodies of your servants as food to the birds of the air, the flesh of your saints to the beasts of the earth. They have poured out blood like water all around Jerusalem, and there is no one to bury the dead.[23]

The crusaders' conception of God was utterly harsh. God's main task was to act as a supreme judge, continuously demanding proof of unhesitating obedience from his followers. Any failure to meet the requirements was punished severely. To protect themselves from God's destroying hand, believers had to be able to convince God of their absolute willingness. In his study of the charters of the First Crusade, Jonathan Riley-Smith emphasises utter negativism as the main factor determining the religiosity of the knights. It was fear and guilt that compelled early crusaders to take the cross.[24] Compared with Guibert of Nogent's scholarly ideal of the crusade as a privileged way to salvation, the ideas of an ordinary crusader seem to have been less optimistic.

According to the chroniclers, crusaders did not believe in unearned mercy. Penance was essential to the attainment of salvation, because sin could not be reconciled without due punishment. As the judgement of God could not be avoided, crusading pilgrims remained anxious about the insuffiency of their sacrifice. How grudgingly the chroniclers mention the love of God towards people during the march to Jerusalem is quite revealing.

Sources stress the importance of judgement and punishment as the most significant parameters defining the relation with God. Nevertheless, the concept of God remains ambivalent. It contains a weak, loving Jesus-figure, an identifiable image of human suffering, whose mercy is not powerful enough to save man from the anger of a fearsome God, the war-hero. Where God is angry, Jesus is mild. When God demands, Jesus comforts and protects. In contrast to God, the Lord of Doomsday, it is Jesus to whom the expressions of affection are directed. A holy grave is the symbol of a good death, the horrors of which Christ in his presence repels.[25]

Crusaders were deeply moved by the death of their companions. Men who were able to use violence efficiently and cleverly had a corresponding insight into the horrors of death, both pre- and post-mortem. The fear of death was vented by revenge for those lost. While chroniclers remain silent as regards to the funeral practices of crusaders, they occasionally, in connection with some fatal setbacks, describe scenes of desecrating Muslim graveyards.[26] The only Christian grave regularly mentioned is the sepulchre of Christ at the centre of the world in Jerusalem. Difficult conditions causing high death rates and increasing anxiety are reflected in the legend of the king of the poor, Tafur who, as a messenger of death, fights his way through the country, devastating, killing and raping until no one is left alive.[27]

Loyalty towards the Christian Family motivated crusading society. Within the framework of high medieval ideas of vassalage and familial obligations, a crusade can be interpreted as a blood feud pursued to take vengeance for the insults suffered by the supreme Lord. In this setting, revenge was a matter of honour. This explains the positive tone which is used to describe the leaders' eagerness to shed the blood of their enemies.[28]

An anonymous chronicler mentions a knight named Guido, who had recently lost his lord. Guido loudly accuses God of leaving his followers to the mercy of the enemy, and threatens Him by claiming that if He will not support the troops, they will also stop calling on His name. The chronicler closes the scene by saying that after the outburst by Guido, none said the name of Christ aloud for several days.[29] Unfortunately, he does not tell us whether this was because of the fear of divine revenge for blasphemy or a manifestation of support for the claims of Guido. If the latter interpretation is correct, this would suggest a degree of reciprocity in the relationship to God.

By declaring that the liberation of Jerusalem was the will of God, the Pope gave the pilgrims a free hand to achieve this goal. During the conquest of Jerusalem crusaders killed many of the inhabitants of the city regardless of their age, sex, or physical or mental health. How then was the persecution of groups such as widows, orphans, the sick and the disabled, which within the Western Church had come under the category of special protection, thus justified? To what extent did the participants estimate the necessity for violence or question its use?

In at least in two cases, we can be sure that a particular crusader was not at all convinced of the justification concerning violence against civilians. These crusaders were the anonymous writer of *Gesta Francorum* and Tancred, a young and ambitious warlord. The anonymous chronicler did not have problems or even particular interest in conventional fighting between armed forces. Violence in a battle was a fact known beforehand, a normal factor, participation in which was at least in principle not obligatory for anyone. A Christian or Muslim joining a battle accepted the risks and did not pity his own, let alone the enemy's destiny. The anonymous author seems to have been able to process this kind of professional violence without guilt, observing the situations without any remorse. Still, the description of the conquest of Jerusalem differs from his previous depictions of the use of violence, not only in the wealth of detail, but in the peculiarity of the tone. Our suggestion is that there was something that struck the chronicler as unusual and made him write the way he did.

The anonymous knight's story of the conquest of Jerusalem differs clearly from the others. Whereas other chroniclers associate the physical leadership of God with the events of conquest, the anonymous chronicler does not mention God once in the context of slaughter. However, he indicates the leadership of God in the case of all other battles. Contrary to the sources that emphasise the greatness of joy after the city has been taken, this author does not hint at any personal delight in the result. Instead he relates the conquest to the suffering and painful death of Christ.[30]

The anonymous chronicler was not the only one to disapprove of the relatively high rate of civilian victims. According to Raymond of Aguilers, after the bloody conquest of Antioch Tancred speaks out in a critical tone: 'Why do we alone have to fight against the entire world? Do we have to kill all of mankind?'[31] During the conquest of Jerusalem the anonymous chronicler mentions that Tancred was furious to witness the killing of inhabitants who had sought protection under his banner.[32] Sources do not reveal the motives for Tancred's resentment. The analysis should remain cautious, since such motives would have been manifold: financial reward, prestige, giving one's word, or, as suggested, pure sympathy.

The sources convey a strikingly split concept of the world, where the wicked necessarily have to act as a counterweight to the pious. This kind of fundamental evil could only be eradicated by extreme means. The chosen people of God represent the good, whereas those outside the Christian circle naturally belong to the bad. The concept of love of one's neighbour clearly did not include non-Christians. Moreover, there was no reason to tolerate, let alone love one's enemy.

> Pilgrims persecuted and slaughtered Saracens up to the Temple of Solomon. Having been gathered there, we battled all the day, so that their blood was shed over the whole temple.[33]

> In the porch of the Temple of Solomon we were riding in blood up to our knees and up to the bits of the horses.[34]

The bleeding wounds of Jesus are a strong symbol of salvation. This keen interaction between pain and eventual glory was clear to the crusaders. Furthermore, there was a correlation between the blood spilt and the degree of success in the struggle, which explains the abundant descriptions of bloodshed in the chronicles. By emphasising the amount of blood, both in Jerusalem and Antioch, the sources convey the idea of an exhaustive offering, sufficient for the purification of the whole group of crusaders. To secure this effect, many had to die. After the conquest of Antioch, Robert of Rheims quotes the preaching of bishop Adhemar, the papal legate: 'Now you have been purged and reconciled for all (your sins) with God.'[35]

It is obvious that bloodshed in holy places was usually a powerful taboo in the high Middle Ages. However, in the sacrificial killings of the First Crusade the case is quite reversed. Here bloodshed was interpreted to have a cleansing effect. The slaughter of Jerusalem purged the holy places in a biblical manner. Even though Solomon Goitein's research has shown that a great many of the inhabitants of the city survived the slaughter, it seems especially important for the eyewitnesses to stress the totality of the killing.[36]

Sources state that tactical skill could not determine the outcome of a battle. Only genuine repentance could bring victory, which is why decisive battles were preceded by formal penitential behaviour. Eyewitness chronicles convey a strong sense of the result of penance as a decisive determinant in fighting. In the primary sources of the First Crusade, piety is practised by social actions, only the result of which reveals the moral rightness or wrongness of the intention.

This is also valid when it comes to the interpretations of violence. If a battle was followed by victory, it was understood that the army was to be seen as in God's favour and the victory viewed as a gesture of blessing. The use of violence against such a background was interpreted as an unavoidable judgement of God. Consistently, failures were taken to be a consequence of sin as an offended God denied his presence and abandoned crusaders to their fate.[37] This interpretation is at least partly against official preaching of the period that generally emphasises the purity of the primary motive as the main factor in defining the good or evil nature of a particular act.

Discipline and order were hard to attain in any medieval army of considerable size. With regard to actual battle, the commander's control was limited to a loosely drafted plan that might, or might not be followed. In general, battles were won or lost by the courage of individual soldiers – or good luck. After the outcome was clear, it would not have been a wise, or even possible, move from the leaders to prohibit violent sacking, during which the tension caused by the combat was discharged.[38]

Commoners who had joined the pilgrimage and followed the crusading army, added their contribution to the general chaos of a battle. In fact, it is quite difficult to draw the line between 'the army', namely, mounted knights and recruited infantry, and the following flock of 'civilian' pilgrims with cruder military equipment. Though some of these pilgrims were only armed with stakes and stones, the majority of civilians had prepared themselves as well as they could, their ability to fight being actually quite good, as Jonathan Riley-Smith has demonstrated.[39] At encounters with the enemy, the pilgrims were involved in fighting according to the abilities and equipment they possessed, actual rank being of secondary importance.

If we ask the sources about the origin of the violence, the answer will undoubtedly be *Deus vult* – it is the will of God. The crusaders' war cry shows that all responsibility was pinned on God.[40] The title of the Chronicle of Guibert of Nogent, *Dei Gesta per Francos*, The Deeds of God by the Francs, clearly reveals that crusaders attributed the violence to divine will. Their role as the chosen people was limited simply to that of being a tool of holy intervention. Faithful to its divine leader, the *militia Christi* followed orders without question.

If the lords took no responsibility, neither did Pope Urban II. In their letter to the Pope after the conquest of Antioch, leaders asked him to take over the leadership of the undertaking: 'by your authority and our courage you will eradicate and destroy all heretics...so that the name of the Christians would be the greatest one among the nations...so that the entire world would obey you.'[41] The expressions used persuade us that the crusaders were waging war in the name of the Pope, the earthly representative of God. According to the contents of the letter, the Pope as head of the Catholic Church was actually using authority over violence. In addressing the letter mighty lords describe themselves as children in their relation to the Pope, the spiritual father of the entire group, thus underlining their subordinate role. The Pope, however, refused to leave Rome, because actual leadership in war, no matter how divinely ordained, would have caused serious damage to the carefully constructed image of the Church of Peace.[42]

Conclusions

The meaning of suffering in the sources is therefore complex. Hardships could be a punishment, test, or manifestation of divine affection, as God tried those that he loved in order to test the strength of their faith. Crusaders found it difficult to perceive which of these reasons applied in their individual cases, yet bad planning and other human factors were rarely blamed for suffering. Crusaders were not able to avoid all sin, but they tended to prefer as small a sin as the situation allowed.[43]

The sources present violence as a necessary means of relieving suffering. The state of peace was to be achieved by painful sacrifice. In practice, causing pain was followed by relieved joy. Indeed, the violence presented in the sources is a necessary contrast to peace and can thus be reduced to complementary anti-war. Joy and death as well as punishment and suffering appear in the sources in complementary pairs. A balance could not be found between the given extremes, but one followed the other on a continuum.

Proving their faith required from the crusaders not only personal suffering, but also causing misery to others. The key concepts for earning one's salvation were obedience and submission. Crusaders were saved by means of violence done to others only because it was God's will, and because any obscure reference to the will of God was sufficient. God's reasons for ordaining such violence were not to be understood by the human mind. In this way, violence remained linked with mystery. The insistence on the incomprehensible therefore explains the justification of practical violence. God could not be understood, only blindly obeyed.

The crusaders could not know that they were beginning a new era in history. For them, the crusade was not only a new, but the one and only way to salvation, in so far as salvation was the only means of staying alive. The Franks were the chosen people, who had an inexorable destiny.

One of the strongest myths associated with the First Crusade is the barbarisation of violence detached from the common Western framework of war. It is a fact that the crusaders used cruel violence to break their enemy. All the same, this has been a typical feature of warfare throughout history. Claiming that the fight was holy sanctified the means used, but did not change them. Surrender and death were the conventional options for the weaker side, and this also held true in religious combat. It is important to note that the commonly observed practices of medieval warfare were also followed by the early crusaders.[44]

The moral identity of the crusaders was based on the operational models given them from above, as well as the necessity of observing these models within the limits of the given physical and mental resources. No one could have spared the enemies of God without endangering his own life, both earthly and eternal. Tancred may have been furious when he saw the people protected by his banner were being slaughtered, but he could not raise his hand against the army of God.

> And when the Lord your God gives your enemies over to you and you defeat them; then you must utterly destroy them; you shall make no covenant with them, and show no mercy to them...And you shall destroy all the peoples that the Lord your God will give over to you, your eye shall not pity them.[45]

NOTES

1 'At nostri tantum patiebantur, dum priores de Turcis posterioribus infarcirentur.' Raymond of Aguilers, p. 247. As regards other primary sources for the First Crusade, we use the anonymous *Gesta Francorum* and the chronicle of Fulcher of Chartres. These three chroniclers participated personally in the crusade. In addition, the letters of Stephen of Blois and Bohemond of Taranto and other leaders of the crusade will be exploited. Concerning the crusade sermon of Clermont, Baldric of Dol, Robert of Rheims and potentially also Guibert of Nogent represent eyewitnesses of the event.

2 France 1999, p. 187.

3 France 1999, pp. 227–228.

4 *Gesta Francorum*, p. 92; Raymond of Aguilers, p. 300; Fulcher of Chartres, pp. 305–306.

5 'Instituit nostro tempore praelia sancta Deus, ut ordo equestris et vulgus oberrans, qui vetustae paganitatis exemplo in mutua versabantur caedes, novum repperirent salutis promerendae genus.' Guibert of Nogent, p. 124.

6 France 1999, p. 205.

7 Pranger 1994, p. 18.

8 *Gesta Francorum*, p. 1.

9 Fulcher of Chartres, p. 229; *Gesta Francorum*, p. 90.

10 Erdmann 1935, p. 13.

11 Raymond of Aguilers, pp. 245, 296; *Gesta Francorum*, p. 90.

12 Raymond of Aguilers, pp. 245, 296; *Gesta Francorum*, p. 90.

13 Matthew 10:37–38. 'Qui non bajulat crucem suam et venit post me, non est me dignus.' Robert of Rheims, pp. 730, 850; 'Si quis vult post me venire abneget semetipsum et tolla crucem suam et sequatur me.' *Gesta Francorum*, p. 1; Fulcher of Chartres, pp. 115–116; Baldric of Doll, p. 16.

14 Coleman & Elsner 1995, p. 8; Sumption 1975, p. 49.

15 According to Robert of Rheims and Baldric of Dol, Pope Urban II was exploiting the idea of Jerusalem as an earthly paradise in the sermon in Clermont; 'Iherusalem umbilicus est terrae...quasi alter Paradisus deliciarum.' Robert of Rheims, p. 729; 'Filii Israel ab Aegyptiis educti, qui, Rubro Mari transito, vos praefiguraverunt, terram illam armis suis, Jesu duce, sibi vindicaverunt; Jebuseos et alios convenas inde expulerunt; et instar Jerusalem coelestis, Jerusalem terrenam incoluerunt.' Baldric of Dol, p. 14.

16 'Pulchrum sit vobis mori in illa civitate pro Christo, in qua Christus pro vobis mortuus est.' Baldric of Dol, p. 14.

17 William of Tyre I, p. 15; Guibert of Nogent, p. 112.

18 Flori 1992, p. 207.

19 'Jerusalem...multotiens a tyrannis hostibus obsessant...Babilonico admirabili tempoere diutino tributaria, que superba cervicositate a Christo suo deviaverat.' Baldric of Dol, p. 11.

20 Van Oort 1991, pp. 118–119.

21 'Paeien unt tort e chrestiens unt dreit.' *Chanson de Roland* LXXIX, p. 1015.

22 In his letter to Flanderians in December 1095, Pope Urban II even writes about 'Barbaric rabies' referring to Muslims. Robert of Rheims, pp. 727–728, speaks of 'immundis gentibus' and 'gens prorsus a Deo aliena', while Guibert of Nogent, p. 114, refers to Antichrist. Baldric of Dol, p. 14, quotes Psalm 79.

23 Ps 79:1–3.

24 Riley-Smith 1997.

25 *Gesta Francorum*, p. 70.

26 *Gesta Francorum*, pp. 42, 80; Robert of Rheims, p. 288; Stephen of Blois in EC X, p. 151.

27 *Chanson d'Antioche* CLXXV, pp. 4115–4118, CCCLIII, pp. 8921–8931.

28 'Por Deu remenbre vos de lui qui tos nos fist ... Que Crestiien por lui la sainte crois presist, et qu'il l'alast vengier del linage Andecrist.' *Chanson d'Antioche* IV, pp. 85, 98–99. 'Raimundus comes de Sancto Egidio, et doctissimus Boamundus, duxque

Godefridus, et alii plures,in Hermeniorum intraverunt terram, sitientes atque aestuantes Turcorum sanguinem.' *Gesta Francorum*, pp. 25, 17. 'Qualiter leo perpessus famem per tres aut quatuor dies, qui exiens a suis cavernis, rugiens ac sitiens sanguinem pecum.' Op. cit. p. 37 on Duke Bohemond.

29 'O Deus uerus, trinus et unus, qua mobre haec fieri permisti ? Cur populum sequentem te in manibus inimicorum incidere permisti et uiam tui itineris tuique Sepulchri liberare uolentes tam cito dimisti … et unus ex nobis non audebi ulterius inuocare nomen tuum… Et fuit hic sermo ualde mestissimus in tota militia, ita ut nullus illorum siue episcopus siue abbas, seu clericus seu laicus, auderet inuocare Christi nomen per plures dies.' *Gesta Francorum*, p. 64. Robert of Rheims, pp. 816–817.

30 *Gesta Francorum*, pp. 90–92.

31 'Numquid nos soli totum mundum expugnabimus? Et habitatores mundi omnes interficiemus?' Raymond of Aguilers, p. 280.

32 *Gesta Francorum*, p. 92; Baldric of Doll, pp. 102–103.

33 'Peregrini, persequebantur et occidebant Saracenos usque ad Templum Salomonis. In quo congregati dederunt nostris maximum bellum per totum diem, ita ut sanguis illorum per totum templum flueret.' *Gesta Francorum*, p. 91.

34 'In porticu Salomonis equittabatur in sanguine usque ad genua, et usque ad frenos equorum.' Raymond of Aguilers, p. 300.

35 'Nunc vero purgati estis, Deoque per omnia reconciliati.' Robert of Rheims, p. 829; 'Occidit omnes Saracenos et Saracenas, maiores et minores', *Gesta Francorum*, p. 75; 'Quid narrabo? Nullus ex eis vitae est reservatus. Sed neque feminis neque parvulis eorum pepercerunt', Fulcher of Chartres, p. 301.

36 Goitein 1952.

37 'Hanc paupertatem et miseriam pro nostris delictis concessit nos habere Deus.' *Gesta Francorum*, p. 34.

38 Smail 1954/1967, pp. 12–13; France 1999, p. 160.

39 Riley-Smith 1984.

40 *Gesta Francorum*, pp. 7, 47; Fulcher of Chartres, p. 233; Raymond of Aguilers, p. 258; 'Sic superati sunt inimici nostri virtute Dei et Sancti Sepulchri,' *Gesta Francorum*, p. 41; 'Deus autem pugnavit pro nobis suis fidelibus contra eos,' Count Stephen of Blois to Countess Adela in EC X, p. 151; 'Dei ordinatione cum armis Iherusalem peregrinati sunt,' Fulcher of Chartres, p. 116; 'Nec mora, adest Dominus, fortis et potens in praelio; protexit filios, prostravit inimicos,' Raymond of Aguilers, p. 247.

41 'Omnes haereses…tua auctoritate et nostra uirtute eradices et destruas…at que Christianum nomen super omne nomen exaltatum facias…totus mundus tibi oboediens erit.' Bohemond of Tarant, Raymond, Count of St Gilles and Toulouse, Godfrey de Bouillon, Duke of Lower Lorraine, Robert, Duke of Normandy, Robert, Count of Flanders and Eustace, Count of Boulogne to Pope Urban II in EC XVI, p. 165.

42 Urban's predecessor, Pope Gregory VII, had been sharply criticised for his military interests. Apparently Urban's policy was to avoid such accusations as far as possible.

43 E.g. 'Horrendum est fratres, horrendum est, vos in Christianos rapacem manum extendere: minus malum est in Sarracenos gladium vibrare.' Baldric of Dol, p. 15.

44 France 1999, pp. 227–228.

45 Deut. 7:2, 16.

BIBLIOGRAPHY

Sources

Anonymous*, Gesta Francorum et aliorum Hierosolimitanorum*. R. Hill (ed.), London 1962.

Baldric of Dol, *Historia Jerosolimitana*. Recueil des Historiens des Croisades, Historiens Occidentaux, vol. IV. Paris 1879.

La chanson de Roland. J. Dufournet (ed.), Paris 1993.

La chanson d'Antioche. S. Duparc-Quioc (ed.), Paris 1976.

Epistulae et chartae ad historiam primi belli spectantes. H. Hagenmeyer (ed.), Innsbruck 1901.

Fulcher of Chartres, *Historia Hierosolymitana.* H. Hagenmeyer (ed.), Heidelberg 1913.

Guibert of Nogent, *Dei gesta per Francos.* Corpus Christianorum, Continuatio Mediaevalis CXXVII. A. R. Huygens (ed.), Turnhout 1996.

Raymond of Aguilers, *Historia Francorum qui ceperunt Iherusalem.* Recueil des Historiens des Croisades, Historiens Occidentaux, vol. III. Paris 1866.

Robert of Rheims, *Historia Iherosolimitana.* Recueil des Historiens des Croisades, Historiens Occidentaux, vol. III. Paris 1866.

William of Tyre, *Willelmi Tyrensi archiepiscopi Chronicon.* Corpus Christianorum, Continuatio Medievalis LXIII–LXIIIA. R. B. C. Huygens (ed.), Turnhout 1986.

Literature

S. Coleman & J. Elsner 1995, *Pilgrimage: Past and Present. Sacred Travel and Sacred Space in World Religions.* London.

C. Erdmann 1935, *Die Entstehung des Kreuzzugsgedankens.* Stuttgart.

J. Flori 1992, *La première croisade. L'Occident chrétien contre l'islam.* Brussels.

J. France 1999, *Western Warfare in the Age of the Crusades, 1000–1300.* London.

S. Goitein 1952, 'Contemporary Letters on the Capture of Jerusalem by the Crusaders', *The Journal of Jewish Studies* 3, pp. 162–177.

J. van Oort 1991, *Jerusalem and Babylon. A study into Augustine's City of God and the sources of his Doctrine of the Two Cities.* Leiden.

M. Pranger 1994, *Bernhard of Clairvaux and the Shape of Monastic Thought.* Leiden.

J. Riley-Smith 1984, 'The First Crusade and the Persecution of Jews', *Studies in Church History* 21, pp. 51–72.

J. Riley-Smith 1997, 'The Idea of Crusading in the Charters of Early Crusaders, 1095–1102', in Actes du Colloque Universitaire International de Clermont-Ferrand, 23–25 June 1995. *Le concile de Clermont de 1095 et l'appel à la croisade.* Rome.

R. C. Smail 1954/1967, *Crusading Warfare (1097–1193).* Cambridge.

J. Sumption 1975, *Pilgrimage. An Image of Mediaeval Religion.* London.

BJØRN BANDLIEN

A New Norse Knighthood?

The Impact of the Templars in Late Twelfth-century Norway

To medieval men there was a certain tension between the virtues of the saints and of the glory of warfare. The symbols of masculinity, the sword, the horse, clothing, sexual control over women, many sons, etc., flourished among the warriors. Among clerics and in monasteries symbols of masculinity had to be obtained in other ways, symbols that were not always recognised by the laity.

This is not to say that kings and aristocrats detested ascetic ideals in the Early Middle Ages. On the contrary, Anthony selling his possessions and going into the Egyptian desert in c. 270, and Martin of Tours laying his weapons before the Emperor Julian in 362, paved the way for those men of the laity who wanted to live closer to God by renouncing women and excessive consumption, and avoiding bloodshed. Although such men tended to gather together in separate communities, several sources indicate that the worlds of the monastery and the warrior band were not mutually exclusive in the Early Middle Ages. Young men could be brought up to a career in the Church hierarchy, but chose or were forced to change the course of their lives. To combine ideals of humility and chastity with an aristocratic life style and warfare was, however, not easy. To some men these conflicting ideals could create critical identity problems.[1]

An extraordinarily attempt to combine aristocratic and monastic norms was the Order of the Temple, founded c. 1119. From this time on, *miles Christi* was no longer a term exclusively attributed to those who were fighting the spiritual war against demons, but rather to those who fought with physical weapons for Christianity.[2] The Templars were a 'new kind of knighthood' (*nova militia*), as Bernard of Clairvaux (c. 1090–1153) put it. *The Rule of the Templars* presents the Order as a revitalisation of a knighthood in error (§ 2), and stresses in monastic terms that the knights should '...despise the deceitful world in perpetual love of God, and scorn the temptations of your body' (§ 9).[3] Several paragraphs restricted the uses of robes (§ 17–19), shoes (§ 22), weapons (§ 52–53) or hair (§ 22) as signs of distinction, and no aristocratic pleasures were permitted, including chess, hawking or hunting (§ 55). They had to forget their family name and their former deeds in secular life (§ 49). The knights should avoid the embraces of women by all means (§ 70–71). Further, they should not raise children or even be godfathers (§ 72). Thus, the Templars both lacked power over women and renounced descendants to carry on their name. They were, in short, stripped of the traditional symbols of social status and masculine identity.

Bernard of Clairvaux tried, however, to defend the masculine identity of the Templars in his *Praise of a New Knighthood* of c. 1130. Part of his strategy was to ridicule the secular knighthood by stating how their tender hands and long hair made them look like women. Their expensive clothing and the adornment of bridles and spurs were the trappings of the weaker sex (II.3). The Templars on the other hand fought a double fight, both against heathens and demons, thus remaining strong and quick, rather than showy and effeminate.[4] He continued:

> They are both gentler than lambs and fiercer than lions, in such a wonderful and peculiar way that I am very nearly incapable of deciding what I think they should rather be called, monks or knights, unless I should perhaps more appropriately name them both, since they apparently lack neither, neither the monk's gentle disposition nor the knights' fierce strength.[5]

Did this new (and rather utopian) vision of the knight, fighting for God rather than for his own name and controlling his lust rather than women, have any impact on Norwegian warriors? I will focus on the twelfth century, especially the time of Sverre, king of Norway from 1179 to 1202.

The idea of going on crusade was picked up by Norwegians fairly early. The travels of Sigurd Jerusalem-farer (reigned 1103–1130) in the first decade of the twelfth century was one of the most successful of the Scandinavian expeditions to the Holy Land, becoming famous throughout Europe, but there are few signs that the image of the Templars had any deep impact in Norway in the first half of the twelfth century. Sigurd himself disputed with the bishop of Bergen because he wanted to marry another woman than his first wife. Both Sigurd and his successors enjoyed the company of women, and the civil wars of Norway in the twelfth century were intensified because of many pretenders born out of wedlock. Although Sigurd's crusade to Jerusalem may also have been motivated by religious intentions, the sagas indicate that the successful expedition was used back home to gain honour in a more traditional manner.[6]

In my view, this reflects a certain continuity of traditional values among aristocrats and warriors in Norway. If we look at what the sources of the king's retinue tell us about the warrior ethos in the eleventh century, especially the skaldic poems composed during the wars of Magnus the Good (1035–1047) and Harald the Hardruler (1046–1066) against the Danes, two themes of special interest emerge. Both have to do with women: first, the Norwegian warriors wanted to control Danish women. To do as they wished with their enemies' wives and daughters was considered a sign of superiority. Second, the skalds repeatedly addressed the women back home when they did their brave deeds in Denmark. Of course, the women were not actually there to watch, but the obsession with women when recounting battles probably reflects the skalds' background in a household society where mothers, wives and mistresses valued their deeds according to the standards of honour. To the extent that they were fighting for a greater cause than their own honour, they were fighting as members of their king's household against members of another king's household, just as they would have fought for their own household against a neighbour back home.[7]

If we take a look at the second part of the twelfth century, we find a grow-ing awareness of a *nova militia* in Scandinavia, especially in Denmark. Most interesting, in this context is the brotherhood founded in 1151 by the aristocrat Vedeman. The idea was to protect Roskilde from the hea-thens in the east. As Janus Møller Jensen has convincingly argued, this organization was inspired by the ideology of the Crusades. Excessive food and drink was banned, the war was explicitly directed towards the heathens, they confessed and received the Eucharist before battles, and they were all equals while in session.[8]

This brotherhood had no equivalent in Norway, but there is an interest-ing saga dating from the end of the century showing a version of such a community. This is the *Saga of the Jomsvikings*, telling the story of a band of warriors living in today's Poland in the tenth century.[9] The *jomsvikings* are presented as a brotherhood consisting of men between 18 and 50 years old, among whom family bonds were abolished and each man should only avenge another *jomsviking*.[10] They were under strict leadership of the master-like Palnatoke, and all possessions they won in battle should be shared equally. Women were strictly forbidden in this masculine society. Alas, they drank and ate a bit too much, promising during a feast to help the Danish king against the Norwegian earl, Haa-kon. Despite their earlier success they were beaten by Haakon and some even ran away from the battle – wanting rather to lie in their mistresses' arms according to skaldic poems. Only Vagn Akason, the bravest of the *jomsvikings*, had any personal success in the battle. He was given his freedom because of his courage, and even managed to get the daughter of one of the Norwegian aristocrats in marriage.[11]

I think we should read the story of the heathen *jomsvikings* with Vede-man and the idea of the new knighthood in mind. The parallels between Palnatoke's warriors and the Templars must have been very clear at the end of the twelfth century. The *jomsvikings* are described as a kind of Noble Heathen – a character very frequently found in Old Norse litera-ture. These noble heathens had it all, except for the true insight that only Christianity could give. In a similar way, the heroic *jomsvikings* were on the right track in establishing a masculine and egalitarian community, but they lacked the right cause to fight for and the strength of mind and moderation in drinking that the *miles Christi* was supposed to have.

On the other hand, Vagn's personal success in marrying the daughter of his enemy reflects domestic values – where women were valued as prizes gained in battle.[12] This twist in the *Saga of the Jomsvikings* neatly reflects the meeting between new and old ideals of the warrior in the last quarter of the twelfth century, the time when Sverre Sigurdsson won, and then with great difficulty defended, the Norwegian throne.

One of the most important moments in *Sverris saga*, and indeed in Sverre's life, was the battle of Fimreite in 1184,[13] in which he managed to kill King Magnus Erlingsson and become sole ruler in Norway. After the battle, Sverre appealed to a traditional warrior ideology in giving the estates and the widows of the defeated magnates to his men. The logic behind this action was the same as in the skaldic poems of the eleventh century and in the story of Vagn Akason's success. To Sverre's warriors, relatively poor and at this point certainly socially dead without their successful leader, the wealth and positions of their enemies were important enough, but the conquest of their women was also a significant symbol of their victory.

Sverre must have consented to this practice of traditional warrior ideals. On being established as king, however, he tried to introduce a new ethic to his retinue. Of course, Sverre had from the start been a most extraordinary pretender through the fact the he grew up as the stepson of a bishop and had become a priest. Thus he was not only an innovative and forceful gang leader, but was also well informed concerning new ideological and political ideas. He used this knowledge both to win loyalty from his retainers and to defame his opponents as morally weak. In doing so, he seems to have tried to establish an independent religious rhetoric of royal authority, independent of the support of the Church.

One of the important elements in the saga's portrayal of Sverre is his almost ascetic virtues. As against both earlier Norwegian kings and his enemies, he never drank so much that he lost control over himself,[14] and he swore on his deathbed that he knew of no other son alive besides Håkon.[15] His moderation in drink was, as Sverre Bagge has pointed out, the political introduction of a more authoritarian monarchy; '...stressing respect and obedience to the king rather than the egalitarian solidarity of the drinking parties.'[16] The saga also values this as a sign of self-control and firmness, however, and indicates that Sverre was morally and military superior to his enemies.[17] Sverre is also the first Norwegian king to claim to be monogamous and was even proud of his lack of mistresses; a unique virtue among twelfth-century kings in Norway.[18] The motivation for this claim may have been partly political, trying to stop the internal struggles and secure his son's succession, and partly based on traditional warrior ethos, since he and his men should not be weakened by women.[19] It also fits into the rhetorical pattern of the saga, however, in portraying the king as even more virtuous than the bishops and clerics of Norway, and thus picturing himself as the real defender of Christian morality.[20] In his visions, he was called by St Olaf[21] and anointed by Samuel himself (ch. 10). He was helped by God and Mary to defeat those who fought an 'unjust war' (*rangliga vandrædi*) against him.[22] In his gratitude, he always let his warriors go to confession before battles, showed mercy to those of his enemies who would receive it after battle, and offered forgiveness and a Christian funeral to those who had died.[23]

This ideal was presented to his retainers through Sverre's speech against drunkenness in 1186 after several internal disputes and battles among his followers. To Sverre, this was a threat to his image as a virtuous king, defending his realm against those who broke the peace. But warriors' disputes provoked by drinking, often about money and women, was increasingly seen as a problem in Norway. Similar episodes occurred in the Orkneys when Norwegian warriors had to stay through the winter on their journey to the Holy Land in the early 1150s, and some decades later when Danish crusaders drank too much in Norwegian towns and seduced women. Such problems are explicitly treated in Sverre's speech. He urged his men to be moderate in drinking, because it first led man into poverty; next to oblivion; then to lust for what is wrong, especially theft and seducing women; further, to stir up violence without a cause, to ruin his health, make the body weak, and in the end lose his soul by yearning for filthy deeds and forgetting God. He then echoes Bernard's praise of the Templars: 'Warriors should be like lambs in peacetime and fierce as lions in war.'[24] According to William of Newburgh, an English clerk writing in the 1190s, this was also inscribed on Sverre's (now lost) seal: *Suerus rex Magnus, ferus ut leo, mitis ut agnus.*[25]

Bernard of Clairvaux would hardly have recognised the birchlegs as a *nova militia*, and Sverre never intended to change his warriors into knights in the way that Bernard dreamed of. Continuous struggles in the 1190s certainly made Sverre's retinue more useful as lions than lambs. The saga is blood-thirsty, sometimes in the extreme when even children are killed by Sverre's men, and dominated as much by the logic of revenge for the killings of his family as with just war. To Sverre, the idea of the New Knighthood was useful in making his warriors more disciplined, obedient and faithful off the battlefield. Furthermore, it probably helped him justify the combination of being ordained a priest while still being a fighting king. He was like the heroic Vikings of Jomsborg, trying to create a masculine sphere to harden his men, but in addition fighting for the just and divine cause like David against Saul. Sverre's moderation in drinking and eating, his bravery facing battles, his devotion to Mary, as well as his sexual self-control, are used in the saga as signs of the sincerity and right intention in warfare.

There are no clear signs that Sverre succeeded in making his own warriors more moderate, even though there are many indications that the Norwegian aristocracy knew the idea of Holy War.[26] It may have been just because the ideals of the *bellum iustum* and *nova militia* were known but still only partially followed in Norway that Sverre and the saga writer used them in working out the rhetoric of his God-given royal authority. He tried to represent something new; if not the *nova militia* of Bernard, at least a *nova norroena militia*.

Still, we do see a glimpse of a more legitimate descendant of Bernard's monkish warrior on Norwegian soil. A brief passage in *Sverris saga* mentions another pretender to the Norwegian throne, Thorleif Breiskjegg. Thorleif and his men represented a kind of warrior that was quite different from Sverre and the birchlegs:

They came to Viken and behaved calmly. They bought the food they needed. Thorleif Breiskjegg had been a monk. There was little strength in his gang. They soon ran short of money, and some of them stole since it was forbidden to them to raid. Many people said that they had heard that Thorleif was a man of such wisdom that nothing surprised him, and that he lived so purely that he seemed to live by monastic rules rather than in the manner of a layman. It was also said that he spoke so well that he could speak in such a manner that no man could get angry with him when he spoke.[27]

In Thorleif we sense a union between the gang leader and the ascetic monk, but as a rival to the throne he was soon put to death. It did not help much that some claimed Thorleif was a saint; he simply did not fit into the plan of the king elected by God and St Olaf. As the saga rather contemptuously tells us at the time he was killed: '[H]is speech for sure did not make his life saveable this time.' The competition for the Norwegian throne was not a game for modest monks, a lesson well learned by the priest and gang leader Sverre.

NOTES

1   See esp. Nelson 1999. She mentions Charles III (c. 839–888), Alfred the Great (reign 871–899) and Gerald of Aurillac (c. 855–909) as examples of rulers or aristocrats who tried uneasily to live as both good Christians and leaders of war bands. This list could easily be extended for instance, with Sigeberht, King of East Anglia, and Oswald, King of Northumbria.

2   On the development on the concept of *militia Christi* from Paul to Constantine, see von Harnack 1981, pp. 27–64. The early Fathers of the Church were sceptical about the bloodshed of the imperial army, but the lives of the military saints up to AD 313 show that there were Christians in the imperial army, and that their problem was less the violence than sacrificing to the gods; see Swift 1983, pp. 71–79 and Helgeland et al. 1985, pp. 48–66. After Constantine, Christians who were not clerics could and should fight for the right causes, but to early medieval warriors the military saints were not models of conduct as much as regional protectors in war; see Holdsworth 1996. Gerald of Aurillac (c. 855–909) is, to my knowledge, the first non-royal saint who *remains* a layperson and is praised for his Christian way of warfare. He did not want to go to war, but Odo of Cluny (c. 878–942) tells us that '...when the unavoidable necessity of fighting lay on him, he commanded his men in imperious tones to fight with the backs of their swords and with their spears reversed...he triumphed by a new kind of fighting that was mingled with piety.' (*De vita Sancti Geraldi*, I.8; transl. from Noble & Head (ed.) 1995, p. 302). More aggressive developments of the concept of the soldier of Christ appeared in the eleventh century with Gregory VII (Pope 1073–1085) saying that all laymen were the vassals of St Peter and that aristocrats should fight with material weapons as a sign of piety instead of becoming monks; see Erdmann 1936, pp. 185–211; Robinson 1973; Cowdrey 1997.

3   The Rule of the Templars clearly echoes the Benedictine Rule, as well as being influenced by the Cistercian call for poverty, simplicity, retirement and purity; see Bulst-Thiele 1992, p. 59.

4   Bernard's praise of the *nova militia* and his condemnation of *malitia* – the luxurious knights – should be read in the context of the Church's growing distinction between 'good' and 'bad' knights in the eleventh century; see Grabois 1992. Clerics such as Anselm of Canterbury, Orderic Vitalis and William of Malmesbury were especially angry at the courtiers of King William II Rufus (1087–1099), accusing them of effeminacy and even sodomy and threatening them with exclusion from sermons and

Christian burial if they did not cut their hair and stop wearing pointed shoes. These should not be taken as signs, as some have done, of a homosexual court culture, but rather as a token of some clerics' self-imposed educational role among the courtiers; see Barlow 1984, pp. 101–110; Bartlett 1994, pp. 50–52; Frantzen 1998, pp. 235–247; Bennett 1999. To William's warriors, however, long hair probably meant youth and strength, as it certainly did in the Early Middle Ages, rather than effeminacy; see Bartlett 1994, pp. 58–59. We should rather take the rhetoric Bernard used as a sign of a struggle about who was manly enough to rule; the 'bad' knights of the traditional, rather independent type, or the new, 'good' knighthood in control of themselves and loyal to St Peter; see McNamara 1994, pp. 15–21.

5 *Praise of the Templars* IV.8; transl. from Carlson 1988, p. 166.

6 Recent evaluation of this crusade can be found in Doxey 1996 and Møller Jensen 2000, pp. 303–304.

7 Bandlien 2001, pp. 41–48 with references.

8 Møller Jensen 2000, pp. 314–317; see Jaeger 1985, pp. 185–190 on Saxo's fierce criticism of German courtiers as against the ideal picture he gives of Vedeman's Lag.

9 This saga was popular in the decades around 1200. It exists in five different versions, as well as being incorporated in *Fagrskinna*, Snorri Sturluson's *Heimskringla*, and Saxo's *Gesta Danorum*. On the relationship between the versions, see Megaard 2000a.

10 *Jómsvikinga saga*, ch. 14.

11 *Jómsvikinga saga*, ch. 35–38.

12 On this ideal, see Bandlien 2001, pp. 61–64. On Vagn Akason and his connections with the Danish aristocracy in the twelfth century, see Megaard 2000b. Saxo never mentioned Vagn, but replaces his role in the battle with a certain Karlsevne. This departure from the saga versions may perhaps be explained by Vagn's position as an ancestor of the family of Trund which many leading Danes belonged to in the later twelfth century.

13 For a short and concise overview of the questions about date and (multiple) authorship of the saga, see Bagge 1996, pp. 15–19. All translations from the saga are my own.

14 *Sverris saga*, ch. 181.

15 *Sverris saga*, ch. 180.

16 See Bagge 1996, pp. 73–74 on the political significance of drinking fellowship and segregation. Sverre's exceptional moderation in drinking is also evident in *Sverris saga*, ch. 7.

17 This is especially clear when the saga writer gives us glimpses of Erling Skakki's leadership before the battle of Kalvskinnet in 1179. He thought that Sverre's men were far away and that his men could sleep safe that night. But one of Erling's men asked him to reconsider: '...some say, my Lord, that you give more attention to getting drunk on ale and wine than giving your men firm orders to rely on.' *Sverris saga*, ch. 34. Erling got angry and said that he was going to stand guard that night himself, if anyone thought him fit to do it. But then he went straight to bed, undressed himself and slept tight until he was attacked by the birchlegs. His son Magnus, who elsewhere in the saga is presented in rather favourable terms, is a great drinker and womaniser, and his men are often weakened because of heavy drinking; see esp. *Sverris saga*, ch. 98, but also ch. 31; 33; 64; 70; 76.

18 Sverre, however, had several children before he married Margret, the daughter of king Erik of Sweden, in 1184. He was accused of bigamy by some Norwegian priests. *Sverris saga*, ch. 122. This is something that indicates that he had had a wife or a concubine in the Faroes. After all, he was twenty-five years old before he went to Norway, and being a priest was no hindrance to marriage in the middle of the twelfth century.

19 Women play a suspiciously marginal role in this saga; see Orning 1997; Bandlien 2001, p. 49. Sverre himself is never pictured as close even to his wife Margret, although he visits his sister a couple of times – mainly to be recognised as her half brother. Women, even Margret, seem to weaken the morale of the warriors and should

be excluded from their sphere, an attitude quite similar to the *jomsvikings'* fear of women. See esp. *Sverris saga*, ch. 47, 145, 160.

20 This theme is also elaborated in *A Speech against the Bishops*, written by a cleric close to Sverre around 1200, defending him against the 'lies' that the bishops told the pope, leading to his excommunication. In *A Speech*, the bishops are said to be immoderate and greedy, and the priests are accused of many luxurious sins; see *En tale mot biskopene*, p. 3. See also Paasche 1915, p. 207 (although he is a bit polemical against Erling) and Bandlien 2001, pp. 52–55, 160–161.

21 *Sverris saga*, ch. 5.

22 *Sverris saga*, ch. 38.

23 Sverre giving mercy (*grid*), forgiveness, or a Christian funeral to men fighting against him: *Sverris saga*, ch. 49, 77, 94, 169, 179. The last episode is most interesting; Sverre managed, after a long siege, to make the *baglar* surrender at Tunsberg in 1202. Despite the baglar's earlier killings of birchlegs, and despite the *níð* directed at Sverre himself, he decides to forgive them: '...now I want to forgive them for God's sake, and in return I hope for forgiveness from Him for all I have done against Him. You [the birchlegs] have not any less soul than I have, and you should remember that. And no man will call you soft men because of that [your forgiveness].' Here the struggle over the interpretation of what was masculine behaviour is apparent as in Britain around 1100. Sverre's adversaries, especially Erling and Magnus, are depicted as much more reluctant to give *grið* or a Christian funeral to fallen enemies (*Sverris saga*, ch. 26, 52, 69, 86, 180), a sign of immoral, uncontrolled and thus unmasculine behaviour. See also Vik 1998, pp. 79–85 on Sverre as God's friend: Sverre forgives his enemies as long as God supports him in battles.

24 *Sverris saga*, ch. 104.

25 William of Newburgh III 6, p. 232. The stamp of a seal with the inscription *verus testis ego, nuntia vera tego* ('true witness I am, true commandments I cover') has been found in Tønsberg. Odd Fjordholm (1973) noted that *ferus* is a possible pun on *verus*, and that both may allude to *Sverus*. He suggested that William of Newburgh cited the obverse of the seal found in Tønsberg.

26 This knowledge existed in Norway in some form or another since about 1100. Several Norwegians and Icelanders went to the Holy Land in the twelfth century, Sverre thought of it himself (*Sverris saga*, ch. 9) and he later allowed a man to take sons of peasants and merchants to Byzantium with him (*Sverris saga*, ch. 127, 129). He also built a castle called Sion in Nidaros. His opponent, Erling Skakki, had been to the Holy Land himself in the early 1150s. Erling made an alliance with Øystein Erlendsson, the Archbishop of Nidaros, in the 1160s, and he probably considered his fight against Sverre as a just war. Øystein had promised him and his men martyrdom if they died in battle against Sverre (*Sverris saga*, ch. 38). After all, Sverre was repeatedly called the 'Devil's priest' by his opponents. Furthermore, the Hospitallers was probably established at Varna by the 1170s or 1180s, perhaps instigated by Erling himself; cf. Gunnes 1997, pp. 35–38. The church of St Olaf in Tønsberg, a circular church on the model of the Holy Sepulchre in Jerusalem, and the biggest of this kind in the Nordic countries, was probably built in the 1160s or 1170s; see Lunde 1993. In sum, Erling may have been influenced of the ideology of just war, while Sverre exploited the rhetorical potential in being a friend and warrior of God.

27 *Sverris saga*, ch. 116.

BIBLIOGRAPHY

Sources

Bernard of Clairvaux, *Praise of a New Knighthood*. C. Greenia (transl.), Kalamazoo 1977.

En tale mot biskopene. A. Holtsmark (ed.), Oslo 1931.

Jomsvikinga saga. Ó. Halldórsson (ed.), Reykjavík 1969.

Odo of Cluny, *De vita Sancti Geraldi*. In *Soldiers of Christ: Saints and Saint's Lives from the Late Antiquity to the Early Middle Ages*, T. F. X. Noble and T. Head (transl.), University Park 1995.

The Rule of the Templars: The French Text of the Rule of the Order of the Knights Templar. J. M. Upton-Ward (transl.), Woodbridge 1992.

Sverris saga etter Cod. AM 327 4°. G. Indrebø (ed.), Kristiania 1920.

William of Newburgh, *Historia rerum Anglicarum*, R. Howlett (ed.), Rolls series 82. London 1884.

Literature

S. Bagge 1996, *From Gang Leader to the Lord's Anointed: Kingship in Sverris saga and Hákonar saga Hákonarsonar*. Odense.

B. Bandlien 2001, *Å finne den rette: Kjærlighet, individ og samfunn i norrøn middelalder*. Oslo.

F. Barlow 1984, *William Rufus*. London.

R. Bartlett 1994, 'Symbolic Meanings of Hair in the Middle Ages', *Transactions of the Royal Historical Society* 6th ser. 6, pp. 43–60.

M. Bennett 1999, 'Military Masculinity in England and Northern France c. 1050–1225', in D. M. Hadley (ed.), *Masculinity in Medieval Europe*. London, pp. 71–88.

M. L. Bulst-Thiele 1992, 'The Influence of St. Bernard of Clairvaux on the Formation of the Order of the Knights Templar', in M. Gervers (ed.), *The Second Crusade and the Cistercians*. New York, pp. 57–65.

D. Carlson 1988, 'Religious Writers and Church Councils on Chivalry', in H. Chickering & T. H. Seiler (ed.), *The Study of Chivalry: Resources and Approaches*. Kalamazoo, pp. 141–171.

H. E. J. Cowdrey 1997, 'Pope Gregory VII and the Bearing of Arms', in B. Z Kedar & J. Riley-Smith & R. Hiestand (ed.), *Montjoie: Studies in Crusade History in Honour of Hans Eberhard Mayer*. Aldershot, pp. 21–35.

G. B. Doxey 1996, 'Norwegian Crusaders and the Balearic Islands', *Scandinavian Studies* 68, pp. 139–160.

C. Erdmann 1936, *Die Entstehung des Kreuzzugsgedankens*. Stuttgart.

O. Fjordholm 1973, '"Sant vitne er jeg…": Seglstampen fra Tønsberg', *Historisk tidsskrift* 52, pp. 197–215.

A. J. Frantzen 1998, *Before the Closet. Same-Sex Love from Beowulf to Angels in America*. Chicago.

A. Grabois 1992, '*Militia* and *Malitia*: The Bernardine Vision of Chivalry', in M. Gervers (ed.), *The Second Crusade and the Cistercians*. New York, pp. 49–56.

E. Gunnes 1997, 'Varna kloster', *Collegium Medievale* 10, pp. 31–89.

A. von Harnack 1981, *Militia Christi: The Christian Religion and the Military in the First Three Centuries*. Philadelphia.

J. Helgeland & R. J. Daly & J. Patout Burns 1985, *Christians and the Military: The Early Experience*. Philadelphia.

C. Holdsworth 1996, '"An airier Aristocracy": The Saints at War', *Transactions of the Royal Historical Society* 6th ser. 6, pp. 103–122.

C. S. Jaeger 1985, *The Origins of Courtliness: Civilizing Trends and the Formation of Courtly Ideals, 939–1210*. Philadelphia.

Ø. Lunde 1993, 'Premonstratensernes kloster i Tunsberg – kirken og klosteranlegget', in J. E. G. Eriksson & K. Schei (ed.), *Seminaret 'Kloster og by' 11.–13. november 1992: omkring Olavsklosteret, premonstratenserordenen og klostervesenet i middelalderen.* Tønsberg, pp. 9–22.

J. McNamara 1994, 'The Herrenfrage: The Restructuring of the Gender System, 1050–1150', in C. A. Lees (ed.), *Medieval Masculinities: Regarding Men in the Middle Ages.* Minneapolis, pp. 3–29.

J. Megaard 2000a, 'Studier i Jómsvíkinga sagas stemma: Jómsvíkinga sagas fem redaksjoner sammenlignet med versjonene i Fagrskinna, Jómsvíkingadrápa, Heimskringla og Saxo', *Arkiv för nordisk filologi* 115, pp. 125–182.

J. Megaard 2000b, 'Vagn Åkesons vekst og fall', in G. Barnes & M. Clunies Ross (ed.), *Old Norse Myths, Literature and Society: Preprints of the 11th International Saga Conference.* Sydney, pp. 327–333.

J. Møller Jensen 2000, 'Danmark og den hellige krig. En undersøgelse af korstogsbevegelsens indflydelse på Danmark ca. 1070–1169', *Historisk Tidsskrift* 100, pp. 285–328.

J. L. Nelson 1999, 'Monks, Secular Men and Masculinity, c.900' in D. M. Hadley (ed.), *Masculinity in Medieval Europe.* London, pp. 121–142.

T. F. X. Noble & T. Head (ed.) 1995, *Soldiers of Christ: Saints and Saints' Lives from Late Antiquity and the Early Middle Ages.* University Park.

H. J. Orning 1997, 'Fra egging til degging? Kvinner i saga og samfunn i norsk høymiddelalder', *Middelalderforum* 2, pp. 36–48.

F. Paasche 1915, 'Sverre prest', *Edda* 3, pp. 197–212.

I. S. Robinson 1973, 'Gregory VII and the Soldiers of Christ', *History* 58, pp. 169–192.

L. J. Swift 1983, *The Early Fathers on War and Military Service.* Wilmington.

K. Vik 1998, *Forestillinger om Gud i Norge på 1100 og 1200 tallet*, unpublished graduate thesis. University of Bergen.

184

VIVIAN ETTING

Crusade and Pilgrimage
Different Ways to the City of God

> Truly that knight, whose soul is dressed in the armour of Faith just as his body is protected by the iron-coat of mail, shall be without fear and feel safe in all respects. Armed with both weapons, he shall fear neither the Devil nor any man.[1]

These words expressed by Bernard of Clairvaux shortly after the founding of the Order of the Knights Templars in 1128 give a good impression of the enthusiasm which characterises the period between the first and the second crusade.

Comprehension of the close connections between crusades, pilgrimages and the European policy of power is crucial to understanding medieval European history. This essay focuses on some of the most obvious examples of these connections in Danish history from the twelfth to the fifteenth centuries. In this period the kings were quite aware that an aggressive policy of power could be linked with the dissemination of the Christian faith to great advantage, and that close relations with the papacy were important to internal policy as well. However, it would be wrong to underestimate the importance of pilgrimage. Medieval society and culture was completely dominated by Christian ideals and symbolism, and the powerful men in medieval Denmark were convinced of their divine obligation to disseminate the faith using spiritual as well as temporal weapons.

During the Viking Age close contacts with the rest of Europe had been established, partly through plundering and partly through trade, but the structure of society itself had remained 'Nordic'. However, when King Harald Bluetooth (Blåtand) was baptised about 965 he started a dramatic change in society. During the next two hundred years a new pattern of life based on European cultural values and Christian belief transformed both the mental and the physical landscape. In this process the king himself played a central role as mediator, and the close connections between the European royal families were an important factor. The king was expected to maintain, exploit and develop these connections, and close contacts and travel were necessary to this end.

Traditional Danish history-writing during the last hundred years is marked by a tendency to regard medieval Denmark and the Nordic countries as rather closed societies which followed the general European development only to a certain degree. In my opinion this picture is wrong because it somehow reflects the nineteenth century's idealistic conception of a nation and its focus on secular history. Another reason for the lack of interest in the Scandinavian participation in the crusades is the sharp criticism of the religious motives and morality informing the crusades, as pointed out by Kurt Villads Jensen.[2] This does not promote understanding and analysis of medieval society, which was influenced by Christian idealism and the general European chivalric culture at all levels. The surviving medieval wall-paintings, altarpieces and sculpture clearly demonstrate that Denmark followed the European trend in the visual arts, in which the Christian knight is glorified. In what follows I will focus on some of the crusades and pilgrimages undertaken by Danish kings in order to show how these journeys were closely interwoven and linked with the European policy of power.[3] Five Danish kings will serve as examples: Erik Ejegod, who reigned from 1095 to 1103, Valdemar II (The victorious), 1202 to 1241, Valdemar IV (Atterdag), 1340 to 1375, Eric of Pomerania, who ruled the Nordic Union from 1397 to 1439, and Christian I, 1448 to 1481. At the same time I will try to illustrate how the ideas of crusade and pilgrimage are reflected in some of the works of art preserved in Denmark.

In 1095 the first crusade was proclaimed by Pope Urban II, who thereby started a new aggressive period in the Christian Church. From an account by the chronicler Albert of Aachen[4] (d. after 1120) we have clear evidence that Danish crusaders participated under the leadership of Prince Sven, son of King Sven Estridsen. Albert refers in detail to the death of the young prince in 1097 during a Turkish attack in Anatolia:

> After the siege and conquest of Nikæa, the son of the king of Denmark, by the name of Sven – a very noble and wonderful man – had been delayed, and the emperor of Constantinople had received him gracefully, whereupon he without interruption went through the whole of Asia Minor, where he heard about the victory of the Christians. He brought 1 500 warriors with him in order to help with the siege of Antioch.

However, the prince was betrayed by the Greeks, who disclosed the campaign to the Turks. Camping in a wood, they were attacked by the Turks, and the prince was killed by a shower of arrows, 'and with him all his followers suffered the same martyrdom by the hand of these godless butchers.' Albert also mentions the death of a certain noble lady called Florina, a daughter of the duke of Burgundy, who followed the company in the hope of marrying the prince. Even though the account of the Chronicler is strongly coloured by his Christian enthusiasm, there can be no doubt about the Danish participation in the crusade.

The Danish King Erik Ejegod went to Italy the next year, where the pope sanctified the canonisation of his brother, the murdered King Canute († 1086), and promised to honour his kingdom with its own archbishopric according to the famous Chronicler Saxo.[5] These decisions were most important achievements, and as a direct result the new archbishopric in Lund was established a few years later. In Erik's journey to Rome he followed the example of King Canute the Great (about 1000–1035) of Denmark, Norway and England, who had gone on pilgrimage to Rome in 1027, where he established a lodging-house for pilgrims from Denmark. Similar to this King, Erik established a lodging-house for pilgrims in Piacenza.

After the conquest of Jerusalem in 1099, the king decided to undertake a pilgrimage to the holy land in company with his queen, Bodil, their son, later King Erik Emune, and a number of noblemen. The main sources for their pilgrimage are Saxo and the Icelandic chronicle *Knytlinga Saga*, which both give quite detailed accounts of this famous journey.[6] The king and his company left Denmark in 1103, their route being briefly described by Saxo, who says that they 'went by sea to Russia, and then Eric travelled over land through this country and a large part of the East until he reached Byzantium.' Presumably they followed the old route of the Vikings along the Russian rivers. In Constantinople (Miklagard) they were welcomed by the Emperor Alexis. At the beginning the Emperor feared that his famous Nordic Varangian guard (Væringerne) would leave him and follow the Danish king but, according to Saxo, he was soon calmed. From Constantinople the pilgrims continued their journey by sea, but the King never reached the Holy land. He became seriously ill when he arrived in Cyprus and the sources relate that he died in the city of Paphos (Baffa) on 10th July 1103. His tomb, however, has never been found and there has been some discussion about the location of his burial place.[7] Queen Bodil continued to Jerusalem, but died on the Mount of Olives and was buried in the church of Our Lady.

About 1164 a convent of the Order of St John was founded in Antvorskov by King Valdemar the Great. This convent became the administrative centre of the Order in the province the 'Dacia', that is, Scandinavia. Thus a clerical order of crusaders was introduced into Denmark, and no doubt this must have been important in spreading the ideas behind the crusades. However the Order had no military functions in Denmark, and the competing Order of the Knights Templars was never established in Scandinavia.

After the fall of Jerusalem in 1187, a Danish crusade was called for by Esbern Snare, a member of the powerful *Hvide* lineage. He was brother of the archbishop Absalon and a close friend of the former King Valdemar I (1157–1182). An unknown contemporary chronicler mentions a meeting in Odense at which the new King Canute had assembled the most powerful men in the country. During the meeting a messenger arrived and related the sad news of the fall of Jerusalem:

> When the king and all those present heard about this, they burst into tears and lamentations; they all became silent and nobody was able to answer the messenger, overwhelmed as they were by this heavy grief.[8]

Finally Esbern Snare rose and delivered a fiery speech, calling upon all present to participate in a new crusade in order to free Jerusalem. He referred to the famous deeds of their ancestors and encouraged them to give up their petty disputes in order to join a greater battle. After this speech fifteen men swore that they would join the crusade, and it was decided to announce the news in all the churches and at the courts. However the fleet was not ready to leave until 1191, since first they had to go to Bergen in Norway to pick up about two hundred Norwegian crusaders. The fleet finally sailed to Friesland through a terrible storm, and continued its journey along the Rhine towards Venice. From here they sailed to the Holy land, arriving in Acre 1192 – almost five years after the fall of Jerusalem. However, the third crusade had ended without success, and King Richard the Lionheart had just signed a peace with Saladin on 7th September 1192 which allowed Christians to visit the holy places in Jerusalem. The Nordic crusaders had come too late. They visited the holy city as pilgrims, and after a short stay decided to return home 'because the peace of the treaty prevented them from fighting.' Unfortunately, these brave men were visited with many troubles on their way back, as some of the travellers went to Constantinople. The journey had been a failure, but the chronicler hid this harsh fact and hailed the journey as a success.

Today we have a tendency to regard medieval Denmark as a very remote province, which played a very limited role in the story of the crusades. As we see this is only true to a certain extent, and evidence of Nordic crusaders can be found in the Holy Land as well. In the church of the Nativity in Bethlehem there are two very interesting paintings, probably from the middle of the twelfth century. They depict two people, who the inscriptions identify with the Nordic saints King Canute the Holy and St Ulaf. The Danish King Canute (murdered 1086) is depicted on a beautiful Byzantine column on the north side of the church. Done in a mixture of Romanesque and Byzantine style this painting represents the oldest known picture of the saint, who was canonised in 1099. The inscription reads: SCS CHNVTUS REX DANORUM. In general we must conclude that the presence of two Nordic saints in this important place of worship indicates a Nordic influence of some importance. In this connection it should be emphasised that the son of the sanctified King Canute, called Charles the Danish of Flanders, was called upon to be crowned as king of Jerusalem in 1123, but rejected the offer.

The close connection between religious motives and European power politics is obvious to modern historians, but perhaps we have difficulty in understanding how medieval man perceived the world and how the will of God was to be fulfilled. To him there was no contradiction between a crusade and a pilgrimage. It was a natural desire to visit and conquer the holy places and spread the word of God both by preaching and the sword. And when these commendable aims could be combined with more worldly desires for power, it was even more interesting to participate in the great crusades. The eagerness and enthusiasm to participate in the crusades was based upon faith, combined with the Christian ideals of knighthood and the romance of chivalry. The legends of the Holy Grail, Perceval and King Arthur were already well-known among the common people about 1200. Frescoes in several medieval churches, such as the Romanesque church Skibet in Jutland, glorify these famous legends. Here a beautiful frieze in the choir shows a row of knights on horseback, and in one of the arcades the Holy Grail is depicted on an altar. In Hornslet church other scenes from the legend show the sick King Mondrian and a fierce battle in the holy war against the infidels.[9]

However, the crusades were not confined to the Holy Land. During the twelfth century the Danish kings became still more involved in the fight against the infidels in the Baltic, primarily the Slavic tribes on the southern coasts near the island of Rügen. Here their base Arkona was attacked several times by Valdemar I (the Great), and finally conquered in 1169. During the reign of Valdemar II (the Victorious) new crusades were launched to fight and convert the infidels in Estonia. In 1210 Pope Innocent III praised King Valdemar for his decision to take the sign of the cross and 'draw the sword of his royal power to subdue a wild and heathen nation.'[10] Accordingly, the Danish conquest of Estonia in 1219 was declared to be a crusade[11] 'against these wild tribes in order to fight for the dissemination of the Christian faith with spiritual as well as temporal weapons.' Later Innocent's successor, Honorius III, confirmed that all conquered land should be attached to Denmark,[12] as an answer to the 'humble request' of King Valdemar II.

Tradition has that the Danish flag with a white cross on a red banner, called *Dannebrog*, came down from the sky in the famous battle of Lyndanise in 1219 – sent by God to show that the Danes should win by the sign of the cross. However the flag is not known to have been used before the middle of the fourteenth century as a symbol of Denmark, and the first time the name *Dannebrog* is mentioned is in the Netherlandic *Armorial Bellenville* from about 1380.[13] In the great seal of the Nordic union from 1397 the flag is held by three lions. The story about the divine offspring of Dannebrog is an interesting mixture of religion, chivalric romance, heraldic tradition and ancient legend. Note the close kinship with the legend of the Roman Emperor Constantine, who saw the sign of the cross in the sky and the words 'Under this sign thou shalt win' during a battle in 312. However, the oldest known written source of the story of Dannebrog is from 1527. The Franciscan chronicler Petrus Olai from Roskilde refers to the legend, but dates the event to 1208 and identifies the place of the battle as Fellin (Viljandi) in the southern part of Estonia.[14] We do not know the origin of the story, but presumably it goes back to the first part of the fifteenth century during the reign of Eric of Pomerania. According to the late medieval chronicler Christiern Pedersen[15] (born about 1480), the flag was greatly honoured by the king and, when he was forced to flee from Denmark, he brought the flag with him: 'He took a banner, called Dannebrog, which God had sent the Danes from the sky with his holy angel, so they could use it in war against their enemies – which they often did and gained great praise and honour.' The direct connection with Eric of Pomerania cannot be verified, but apparently the story of the divine origin of the banner was firmly established during the fifteenth century.

Several other examples of this symbolic use of the cross in the official presentations of Denmark and the royal house can be mentioned. A famous triangular relief stands over the portal in the southern transept of the cathedral in Ribe has been much discussed among scholars. The relief shows Christ in the middle, handing over a cross to his mother, the holy virgin, dressed as the queen of Heaven. In her role as a mediator between God and mankind, she gives the cross to a secular king, and behind him stands a queen. At the same time, Christ takes the hand of a presumably young, beardless man. Below this a crowd of people symbolises mankind. The inscription in the centre of the relief says 'Civitas Hierusalem', which in this connection means the heavenly Jerusalem – a depiction of the spiritual Church. On each side angels carry bands with inscriptions: 'VENITE ASCENDAM AD MONTEM DEI' 'Come, let us go to the mountain of God,' and 'BEATI PAUPERES SP(T?)V QUONIAM REGNUM DEI POSSIDEBITIS' 'Blessed are the meek, for Thou shall inherit the kingdom of God.' Several scholars have tried to identify the persons in this relief, which clearly plays on the idea of 'taking the cross' – a well-known reference to crusaders. Some identify the king with Christoffer I, who died in 1259 during a conflict with Archbishop Jacob Erlandsen and was buried in the cathedral in Ribe. The king had been excommunicated at the time of his death, and the relief was perhaps set up by his widow, Queen Margaret and his son Erik (Glipping) in order to show that he had been a repentant Christian. Other scholars identify the king as Valdemar II (The Victorious) in his role as a crusader king. The letter alluded to above from Pope Innocent III to Valdemar II in 1215 mentions the practice 'of fastening the sign of the cross to their shoulders.' Here again the symbol of the cross is obvious. However we will never agree on an interpretation of the relief – perhaps it simply symbolises the relation between God and mankind, and the obligation to 'take the cross' in order to be saved.

As medieval society during the High Middle Ages tended to be increasingly secularised, eagerness to arrange and participate in new crusades faded. Nevertheless pilgrimage and policy were still closely interwoven. The Danish King Valdemar IV (Atterdag) went on several long trips through Europe, which partly served to enlist support to fight his enemies: the Hanseatics, Sweden, Holstein and Mecklenburg, and partly served to exploit the possibilities of church policy.[16] He even tried to intervene in the war between France and England, and proposed to lead an army of 12 000 men to England, which he proclaimed 'rightly belonged to Denmark.' In 1347, after the sale of Estonia to the Teutonic Order, Valdemar went on a pilgrimage to Jerusalem, where he was made a knight of the holy grave. Not much is known about this journey in contrast with another, which the king undertook in 1363–1364, on which he visited the German Emperor Charles IV in Prague, and continued to Strasbourg and the Papal court in Avignon. Here he was received by the Pope Urban V, who bestowed on him the honourable Golden Rose, which according to tradition was granted to defenders of Christianity. As expected, King Valdemar brought with him a large number of petitions, and many were granted by the pope.[17] The most important of these was perhaps permission to use the punishment of the Church against potential enemies inside and outside the borders of Denmark. Here again we see the close connection between the

Church and the secular power. The Swedish historian Sven Tägil wrote a detailed and interesting thesis in 1962 about the foreign policy of King Valdemar IV, which sheds light on this interesting point.

The famous daughter of King Valdemar IV, Queen Margaret I, surprisingly enough, never went on an extended European trip, concentrating her energy on Nordic affairs. All we hear of is a journey to Aachen in 1385.[18] When the Byzantine Emperor Manuel Paleologus on his great European journey in 1402 tried to enlist support to fight the Turkish empire, the queen was not motivated to help him, even though he had sent her a relic with a piece of Christ's coat.[19] However, shortly before her death in 1412 she made a testament which stated, that after her death no less than 125 people should go on pilgrimage all over Europe on her behalf to pray for her soul[20]. Apparently these arrangements had only religious purposes, even though the queen had exercised strong authority during her reign.

Queen Margaret's stepson, Eric of Pomerania, who was crowned king of the Nordic Union in 1397, had strong European connections. Between 1423 and 1425 he went on a pilgrimage to Jerusalem, but the political interests in the voyage were obvious.[21] We have several sources for this journey, which no doubt was related to the king's effort to fight his enemies from Holstein. King Erik was accompanied by many of the most important men from Scandinavia: the archbishop of Uppsala, the bishop of Roskilde and many noblemen, about fifty in all. After a long delay in Pomerania the king finally met the German Emperor Sigismund, who delivered the judgement that the whole of Schlesvig should belong to Denmark. After this most important achievement the journey continued to the holy land through Venice, where the king was received by the Doge. It is said, that from then on the King was disguised as a servant for safety reasons, but on his return from Jerusalem he was unmasked by a delegate from the sultan of Damascus. The king had to pay a large ransom to secure his release before he could return.[22] The story is told by the esteemed German writer Herman Korner, but there are no other sources for this event, even though we know that the king had to raise several loans. On his journey home he visited the emperor again and continued to King Vladislav in Poland, and the grandmaster of the Teutonic Order in Thorn. In general, the journey must be described as very successful.

It is tempting here to mention the efforts to organise a crusade against the Turks, which was later proposed by the Danish King Christian I in 1471. After the conquest of Constantinople in 1453 and the fall of the Byzantine Empire, the Turks constituted a serious danger to the Christian world. The pope and the German emperor tried several times to organize a new crusade, but their efforts were fruitless. Christian I mentioned his new plans for a crusade in the German Reichstag in 1471,[23] proposing to form a Christian alliance and attack the infidels both by the sea and land. However, the king emphasised that in order to realise the plan, it was necessary that the other European countries help to fight the rebellion in Sweden. In fact this rather naive suggestion was well received by all present, but the crusade was never undertaken. Perhaps the king wanted to make a good impression on the German Emperor Frederick III, and in that case it was a good investment. On his journey to Rome three years later in 1474 the Emperor endowed the king with the duchy of Holstein, and Pope Sixtus IV sanctified the founding of a university in Copenhagen. At the same time Pope granted the king the honourable Golden Rose, which later was exhibited in the cathedral in Roskilde. On his way home Christian visited Mantua, which was the seat of the Gonzaga family. The countess Barbara was sister of the Danish Queen Dorothea, and they had arranged a splendid reception with banquets and tournaments. The poet Filippo Nuvoloni gave a high-flown speech before the king in Latin, which was printed soon afterwards in Mantua. In this interesting speech he praises the king who, in contrast to his savage ancestors, came to Italy as a pilgrim. After the speech Christian I bestowed on the poet his new Order of the Mother of God – now called The Order of the Elephant, a parallel to the English Order of the Garter and the Burgundian Toison d'Or. The king received a copy of the print, which later was translated into Danish by Christiern Pedersen about 1520. In this text he adds several passages, which mention how the king 'advised all Christian kings, lords and princes that they all should fight like men against the enemies of the holy Christian faith, that is, Turks, Jews, pagans and heretics.' In general, the trip in 1474 is a good example of the intermingling of crusades, pilgrimages and European policy which characterise the voyages of kings during the Middle Ages.

To sum up, crusades and pilgrimages not only served religious purposes, but were closely interwoven with the complicated chess game, that constituted European politics. However, it would be wrong to regard the journeys just as cynical ways to implement temporal aims. No doubt the religious aspects of the journeys were taken most seriously, and what we today regard as a dubious and ambiguous mixture of faith and policy was not seen that way at the time. Pilgrimages were in no way reserved for the rich and the powerful, and this is testified by numerous sources, written as well as archaeological. Pilgrim-badges are often found in excavations; where the deceased was buried with two scallop-shells from Santiago de Campostella in Spain. Professional pilgrims could travel on behalf of others, and the pilgrim Jonas is described in the following way on this tombstone from the church of the great Cistercian monastery in Sorø: 'The abbot's dear man lies buried here, Jonas, taken away from us and united with the saints. Twice he reached Jerusalem, three times he visited Rome and once he went to St Jacob' (translated from the Latin inscription). Pilgrimages and crusades opened up the world, and perhaps the feeling of European identity was created and grew out from the meetings and clashes with foreign, non-Christian powers and cultures.

NOTES

1   Translated by the author from C.P.O. Christiansen: Bernhard af Clairvaux 1926, pp. 268–269.
2   Jensen 2000a; Jensen 2000b; also his introduction for this volume.
3   Riant 1865.
4   Albert von Aachen, pp. 148–149.
5   Olrik (ed.) 1908, pp. 87–88.
6   *Sakses Danesage*, pp. 91–96; *Knytlinge Saga*, pp. 114–116.
7   Riis 2000; Ræder 1871.
8   SM, vol. II, pp. 465–467.
9   Norn 1982, pp. 18–36. See also Nyborg & Jensen 1998.
10 DD, 1 rk. IV nro. 173: 7th May 1210 (Innocent III).
11 DD, 1 rk. V nro. 61: 29th December 1215 (Innocent III).
12 DD, 1 rk. V nr. 145: 9th October 1218 (Honorius III).
13 KLNM, vol. 21, pp. 135–137.
14 SM, vol. I, p. 459.
15 Pedersen 1534/1850–1856, vol. V, p. 488.
16 Tägil 1962.
17 DD, 3 rk. VII nr. 36 ff.
18 Daenell 1900-1902, pp. 190–194.
19 SD IV, nr. 2948.
20 Erslev 1881-1882. KS, 3 rk. vol. III, pp. 377–379.
21 Mollerup 1882.
22 *Chronica Novella*.
23 Etting 1998, pp. 131–159.

BIBLIOGRAPHY

Sources

Albert von Aachen, *Geschichte des ersten Kreuzzugs. Erster Teil: Die Eroberung des heiligen Landes*. Jena 1923.
Bernhard af Clairvaux, *Hans liv fortalt af samtidige og et utvalg af hans vær*ker *og breve*. C. P. O. Christiansen (ed.), København 1926.
Die Chronica Novella des Hermann Korner. J. Schwalm (ed.), Göttingen 1895.
Diplomatarium Danicum. F. Blatt (ed.), København 1938–2000. Translated to Danish in *Danmarks Riges breve*.
Kirkehistoriske Samlinger, København 1849 ff.
Knytlinga Saga. J. P. Ægidius (ed.), København 1977.
Sakses Danesaga. Svensønnernes og borgerkrigenes tid (1076–1157). J. Olrik (ed.), København 1908.
Scriptores Minores Historiæ Danicæ Medii Ævi, I–II. M. C. Gertz (ed.), København 1922.

Literature

E. R. Daenell 1900–1902, 'Om en hidtil upåagtet Rejse til Aachen af Dronning Margrethe i 1385', *Historisk Tidsskrift* 7 vol.3.
Danmarks Historie. Ed. Olaf Olsen. Vol. 1–16. København 1988–1991.
K. Erslev 1881–1882, *Tre Gavebreve fra Drinning Margarethe fra Aaret 1411*. In KS 3 vol. III, pp.377–379.

V. Etting 1997, *Margrete den Første. En regent og hendes samtid*, 2nd edition. København.

V. Etting 1998, *Fra fællesskab til blodbad. Kalmarunionen 1397–1520*. København.

K. V. Jensen 2000a, 'Temaer i korstogshistorien – et historiografisk rids', in *Krig, korstog og kolonisering. Den jyske Historiker* 89, pp. 8–30.

K. V. Jensen 2000b, 'Danmark som en korsfarerstat', in *Krig, korstog og kolonisering. Den jyske Historiker* 89, pp. 48–68.

Kulturhistorisk Leksikon for Nordisk Middelalder. Vol. I–XXII. København 1956–1978.

W. Mollerup 1882, 'Kong Erik af Pommerns Udenlandsrejse 1423–1423', *Historisk Tidsskrift* 5 III.

O. Norn 1982, *At se det usynlige. Mysteriekult og ridderidealer*. København.

E. Nyborg & J. M. Jensen 1998, 'Messeoffer, gralsriddere og snakkekvinder. Genfundne og nyopdagede kalkmalerier i Ølsted kirke', in *Nationalmuseets Arbejdsmark*, pp. 54–71.

C. Pedersen 1534 (ed. 1850–1856), *Danske Skrifter*, 1–5. C. J. Brandt (ed.), København.

P. Riant 1865, *Expeditions et pelerinages des Scandinaves en Terre Sainte au temps des Croisades*. Paris.

P. J. Riis 2000, 'Hvor blev Erik Ejegod begravet?' in *Som kongerne bød – fra trelleborge til enevælde. Festskrift til dronning Margrethe*. København.

J. G. F. Ræder 1871, *Danmark under Svend Estridsen og hans sønner*. København.

S. Tägil 1962, *Valdemar Atterdag och Europa*. Lund.

KURT VILLADS JENSEN

Crusading at the Fringe of the Ocean
Denmark and Portugal in the Twelfth Century

Why did the Danish King Valdemar II the Victorious in 1214 marry the sister of the Portuguese King Afonso II the Fat. This question has intrigued modern Danish historians for whom Portugal is a small country very far away. It has also intrigued modern Portuguese historians for whom Denmark is a small country with a short history of only a thousand years, inhabited by big Viking-like types who cannot speak the civilised languages of Southern Europe. An obvious explanation for the historians of the late nineteenth century was that Berengaria was extremely beautiful and had 'disarmed and conquered one of the most valiant fighters of Northern Europe of her time.'[1] Another explanation might perhaps also be that both Valdemar and Afonso – like their fathers and grandfathers, also named Valdemar and Afonso – were both important crusader kings. This makes it worth while looking more closely at both how their crusades were organised and pursued, and how these crusades at the fringe of the ocean fitted into the general crusading movement in the High Middle Ages.

I will attempt to sketch briefly how such a comparison between Denmark and Portugal might offer a better understanding of dynamics of small countries in the periphery of Europe and to indicate some of the conclusions that may be drawn from such a comparison. The intention is primarily to outline some ideas for further discussion rather than to present the results of a research project.

When pope Urban II preached the first crusade in 1095, he was addressing an audience of Frenchmen. All the earliest sources for his speech agree on this point, but it was soon elaborated upon by later historians writing some ten to twenty years after the event. They stressed three things. First, that the actual conquest of Jerusalem had been made possible by the military effort of the French. Second, that the news of Urban's sermon had spread very quickly to the remotest parts of Christianity, across the Ocean, which means to England, or to the fringe of the Ocean, which means both to the Iberian Peninsula and Scandinavia and Scotland. The crusade was thus a common Christian enterprise. Third, they stressed the difference

195

between Frenchmen and others by describing those from the fringe of the ocean as barbarians who were of no military account but supported the crusade by their prayers. One of the best-known examples of this is William of Malmesbury's remark in the early 1120s, that the sermon of Pope Urban was such a success that the Welsh left their poaching to join the crusade, the Scots their familiarity with flies, the Norwegians their gorging on fish, and the Danes their incessant drinking.[2]

This approach of the first historians created a tradition and is one reason why there has been very little research done in crusading on the periphery of Europe – they were barbarians and did not really count in the conquest. A second reason is the general lack of medieval sources from Scandinavia. A third reason is that people from Scandinavia sailed to the Holy Land and were therefore encountered comparatively less on their way than those who went overland, so that fewer would note the movements of the Scandinavians. A fourth reason, and probably the most important, is the historiographical tradition. A very nationalistic and isolationistic historical approach developed during the twentieth century in the small countries on the periphery. In the Scandinavian countries, Portugal, Hungary, Czechoslovakia, and many other such countries, the national history has been understood as uninfluenced by anything from outside, be it feudalism, or crusading. In Portugal, historians could rely upon the authority of no less than Carl Erdmann, who stated definitively in 1940 that there had been no proper crusades in Portugal before 1219. In Denmark, historians during the twentieth century have tended to see Danish crusades to the Mediterranean or the Baltic as simply a pretext for political expansion and looting – in short, as a continuation of Viking Age raids.

A way to escape the burden of such a heavy historiographical tradition is to compare similar countries. From a crusading perspective, Denmark and Portugal were the most similar countries in the two first centuries of crusading, both with access to the sea, and a religious frontier with the heathen Wends or Muslims which was expanded by wars understood by contemporaries as crusades. There had been a similar development in these two countries since the late eleventh century with religious wars against neighbouring heathens and regular contacts between the two powers. Around 1100, the royal family of Denmark and the ducal family of Portugal were connected through intermarriage with the princely families of Flanders and Burgundy, and members of both families participated in the very early crusading. Because of this engagement in the crusades, at home and in the Mediterranean, both countries became strong monarchies under King Valdemar I the Great, who died in 1182, and Afonso I Henriques in Portugal, who died in 1185.

A characteristic feature of many expanding powers in the periphery was that they were extremely dependant upon foreigners from outside. Portugal is a good example. The father of Afonso Henriques was a knight from Burgundy, related to the later Pope Calixtus, Abbot Hugh of the Great reform monastery of Cluny, and the royal family of Hungary. He went to Galicia in Northern Spain, married the daughter of the king of León and was given the Duchy of Portugal, an ill-defined and mainly Muslim dominated area, to conquer and govern. From this position, he began to expand his territory.[3]

In Denmark, the father of Valdemar the Great was Duke Canute, son of a Danish king, but brought up by a foster family. He was given the area of the heathen Abodrites along the Baltic Sea in North-Western Germany by the German count and later king Lothar to conquer – a clear parallel with the duchy of Portugal – and Canute was also given the Duchy of Schleswig in Southern Denmark by the Danish king. This father of Valdemar was married to a Russian princess – hence the strange name of Valdemar from Vladimir – and Canute's main political sphere was probably in the heathen areas along the Baltic more than in Denmark proper.[4]

The two fathers died before the sons were old enough to rule. Valdemar's father was killed in 1131, even before Valdemar was born, and Afonso was perhaps five years old when his father died. They disappear from history; Valdemar was probably brought up by his mother in Russia,[5] Afonso Henriques was certainly brought up by his mother, who lived a hard life with a young Galician lover and seems to have cared little for her child.[6] At least he later rebelled openly against her. When they became adults, fifteen years old, the two boys declared themselves rulers. Afonso did so in the mid 1120s by girding himself with the sword; Valdemar did so by attempting to canonize his murdered father. This happened in 1146 but was prevented by the archbishop claiming that no authorisation had been given by the pope.[7] After these two dates, both Valdemar and Afonso were fighting wars almost every year against rivals for their position and especially against infidels.

Both rulers had a crusading background, which they exploited from the beginning of their careers. The father of Valdemar had fought against Abodrites and other Wends, and his father had been King Eric the Good who went on a crusade towards Jerusalem as early as 1103. In the same year, Afonso's father travelled with a cleric who stayed for several years in the church of the Holy Sepulchre in Jerusalem, and when he came back to Portugal, he was persuaded by Afonso to found the monastery of the Holy Cross in Coimbra.[8] This was a convent that was organised so as to closely imitate the Holy Sepulchre, and which came to play an important role in Afonso's conquest of Muslim territory in formulating a crusading ideology, as did other convents of the Holy Cross like the contemporaneous ones in Barcelona and Bologna.

There is a close parallel to the Portuguese Holy Cross convent in the Danish monastery in Ringsted, which was re-founded in the same year, 1135, as the centre for the cult of a crusader saint, Valdemar's father. This later came to play a very important role in the conquest and missionising of Wendic areas, and especially in writing the *vitae* and liturgy that turned Valdemar's father into a crusader saint of the frontiers.

Afonso and Valdemar fought wars for some forty to fifty years, but rather than describe all these wars in detail, it is more important here to indicate some characteristic developments in this process. An overall concern of these two rulers seems to have been to liberate themselves from the influence of the great noble families.[9] In Portugal this can be seen in the shift of the royal centre from the north towards the south, following the advance of the *reconquista*. In Denmark, a similar shift took place from West to East, from Odense to Ringsted and probably to Vordingborg in the southern part of Zealand.

This physical translocation of royal administration and royal presence was followed by the creation of new military structures dependant upon the king and only to a much lesser extent upon the nobles. In Portugal, the military expansion was followed by the establishment of local towns or local communities – *concelhos* – which were granted royal privileges if they provided warriors for the annual summer expeditions against the Muslims. These small towns were 'organised for war'[10] from top to bottom of the social hierarchy so that ordinary citizens should provide foot soldiers or, along the coastline and the big rivers, men for the battleships; other citizens were specialised warriors as for example crossbow-men; and a few were mounted warriors – a kind of urban knight. These petty knights were newcomers to the town; they had to have a horse, they formed the upper strata of the *concelho*, and formed a confraternity in which members helped each other with provisions and equipment.

In Denmark, there are some indications of similar new militarised city groups. The kings would grant privileges to cities to gain their support, some of which were actually able to provide both foot-soldiers and cavalry. The city of Schleswig of Valdemar's father had a structure with a confraternity with warriors strong enough to kill a king as it did with King Niels in 1134 to avenge the murder of their Duke Canute.

In the late twelfth century the military role of the *concelhos* in Portugal diminished, and the military orders increasingly took over their function as the instrument of the king. Templars and Hospitalers had been introduced early into Portugal, and very soon acquired far-reaching privileges and large areas of land if they could conquer and settle it. In 1129, when Afonso tried hard to gain an independent position, he had granted land to the Templars because he 'was a brother in your brotherhood.' He must then have been a member of the order or, rather, attached to the order in some way.[11] In Denmark, the knights Hospitalers seem to have had a specially privileged position from the 1160s when king Valdemar granted them a special tax of one penny from every house-hold in Denmark.[12] This is the first example of such a general taxation in favour of a military crusading order as far as I know.

One problem with military orders was, however, that the members had to be celibate. In spite of all the good arguments one could produce in favour of such an institution, it might have prevented some nobles from entering the orders. The solution was simple. In 1170, a prince of León created the order of Santiago which also accepted married members.[13] This order came to Portugal in 1172 and soon became the one most favoured by king Afonso.

In Denmark, we get small glimpses of confraternities, about whose role we know little, but which are possible to understand as similar new, local military orders. About 1170, a number of confraternities of Duke Canute existed. The king became a member of these confraternities, which comprised merchants, warriors and peasants, and were centralised under the main confraternity in Ringsted itself where the cult of Duke Canute was. These confraternities of Duke Canute probably formed a royal military order similar to that of Santiago. Further, the picture of Duke Canute on the seal of the confraternity of Schleswig is exactly like that of Santiago, on seals, murals, etc., from Galicia and Portugal in the thirteenth and fourteenth centuries. It is therefore very probable that we do have a military religious crusading order, created by the king, in which the members could continue to be married but still go on crusade.[14]

Apart from towns and orders, the king also tried to control and regulate the general levy of local armies and of the army for the whole country. About 1170, the *leding* in Denmark, the naval conscription, was probably reorganised, and the king seems to have gained much more control over it than before. In principle, the whole country was divided into units which were all to provide ships and men. One third of the *leding* would be permanently mobilised, another third the next year, etc., and the whole *leding* could be summoned by the king for crusades into the Baltic.[15] In Portugal, similar reorganisations also took place about 1170 when Afonso I gained more control over the military contingents of the *concelhos*. Especially in the north, ships were manned by royally controlled conscription from towns and coastal areas, which seems to have functioned very much like the Danish *leding*. During the twelfth century, a fleet was built up which became important in the king's wars in the 1180s.[16]

In these incessant wars, the kings often had a very weak basis among the local families and were therefore also dependant upon the help of non-locals who owed their loyalty to the king alone. In Denmark, Valdemar and other kings used German knights, and they would ally themselves with Wendic princes who fought for the king, not only against their heathen families but also within Denmark against the king's rivals, as did the heathen Niklot in the 1150s, serving King Svend against other Danish claimants to the throne.[17] Some of these outsiders were granted large areas of land to govern, as was Niklot's son who married the sister of king Valdemar and was enfeoffed with the big southern Danish island of Lolland. In Portugal, there was a constant flow of foreign knights who stopped on their way to the Holy Land and joined the king's expeditions. Some were famous kings themselves like Sigurd Jerusalem-farer from Norway, who attempted to conquer Muslim Lisbon in 1109.[18] Others were anonymous English, French, Flemish, German, and Scandinavian crusaders.[19]

This is a well-known fact, but one might wonder then why it was so important for the kings to rely upon foreign knights. One explanation might be that the local nobles were not automatically inclined to fight in their local areas. Or, to put it differently, there seem to have been some kind of peaceful *convivencia* in both Denmark and Portugal between the Christians and the heathens before these foreign kings began their crusading.

In Denmark, there seems to have been a not insubstantial Wendic population in the eleventh and twelfth centuries, and there were dynastic relations between Danish and Wendic princes from the ninth century onwards.[20] In Portugal, the Christian population had lived as *mozarabs* under Muslim rule – they had adopted the Arab language and culture but could normally continue their Christian rite. One of the main goals of attack from the new foreign knights was this *convivencia*. It happened physically in Lisbon in 1147 when the crusaders, by a regrettable mistake, killed a Christian mozarab bishop; and it happened on several occasions when the Mozarabs rebelled against King Afonso – some even fled to Muslim territory to be able to practise their Christianity in peace.[21]

There may be some comparable examples from Denmark. About 1150, king Svend donated a huge golden bowl to the Wendic God Svantevit in Arkona on the island of Rügen – a political act to placate his pagan allies, a sign of mutual respect, perhaps even an indication that the cult of Svantevit was actually a kind of syncretic pagan/Christian phenomenon. In any case, it is a sign that the religious border was not fixed and not impossible to penetrate.

That a kind of *convivencia* existed can also be argued from the fact that it was vehemently attacked by the Danish historian Saxo who wrote about 1200. His work was an important element in an ideological war against *convivencia*. According to Saxo, there have always been wars between Danes and Wends. The Wends had always attacked Danish land and robbed and killed and burned, and it had always been the prime duty of Danish kings to fight back against them, to defend the Patria, the Christian fatherland.[22]

Portugal does not have a great, twelfth-century narrative comparable to Saxo, but in smaller chronicles, saints' Lives, and genealogies of the nobility, we observe the same picture of an age-old confrontation, an uninterrupted *reconquista* since the early eighth century battle of Covadunga in 722/724.[23]

Saxo and the Portuguese sources are clearly creating a mythic past characterised by confrontation. In cases where we can complement this picture with older sources it is apparent that it is a fabrication. There had been no concerted *reconquista* for 400 years. The twelfth century picture is a successful attempt to turn *convivencia* into confrontation and thus represents the view of the crusading kings and foreign knights attempting to extend the border of Christianity. It is an attempt in a fluid frontier zone to create a fixed, conceptual borderline that could not be transgressed, except in war.

This understanding of fighting a necessary war and its importance for its proponents is reflected in a number of sources; for example, in both Danish and Portuguese kings' designating themselves as *pacis restaurator*, *patriae liberator*, or simply as crusaders who converted infidels. When Valdemar I was buried he had a leaden plaque with him in his tomb stating that here lay Valdemar, son of Saint Duke Canute, who first converted the Wends to Christianity. This was thus what he himself wanted to be remembered for. Afonso wrote in 1147 that he was the most loyal of all the pope's vassals because the others fought to get land for themselves, but he had given all he had conquered to the Church; and was therefore entitled to more privileges from the Church than other rulers.

We may claim therefore, I think, that the arrival of new knights and new kings in the periphery led to a militarization of societies, which became organised for crusading, and to an ideological war by creating a mythical past in the image of the crusaders. How far, then, were these changes co-ordinated?

As concerns the ideological war it is obvious that the historians and the theologians were part of the same environment, often educated in the same places, and reading each other's literature. Not only do they depict their contemporary wars from a crusading perspective, but they also give their countries' histories the same origin. Both in Portugal and Denmark, almost all chronicles – Saxo being a notable exception – began with a long quotation form Isidor of Seville on the history of the Goths, thereby again stressing the stretching continuity back to Antiquity and therefore substantiating an age-old claim to the land now threatened by the infidels.[24]

As concerns military organisations it is more complicated. The various branches of the international military orders would certainly have known about each other's activities. As to the local military orders, it is very tempting to see a connection between the creation of the Order of Santiago and the Confraternity of Duke Canute, but it cannot be demonstrated.

As concerns military action, particular crusades, it is difficult not to see a connection. The clearest example is in 1147, when two Danish kings became engaged in the Second Crusade and led a Danish army against the Wendic city of Dobin, which was also attacked by a Saxon army. On the Iberian peninsula in the same year, Tortosa on the North East coast, Almeria on the South coast, and Lisbon on the west coast were all conquered by local kings with the help of foreign crusaders, from Genoa and France and all over Western Europe. The Second crusade proper left for the Holy Land at the same time. It was one war on many frontiers, as it was described by contemporary chroniclers.[25]

In 1168, Valdemar and Afonso both decided to attack the nearest and strongest pagan city, but with very different results. Valdemar actually conquered Arkona on Rügen, his father Canute being then papally canonised because of Valdemar's crusading. The crusade in the Baltic was expanded as far as Finland, and Valdemar could prepare a new crusade east of Rügen.

Afonso conquered the city of Badajoz in 1169 together with his loyal general, Geraldo Sem Pavor, Geraldo the Fearless. A Muslim counter siege was, however, immediately arranged. During one of the battles outside the city, Afonso broke through the line of the enemies and galloped back to the city and through the city gate but had not noticed that the grille had not been fully raised, and banged his head into an iron beam and was taken prisoner.[26] Afonso never recovered fully from the incident, and so he concluded a truce with the Muslims for eight years. When war was resumed in 1178, the papal response came immediately. Pope Alexander now for the first time recognised Afonso's title as king of the Portuguese in his famous bull *Manifestis comprobatum*,[27] doing so explicitly because of Afonso's lifelong crusading. If Afonso had been less tall and had not banged his head against the grille, this recognition would have come in 1170. In the same year that Valdemar obtained his great privileges from Pope Alexander. It would have been tempting to see the two crusades as co-ordinated in some way.

The last example from the fifth crusade is less speculative. Three expeditions set out when general crusades were preached all over Western Europe after the fourth Lateran council. The first was in Portugal where the new king, Afonso II, conquered the strong fortress of Alcáser do sal in 1217 with help from foreign crusaders, including some from the north. The second expedition was that of Valdemar II who, with 1500 ships, conquered Estonia in 1219, greatly helped by the new Wendic Danes from Rügen who only fifty years before had themselves been the target for crusading. The third expedition was the mainly French crusade to Egypt, which, after initial success, ended in a military catastrophe. Again, these efforts must have been co-ordinated.

The question of how such co-ordination could actually have been established, could possibly be answered by suggesting two different ways of communication. One is papal initiatives or papal responses to other's initiatives - through papal legates and the existing ecclesiastical structures of bishops and religious orders. But the other answer must be that the rulers and the knights on the periphery knew very well about the actual warfare in the other countries. Their societies were organised in the same way – they were crusading societies both in practical and ideological terms – and warriors moved freely from one country on the periphery to another and took part in the crusades.

What then are the results of such a comparison between Denmark and Portugal? It offers a better understanding of some details, such as why the two royal houses of Denmark and Portugal married into each other in 1214. The usual answer has been that the Portuguese princess Berengaria was extremely beautiful. So she was; we know thus from the Danish medieval sources and from her well-preserved skull in Ringsted, but another reason has certainly been that the two kingdoms had undergone parallel development for almost a century with similar military institutions, etc., and that they had very good contact with each other, all because of crusading. In that respect, a dynastic alliance is no surprise.

Of more interest, however, is that such a comparison demonstrates how easily ideas and organisations could be exchanged and copied in the Middle Ages between countries with a similar geopolitical location. It also shows how important the crusading movement was to the rulers and political agents of these countries as a means of gaining a position in competition with other rulers and rivals to the throne. It also shows, I hope, that institutions in Denmark should not be understood as internal developments of older Danish institutions. They should rather be seen as the result of competition and co-operation with other contemporary countries. With such an insight, we could begin to understand the past not from not only diachronically, but synchronically as well.

NOTES

1   Cf. Bruun 1893; Cordeiro 1893/1984. The quotation is from Cordeiro, introduction. His book was re-edited in 1984 on the occasion of the visit of the Danish Queen to Portugal, with an introduction by José Mattoso and with the same conclusion that the beauty of Berengaria was a decisive factor in the Danish-Portuguese liaison.
2   William of Malmesbury. Cf. Jensen 2002a.
3   See in general Mattoso 1993.
4   Gaetke 1999; Hermanson 2000.
5   In the magnate family of Skjalm Hvide according to *Saxonis Gesta Danorum* (c. 1200), but in Russia according to the later *Knytlinga saga*, which is probably more reliable in this respect; cf. Lind 1992.
6   The Galician's name was Fernando Pérez de Traba, cf. Barton 1997: passim.
7   VSD 202, pp. 216–217.
8   Sousa Viterbo 1914.
9   Mattoso 1982.
10 Powers 1988.
11 DMP, I 1 no. 96; cf. Barber 1994, pp. 32–33.
12 DD, 1:7 no. 156.
13 Lomax 1965.
14 Jensen 2002b.
15 Lund 1996.
16 Serrão & Oliveira Marques 1986.
17 *Saxonis Gesta Danorum*, XIV, XVII; Helmold, *Chronica slavorum*, 300.
18 Machado 1948.
19 Oliveira Marques 1993, pp. 25–41.
20 Harck & Lübke (ed.) 2001; Selch Jensen 2000.
21 Mattoso 1995, pp. 320–340.
22 Jensen 2002c.
23 Krus 1994a.
24 For Denmark, *Annales danici*; for Portugal especially, *Annales Domni Alfonsi*; *Annales Portugalenses Veteres*; cf. Krus 1994b.
25 Constable 1953; Phillips & Hoch (ed.) 2001.
26 Gonzaga de Azevedo & Gomes dos Santos 1935, vol. 4, pp. 124–130.
27 PL, 200, col. 1237.

BIBLIOGRAPHY

Sources

Annales danici medii ævi. E. Jørgensen (ed.), København 1920.
Annales Domni Alfonsi Portugallensium Regis, in M. Blöcker-Walter 1966, *Alfons I. von Portugal.* Zürich, pp. 151–161.
Annales Portugalenses Veteres, in P. David, *Études historiques sur la Galice et le Portugal du VIe au XIIe siècle.* Lisboa 1947, pp. 291–312.
Helmold, *Chronica slavorum*. B. Schmeidler & H. Stoob (ed.), Darmstadt 1963.
Knytlinga Saga, in Det Kongelige Nordiske Oldskrift-Selskab (ed.), *Jomsvikinga Saga og Knytlinga tilligemed Sagabrudstykker og Fortællinger vedkommende Danmark, ... oversatte af C. C. Rafn.* København 1829, pp. 157–355.
William of Malmesbury, 'Gesta regum Anglorum = The history of the English kings', in R. A. B. Mynors, R. M. Thomson, M. Winterbottom (ed.), *Oxford medieval texts*, vol. 1–2: 2nd vol. Oxford 1998.

Literature

M. Barber 1994, *The new knighthood: a history of the Order of the Temple*. Cambridge–New York.

S. Barton 1997, *The Aristocracy in Twelfth-Century León and Castile*. Cambridge.

C. Bruun 1893, 'Berengaria af Portugal, Valdemar II Sejers Dronning. En Historisk Undersøgelse', *Aarbøger for nordisk Oldkyndighed og Historie*, II, 8, pp. 46–120.

G. Constable 1953, 'The Second Crusade as seen by contemporaries', *Traditio* 9, pp. 215–279.

L. Cordeiro 1984, *Berengela e Leonor rainhas da Dinamarca*. Lisboa.

C. Erdmann 1940, *A Ideia de Cruzada em Portugal*. Coimbra.

H.-O. Gaethke 1999, *Herzog Heinrich der Löwe und die Slawen nordöstlich der unteren Elbe*. Frankfurt am Main.

L. Gonzaga de Azevedo & D. M. Gomes dos Santos. 1935–. *História de Portugal*, 6 vols. Lisboa.

O. Harck & C. Lübke (ed.) 2001, *Zwischen Reric und Bornhöved: die Beziehungen zwischen den Dänen und ihren slawischen Nachbarn vom 9. bis ins 13. Jahrhundert; Beiträge einer internationalen Konferenz, Leipzig, 4.–6. Dezember 1997*. Stuttgart.

L. Hermanson 2000, *Släkt, vänner och makt. En studie av elitens politiska kultur i 1100-talets Danmark*. Göteborg.

K. V. Jensen 2002 a, 'The Barbarization of the Northerners as a result of the First Crusade', [http://www.sdu.dk/Hum/kvj/barbarization.htm].

K. V. Jensen 2002b, 'Knudsgilder og korstog', in L. Bisgaard & L. Søndergaard (udg.), *Gilder, lav og broderskaber i middelalderens Danmark*. Odense, pp. 63–88.

K. V. Jensen 2002c, 'The Blue Baltic Border of Denmark in the High Middle Ages. Danes, Wends and Saxo Grammaticus', in D. Abulafia & N. Berend (ed.), *Medieval Frontiers: Concepts and Practices*. Aldershot, pp. 173–193.

L. Krus 1994a, *Pasado, memória e poder na sociedade medieval portuguesa: estudos*. Redondo.

L. Krus 1994b, *A concepção nobiliárquica do espaço ibérico: 1280–1380*. Lisboa.

J. Lind 1992, 'De russiske ægteskaber. Dynasti- og alliancepolitik i 1130'ernes danske borgerkrig', *Historik tidsskrift* (Danish) 2, pp. 225–261.

D. W. Lomax 1965, *La Orden de Santiago, 1170–1275*. Madrid.

N. Lund 1996, *Lith, leding og landeværn*. Roskilde.

L. S. Machado 1948, 'Circunstâncias do ataque a Lisboa por Sigurdo da Noruega (1109)', *O Instituto. Revista Científica e Literária* 111, pp. 205–247.

J. Mattoso 1982, *Ricos-homens, infanções e cavaleiros : a nobreza medieval portuguesa nos séculos XI e XII*. Lisboa.

J. Mattoso 1993, *Nova História de Portugal*. Lisbon.

J. Mattoso 1995, *Identificação de um país: ensaio sobre as origens de Portugal, 1096–1325*. Lisboa.

Nova História de Portugal, v. 2. A. H. de Oliveira Marques (ed.), Lisboa 1993.

—, v. 3. M. H. da Cruz Coelho e A. L. de Carvalho Homem (ed.), Lisboa 1996.

Saxonis Gesta Danorum. Hauniæ 1931.

A. H. R. de Oliveira Marques 1993, *Hansa e Portugal na Idade Média*, 2nd edition. Lisboa.

J. Phillips & M. Hoch (ed.) 2001, *The Second Crusade: scope and consequences*. Manchester.

J. F. Powers 1988, *A Society Organized for War. The Iberian Municipal Militias in the Central Middle Ages, 1000–1284*. Berkeley.

J. Serrão & A. H. R. de Oliveira Marques 1986, *Nova história da expansão portuguesa*. Lisboa.

C. Selch Jensen (ed.) 2000, *Danmark og Venderne*. Odense.

F. M. de Sousa Viterbo 1914, *O mosteiro de Sancta Cruz de Coimbra*. Coimbra.

Part III

Crusading Movement at
the Baltic Sea Region and Beyond

CARSTEN SELCH JENSEN

The Early Stage of Christianisation in Livonia in Modern Historical Writings and Contemporary Chronicles

In the last decades of the twelfth century, Livonia became the target of a series of direct attempts to convert its pagan population. These missionary activities seem to have been carried out mostly by German clerics from the archbishopric of Bremen. The story of these early missionaries in Livonia has become known to us mainly through chronicles of the early thirteenth century – primarily Arnold of Lübeck, who wrote around 1210, and Henry of Livonia from the 1220s.[1]

These early chronicles and various other sources have provoked discussion over the years among the scholars of the Baltic crusades on the nature of these early attempts to convert the Livonians. Some of these scholars in turn seem to have differentiated between two types of conversion in Livonia. First, there was an early peaceful mission mainly carried out through preaching by those clerics present in Livonia. This peaceful mission was then followed by a more violent conversion by the sword – that is to say, the crusades.

It is also assumed that this significant shift in the nature of the conversion happened some time during the early part of the Christianisation of the Livonians, although it has been dated differently by various scholars. Most seem to think that this change in the means of conversion happened shortly after the first bishop of Livonia had died in 1196. From that time onwards the conversion of the Livonians all happened with the aid of crusader armies. Hereafter the missionary work in Livonia had a profoundly violent character, dominated, as it was by almost continual fighting between the crusaders and the Livonians.[2]

In my opinion this is a false assumption without real foundation in the medieval chronicles or in the sources in general. It is therefore my intention in this short article to reconsider the nature of the early missionary activities in Livonia, by examining the information given to us in the two chronicles mentioned above on the episcopacy of Meinhard from his appointment in 1186 until his death in 1196. A few remarks on the following two bishops, Bertold and Albert will end this discussion around the year 1200.[3]

The Early Christianisation of Livonia during the Reign of the First Missionary Bishop

According to Arnold of Lübeck and Henry of Livonia, Meinhard was the first missionary to bring the word of God to the Livonians.[4] He originated from the monastery of Segeberg in Holstein, and apparently visited Livonia several times in the early 1180s before finally deciding to stay there and commit himself fully to the work of preaching and baptising in the area around the river Dvina.[5]

It is reasonable to assume that this mission amongst the Livonians had been planned for some time and masterminded by the ecclesiastical leaders of the archbishopric of Bremen, who had chosen Meinhard to carry the word of Christ to the pagans of Livonia.

As mentioned, Meinhard undertook several journeys to Livonia before he eventually decided to settle down, and sometime during the fall of 1184 took upon him the burden of a full-time missionary in a pagan and doubtless also hostile milieu, presumably accompanied by a few other clerics.[6] Well aware of the political situation in the area along the river Dvina, Meinhard got permission to preach the word of God from the ruling Russian duke of the nearby Polotsk, who was very kind towards Meinhard, even though this German priest represented the Roman Church. Obviously Duke Vladimir did not consider him a threat to his supremacy in the area.[7] Had he been able to look into the future, he may have felt different. Now he gave his blessings to Meinhard, and gave him permission to start preaching and baptising the pagans.[8]

Meinhard then chose the village of Üxküll as the site were he wanted to build the first church in Livonia.[9] Over the succeeding years he and his followers may on several occasions have regretted the choice of this place as the centre for their missionary activities. Although Üxküll was quite a big village situated near the Dvina, it was also a very isolated spot far away from the coast. Because of some very shallow places in the river, it was absolutely impossible for the big ships from Gotland and Lübeck to sail that far. This meant that in times of rebellion amongst the Livonians Meinhard and his fellow missionaries were too easily isolated and cut off from reinforcements. It was only with the utmost difficulty that they could be rescued from downstream.[10] But these difficulties were still in the future – for now Meinhard concentrated on the conversion of the people living around him in Üxküll and its immediate surroundings.

The efforts of Meinhard were soon to show some progress in the area, when he decided to use military engineering as a part of his missionary work. What he wanted to do was to build a castle out of dressed stone – a way of building that seems to have been relatively unknown to the Livonians at the time.[11]

In the early winter of 1185, marauding Lithuanians attacked Üxküll, forcing the inhabitants (including Meinhard) to hide in the forests. That experience made Meinhard promise the Livonians that he would help them build a stone castle as a protection against their Lithuanian enemies if they would accept baptism in return. The people of Üxküll accepted, and so did the people of the nearby Holme the following year on the same conditions and for the same reason.[12]

Thus in the spring of 1186 Meinhard arranged for some stone-masons from Gotland to come to Üxküll and begin the construction of the first stone castle in the country built in connection with a larger fortified church.[13] At the time of this construction work, Meinhard was formally appointed bishop of Livonia by the archbishop of Bremen, and the country now had its own bishop, responsible for the future Christianisation of the region.[14] The fortified church was then to become the first episcopal see of Livonia.

According to some historians there seems to have been little need for swords and crusaders in this first missionary work of Meinhard thus far, stressing his apparent intention of converting the people of Livonia through preaching and not by the sword. It is important however to bear in mind that Meinhard did arrange for craftsmen to construct a fortified church in Üxküll in connection with the stone castle that he had promised the Livonians in return for their conversion. In this way he demonstrated his intention of protecting the Church in Livonia, not only against marauding Lithuanians, but seemingly also against any opposition amongst the Livonians. We know that there were several other fortified places in the area that had been built by the Livonians as shelter against their enemies.[15] Meinhard could have chosen to strengthen these wooden fortresses instead of building a new castle out of dressed stone – but he did not. What he really wanted was a fortified place for himself as new bishop of Livonia – a place that could protect him and the converts.

Accordingly, Meinhard first bought a piece of land for the church and then also paid one fifth of the cost of the castle, thus perhaps minimising the risk of being driven away should there be any disagreement later on concerning the ownership of the place. It may also be that his payment of land and construction work was part of the deal with the Livonians: only in this way could he persuade them to accept baptism in return for protection.

Thus the construction of a fortified place indicates that Meinhard did accept the use of military force as a way to preserve and enhance the Christianisation of the Livonians, even though it was in a defensive way. Meinhard's missionary strategies bear great resemblance to those used by other missionaries, settlers and crusaders in the other medieval frontier societies. Both in Spain and the Holy Land we see how castles were built to protect colonists and important institutions as a part of a well-tried strategy along the borders of Western Christendom.[16]

Henry of Livonia tells us in his chronicle that some neighbouring pagans came to Üxküll when the castle and the church had been built. On their arrival they immediately tried to tear down this new stone building; naturally, without success. Instead some men armed with crossbows manned the walls of the castle and drove the pagans off.[17] We have to ask who these men, armed and fighting like traditional Western crusaders, were. It has been suggested that they were in fact the stone-masons who had armed themselves as the pagans attacked the castle and church in Üxküll.[18] It seems more likely though that Meinhard or some of the German merchants had brought with them a small group of men-at-arms to protect the craftsmen during the construction work. These same men now manned the new castle and became its first garrison so to speak. Naturally, Meinhard could have chosen to use Livonians for the garrisoning, but the castle and the church was not constructed exclusively for the protection of the native population – since it was primarily to be his own episcopal see. He may have thought it wiser to use fellow Christians from Gotland (or Germany) as a garrison. In this the men-at-arms in the castle bear a strong resemblance to those *servi episcopi* that later formed the private fighting force of Bishop Albert of Livonia, thus indicating that the Livonian bishops had fighting men of their own as early as during the time of Meinhard.[19] In any case we have here the very first references to an armed clash between Western Christians and native Livonians as a part of the Christianisation process in the country.

Meinhard continued his work for the next ten years with a firm base at the castle and the church, but he experienced what seems to have been growing opposition amongst the people of Livonia to his work. And not only among those who were still pagans, but also amongst the newly baptised, who seem to have turned their backs on him.[20] The hostilities were so bitter that Meinhard and his followers decided to give up the work and return to Germany in the early 1190s. It is not quite clear what provoked the rebellion after more than ten years of Christianisation. It has been suggested that the opposition was the work of the pagan priesthood, who could no longer ignore the relatively successful attempts by Meinhard to convert the population to Christianity. By doing so he seriously undermined the authority and power of these pagan priests and thus provoked their violent resistance and hatred.[21] They may therefore have tried very hard to turn the people against the Christian priests, thus hoping to destroy this new religious belief before it became too strong and powerful.

At Easter 1195 (or 1196), Meinhard decided to follow the German merchants back to Gotland because of the rebellions amongst the Livonians. According to Henry of Livonia, he only agreed to stay behind because he was promised that an (crusader) army of Germans, Danes and Norwegians would come to his rescue should he need it.[22] In return the Livonians also agreed to submit to Meinhard and the Christian faith in fear of what these crusaders would do to them if they actually came to the aid of the bishop.

It is not quite clear who promised Meinhard the aid of the crusaders - but it probably came from the German merchants from Gotland present in Livonia at the time. They would have known about such an army from previous crusades in the region.[23] A few years before in 1191 a Danish army had in fact passed Gotland and perhaps even anchored outside Visby.[24] In 1196 another army from Denmark was again sailing in the Baltic, heading for Estonia.[25] It may very well be that it was that same army that the merchants were talking about as the rescuers of Meinhard.

Meinhard did decide to stay in Livonia but, contrary to the promises of the Livonians, the opposition increased and the bishop was more or less trapped in his church at Üxküll, unable to escape to Gotland.[26] When he tried to leave the country once more, this time through Estonia probably hoping to link up with the Danish army, he learned that there were plans to kill him as soon as he left the safety of his fortified church in Üxküll. Thus he also gave up this second attempt to leave the country. Overwhelmed by his misfortune and the hostility amongst the Livonians, Meinhard fell ill shortly afterwards and eventually died sometime during the late summer or autumn of 1196.

Shortly before his death, Meinhard had managed to send a cleric named Theoderich secretly to Rome to ask the pope for help.[27] Pope Celestine III was very pleased to hear about the work done by Meinhard and his followers in Livonia. What he did not like to hear of was the many converts turning their backs on the Church and rejecting their baptism. According to the canonical laws the Church could not force anyone to accept the Christian faith, but once baptised by their own free will they could be forced to hold on to their new faith.[28] To make sure that the converted Livonians would do so, Celestine accordingly granted full remission of sins to all those who would take the cross and go to Livonia to help protect the Christian Church.[29] Even though the letter mentioned by Henry of Livonia is not preserved, it seems possible that Celestine did in fact call for a crusade against the Livonians in 1196. It is known that the lands around the Baltic sea had been part of the crusading movement prior to 1196, thus verifying the information in the chronicle of Henry of Livonia. In 1168 a Danish crusader army had conquered the main shrine of the Wends in Arkona after a series of hard-fought wars that forced the Vends to accept Christianity.[30] These wars against the Vends also included German crusaders. A few years later in the early 1170s Pope Alexander III called for another crusade, this time against Estonians and other pagans in the region. In one of several letters concerning these matters Alexander urged the people of Denmark, Norway and Sweden to take upon them the task of defending and spreading Christianity in Estonia. In return the crusaders would receive the same indulgence as had been given to the crusaders in the Holy Land.[31] In this way the pope placed the crusades to the Holy Land and crusades against the Estonians on an equal footing as early as the 1170s. Within the same period, the Swedes also seem to have attacked Finland on what appear to have been regular crusades.[32] The Danes also continued their engagements in the Baltic after the attack on Estonia in the 1170s. As has already been mentioned, a Danish army attacked Finland in 1191 and then again attacked parts of Estonia in 1196.[33]

Thus for decades Danes, Swedes and Germans had been fighting as crusaders around the Baltic with the blessing of the popes – fighting for the defence of the Church and with the promise of indulgence. It therefore seems quite possible that Pope Celestine III did react promptly in 1196 to the reports of Theoderich and promised indulgence to all those who would go to Livonia to defend the Church and help the clerics living there. In this there was really nothing new compared to what had already been going on for decades in the region. This also makes it seem probable that Meinhard was in fact promised the help of crusaders from Germany, Denmark and Norway in 1195 or 1196. Both the Germans and the Danes were active at the time as crusaders and therefore could willingly have given their assistance to Meinhard when he was in need of help.

Some Final Remarks on the Nature of the Early Christianisation of Livonia

Theoderich did take full advantage of the papal crusading bull by staging a crusade sometime during 1197. A new bishop of Livonia was appointed at the same time. His name was Bertold, and he was later to die in a battle between his own crusader army and the Livonians that took place in the summer of 1198.[34] A third bishop of Livonia was then appointed. This was Albert, who arrived in 1200 accompanied by no less than 23 ships, giving him an army of some 2000 foot soldiers and knights – a truly powerful army ready to support him from the moment they set foot on the land.[35]

Thus the succeeding bishops continued the work of the first bishop of Livonia in much the same way. They all needed to protect the Church in Livonia, either by building castles and fortified churches or by bringing in armies of crusaders from the West. At the same time they all brought with them clerics to preach the word of God to the pagans in Livonia.[36]

It is therefore very difficult (and in fact misleading) to keep differentiating between two distinctly different types of conversion in Livonia between 1185 and 1200 – conversion by preaching or by the sword. We find that both types of Christianisation existed side by side throughout the period. Neither Meinhard nor his successors seem to have experienced any contradiction between preaching to and waging war against the pagans at the same time. According to the theories on the just war (*bellum justum*) that also influenced the crusading movement, the bishops were simply protecting the Christian Church as well as the newly baptised people of Livonia against any (pagan) attack. Thus the crusaders in the Baltic lands did not fight to convert the pagans, but for the defence of the Church. They had indeed been doing so since the very first crusades against the Wends and the Estonians and were acting for the same reasons in the 1180s and 1190s during the time of Meinhard, Bertold and Albert. Thus the real differences in the nature of the missionary work during the incumbency of these first three bishops were not in their use of force to defend the Church: strongholds, men-at-arms and even crusaders were used throughout the period as a means to secure the Church in the entire Baltic region. At the same time there were attempts to convert the Livonians in a peaceful way by clerics who preached the word of God to the pagans.

The real difference between Meinhard, Bertold and Albert is to be found in the length of time that the crusaders had to spend in Livonia. The crusaders that came to Livonia together with Albert after 1200 were expected to stay there for a much longer period of time than had been normal hitherto. When Albert eventually founded a new town in Livonia by the name of Riga in 1202, it acquired the presence of the crusaders and the colonists all year around, with the city walls actually making it possible for the colonists to live there day in and day out.[37] The presence of the Germans in Livonia from then on became permanent and not just for short periods of time, and Albert had to spend a considerable amount of time in northern Germany each year preaching the crusades and gathering crusaders for the next season's campaigns in Livonia.

In my opinion, the permanent presence of colonists, merchants and crusaders marked the real change in the nature of the early missionary activities and crusades in Livonia and not the use of force compared to peaceful preaching.

NOTES

1   Hucker 1989, p.52. See also *Arnoldus*; *Heinrici*.
2   As example, see Biezais 1969; Christiansen 1997, pp. 79f.; Rebane 1989, p. 180; Hellmann 1989, pp. 31, 34; Hucker 1989, p. 40. See also the article by B. Bombi in this anthology. Some scholars even suggest that violent conversion dominated the region even before the first attempts to convert the Livonians and thus dated back to the early 1170s; Abers 1958.
3   For a much more comprehensive version of this article, see Jensen 2001a.
4   *Heinrici*, I, 2. *Arnoldus*, 5, 30.
5   *Arnoldus*, 5, 30.
6   Hellmann 1989, pp. 19–23.
7   *Heinrici*, I 3.
8   *Heinrici*, I 3.
9   *Heinrici*, I 3.
10 Jensen 2000, pp. 71-72.
11 Jähnig 1989, p. 127. Se also Caune 1996, pp. 19–28.
12 *Heinrici*, I, 5-7.
13 *Heinrici*, I 5-7; Jähnig 1989, p. 127. Jähnig seems to think that the church and castle were built in 1185.
14 *Heinrici*, I, 8.
15 Hellmann 1989, p. 24.
16 Jiménez 1996, p. 74; France 1999, p. 91.
17 *Heinrici*, I, 6.
18 Hellmann 1989, p. 27.
19 Concerning the *servi episcopi* see *Heinrici*, X, 8 as an example.
20 Some of the Livonians who had been baptised, according to Henry, washed it off by taking a bath in the river, thus cleansing themselves of Christianity. This took place immediately after the construction of the castles. *Heinrici*, I, 9. See also ibid. I, 11. According to modern scholars it is more likely that Henry is referring to the local use of saunas and wrongly believed this strange behaviour to be some kind of pagan ritual. Lind 2004.
21 Urban 1998, p. 196.
22 *Heinrici*, I, 11.
23 *Heinrici*, I, 11. Hellmann 1989, p. 30.
24 Kroman 1980a, p. 110; Kroman 1980b, p. 168.
25 Kroman 1980a, p. 110; Kroman 1980b, p. 168.
26 *Heinrici*, I, 11.

27 *Heinrici*, I, 12.
28 Angenendt 1997, pp. 470f.
29 *Heinrici*, I, 12.
30 Traditionally Danish scholars have dated this event to the year of 1169. Resent research however seems to indicate that the year of the Danish conquest of Arkona took place in 1168. Lind 2004, p. 77.
31 DD, 1, 3, 27.
32 See the article of John H. Lind in this anthology. See also Schmidt 2000.
33 Kroman 1980, pp. 110, 168.
34 *Arnoldus*, 5, 30.
35 *Heinrici*, IV 1; Brünjes 1997, p. 211.
36 Jähnig 1989, p. 143.
37 Jensen 2001b.

BIBLIOGRAPHY

Sources

'Arnoldus Lubicensis, Chronica slavorum', in *Quellensammlung zur mittelalterlichen Geschichte (Fortsetzung, CD-ROM)*. Berlin 1999.
Heinrici, Chronicon Livoniae. L. Arbusow & A. Bauer (ed.), Darmstadt 1959.

Literature

B. Abers 1958, 'Zur päpstlichen Missionspolitik in Lettland und Estland zur Zeit Innocenz' III', *Commentationes Balticae* IV–V,1, pp. 3–18.
A. Angenendt 1997, *Geschichte der Religiosität im Mittelalter*. Darmstadt.
H. Biezais 1969, 'Bishof Meinhard zwischen Visby und der Bevölkerung Livlands', in S. Ekdahl (ed.), *Kirche und Gesellschaft im Ostseraum und in Norden vor der Mitte des 13. Jahr*. Acta Visbyensia III. Visby, pp. 77–98.
H. S. Brünjes 1997, *Die Deutschordenskomturei in Bremen. Ein Beitragzur Geschichte des Ordens in Livland*. Marburg.
A. Caune 1996, 'Steinburgen des 12.–16. Jahrhunderts im Dünamündungsgebiet', in M. Josephson & M. Mogren (ed.), *Castella Maris Baltici II*. Nyköping, pp. 19–28.
E. Christiansen 1997, *The Northern Crusades*, London.
J. France 1999, *Western Warfare in the Age of the Crusades 1000–1300*. New York.
M. Hellmann 1989, 'Die Anfänge christlicher Mission in den baltischen Ländern', in M. Hellmann (ed.), *Studien über die Anfänge der Mission in Livland*. Vorträge und Forschungen, Sonderband 37. Sigmaringen, pp. 7–38.
B. U. Hucker 1989, 'Der Zisterzienserabt Bertold, Bishof von Livland, und der erste Livlandskreuzzug', in M. Hellmann (ed.), *Studien über die Anfänge der Mission in Livland*. Vorträge und Forschungen, Sonderband 37. Sigmaringen, pp. 39–64.
B. Jähnig 1989, 'Die Anfänge der Sakraltopographie von Riga', in M. Hellmann (ed.), *Studien über die Anfänge der Mission in Livland*. Vorträge und Forschungen, Sonderband 37. Sigmaringen, pp. 123–58.
C. S. Jensen 2000, 'Byer og borgere i 1200-tallets baltiske korstog', *Den Jyske Historiker* 89, pp. 68–88.
C. S. Jensen 2001a, 'The Nature of the Early Missionary Activities and Crusades in Livonia, 1185–1201', in L. Bisgaard & C. S. Jensen & K. V. Jensen & J. H. Lind (ed.), *Medieval Spirituality in Scandinavia and Europe. A Collection of Essays in Honour of Tore Nyberg*, Odense, pp. 121–37.
C. S. Jensen 2001b, 'Urban Life and the Crusades in Northern Germany and the Baltic Lands in the Early Thirteenth Century', in A. Murray (ed.), *Crusade and Conversion on the Baltic Frontier, 1150–1500*. Ashgate, pp. 75–94.

M. G. Jiménez 1996, 'Frontier and Settlement in the Kingdom of Castile (1085–1350)', in R. Bartlett & A. Mackay (ed.), *Medieval Frontier Societies*. Oxford, pp. 49–74.

E. Kroman 1980a, 'Ældre Sjællandske Krønike', in E. Kroman (ed.), *Danmarks Middelalderlige Annaler*. Copenhagen, pp. 106–116.

E. Kroman 1980b, 'Ryd Kloster Årbog', in E. Kroman (ed.), *Danmarks Middelalderlige Annaler*. Copenhagen, pp. 149–176.

J. H. Lind 2004, *Danske Korstog – Krig og Mission i Østersøen*. Copenhagen.

P. Rebane 1989, 'Denmark, the Papacy and the Christianization of Estonia', *Gli Inizi del Christianesimo in Livonia-Lettonia*. Rome, pp. 171–201.

I. Schmidt 2000, 'De skandinaviske kongemagters korstogserobringer', *Den Jyske Historiker* 89, pp. 112–132.

W. L. Urban 1998, 'Victims of the Baltic crusade, *Journal of Baltic Studies* XXIX/3, pp. 195–212.

TORBEN K. NIELSEN

Mission and Submission
Societal Change in the Baltic in the Thirteenth Century

The conversion of the Baltic societies and the ways in which this conversion came about can be partly illustrated by looking into the fate of one of the local Baltic leaders during the first decades of the thirteenth century. In Henry of Livonia's *Chronicon Livoniae* Caupo appears in several different connections. The *Chronicon Livoniae* is no doubt one of the most important sources for the Christianisation of the Baltic from 1186 to 1228. The Chronicle, which Henry completed around 1225 with additions from 1227–1228, takes as its point of departure the story of the German missionary bishop, Albert of Buxhöveden and his establishment of the missionary base in Riga.[1] Henry of Livonia himself worked in the Baltic as a priest, arbitrator, and translator, and large parts of his Chronicle mention incidents and events in which Henry actively participated. Henry's Chronicle includes a lucid and vivid description of the wars in the Baltic by the German and Danish crusading forces. In so doing, Henry furnished later scholars with many invaluable details especially concerning the military technology employed in these years and the many native tribes in the region.[2]

For Henry Christianity clearly was a superior culture which had taken upon itself to evangelise in the Baltic region and ultimately convert the Baltic peoples. This, however, was a task in dire need of local support. Occasionally, the Christian crusaders and missionaries were able to gain support from local leaders – Caupo among others. The importance of Caupo, both historically and symbolically, is underlined by the fact that, beside playing a leading role in Henry's Chronicle, Caupo also appears in one of the stories from Caesarius of Heisterbach's *Libri octo miraculorum* of about 1245. Furthermore, he has several entries in the *Livonian Rhymed Chronicle* of about 1290.[3] We shall meet Caupo several times in the pages of this article.

Christianising the Pagan Elites

In 1199 the German nobleman and prelate, Albert of Buxhöveden, was appointed missionary bishop of Livonia by the German Archbishopric

216

of Hamburg-Bremen. As such, Albert succeeded his immediate predecessors, Meinhard, who had died in 1186, and Bertold, who was killed by the pagans in 1198. Unlike his predecessors, Albert chose from the very beginning not to act solely as a humble servant of the Lord, wanting to convert the pagans by the Word alone. Albert quickly recognised that military strength would be decisive in the success of his campaign. Accordingly, he initiated his career as missionary bishop not by going to the Baltic on crusade; instead he headed for Gotland in the summer of 1199 where he signed about five hundred men with the cross to go to Livonia.[4] From Gotland his journey went to Denmark, where he gained solid support from King Canute VI, Duke (and later to be King) Valdemar, as well as the Danish Archbishop Absalon. Continuing to Germany and joining with King Philip of Swabia, Albert again signed many pilgrims with the Cross. Having assured Philip that the German pilgrims would be granted the papal privileges of plenary indulgences and protection of property normally given to the pilgrims and crusaders going to Jerusalem, Albert also gained the support of the German king. With this support, Albert sailed to Livonia in the summer of 1200 together with two German dukes, Conrad of Dortmund and Hartberg of Iburg. He directed his fleet into the mouth of the Dvina River; and it was from here that the German mission to Livonia would make its departure.[5]

Albert of Riga's first time in Livonia was difficult, since he was exposed to violent opposition from the neighbouring regional tribes. The establishment of the missionary base could only be carried out through negotiations with the Balts; negotiations that would take place on the basis of military strength and with the foundation of other religious or clerical institutions to support and protect the Christian pilgrims as well as preach the Word.[6] Such was the situation in the summer of 1200, when Albert, shortly upon arrival, found himself surrounded by hostile pagan opposition. In this situation the bishop was to be saved only thanks to a small band of Friesian warriors. The Friesians were reputed to be fierce and efficient warriors, and on this occasion they would fully live up to their reputation in that they resolutely burnt the crops and fields of the pagans on their way to rescue the besieged bishop. The Baltic leaders for their part apparently considered this a sign of great military strength and were quick to renew the peace by accepting baptism and gave hostages to the Germans.[7]

We know such militarily supported attempts at conversion were also directed against the elites of pagan society prior to 1200. Christian missionising had proven itself to be most successful in areas where local leaders personally accepted a change of faith, and where such royal conversion was followed by forcible Christianisation of the population. The Christianisation of Denmark under the reign of King Harold Bluetooth serves as a fine example of top-down missionary and conversion efforts.[8]

The pagan leader Caupo was one of the tribal elders Albert of Riga had to deal with in 1200. Henry of Livonia tells us how Caupo and some other leaders were invited to a drinking party in the German camp to celebrate successful peace negotiations. However, the deceitful Germans simply imprisoned the Balts and demanded that they present 30 of their better boys as hostages. Caupo and other Livonian leaders accepted, for fear of being transported across the sea to Germany themselves as hostages.[9] Since we hear about such hostage-taking several times in Henry's Chronicle, it is obvious that this was an integral part of waging war in the region and, I imagine, other regions as well. However, here the hostage-taking may have had other implications apart from being a means of waging war. I shall return briefly to this.

Possibly Caupo was baptised following these incidents.[10] We do not know, but he surely must have converted when he travelled to Rome, of all places, in 1203. With Albert of Livonia's second in command, the Cistercian Theoderich, acting as guide, Caupo visited the Eternal City and Pope Innocent III. In Henry's Chronicle this journey is conveyed as an educational tour: a classic, but still very special, pilgrimage. Thus, Caupo is portrayed as the 'model pagan' in a sense, converted, baptised, and penitent. On finally reaching Rome, the travellers were greeted by the pope, who, very conveniently, thanked Caupo for the conversion of 'the Livonian tribe' – of course a gross misrepresentation.[11]

Both Caupo and Theoderich were offered splendid gifts by the pope. Theoderich received a beautiful copy of the Bible of Gregory the Great and Caupo was handed one hundred gold pieces, a papal blessing and an amicable goodbye.[12] Innocent in Rome was very aware of the importance of local and newly converted princes as allies in the continued struggle for conversion and conquest.[13]

It is interesting to note that, in connection with this journey to Rome, Henry of Livonia actually calls Caupo king or *Rex* – and this is the only designation of a Baltic leader as such in the entire Chronicle. That Caupo played a very important role in Livonia before the Germans arrived on the scene is also made clear in the *Livonian Rhymed Chronicle*, which describes him as virtuous, noble and rich. Obviously these sources depict Caupo as honourable, albeit a former pagan. Caupo is presented as a model for imitation to be followed by the other members of the Livonian pagan elites. The modelling of Caupo is thus based on the common assumption that, were the mission to succeed, it would be necessary first to convert the pagan leaders. In the history of the Christian mission it is a commonplace that conversion – if successful – should be aimed primarily at the leading strata of pagan society, the assumption being that if the leaders are converted, the people will follow. Christian missionising was most successful in areas where local rulers first changed their beliefs and gave way to Christianisation of their own population. This seems to be the case in Livonia as well. Accordingly, we learn from the *Livonian Rhymed Chronicle* that it was

> a blow to the heathens that Caupo and his followers had accepted Christianity. This soon became known throughout the land and a great outcry arose. The Lithuanians and Russians were enraged and the Estonians, Letts, and Öselians also, for the news that Christianity had come to Livonia was hard for them to bear. And the complaint of the pagans was that the Christian numbers increased day by day.[14]

On their way back from Rome, we are told, Caupo, Theoderich, and the accompanying ships, carrying pilgrims, provisions and weapons, 'made the people of Riga, who had been very sad, happy with their arrival,' because the city was once again threatened by pagans. Perhaps it was precisely the impression of Caupo as an ardent believer, a neophyte, and a loyal ally of the Germans that made Henry of Livonia write that 'to the extent that the joy of the Christians was increased, so the multitude of the pagans was made sorrowful and confused.'[15]

Baptism and Submission

The Christian missionary activity has been described as being made out of two objectives, a positive and a negative one. The positive objective was to ensure the free acceptance of the Christian faith; the negative one to wipe out paganism. The symbol of having accepted Christianity was baptism, which St Augustine considered should only to be offered to people who, by their own free will and their actual behaviour, demonstrated their real and deep conversion to the Christian faith. Later these Augustinian baptismal preconditions were reduced to only demanding from the person wanting to be baptised a short version of the creed, particularly the parts involving the renunciation of paganism and the punishment for apostasy.[16] Only after baptism would the Christian mission undertake the necessary parochial work, i.e., educating the neophytes in the Creed and other tenets of the faith as well as establishing institutions of confession and penance.[17]

Traditionally baptism would take place in three different ways: *immersio*, *infusio*, and *aspersio*, each involving different levels of liturgical display. The most elaborate baptismal liturgy, the *immersio*, was also the most commonly used in Western Europe in the Middle Ages. This consisted of prolonged exorcist rituals before a three-fold immersion of the entire body in the baptismal font, followed by the laying on of hands, and formal abjurations of one's former faith, before the final blessings. This, however, was a liturgy apparently very seldom used with members of the defeated Baltic tribes.[18] We have ample evidence in Henry's Chronicle that the rather simplified *aspersio* liturgy was the one in use. Caesarius of Heisterbach tells of the excessive use of the reduced *aspersio* liturgy in the Baltic.[19] After a fierce battle in 1211 Henry of Livonia writes:

> The Esthonians rejoiced greatly over peace simultaneously with the Livonians and Letts, and they promised to receive the sacrament of baptism on the same terms. When hostages had been given and peace had been ratified, therefore, they received all the priests into the fort. The priests sprinkled all the houses, the fort, the men and women, and all the people with holy water. They performed a sort of initiation and catechised them before baptising but postponed administering the sacrament of baptism because of the great shedding of blood, which had taken place. When these things had been done, therefore, the army returned to Livonia and they all glorified the Lord for converting the tribes.[20]

Henry obviously gives a very pious explanation of why the full baptismal liturgy was postponed. On other occasions, the full liturgy would be postponed on account of pressing military needs, often in the shape of an approaching enemy. And apparently there was good reason for this. We learn from Henry, writing of yet another 'final' victory over the fierce Öselians, that the baptismal liturgy was very time-consuming:

> The sons of the nobles were given up. The venerable bishop of Riga joyfully and devotedly catechised the first of them and watered him from the holy font. Other priests poured water on the other hostages. The priests were led with joy into the town in order to preach Christ and throw out Tharapita, the God of the Oesilians. They consecrated a fountain in the middle of the fort, filled a jar, and, after catechism, baptised first the elders and upper-class men and then the other men, women, and boys. From morning to evening the men, women, and children crowded very closely around, shouting: 'Hurry and baptise me,' so that even these priests, of whom there were sometimes five, sometimes six, were worn out with the work of baptising. The priests, therefore, baptised with the greatest devotion many thousands of people, whom they saw rush with the greatest joy to the sacrament of baptism; and they, too, rejoiced, hoping that the work would count for the remission of their sins. What they could not accomplish on that day, they completed on the next day and the third day.[21]

One important reason why the priests had to hurry so much was the status given to the neophytes in their baptism. Baptism was a sacrament, but in fact also an important legal act. Baptism would place the neophyte in a legal relationship with the local church acting as a representative of divine will on earth. Given these realities it was vital to know exactly which authority the neophytes would belong to, whether Danish, German, or Swedish, or whether the neophytes were submitted to the authority of the Sword Brothers.[22] At times there was in fact a fiercely competitive atmosphere between the crusading powers on this issue. Henry records an argument in 1220 between German and Danish missionaries:

> The Wierlanders of the first province, called Purdiviru, received them and everyone from fourteen villages was baptised by them, including Tabelin, their elder, who was later hanged by the Danes because he had received baptism from the Rigans and had placed his son as a hostage with the Brothers of the Militia. The rest of the Wierlanders from the other provinces dared not receive the Rigan priests because of the threats of the Danes, but summoned the Danes, as they were so near, and they were baptised by them. The Wierlanders believed that the Christians had one God, both for the Danes and the Germans, and one faith and one baptism. They thought that no discord would come of it and so they accepted, unconcernedly, the baptism of their Danish neighbours. The Rigans, however, held that Wierland was theirs, since it had been subjected to the Christian faith by their men, and sent the aforesaid priests to baptise here. But the Danes desired to take over this neighbouring land for themselves and sent their priests, as it were, into a foreign harvest. They baptised some villages and sent their men to the others to which they could not come so quickly, ordering wooden crosses to be made in all the villages. They sent holy water into the villages by the hands of the peasants

and instructed then how to splash the water on women and children. They tried hereby to anticipate the Rigan priests and sought in this manner to put the land into the hands of the Danish king.[23]

The competition to convert the largest numbers of Balts was obviously due to the fact that the neophytes, by their baptism, would not only acknowledge the Christian faith, but also the Christian obligations known in Henry's words as *iura christianitatis*. It is interesting to note that in almost every incident in Henry's Chronicle in which the Balts were conquered and were to acknowledge Christianity, they would also have to acknowledge an accompanying secular authority, which would levy taxes and other obligations on the former pagan population. In 1212 Caupo appeared as an arbitrator in a conflict between a Lett tribe from Autine on the one side and the Sword Brothers on the other. The Letts had complained to their new religious master, Bishop Albert of Livonia, over the unjust taxes and duties claimed by their new secular rulers, the Sword Brothers. The incident as reported in Henry's Chronicle underlines wholly new ties of dependency and economic submission which were the consequences for the Letts of their conversion. In Henry's Chronicle negotiations ended in no result, after which several former pagan tribes actually joined forces, threatening to renounce their new faith. In the midst of all this, we find Caupo, who, according to Henry, solemnly declared never to waver in his new-found beliefs. However, he promised to intercede with the bishop for his fellow tribesmen so that 'the Christian law might be lightened for them.'

The Balts in this situation turned down the proposal from Caupo to act as a negotiator and chose to fight against the unjust taxes on bees, trees and fields – only to witness the subsequent imprisonment of the Livonian elders and the burning down of their castles. Bishop Albert of Riga harshly criticised the Sword Brothers over this incident and promised the Balts that they should receive their properties again.[24]

Both this and other stories and the overall tone of the language in the Chronicle suggest that conversion was not merely a matter of religion, but a profound change in society involving new ties of dependence, new structures of economic exploitation and completely new kinds of rule. We learn in Henry's Chronicle, that the German missionaries introduced a new system of jurisprudence. A system of *Vogts* (in German) or *advocatus* (in Latin) was apparently a great success in the first years of Livonian Christendom. Henry tells the story of a German *advocatus*, whose services were greatly appreciated by the Balts:

> The people of Treiden, indeed, after they had accepted the mysteries of holy baptism and, with it, the whole spiritual law, asked their priest, Alabrand, just as he administered spiritual law for them, likewise to administer civil cases according to the law of the Christians, which by us is called secular law. The people of Livonia were formerly most perfidious and everyone stole what his neighbour had, but now theft, violence, rapine, and similar things were forbidden as a result of their baptism. Those who had been despoiled before their baptism grieved over the loss of their goods. For, after baptism, they did not

dare to take them back by violence and accordingly asked for a secular judge to settle cases of this kind. Hence the priest Alabrand was the first to receive the authority to hear both spiritual and civil cases. He, administering quite faithfully the office enjoined upon him, both for the sake of God and because of his sins, exercised his authority in cases of rapine and theft, restored things unjustly seized, and so showed the Livonians the right way of living.[25]

Still other areas of social importance were influenced by conversion to Christianity. We hear several times in Henry's Chronicle how women and children were simply abducted, how child hostages were demanded – and accepted. In fact, on several occasions, Henry is quite explicit concerning the fate of surviving women and children. When Christian armies had massacred entire villages, slaughtering every man, we learn how the women and children were spared, but held captive, some of them even sent to Germany. What, besides normal military procedure, could the reason for this be? A letter from pope Innocent III dated 1201 might enlighten us here. The papal letter is a response to several specific questions and requests concerning the former pagans in the Baltic put to Innocent by Albert of Livonia. The pope writes of the Baltic marriage-strategy and how it was common practice among the Baltic widows simply to remarry the brother of their deceased husbands, i.e., the original brother–in-law. According to canon law, such *Levirate* marriages were strictly forbidden. However, the pope had been informed that were the Balts not allowed to continue with this practice, the conversion of Livonia would be in grave danger, and massive apostasy would unavoidably result.[26] Innocent allowed the Balts to retain their customs in this matter under certain circumstances.

In this way, the papal letter helps us understand the explicitness of Henry of Livonia when it comes to the defeated women and children. It is apparent that abducting women and children was not a military strategy known only to the Christian crusading armies, but of course also to the Balts themselves. The idea of such abduction was probably the same, whether the victors in battle were pagans fighting other pagans or Christians fighting for conversion. It is obvious from the papal letter that a widow would remarry the brother of her deceased husband in order to uphold her previous kinship relation, and that she believed that she would hereby pass on the lineage of her husband to coming generations. Abducting women and children would effectively put an end to existing pagan dynasties in the area. Thus the Christian victors would achieve two objectives through abduction and hostage-taking. Firstly, the Christians would hereby initiate effective destruction of pagan kinship relations. The introduction of Christian principles of marriage (non-incestuous marital connections; consent between the marital partners; the indissolubility of marriage) would in time efficiently obliterate the Baltic marriage and kinship structure and hereby destroy the former pagan societies from within. Secondly, the Christians would seize a great opportunity to secure the new Christian faith and its rules in the region, through education and instruction of the hostages taken.

Desacralisation of Paganism

Following initial conversion and baptism, proper Christianisation would take place with the aid of preachers explaining the principal articles of faith. Church-building and the creation of socio-religious role models like our friend Caupo would be a part of this. However, proper Christianisation would presuppose yet another element of social change – the extinction of pagan practices and beliefs, as well as the physical remains of paganism in the landscape. A process of desacralisation of pagan cult places would follow initial conversion.

Baltic pagan religion was strongly marked by magic rituals and practices. The Balts believed in the existence of a number of different gods, each with different attributes and powers. Beside magical beliefs and the matching cultic practices, the Baltic religion was characterised by some sort of animism and the worship of ancestors. One of the few gods actually mentioned by name in Henry's Chronicle is Tharapita, the main god for the inhabitants of the island Ösel. This was a god who was believed to provide help to his followers when experiencing a crisis. Other gods or, in Christian terms demons, would populate the many groves and trees in the Baltic, and at times appear to foretell the future or to decide in matters of public interest.[27] Through specific rituals and prayers, the god could be called upon to give advice, as in 1211, when bellicose Öselians laid siege to Caupo's castle. During the siege the pagans sacrificed several animals, through which they sought to receive the advice of their gods. In one case the sacrifice produced the sinister omen that 'the flesh, which they cut off, fell on the left side, which indicated that their gods were displeased.' Consequently (!), the pagans lost the battle.[28] On another occasion we learn of a sacrifice made by Livonians under siege themselves. The pagans immolated goats and dogs, and tossed the animals from the surrounded castle 'in the face of the Bishop and the whole army to mock Christianity.'[29] The cultic practices associated with paganism in the Baltic could also include human sacrifice. However, it is uncertain whether human sacrifice was actually a rather recent cultic invention, perhaps even provoked by crusading activity in the area. Henry gives the terrifying story of the martyrdom of the Danish *advocatus* Hebbe, with a clear allusion to Jeremiah 15:3:

> After this the Saccalians went into Jerwan. There they seized the magistrate, Hebbus, and brought him with the other Danes back to their fort and tormented him and the others with a cruel martyrdom. They tore out their viscera and plucked out Hebbus' heart from his bosom while he was still alive. They roasted it in the fire, divided it among themselves, and ate it, so that they would be made strong against the Christians. They gave the bodies of the Danes to the dogs to gnaw and to the birds of the air.[30]

Of course, paganism like this could not be tolerated and must be eliminated. Other elements of paganism also had to be demolished. In 1220 German priests tore down a holy place, apparently the birthplace of the god Tharapita. In this holy place, which was a grove in a beautiful forest, the priests found numerous figures of a pagan pantheon. The priests tore down the

223

images and destroyed the place entirely: 'the Natives wondered greatly that blood did not flow' from the statues, and 'they believed the more in the priests' sermons,' Henry states coolly.[31] Desacralisation of pagan cults could also take place in the shape of direct assistance from the Christian God through miracles brought to public knowledge through the works of the missionaries. Maybe one of Henry's main purposes in writing his Chronicle was to show how God intervened in the physical world. Henry relates a story from 1223 of a German merchant, living in the house of an Estonian, who was killed by his pagan landlord. Some time after the killing, the wife of the Estonian gave birth to a son, who bore on his body the fresh marks of the stabbing suffered by the German merchant. The wounds on the boy healed, but the scars remained visible. 'Many people saw this and were astonished, bearing witness to and proving God's vengeance, for the murderer was slain at once by the Christian army.'[32]

Massacres and Warfare

Whether Caupo himself would help spread the gospel in Livonia is doubtful, but it is beyond doubt, however, that he was a master of another basic element of Christianisation. Caupo is depicted as a very efficient and clever warrior. Henry states that Caupo was 'the very faithful, who never neglected the Lord's battles and expeditions.'[33] In 1206 Caupo apparently led an army against his own former castle, which at the time was held by Caupo's still pagan relatives and friends. Following a short siege, the inhabitants of the castle were dealt with firmly. They were hunted down and the castle looted and burnt. In 1210 Caupo's military skills again came in handy. Henry of Livonia recalls how a joint force of Germans, Livonians and Letts pursued some Estonians. In this incident, Caupo is described as the strategic mind who patiently waits to go into combat. Contrary to the shrewd (i.e., Christianised) Caupo, the Letts hurled themselves into battle with the inevitable result that enemy forces surrounded them. In this case, Henry of Livonia puts some powerful biblical statements concerning the necessity and the devoutness of just warfare into the mouth of Caupo.[34]

That Caupo was very useful in warfare is further evidenced by his not being the least soft on even his former allies and relatives. Henry's narrative contains stories of how Caupo conducted regular massacres on Baltic, pagan communities in both 1211 and 1212. What strikes a modern reader is therefore not the many stories of decapitation, torture, massacres, hostage taking, robbing and pillaging – in short genocide. What is really terrifying is the impression of every-day ritual in these stories. In the Chronicle some of the worst human atrocities are presented in a very low-key tone. From a battle in 1211:

> Caupo, Bertold of Wenden and his men, and the bishop's men immediately rose up and went into the nearest Saccalian province. They burnt all the villages to which they could penetrate, killed all the men, brought the women back as prisoners, and returned to Livonia.[35]

Later that same year, Caupo conducted a retaliation campaign against the Estonians:

> The Esthonians went on all night and came in the morning to Raupa. They burned the church and the church property and went around the whole province consigning villages and houses to the flames, killing men, dragging women and children out of their hiding places of the forests, and taking them captive. The Rigans heard this, went out with the pilgrims, and came to Treiden. The pagans, however, feared their arrival and, after three days, swiftly returned to their own land with all their loot. Caupo with some Germans and others followed them in Saccalia, burnt the forts of Owele and Purke as well as many villages, took much booty, killed many men, and led off the women and children as captives.[36]

However, although the Chronicle is crammed with laconic statements like these on the pure necessities of war, Henry also ascribed to Caupo the very Christian ability to express grief and sorrow in this connection. Thus, Caupo's very special position in Henry's Chronicle is emphasised yet again. The character of Caupo serves the purpose of underlining that man's real and inner feelings and emotions could only be expressed through the Christian belief. This will also account for the rather unusual paragraph in which Caupo's own grief and sorrow is expressed through very consciously chosen biblical imagery. This imagery, whose composition, starting as it does with the Old Testament, followed by the Gospels and ending with a quotation from the Apocalypse, indicates that the heavy fighting in remote Baltic regions would also be included in the great history of Christianity. The biblical references serve to place the conversion of the Livonians firmly in the overall Christian history of salvation. During heavy fighting in 1210, some newly converted Lettgallians and the Rigans were defeated by a larger Estonian army:

> The Esthonians, however, followed both the Germans, the Livonians, and the infantry of the Letts from right and left. They captured about a hundred of them, killed some, and, leading the others back towards the Sedde, tortured them in a cruel martyrdom. Of the fourteen of the latter, they roasted some alive, and, after stripping the others of their clothes and making crosses on their backs with their swords, they cut their throats, and thus, we hope, sent them into the heavenly company of the martyrs. Then the Esthonians, taunting the Christians, returned to their country and sent men through all the provinces to persuade them to swear and join together with one heart and mind against the Christian name. Caupo, the Livonians, and the Letts returned from the fight, bewailed their dead, and were joined by the whole church in grieving over the newly baptised who had been butchered by the pagans. The church, indeed, was like an arch, always bent but never broken; like the ark of Noah, raised up by great billows but not crushed; like the bark of Peter, shaken by waves but submerged; like a woman whom the dragon followed but did not overtake. For consolation followed after this tribulation, and after sadness God gave joy.[37]

Evangelisation and Social Remodelling

Changing the pagan Baltic societies could not be accomplished simply through war, human atrocities and the accompanying breakdown of age-old kinship structures and governmental systems. Founding new Christian institutions would be equally necessary in efficiently remodelling these societies. A story in Caesarius of Heisterbach highlights Caupo's status as a role model for the neophyte elites and perhaps for experienced Christians as well. Caesarius's collection of exempla constituted of stories of miracles was designed especially to be used by novices in the Cistercian monasteries, and was to be read aloud, preached and contemplated upon. In this way, the stories would become efficient devices for moral and ethical progress. The stories and their moral content could be used to meditate upon sin, guilt and the possibility of redemption.[38]

In Caesarius of Heisterbach's *Libri VIII miraculorum* Caupo appears as a military leader. During a raid, one of his servants fell mortally ill and was in dire need of a priest, for 'without the medicine of confession, salvation is impossible,' Caupo told his servant.[39] Since, however, no priest was available, Caupo urged the servant to confess his sins to him. Being unaware of confession's faculty of purifying, the dying servant chose the wrong strategy, maintaining upon several pledges from Caupo, that he had no sins to confess, whereupon he drew his last breath in the arms of his master. In Caesarius' story the dead servant was later to return to life, only to account for terrible and horrifying torments after death. The servant had been transported to a 'place of punishments,' where he was forced to eat some very spicy and strong fish. After this horrifying experience, the servant was moved to another place, where he was forced to drink boiling mead; and finally the servant was transported to a third place, where he had a cartload of hay burnt on his back. These punishments were meted out for three specific sins, the fish for having cheated a fellow fisherman, the mead for having stolen some honey to make mead, and the burning hay for having transported hay from his field to his house on a Sunday. Lastly, the unhappy servant was released from his punishments and returned to life on the explicit order that he must tell of the punishments visited on sinners who disregard the 'help of confession.'

Perhaps not only Cistercian novices in Western Europe, but also neophytes in the Baltic, could have made good use of such stories of godly intervention in the physical world. However, it was not only acting as a lay curate ready to hear confessions that Caupo would serve as a model worthy of imitation. In yet another way, Caupo also served as the ideal neophyte. We are told that Caupo upon return from Rome 'became most faithful, and because of the persecution of the Livonians, fled to the town and lived there with the Christians for almost a whole year,' apparently taking up Christian habits and customs.[40]

Although, as a convert, Caupo at this point (1205) would be considered quite exceptional, he was no longer alone in this. More Livonian elders were converted, and the Germans would provide a proper upbringing and instruction in Christianity for the newly converted. Henry notes how

Albert of Livonia took 'the elders of Holm with him to Germany so that by seeing and hearing Christian customs there they, who had always been unfaithful, might learn to become faithful.'[41] Upon a visit by the Danish Archbishop Andreas Sunesen to Riga in the winter of 1206–1207, the Riga mission sent out priests into the newly conquered, but presumably still pagan areas. The message from the Danish Archbishop was that the priests should build churches, divide the regions into parishes, and instruct the inhabitants in the Faith – of course only after demanding hostages from the leading families.[42] After all, there was no need to take unnecessary risks.

Such ideas of religious instruction lay behind the idea of staging a theatre show in the city of Riga in 1205. Henry of Livonia tells us how the theatrical display of the Old Testament battles between Gideon and the Philistines was acted out so energetically that the inhabitants precipitately fled the City Square for fear of being hurled into the rumbustious fights on the stage. The direct intention was 'that the pagans might learn the rudiments of the Christian faith by an ocular demonstration.' In Henry's Chronicle the story is also used as a prophecy or literary allusion to the many trials and tribulations the Balts were to encounter in the following years. The combination of warfare and Christian instruction and education would secure the Christianisation of the Baltic:

> Certainly, through the many wars that followed, the pagans were to be converted, and, through the doctrine of the Old and New Testaments, they were to be told how they might attain to the true Peacemaker and eternal life.[43]

As would be expected, Caupo would die as he had lived – by the sword. In a battle in 1217 a lance ran through Caupo and he died shortly after. Of course, only after confessing his sins, saying his prayers and professing his Creed, receiving his viaticum, and leaving all his property and his estates to the Church. Thus, the Chronicler carefully constructed both his death and his last words. Neither the weapon that killed him nor the way Caupo was killed was of course at all accidental. We are explicitly told that the lance penetrated Caupo's side, and in the Livonian Rhymed Chronicle, the references to the Passion of Christ are also clear. This work is explicitly states that Caupo received four wounds, and that he repeatedly said: 'God received five wounds for me and I only regret that what befell Him has not befallen me.' He died in peace.'[44]

Caupo's exemplary status as a transitional figure between paganism and Christianity was further enhanced through the story of his funeral. Henry recalls how both 'Count Albert, the abbot, and all who were with them, mourned over him. His body was burned and the bones were taken away to Livonia and buried at Cubbesele.'[45] Thus, Caupo's funeral displays obviously syncretistic features, with the application of both pagan and Christian burial rituals. In this way, Caupo's story, from his initial capture via baptism and conversion to his last journey, is a consciously constructed story of one man's necessary journey towards God. At the same time, however, it is an expression of the gradual militarisation,

Christianisation and colonisation undertaken in the Baltic in the thirteenth century. Henry's Chronicle, with his inclusion of the story of Caupo, is the story of a number of pagan societies which had to submit to a Christian Europe under heavy and violent expansion.

NOTES

1   On Albert see Gnegel-Waitschies 1958.
2   Cf. the Introduction in Henry of Livonia.
3   Tamm 1996; *Livonian Rhymed Chronicle*, pp. 5, 6, 8; *Livländische Reimchronik*, lines 269, 280, 310, 388, 513.
4   Heinricus, ch. III 2; Henry of Livonia, p. 35.
5   Heinricus, ch. III 4–; Henry of Livonia, pp. 35–36; Heinricus, ch. IV 1; Henry of Livonia, p. 36.
6   Cf. C. S. Jensen 2000.
7   Heinricus, ch. IV 3; Henry of Livonia, p. 37.
8   K. V. Jensen 2000, pp. 52–53. Examples can be found among the Western Slavs on the southern shore of the Baltic. Saxo Grammaticus's stories are illuminating in telling how personal conversions among the leaders of the pagan countries had significant influence on the fate of the mission and submission of the area. (*Saxonis Gesta Danorum* books 14–16) However, the Abodrite kingdom in this region has been called 'one of the very few instances in the Western missionary history, where the conversion of the princely family did not pull the conversion of the entire realm with it.' Hellmann 1989, p. 15 quoting Fritze 1960. However, normally it was believed that the conversion of the pagan princes and nobles would pave the way for Christianisation involving preaching campaigns, church-building and the division of the landscape into the ecclesiastical/administrative parochial system. Still, results of the missionary attempts would often be hard to maintain. Were the Christian armies to pull out of the conquered regions, the risk of apostasy would be imminent. Saxo and Helmold not only tell of successful mission and conquest, but also – and very much so – of such relapses.
9   Heinricus, ch. IV 4; Henry of Livonia, p. 37.
10 Details in Henry's Chronicle suggest that Caupo had received baptism at this time. Hellmann 1989, p. 29. Other sources, however, claim that the first German missionary bishop, Meinhard, had already converted Caupo. *Livländische Reimchronik*, lines 385ff; *Livonian Rhymed Chronicle*, p. 6.
11 The Livonian Rhymed Chronicle actually quotes the report from Theoderich to Innocent III: 'There are numerous pagans by whom we are oppressed. They do much harm to Christianity, as we will tell you, father. One group is called Lithuanians. Those pagans are arrogant and because of their great might, their army does much harm to pure Christianity. Nearby lies another group of pagans named Semgallians, who have great strength of numbers and dominate the lands around them. They impose hardships without relief upon those who live near them. The Selonians are also pagans and blind to all virtue. They have many false gods and perform evils without number. Nearby is another people named Letts. All these pagans have most unusual customs. They dwell together of necessity, but they farm separately, scattered about through the forests. Their women are beautiful and wear exotic clothing. They ride in ancient manner and their army is very strong whenever it is assembled. Along the seashore lies an area named Kurland. It is more than three hundred miles long. Any Christian who comes to this land against their wishes will be robbed of life and property. The Öselians are evil heathens, neighbours to the Kurs. They are surrounded by the sea and never fear strong armies. In the summers, as we have cause to know, they raid those neighbouring lands, which they can reach by ship. They have attacked both Christians and pagans and their greatest strength lies in their fleet. The Estonians are

also pagans and there are many mother's sons of them. That is because their land is wide and extensive. I cannot begin to describe it. They have so many powerful men and so many provinces that I do not wish to say anything more about them. The Livonians are also heathens, but we have hope that God shall sunder them from that, just as He has with Caupo, who has come here with us. God's gentle wisdom has brought him to Christianity. His tribe is large and most of it has come to us and has accepted baptism' *Livonian Rhymed Chronicle*, pp. 5-6; *Livländische Reimchronik*, lines 322–384.

12 Heinricus, ch. VII 3; Henry of Livonia, p. 43.

13 Theodorich himself might have had another purpose for this journey besides accompanying a noble neophyte on his first pilgrimage. His main purpose may easily have been papal recognition of the new monastic order, The Sword Brothers, which was founded the year before in 1202. Urban 1975, p. 52; Benninghoven 1965, p. 39. See also Heinricus, ch. VI 4; Henry of Livonia, p. 40.

14 *Livländische Reimchronik*, lines 279–281; *Livonian Rhymed Chronicle*, p. 5.

15 Heinricus, ch. VIII 2; Henry of Livonia, p. 46.

16 Kahl 1983, p. 125.

17 Blanke 1963a, pp. 347–348.

18 Tamm 1996, p. 74.

19 In Caesarius of Heisterbach the *aspersio* liturgy actually caused worries about how both canon law and Christian dogmatics would respond to the validity of such baptism. Tamm 1996, p. 38.

20 Heinricus, ch. XIV 11; Henry of Livonia, p. 107.

21 Heinricus, ch. XXX 5; Henry of Livonia, p. 244.

22 The Russian Church was also involved in the competition for the souls in the Baltic. In Henry's Chronicle we read how in 1208 a Lett tribe near Ymera 'cast lots and asked the opinion of their gods [!] whether they should submit to the baptism of the Russians of Pskov or, on the other hand, to that of the Latins,' Henry of Livonia, p. 75. Cf. Heinricus, ch. XI 7.

23 Heinricus, ch. XXIV 1; Henry of Livonia, p. 188.

24 Heinricus, ch. XVI 3; Henry of Livonia, pp. 123–124. We hear of rebellion and uprising whenever the level of economic exploitation was considered too high. See Heinricus, ch. XV 5, XVI 4 et passim. Apparently, the Christian powers acknowledged the necessity of a relatively slow remodelling of the Baltic societies. Henry of Livonia said of the new methods of government that 'this Christian law [of making use of judges or magistrates, TKN] pleased the Livonians the first year because the office of magistrate was administered by faithful men of this kind. Afterwards, however, this office was very much degraded throughout all Livonia, Lettgallia, and Estonia at the hands of diverse secular judges, who used the office of magistrate more to fill their own purses than to defend the justice of God.' Heinricus, ch. X 15; Henry of Livonia, p. 67. The papal legate, William of Modena, admonished the Germans during a visit in Livonia in the 1220s, not to 'hurt their subjects by excessive exactions and undue harshness. They were to bring in Christian customs and abolish pagan rites, and to teach and instruct them both by their words and by their good example.' Heinricus, ch. XXIX 5; Henry of Livonia, p. 234.

25 Heinricus, ch. X 15; Henry of Livonia, p. 67.

26 Maccarone 1989, pp. 78–80; Brundage 1973, p. 316.

27 See, for example, Heinricus, ch. X 14; Henry of Livonia, p. 66. On Tharapita see Heinricus, ch. XXIV 5; Henry of Livonia, pp. 193–194.

28 Heinricus, ch. XV 3; Henry of Livonia, p. 110. It is of course interesting to note how in Henry's account the sinister omen for the pagans was a foretelling of Christian victory. At times in Henry's Chronicle, the pagan pantheon was rejected as mere superstition, whereas at other times decisions by the pagan gods were used to enhance the power of the Christian God.

29 Heinricus, ch. XVI 4; Henry of Livonia, p. 127.

30 Heinricus, ch. XXVI 6; Henry of Livonia, p. 209.
31 Heinricus, ch. XXIV 5; Henry of Livonia, pp. 193–194.
32 Heinricus, ch. XXVI 10; Henry of Livonia, pp. 210–211.
33   Heinricus, ch. XX 2; Henry of Livonia, p. 162.
34 The allusion was to 1 Macc. 9:8. Heinricus, ch. X 10; Henry of Livonia, pp. 61;
    Heinricus, ch. XIV 8; Henry of Livonia, p. 101.
35 Heinricus, ch. XIV 12; Henry of Livonia, p. 107. It is necessary to point out in this
    depiction of a period of almost continuous warfare that the Baltic was a region of
    strife and war even before the arrival of the Christians. The many different Baltic
    tribes apparently waged war against each other and engaged in often very volatile
    alliances. Veritable massacres are often mentioned in Henry's Chronicle, cf. ch. IX
    4, XII 6, XIV 11, XIV 12, XV 2, XV 7, XIX 3, XIX 9, XX 6, XXIII 7.
36 Heinricus, ch. XV 2; Henry of Livonia, p.109.
37 Heinricus, ch. XIV 8; Henry of Livonia, p. 102.
38 Nielsen 1993, pp. 129–131. Collections of exempla were of growing importance dur-
    ing the first decades of the thirteenth century. This has made scholars characterise the
    century as marked by a 'pastoral revolution' in the sense of being marked by serious
    ecclesiastic endeavours to encapsulate and meet a growing interest among lay people
    for education in the faith. See, e.g., Bolton 1983; Morris 1989, pp. 478–504.
39 'Amice, dicunt nobis sacerdotes nostri, quod nullus peccatorum sine medicina confes-
    sionis salvari possit.' Quoted from Tamm 1996, p. 38.
40 Heinricus, ch. X 10; Henry of Livonia, p. 61.
41 Heinricus, ch. X 9; Henry of Livonia, p. 60.
42 Heinricus, ch. X 14; Henry of Livonia, pp. 65–66.
43 Heinricus, ch. IX 14; Henry of Livonia, p. 53. Cf. also Schneider 1989.
44 Livonian Rhymed Chronicle, p. 8; Rheimchronik, line 525.
45 Heinricus, ch. XXI 4; Henry of Livonia, p. 163.

BIBLIOGRAPHY

Sources

Heinricus, *Heinrici Chronicon Livoniae. Editionis quam paraverant L. Arbusow et
    A. Bauer textum denuo imprimendum curavit Albertus Bauer.* Darmstadt 1959.
Henry of Livonia, *The Chronicle of Henry of Livonia. A Translation with Introduction
    and Notes.* J. A. Brundage (ed.), Madison 1961.
Helmoldus, *Helmoldi presbyteri Bozoviensis Chronica slavorum.* B. Schmeidler &
    H. Stoob (ed.), Darmstadt 1983.
Livländische Reimchronik mit Anmerkungen, Namenverzeichnis und Glossar. Leo Meyer
    (ed.), Paderborn 1876.
Livonian Rhymed Chronicle. J. C. Smith & W. L. Urban (ed.), Bloomington 1977.
Saxo, *Saxos Danmarkshistorie.* Translated into Danish by Peter Zeeberg. København.
Saxonis Gesta Danorum. J. Olrik & H. Ræder (ed.). Copenhagen 1931.

Literature

F. Benninghoven 1965, *Der Orden der Schwertbrüder.* Köln–Graz.
F. Blanke 1963, 'Die Missionsmethode des Bischofs Christian von Preuen', in H. Beumann
    (ed.), *Heidenmission und Kreuzzugsgedanke.* Darmstadt, pp. 337–363.
B. Bolton 1983, *The Medieval Reformation.* London.
J. A. Brundage 1973, 'Christian Marriage in Thirteenth-Century Livonia', *Journal of
    Baltic Studies* 44, pp. 313–320.

W. Fritze 1960, 'Probleme der abodritischen Stammes- und Reichsverfassung und ihrer Entwicklung vom Stammesstaat zum Herrschaftsstaat', in H. Ludat (ed.), *Siedlung und Verfassung der Slawen zwischen Elbe, Saale und Oder*. Giessen.

G. Gnegel-Waitschies 1958, *Bischof Albert von Riga. Ein Bremer Chorherr als Kirchenfürst im Osten (1199–1229)*. Hamburg.

M. Hellmann 1989, 'Die Anfänge christlicher Mission in den baltischen Ländern', in M. Hellmann (ed.), *Studien über die Anfänge der Mission in Livland*. Sigmaringen, pp. 7–35.

C. S. Jensen 2000, 'Byer og borgere i 1200-tallets baltiske korstog', *Den jyske Historiker* 89, pp. 68–88.

K. V. Jensen 2000, 'Danmark som en korsfarerstat', *Den jyske Historiker* 89, pp. 48–67.

H.-D. Kahl 1983, 'Zur Problematik der mittelalterlichen Vorstellung von "Christianisierung"', in Zenon 1983, pp. 125–128.

M. Maccarone 1989, 'I papi e gli inizi della Cristianizzazione delle Livonia', in *Gli inizi del Cristianesimo in Livonia-Lettonia (a cura di Michele Maccarone)*. Libreria Editrice Vaticana.Cittá del Vaticano, pp. 31–80.

C. Morris 1989, *The Papal Monarchy. The Western Church from 1050 to 1250*. Oxford.

T. K. Nielsen 1993, 'Processen i Sens 1140 – problemer i europæisk middelalder', *Den jyske Historiker* 65, pp. 116–134.

R. Schneider 1989, 'Straentheater im Missionseinsatz. Zu Heinrichs von Lettland Bericht über ein groes Spiel in Riga 1205', in M. Hellmann (ed.), *Studien über die Anfänge der Mission in Livland*. Sigmaringen, pp. 107–122.

M. Tamm 1996, 'Les Miracles en Livonie et en Estonie à l'époque de la christianisation (fin XIIème – debut XIIIème siecles)', in J. Kivimäe & J. Kreem (ed.), *Quotidianum Estonicum. Aspects of daily life in Medieval Estonia*. Medium Aevum Quotidianum. Sonderband V. Krems, pp. 29–78.

W. Urban 1975, *The Baltic Crusade*. De Kalb.

BARBARA BOMBI

Innocent III and the praedicatio to the Heathens in Livonia (1198–1204)

In his seminal work of 1984, Benjamin Kedar demonstrated that a sea-change was occurring in the attitudes of crusaders towards the peaceful conversion to Christianity of Moslems in the Holy Land during the twelfth century.[1] In Kedar's opinion, the two most significant proponents of this change were Pope Eugenius III and Bernard of Clairvaux. By 1147 Eugenius and Bernard were not only promoting conversion as a major objective in the Holy Land but also in their support for the German expedition against the Wends in Northern Europe.[2] Kedar's work raises two valid questions. Firstly, how did the relationship between crusade and mission develop from the second half of the twelfth century onwards? Secondly and more importantly, was there a papal plan for the conversion of pagan Wends in Northern Europe? These two questions must have seemed of particular relevance at the turn of the twelfth century when Albert of Buxhöveden, *ministerialis* of the cathedral church of Hamburg, became the third bishop of Livonia in 1199 and began to promote mission and crusade against the heathens of his bishopric, at the same time requesting papal support from Innocent III for this endeavour.

In fact, the North-Eastern lands of Saxony had already felt the impact of German settlement as a result of Henry the Lion's expansionist policy beyond the Elbe and the support of Hartwig II, archbishop of Hamburg-Bremen (1185–1207). Hartwig was responsible for sending the Cistercians to preach the Gospel to the heathens and also for the many canons regular foundations of central Germany. Furthermore, in about 1185, Meinhard, a canon regular from Segeberg in Mecklenburg, travelled to Livonia in a fleet of ships belonging to German merchants and began to preach the Gospel to the heathens. In 1187, Hartwig ordained Meinhard as bishop of Üxküll, obtaining confirmation from Pope Clement III in 1188. Meinhard and his preachers were supported by Hartwig, the Saxon nobility, and above all the merchants of Mecklenburg's harbour towns, were eager to gain access to the Baltic in order to trade with Russian merchants. Meinhard was briefly succeeded by Berthold (1196–1198) who organised a crusade in 1197 against the Livonian heathens during the pontificate of Celestine III. Albert was then appointed to the troubled bishopric. Albert's family was close to Hartwig, and he was capable of coping with the complicated German policy occasioned by the divisive double imperial election of Philip of Swabia and Otto IV of Brunswick in the middle of 1198. After Albert's consecration in Hamburg at the beginning of 1199, he began to preach a crusade against Livonians in Saxony and Westphalia, gaining the support of Canute VI, King of Denmark, and his brother Valdemar as well as that of Archbishop Absalon of Lund, according to Henry of Livonia's *Chronicon Livoniae*.[3] Word of Albert's preaching, together with some requests probably made by him, soon reached to Rome, where on 5th October 1199 Pope Innocent III responded in his letter, *Sicut ecclesiastice religionis*, addressed to all the faithful living in Saxony and Westphalia and in the lands beyond the Elbe.[4]

The *arenga* of Innocent's letter expounded the topic of the peaceful conversion of heathens. The Pope reminded his audience that the Christian religion did not allow heathens be forced to believe:[5] pagan conversion had to take place *sponte*, willingly. Moreover, the work of preaching was first and foremost the duty of the Apostolic See, referred to by Innocent as *mater omnium generalis* and regarded by Imkamp as *Primatstitel*.[6] Thus the papacy had the duty of carrying out this work in order to take care of converted peoples, and it had to urge the faithful to defend the new converts. In fact, if new Christians were not helped and defended, they might immediately relapse into sinfulness, regretting their conversion.[7] As Kedar has pointed out, forced conversions had been prohibited in Gratian's *Decretum* (C. 1 q. 45 c. 3), again in the commentary on Gratian's text, the *Summa Decretalium* of Bernardo of Pavia (1190) and, not long after, in the *Summa de casibus poenitentiae* of Raimond de Peñafort.[8] Moreover, Innocent had already issued the same express prohibition in a letter concerning Jewish conversion on 15th September 1199.[9] In this letter the pope stated that no Christian should force a Jew to be baptized, and confirmed that conversions might only be carried out *sponte*, after an expressed desire. Finally Innocent argued that true faith could not result from force but must be voluntary.[10]

The focus of his *arenga* on the voluntary conversion of heathens led the pope on to the *narratio*. After recalling the work of Meinhard, the first preacher to arrive in Livonia, Innocent reminded the faithful of Saxony and Westphalia how the first bishop of Livonia had 'let down the nets of his preaching in order to make catches among the barbarian peoples' (*laxare praedicationis sue retia in capturam inter populos barbaros*).[11] With regard to these circumstances, Innocent's metaphor of the *navicula beati Petri* or 'ship of St Peter', from the Gospel of Luke 5:4, has been cited by both Maccarrone and Imkamp as a fundamental example of Innocent's 'theology of primacy.'[12] After giving a particular account of the heathens' religion, Innocent underlined the result of preaching, although he stressed that regression to paganism might occur at any time with its threat 'to wipe out the memory of the Christian name' (*christianis nominis memoriam abolere*).[13]

Thus, Innocent moved on to the *dispositio*: the pope granted *remissio peccaminum* ('remission of sins') to anyone joining the forces assembled *in nomine Domini* to defend *potenter et viriliter* converts and Christians in Livonia should the Livonians refuse to accept or observe truces made with Christians. Furthermore, he stated that anybody taking the vow to visit the *limina sanctorum*, namely anybody going on pilgrimage to Rome, could commute his vow *in defensionem Livoniensis ecclesiae*. The pope ended his letter by placing Christians and anyone who would have gone on pilgrimage to Livonia *sub beati Petri protectione*.[14]

Maccarrone explained Innocent's decisions as a clear call to a crusade against heathens, following the example of Eugenius III's appeal for a crusade against the Wends (1147) and Alexander III's call for evangelisation in Estonia (1170).[15] Maccarrone regarded the lack of the expressions *cruce signati* and *signum crucis* in this rescript as a papal device to avoid withdrawing the faithful of central and northern lands from participation in the Crusade to the Holy Land.[16] On the other hand, as he points out, Albert, bishop of Livonia, who had requested the proclamation of a crusade to Livonia, was not satisfied by the papal response, because the indulgence granted for the Livonian pilgrimage was legally the same as the pilgrimage to Rome. At Christmas 1199, Albert was present in Magdeburg at the court of Philip of Swabia, where he obtained a *sentencia* that placed *peregrinatio* to Livonia on the same level as the crusade to the Holy Land.[17]

In my opinion, we have to begin with the *arenga* to grasp the sense of the final arrangements made by the pope. Underlining the primacy of the Apostolic See, Innocent began his letter by pointing out the prohibition of *coactio ad fidem* in canon law and then recalling Meinhard's preaching, which had been carried on without violence. Innocent had thus deliberately omitted any reference to the second Livonian bishop, the Cistercian Bertold, who had organized a crusade to the Livonians between 1197 and 1198. As I have argued elsewhere,[18] some evidence shows that the crusade promoted by Bertold was contrary to the policy of the Curia, at which cardinal Lothar of Segni, later Pope Innocent III, was then present.[19]

It could be argued that Innocent wished to limit pagan attacks, thus avoiding another crusade against heathens similar to that undertaken by Bertold. The Pope thus begins the *dispositio* by stating that the troops, assembled *in nomine Domini*, were to defend Christians and converts only if the Livonians refused to accept and respect any truce. Moreover, in 1198 Innocent took the same steps about preaching in Iceland, allowing preachers to defend themselves against heathen attacks *in extremo examine*, without the need to resort to lay support.[20]

The need to recruit forces to defend preachers in Livonia had been also suggested by an odd German situation. Problems with the imperial election had led Otto IV of Brunswick to withdraw from the policy of territorial expansion into eastern lands begun by his father, Henry the Lion. The imperial controversy had also affected archbishop Hartwig II of Hamburg-Bremen and bishop Albert of Livonia, who supported Philip of Swabia in 1199. Innocent set himself up as judge of this situation, summoning an army to defend preachers without altering canon law against *coactio ad fidem*. For this reason, the pope granted remission of sins to pilgrims going to Livonia, pointing out that their indulgence was equivalent to that given for Roman pilgrimage, rather than a crusade indulgence, as Pitz has also shown.[21] Furthermore, the pope had issued a similar indulgence on 13th May 1198 to anyone about to employ 'the spiritual sword' (*gladium spirituale*) against heretics in Southern France, granting them the same *indulgentia peccatorum* as that granted to pilgrims to Rome and Santiago de Compostela.[22] It could thus be argued that Innocent was trying to distinguish the indulgence given for the crusade to the Holy Land, which was characterised by granting of spiritual and material benefits, from what had become an offensive war against heathens after the crusade against the Wends in 1147 as well as from the *remissio peccatorum* given anyone defending preachers both inside and outside the *Christianitas*.[23]

Circumstances altered some years later in 1204 when Albert, needing to create a lasting organization to defend preachers in Livonia, asked for Innocent's proclamation of a new crusade against heathens. At that time the pope changed his mind about the requests of the bishop of Livonia. He took into consideration the election of Otto IV (March 1201), who had allied his forces with those of Valdemar II, King of Denmark, in Dithmarschen and Mecklenburg. Thus, on 12th October 1204, Innocent answered the requests of Theodorich and Caupo, who were sent by Bishop Albert to Rome at the end of 1203 in order to seek papal support for a new crusade against Livonians following the failure of the Fourth Crusade and the sack of Constantinople in April 1204.[24]

This letter, dated 12th October 1204 and beginning *Etsi verba evangelizantium pacem*, was not addressed to Albert of Livonia but was directed to the archbishop of Bremen, his suffragans and the abbots, priors and clergy of the province of Bremen. This was perhaps a strange choice, since in 1199, Bishop Albert promoted his preaching on the Livonian crusade independently of Hartwig, who had been involved in the struggle of the Staufen against the Guelphs.

It could be argued that the same Albert had asked Innocent for Hartwig's support for the Livonian mission during the journey of Theodorich and Caupo to Rome. On the other hand, it might be stated that the pope wanted Hartwig and the clergy of Hamburg-Bremen to manage the conversion of heathens in opposition to Albert's request for independence from metropolitan jurisdiction. Innocent was certainly reassured about Hartwig's loyalty to Otto IV, also underlined in another papal letter dealing with the question of jurisdiction over Stade on 5th April 1204.[25] According to Pitz, this rescript addressed an area concerned with Albert's preaching, which now took advantage of papal arrangements.[26]

To return to Innocent's letter to the clergy of Bremen, its *arenga* begins by citing Gregory the Great's commentary on Job. 40:16–18, which points out the regenerative power of baptism and, through Jesus's example, the need to profess faith through words as well as actions. The *arenga* declares that the conversion of the heathens should be supported everywhere, *etiam in fines orbis terre*, because of its message of universal Salvation.[27] Innocent emphasised the importance of preaching the Gospel to the heathens by citing the example of St Paul's mission to the pagans in 2 Cor. 4:4–6.[28] He then referred to Matt. 13:18–23, which states that the preaching would be successful as long as it had been understood.[29] Finally, according to Gregory the Great's commentary on Isaiah 41:19, Innocent ended the first part of the *arenga*, characterised by its theological content.[30]

In the second part of the *arenga*, ecclesiological topics mirror the events that brought about Livonia's conversion to Christianity. Using Gregory the Great's idiom *opus bonum*, which should be translated as mission, Innocent called to mind that heathens could obtain salvation through preachers who irrigated the spiritual aridity of pagans by drinking deep from the fountains of Faith. [31] Thus the Pope stated that the faithful obtained virtues, represented by the cedar tree, while pagans received suffering, signified by thorns. Pagan souls would be cleaned from sin 'per sanctae praedicationis officium et comminationem iudicii.' Comfort, represented by the myrtle as well as the olive, which stands for Lord's mercy, will thus be bought.[32]

This topic of the Lord's mercy on human sufferings introduces the *narratio*. Innocent highlights the central task of the papacy in the conversion of heathens, stating that, pagans came *ad agnitionem fidei* as a result of the *opus efficace* of Bishop Albert. Moreover, Innocent reminded Archbishop Hartwig that Albert had divided preachers into *tres religiosorum ordines*, monks and canons regular, 'qui discipline insistentes pariter et doctrine spiritualibus armis contra bestias terre pugnent,' and *fideles laici*, 'qui sub Templariorum habitu barbaris infestantibus ibi novellam plantationem fidei Christiane resistant viriliter et potenter.'[33]

The Livonian mission was necessarily organised on two different levels, as Innocent had already established in his letters *Sicut ecclesiastice religionis* (5th October 1199) and *Is qui ecclesiam suam* (19th April 1201). Preachers, monks and canons regular were employed to carry on the conversion of heathens using spiritual weapons, whereas the *fideles laici*, who were assembled by Albert and Theodorich as the *Militia Christi* between 1202 and 1203 and accepted the *habitus* of the Templars, were to defend the mission (*novella plantatio fidei*) with the sword. Furthermore, Innocent cast his mind back to the letter of 5th October 1199, *Sicut ecclesiastice religionis*, in which he had left the defence of both preachers and the faithful in Livonia to the forces brought together *in nomine Domini*. At that time, the pope made use of the same expression, *potenter et viriliter*, with relation to the *exercitus*.[34]

Innocent therefore took up the request of Theodorich and Caupo.[35] Actually, the Pope agreed that the indulgence given to the *clerici et sacerdotes* as well as to the *laici* taking the vow for the crusade to the Holy Land could be commuted into that granted for the mission to the heathens. This was the case of pilgrims unable to go to the Holy Land because of their age or physical disease. By such means, pilgrims would have been able to come to Livonia *contra barbaros* in order to defend preachers *viriliter et potenter*.

Therefore, in the *dispositio* of *Etsi verba evangelizantium pacem*, Innocent overrode regardless the arrangements he had set down in 1199 when, in *Sicut ecclesiastice religionis*, he stated that the indulgence granted for the Livonian pilgrimage was legally the same as the pilgrimage *ad limina sanctorum*.[36] Moreover, the Pope agreed that the Livonian pilgrimage could be preached around the diocese of Hamburg-Bremen, except in places under interdict and excommunication in accordance with the canons concerning the crusade.[37] Innocent ended *Etsi verba evangelizantium pacem* with the hope that the work of preachers could be made easier and more successful as a result of his arrangements.[38]

Innocent's *Etsi verba evangelizantium pacem*, is characterised by the commutation of the indulgence given for the crusade to the Holy Land, not for charity or penance, but for the Livonian pilgrimage. Actually, according to the papal letters included in the *Liber Extra* of Gregory IX under the rubric 'De voto et voti redemptione', Alexander III had already established that the vow to go on pilgrimage to the Holy Land might be commuted into alms-giving: 'Vota possunt elemosynis redimi, vel in aliud commutari, interdicente superioris auctoritate, et iusta causa redimendi vel mutandi.'[39] Afterwards, in his letter sent to Garnerius, bishop of Troyes, on 15th March 1198, Innocent stated terms for commuting the indulgence for the crusade to the Holy Land for charity, on account of physical illness and old age.[40] *Etsi verba evangelizantium pacem* in which Innocent III considered the mission to the heathens as an exception to the commutation of the crusade vow together with charity and penance, which were taken into account by canon law, was never included in the *Liber Extra*.

In another letter, addressed to the archbishop Andreas of Lund on the 13th November 1204, Innocent released a *villicus* from excommunication, which he had incurred by assaulting a priest.[41] Furthermore, the pope stated that that *villicus* did not have to come to Rome, 'ita quod expensas, quas esset facturus in itinere ad sedem propter hoc apostolica veniendi, mittat in subsidium Terrae sanctae vel in Christianorum auxilium, qui laborant in partibus illis contra perfidiam paganorum'; he just had to pay for the journey according to his means (*iuxta proprias facultates*).[42]

This point may also provide an answer to my first question. In 1199 Innocent tried to distinguish between a crusade to the Holy Land and the mission to heathens, which was legally considered the same as pilgrimage *ad limina sanctorum*. Moreover, according to Herde, between the end of the twelfth and the beginning of the thirteenth century canon law stated that the Saracens were not to be attacked or killed, but tolerated if they lived in peace with the Christians.[43] However, after 1204, the Pope changed his mind and commuted the indulgence to go on crusade to the Holy Land into the pilgrimage to Livonia, which was to be considered as a struggle with the spiritual sword as well as the material one for defending preachers against the heathens.

This further point also has implications for the answer to my second question. There was no papal plan to organise the conversion of the heathen to Christianity from the second half of the twelfth century. In accordance with his decisions, Innocent granted the requests put forward by Albert, bishop of Livonia, and agreed with the state of affairs brought about as a result of the mission and crusade to Livonia, supported by the ecclesiastical foundations of central-northern Germany and after 1206 by the Scandinavian Church and the Danish monarchy. At that time, the Apostolic See made use of crusading as an instrument to defend and ensure the development of preaching. This impressive example seems to have struck a new balance between the centre and the periphery of Christianity.

NOTES

1   Kedar 1984, pp. 60–61, 66–68.
2   Kedar 1984, pp. 70–71.
3   *Henrici*, ch. 3, § 2, p. 12.
4   *Register* II, pp. 182, 348–349. See also Maccarrone 1989, pp. 31–79; Haller 1952, p. 364; Pitz 1971, pp. 7–10.
5   *Register* II, pp. 182, 348: 'compellere ad credendum'.
6   Imkamp 1983, p. 266.
7   *Register* II, pp. 182, 348: 'Sicut ecclesiastice religionis censura compelli non patitur ad credendum invitos, sic sponte credentibus apostolica sedes, que mater est omnium generalis, munimen sue protectionis indulget et fideles ad defensionem eorum salubris monitis exhortatur; ne, si nuper conversis negatum fuerit defensionis auxilium, vel in primos revertantur errores vel eos saltem peniteat credidisse.'
8   Kedar 1984, pp. 73–74; Kedar 1985, pp. 329–330. See Gratiani *Decretum*, C. 1 q. 45 c. 3: 'Sequitur: "non percussorem". Non enim oportet episcopum ita esse irascibilem et perturbati sensus, ut percutiat, qui debet esse patiens : sed sequantur eum, qui dorsum posuit ad flagella. ...c. 3 Non asperis, sed blandis verbis ad fidem sunt aliqui provocandi.' See also Condorelli 1960, p. 29.
9   *Register* II, 276, (302), pp. 535–537.
10   *Register* II, 276, p. 536: 'Statuimus enim, ut nullus Christianus invitos vel nolentes eos ad babtismum per violentiam venire compellat; sed si eorum quilibet *sponte* ad christianos fidei causa confugerit, postquam voluntas eius fuerit patefacta, sine qualibet efficiatur calumpnia christianus: veram quippe christianitatis fidem habere non creditur, qui ad christianorum babtisma non spontaneus sed invitus cognoscitur pervenire.'
11   *Register* II, 182, (191), p. 348.
12   Maccarrone 1940, pp. 13–15; Imkamp 1983, p. 276.
13   *Register* II, 182, (191), p. 349.
14   See Labande 1966, pp. 283-291. According to Maccarrone 1991, p. 257 the expression *limina sanctorum* had already been used in the fourth century to mean pilgrimage to Rome, then called *limina apostolorum*.
15   Alexandri III *Epistole*, PL 200, col. 861A.
16   Maccarrone 1989, p. 55.
17   *Henrici*, ch. 3, § 2, p. 16: 'Reversus in Theuthoniam in natali Domini Magdeburch plures signat. Ubi rex Philippus cum uxore coronatur. Et coram eodem rege in sentencia queritur, si bona in Lyvoniam peregrinancium sub tuicione pape ponantur, sicut eorum, qui Ierosolimam vadunt. Responsum vero est ea sub protectione apostolici comprehendi, qui peregrinacionem Lyvonie in plenariam peccaminum remissionem iniungens vie equavit Ierosolimitane.'
18   Bombi 2000.
19   Maleczek 1984, p. 104. See also Tillmann 1954, pp. 1–15; Maleczek 1982, pp. 564–576.

20 *Register* I, 320, p. 465: 'tamquam in extremo examine, quando unusquisque onus suum portabit, illi possint eos a ventura ira defendere, qui pro suis sceleribus eternis incendiis reservantur'.

21 Pitz 1971, p. 18. According to Roscher 1969, p. 200, Innocent III granted a crusade indulgence in 1199.

22 *Register* I, 165, p. 235: 'Omnibus autem, qui pro conservatione fidei christiane in tanto discrimine, quod ecclesie imminet, ipsis astiterint fideliter et devote, illam peccatorum suorum concedimus indulgentiam, quam beati Petri vel Jacobi limina visitantibus indulgemus.'

23 See Zerbi 1992, p. 290.

24 *Register* VII, 139, pp. 225–226.

25 Lappenberg 1842, pp. 304, 347.

26 Pitz 1971, p. 27.

27 *Register* VII, 139, p. 225. See also Gregorii Magni, *Moralia* 33, ch. 6, 12, pp. 1681–1682. Innocent III's references to Gregory the Great's commentary on the Bible in this *arenga* seem to agree with the piece of information given by Henry of Livonia. According to *Henrici*, ch. 7, § 3, p. 21, the Pope presented Bishop Albert a manuscript by Gregory the Great during Theodorich and Caupo's journey to Rome: 'Transactis diebus aliquantis idem venerabilis papa Innocentius predicto Cauponi dona sua, videlicet centum aureos, porrigit et in Theutoniam redire volenti magno caritatis affectu valedicens benedicit et bibliothecam beati Gregorii pape manu scriptam episcopo Lyvoniensi per fratrem Theodoricum mittit.'

28 *Register* VII, 139, p. 225.

29 *Register* VII, 139, pp. 225–226: 'Licet enim lumen vultus Domini signatum fuerit super eos, ut invisibile eius possent conspicere intellecta, quia tamen, cum cognovissent Dominum, ipsum sicut Deum glorificare minime curaverunt, facti sunt velut arida in Ade opere maledicta, spinas et tribulos germinans, que fructum afferre debuit tricesimum, sexagesimum et centenum.'

30 *Register* VII, 139, p. 225. See also Gregorii Magni, *Homiliae*, 1, 12–13, 20, 164.

31 *Register* VII, 139, p. 225.

32 *Register* VII, 139, p. 225.

33 *Register* VII, 139, p. 225.

34 *Register* I, 182, p. 349.

35 *Register* VII, 139, pp. 226–227.

36 *Register* VII, 139, p. 227: 'Nos igitur eius precibus benivolum prebentes favorem postulata ipsi duximus indulgenda, ut sermo Dei in eos currere valeat et Christiana religio propagari.' On the indulgence granted by Innocent III in Southern France, see above, n. 22.

37 *Register* VII, 139, p. 227. See also Pitz 1971, p. 27.

38 *Register* VII , 139, p. 227.

39 *X*, 3. 34, 1.

40 *Register* I, 69, p. 103: '… licentiam concedimus votum peregrinationis taliter commutare, ut omnes expensas, quas fueras in eundo, morando et redeundo facturus, alicui religioso committas in necessarios usus terre, illius sine diminutione qualibet transferendas. Sic enim et orientali provincie, que plus tuis quam te in articulo necessitatis instantis indiget, tua subventione proficies et Trecensi ecclesie tua presente et regimine utilius providebis ac per hoc anime tue salubrius consuletur.' This letter quotes of Alexander III's decretal, which was copied in 3. 34 7: 'Commutat Papa votum ultramarinum in vigilias, orationes et ieiunia, tunc maxime, quum cessat causa, quae induxit ad vovendum; ita etiam quod expensae fiendae in eundo, morando et redeundo, integraliter mittantur in terrae sactae subsidium.' See also *X*, 3. 34. 9: 'Votum ultramarinum certis casibus redimi et commutari potest, nec tamen per alium, quam per Papam, vel cum ipsius speciali mandato.'

41 *Register* VII, pp. 271. See also *X*, 5. 39. 5: 'Percutiens clericum vel religiosum excommunicatus est, nec ab alio quam a Papa absolvitur, praeterquam in mortis articulo.' The

same sanction is taken up in *X*, 5. 39. 19: 'Excommunicatus pro iniectione manum in clericum, vel incendiarius post publicationem a solo Papa absolvitur.'

42 *Register* VII, pp. 271.

43 Herde 1967, pp. 365–366. On the thirteenth century, see also J. Muldoon 1979, *Popes, lawyers and infidels*, Philadelphia PA.

BIBLIOGRAPHY

Sources

Die Register Innocenz' III., 1. Pontifikatsjahr, 1198/99, Texte. Publikationen der Abteilung für historische Studien des Österreichischen Kulturinstituts in Rom, II/I. O. Hageneder & A. Haidacher (ed.), Graz – Köln 1964.

Die Register Innocenz' III., 2. Pontifikatsjahr, 1199/1200, Texte. Publikationen des Österreichischen Kulturinstituts in Rom, II/I. O. Hageneder & W. Maleczek & A. A. Strnad (ed.), Graz – Köln 1979.

Die Register Innocenz' III, 7. Pontifikatsjahr, 1204/1205, Texte und Indices. Publikationen des Österreichischen Kulturinstituts in Rom, II/I. O. Hagenender & A. Sommerlechner & H. Weigl (ed.), Graz – Köln 1997.

Gregorii Magni, *Homiliae in Evangelia*. Corpus Christianorum, Series Latina 141. R. Étaix (ed.), Turnhout 1999.

Gregorii Magni, *Moralia in Job*. Corpus Christianorum, Series Latina 143b. M. Aadriaen (ed.), Tournhout 1985.

Henrici Chronicon Livoniae. MGH in usum scholarum 31. L. Arbusow & A. Bauer (ed.), Hannover 1955.

Literature

B. Bombi 2000, *Innocenzo III e la «praedicatio» ai pagani del Nord Europa. Crociata e Missione (1198–1216)*. PhD Diss. Milano.

M. Condorelli 1960, *I fondamenti giuridici della tolleranza religiosa nell'elaborazione canonistica dei secoli XII–XIV*. Milano.

Corpus Iuris Canonici I, E. Friedberg (ed.), Leipzig 1922.

J. Haller 1952, Das Papsttum. Idee und Wirklichkeit, III. Stuttgart.

P. Herde 1967, 'Christians and Saracens at the time of the Crusades. Some Comments of contemporary Medieval Canonists', *Studia Gratiana* 12, pp. 359–376.

W. Imkamp 1983, *Das Kirchenbild Innocenz' III. (1198-1216)*. Päpste und Papsttum 22. Stuttgart.

B. Z. Kedar 1984, *Crusade and Mission. European Approaches towards the Muslims*. Princeton.

B. Z. Kedar 1985, 'Muslim conversion in canon law', in S. Kuttner & K. Pennington (ed.), *Proceedings of the Sixth Iternational Congress of Medieval Canon Law (Berkeley, 28 July–2 August 1980)*. Monumenta Iuris Canonici 7. Città del Vaticano.

E.-R. Labande 1966, '«Ad limina»: le pélerin médiéval au terme de sa demarche', in P. Gallais & Y. Rion (ed), *Mélanges offerts a R. Crozet*, I. Poitiers, pp. 283–291.

M. Maccarrone 1940, *Chiesa e stato nella dottrina di papa Innocenzo III*. Lateranum, n. s., 6/3–4. Roma.

M. Maccarrone 1989, 'I papi e la cristianizzazione della Livonia', in Gli inizi del cristianesimo in Livonia-Lettonia, Atti del colloquio internazionale di storia ecclesiastica in occasione dell'VIII centenario della Chiesa in Livonia (1186–1986) (Roma, 24–25 giugno 1986). Città del Vaticano: 31–79; now in Id., 1995, in R. Lambertini (ed.), Nuovi Studi su Innocenzo III. Nuovi Studi Storici 25. Roma, pp. 369–420.

J. M. Lappenberg 1842, *Hamburgisches Urkundenbuch*, I. Hamburg.

M. Maccarone 1991, 'Il pellegrinaggio a San Pietro. I «limina apostolorum»', in P.Zerbi & R. Volpini & A. Galuzzi (ed.), *Romana Ecclesia Cathedra Petri*. Italia Sacra 47, Roma.

W. Maleczek 1982, 'Ein Brief des Kardinals Lothar von SS. Sergius und Bacchus (Innocenz III.) an Kaiser Heinrich VI.', *Deutsches Archiv für Erforschung des Mittelalters* 38, pp. 564–576.

W. Maleczek 1984, *Papst und Kardinalskolleg von 1191 bis 1216. Die Kardinäle unter Coelestin III. und Innocenz III*. Publikationen des österreichen Kulturinstitut in Rom. Abhandlungen 6. Wien.

J. Muldoon 1979, *Popes, lawyers and infidels*. Philadelphia.

E. Pitz 1971, *Papstreskript und Kaiserreskript im Mittelalters*. Bibliothek des Deutschen Historischen Instituts in Rom 36. Tübingen.

E. Roscher 1969, *Papst Innocenz III. und die Kreuzzüge*. Göttingen.

H. Tillmann 1954, *Papst Innocenz III*. Bonner historische Forschungen 3. Bonn.

P. Zerbi 1992, 'La "militia christi" per i cisterciensi', in 'Militia Christi' e Crociata nei secoli XI-XIII, Atti dell'undecima Settimana internazionale di studio (Mendola, 28 agosto–1 settembre 1989). Miscellanea del Centro di studi medoevali 13. Milano.

IBEN FONNESBERG SCHMIDT

Pope Alexander III (1159–1181) and the Baltic Crusades

R ecent years have seen considerable interest in the conversion of the
Baltic region, resulting in an extensive literature on the missions
and crusades there. The formulation of a papal policy on the Baltic crusades has, however, not been examined in much detail. The studies that
have been done on papal policy in the period after Pope Eugenius III's
proclamation of a crusade against the pagan Slavs in 1147 have focused
mainly on his policy for the 1147 crusade or the pontificate of Innocent
III (1198–1216)[1] and have not attempted to analyse papal policy in the
intervening period or after Innocent's pontificate. This lack of research
may reflect the fact that many historians seem to have assumed that the
papacy's Baltic policy found its final form with the proclamation of the
crusade of 1147 and have therefore not set out to examine whether Eugenius's successors maintained his policy. Furthermore, many of those
German, Danish, Swedish and Finnish scholars who have produced the
bulk of the works on the Baltic crusades have approached the topic mainly
with an eye to their own national history and have had little interest in
papal history or even the interaction between the local powers of the
Baltic region and the papacy.

I therefore chose the formulation of papal policy on the Baltic crusades
as the subject of my PhD thesis which examined papal policy on the crusades in the Baltic region from Pope Eugenius III's proclamation of the
crusade against the Slavs in 1147 to the end of Innocent IV's pontificate in
1254. The papacy's perception of these campaigns, the intentions stated,
the rewards granted, and the extent of papal involvement in the organization and implementation of the campaigns were analysed. Furthermore,
the question of whether various popes believed these Baltic crusades to be
on a par with those undertaken in aid of the Holy Land was discussed, as
was the character and importance they ascribed to these Baltic enterprises.
The impetus behind the extension of the crusade concept from the Holy
Land to the Baltic was also examined.

The analysis was inspired by the pluralist definition of crusades as
formulated by Jonathan Riley-Smith which states that a crusade was a
penitential war which ranked as, and had many of the attributes of, a pil-

grimage. It manifested itself in many theatres. The cause – the recovery of property or defence against injury – was just in the traditional sense, but was related to the needs of all Christendom or the Church, rather than those of a particular nation or region. A crusade was legitimised by the pope, rather than by a temporal ruler. At least some of the participants took a vow which subordinated them to the Church and ensured some papal control over them in matters other than the actual waging of war. Pilgrimage terminology was often used of them; and some of the privileges they enjoyed, particularly the protection of themselves, their *familiae* and properties, were associated with those of pilgrims. They believed themselves to be penitents and as such they were granted full remission of sins, which was reformulated after 1198 as a plenary indulgence.[2]

In order to determine the papacy's policy on, and perception of, the Baltic crusades, particular attention was given to the indulgence granted to their participants. The formulations of the indulgences granted to crusaders going to the Holy Land were compared to the formulations of those granted to crusaders in the Baltic, and the differences or similarities in their characteristics, in particular whether the indulgence was plenary or partial and what kind of services merited one, were used to clarify the papal stance on the Baltic expeditions. The papal decision about whether a specific act merited an indulgence and, if so, which indulgence would be granted for the deed, was of course a deliberate one. The indulgence granted must therefore be assumed to reflect the importance ascribed to the deed by the pope, so that the significance of an act was indicated by the indulgence granted to it. The indulgence is therefore a central parameter in the analysis of the papal policy on the Baltic crusades and can be used to clarify the importance ascribed to these crusades by the papacy. But the temporal privileges granted to crusaders (such as papal protection), the justifications offered for these crusades and the terminology employed were also taken into account in the analysis of papal policy. This was supplemented by an analysis of the extent of the papacy's involvement in the organisation of these campaigns and its attempts to control them. Its stand on these issues with regard to the Baltic crusades was compared to that on crusades fought elsewhere. Some aspects, however, cannot be addressed because of the character and scarcity of the source material. The evidence does not allow us to determine whether the participants in all the various Baltic campaigns in the period from the middle of the twelfth century to the middle of the thirteenth took a vow or what form such a vow may have had, although some certainly did so; nor do the sources allow us to describe in any detail the preaching for, and organisation of, the Baltic crusades in that period.

The examination of the papal policy on the Baltic crusades showed that the policy varied greatly in the twelfth century. With Eugenius III's proclamation of a crusade against the Slavs as part of the Second Crusade in the bull *Divina dispensatione* of April 1147 the idea of the crusade was applied to warfare against the pagans in Northern Europe, and Eugenius put the campaigns on an equal footing with the crusades in aid of the Holy Land. He granted participants in the Baltic crusades a full indulgence as well as some temporal privileges and set in place measures to ensure papal representation in this crusade – as in the crusade to the Holy Land – through a papal legate, Bishop Anselm of Havelberg, who was to be assisted by Bishop Henry of Olmütz.[3] Eugenius's policy was not, however, followed by his successor, Alexander III.

The Mission to Finns and Estonians during the Pontificate of Alexander III

After the Second Crusade, the North German and Scandinavian princes continued their expeditions against the neighbouring pagans. They do not, however, appear to have attempted to receive papal authorisation for their campaigns or to have sought an indulgence for the participants. In contrast, the Danish Church sought papal support to strengthen a newly planned missionary campaign in the Eastern Baltic region through papal authorisation and privileges. This mission, planned by the Danish Archbishop Eskil (1137–1177), was to target the Estonians.

In the papal schism of 1159–1177 the Danish King Valdemar (1157–1182) had sided with the German emperor to support the antipope Victor IV (1159–1164) while Archbishop Eskil had supported Alexander III; this situation had forced Eskil into exile in 1161.[4] The conflict was resolved in the mid-1160s when Valdemar approached Alexander, leading to the return of Eskil towards the end of 1167.[5] Eskil had begun his exile with a pilgrimage to Jerusalem, but spent most of his time in France, mainly in Paris and Rheims, although in 1164 he also visited Sens where he met Alexander.[6] He had previously formed a close friendship with Peter of Celle,[7] abbot of Montier-la-Celle and later of St-Rémi in Rheims, and when he took refuge during his exile with Peter in Rheims, they planned a mission among the pagan Estonians. The missionary was to be a monk called Fulco, who had been brought up in Montier-la-Celle and was now consecrated as bishop of the Estonians by Eskil.[8] Eskil's interest in mission may have been influenced by Bernard of Clairvaux's criticism of the lack of missionary efforts as expressed in *De consideratione*, the work composed by Bernhard as advice to Pope Eugenius III, his former pupil.[9] Eskil was inspired by Bernard and the Cistercian order throughout his life. He introduced the Cistercian order in Denmark and Sweden in the 1140s. He had met Bernard during a visit to Clairvaux in the early 1150s – and may have visited the abbey again in the 1160s during his exile – and decided to retire to Clairvaux in 1177.[10]

Eskil and Peter were the central figures behind the new missionary plans. The Danish king had hitherto directed his expansionary and missionary efforts towards the central part of the Baltic region, the lands immediately south-east of his realm, and continued to do so in the following decade.[11] Eskil's project, in contrast, was targeting the peoples further east, the Estonians in the easternmost part of the Baltic region. This is likely to have been inspired by his involvement with the Swedish Church, which was at this time becoming increasingly engaged in missions in that part of the Baltic region, in Finland. When Eskil had been elected archbishop of Lund in 1137, his see had encompassed not only the Danish church province, but also those of Norway and Sweden. Sweden was granted its own metropolitan see in 1164, but Eskil's relations with the Swedish Church remained strong, as he was appointed *primas Suecie* in 1157. He maintained contact to the Swedish Church even while in exile personally giving the new Swedish archbishop, the Cistercian Stefan, the *pallium* in Sens in the late summer of 1164.[12]

Eskil and Peter appealed to Pope Alexander to support the mission in the Eastern Baltic. This course of action may have been taken because the plans were hatched while Eskil was in exile and would not receive assistance from the Danish king. After his return in 1167, there was a period of co-operation between the two,[13] but Eskil may either not have felt convinced that Valdemar would provide sufficient backing, or may simply have wished to secure the broadest possible assistance. Furthermore, in *De consideratione* Bernard had reminded Pope Eugenius of his duty in the matter of the conversion of pagans.[14] Eventually, in September 1171 or 1172, Alexander issued a series of letters concerning the mission in the Eastern Baltic. One letter concerned the apparently ongoing, but only partly successful, Swedish mission among the Finns: in response to local complaints about the recurrent apostasy among newly converted Finns, Alexander warned the Swedish archbishop and his suffragans to take precautions against such dangers.[15] The pope also issued three letters concerning the planned mission to the Estonians encouraging all Danes to support Bishop Fulco financially, and recommending that the Norwegian archbishop allow an Estonian monk, Nicholas, then in a Norwegian monastery, to accompany Fulco.[16] He furthermore issued a letter, *Non parum animus*, to the Christian princes and peoples of Denmark, Sweden and Norway in which he promised an indulgence to all those who fought the pagan Estonians threatening the Christians; this letter will be discussed more fully below.[17] That this letter was addressed to all Scandinavian princes adds credence to the suggestion that the mission was Eskil's project, not Valdemar's, and that he was behind the petitions to the pope. Had it been in reply to a request from the Danish king, it would have been more likely to be addressed only to him, as he probably would have tried to maintain sole control over the campaign. Relations between Valdemar and both the Swedish and Norwegian kings were strained,[18] making it improbable that he would have planned a joint expedition with them. It is unlikely that the pope would have interfered with the organization of the mission and have extended the appeal to all Scandinavian princes on his own initiative in his reply. A later letter, in which Peter informed the Swedish king of Fulco's enterprise, also indicates that Eskil and Peter did not intend to have the mission backed exclusively by the royal power of Eskil's Danish church province.[19]

It cannot be proved with any certainty that Alexander's grant of an indulgence to those who fought the pagans in defence of the Christians answered Eskil's request. The petition itself is lost, and there is no internal evidence in the papal reply to prove beyond doubt that a request for an indulgence was made. The letter does, however, state that the papal letter was based on reports from the region and it is therefore possible that the Danish petition for support for the fight against the pagans had contained such a request. Regardless of how it came about, this new grant of an indulgence to those who fought the pagans in the Baltic was prompted by plans for a mission in the region proposed by the Danish archbishop and Abbot Peter, not by the actions of the local princes.

Alexander III and the Mission in the Baltic

It seems that Alexander at first had been unwilling, or at least hesitant, to support the mission in the Eastern Baltic region.[20] A letter from Abbot Peter to the pope shows that Fulco had visited the curia sometime before the issue of the papal letters in September 1171 or 1172, presumably to receive papal support for his mission, but had been unsuccessful. Fulco returned to Peter in Rheims, who now wrote to Alexander to recommend Fulco, begging the pope to look kindly upon Fulco's requests and mission, stating that 'You should thus not be vexed when you are asked for help to propagate the Catholic faith, as the praise of both God and our Lord Jesus Christ will be increased, you will accumulate merit, and the infidel people will gain salvation.'[21] Such hesitancy in supporting Fulco's mission could have been due to a general papal policy on mission. Since the Early Middle Ages the popes had taken a passive stand, merely supporting and approving missions already organised and endorsed by local princes and bishops. The only major exceptions were Pope Gregory I (590–604), who famously initiated the conversion of England, the co-operation between Boniface (672 or 675–754) and Popes Gregory II (715–31) and Gregory III (731–41) on the mission in Germany, and the involvement of Nicholas I (858–67) in the mission to the Bulgars.[22] Alexander may have had no wish to break with this line to take on an active role in a mission's early stages. A lack of interest in engaging actively in mission may perhaps also be detected in his response to a Turkish sultan, the ruler of Konya, who had approached him to ask for instruction in the Christian faith. In return Alexander sent him an *Instructio fidei*, but does not appear to have taken this chance to extend the faith by sending missionaries to the sultan's realm.[23] Later, in 1175, he did however display some interest in mission, when he approved the new Order of Santiago and took it under papal protection in a bull of 5th July 1175 drafted by Cardinal Alberto de Morra, the future Pope Gregory VIII. He confirmed that the order should urge its members to wage war to protect the Christians and convert the Saracens to Christianity.[24]

Alexander's reluctance to support the mission in the Baltic was, however, only temporary. At Tusculum in September 1171 or 1172 he issued the three letters concerning Fulco's mission among the Estonians and the letter concerning the mission among the Finns mentioned above. He also issued five letters to the Swedish Church which dealt with irregularities – such as simony and refusal to pay tithes – and the newly elected bishop of Linköping, all matters which may have been reported by Archbishop Eskil, who was primate of Sweden and was mentioned in two of the letters.[25] All these letters have survived only as copies in Abbot Peter of Celle's letter-book, indicating that Peter had acted as intermediary between Eskil and the curia. It is possible that the pope's change of attitude and new willingness to support Fulco's mission was due to the renewed appeals from Peter and Eskil, but another possibility presents itself. Perhaps Peter had asked for, and received, support for this cause from Archbishop Henry of Rheims. Henry, born in the early 1120s, was the third child of King Louis VI of France (d. 1137) and Adelheid of Savoy and was set for a career in the ecclesiastical hierarchy. Around 1145 he experienced a sudden *conversio* and became a monk in the Cistercian abbey of Clairvaux, at the time led by Bernard. Henry was, however, soon tempted away from monastic life and became bishop of Beauvais in 1149 before being elected Archbishop of Rheims in 1162.[26] He supported Pope Alexander right from the beginning of the papal schism, and the council of July 1160 at which the French bishops decided to support Alexander in the schism was held at Beauvais. The two appear to have had a close relationship, and more than 400 letters from Alexander to Henry have survived.[27] Henry became an influential papal aide, and in the late 1160s and early 1170s Alexander gave him the important task of coordinating French recruitment to the crusade to the Holy Land.[28]

Abbot Peter enjoyed good relations with Archbishop Henry as evidenced by the fact that Henry entrusted his affairs to Peter when Henry later visited the curia.[29] Henry appears to have sent letters to the curia at the same time as Peter sent the letters concerning Fulco's mission; he and the Church in Rheims also received several letters from Alexander, issued in Tusculum in September in either 1171 or 1172.[30] It is thus possible that an envoy from Rheims visited the papal curia carrying both the letters of Henry and of Peter and Eskil, thereby allowing the men advocating Fulco's mission to benefit from the good relations between Henry and the pope.

Among the papal letters issued in September 1171 or 1172 is *Non parum animus* of 11th September addressed to kings, princes and the faithful in the Danish, Swedish, and Norwegian kingdoms in which Alexander promised an indulgence to those who fought against the Estonian pagans. This short letter starts with a description of the threat posed by the pagan Estonians to the Christians in the region. The pope had received reports, presumably from Eskil, of the Estonian attacks on Christians and missionaries: 'We are deeply distressed and greatly worried when we hear that the savage Estonians and other pagans in those parts rise and fight God's faithful and those who labour for the Christian faith and fight the virtue of the Christian name.'[31] The pope then exhorts the addressees on ten points: to serve God in all respects; to love mercy, justice and fair trials; to refrain from pillaging and unjust deeds; to serve God piously; to honour the Roman Church and recognise it as their mother and teacher; to obey the bishops, priests and prelates; to give tithes and other dues to their clergy; to honour their clergy as their fathers and shepherds; and to defend their clergy and its rights.[32] Finally, the letter returns to the subject of the pagans, the pope exhorting the addressees to defend and expand the Christian faith: 'gird yourselves, armed with celestial weapons and the strength of Apostolic exhortations, to defend the truth of the Christian faith bravely and to expand the Christian faith forcefully …'[33] The letter finishes by promising an indulgence to those who fight against the pagans. Participants receive a year's remission of sin, although those who die in this battle receive a full indulgence:

> Trusting God's mercy and merits of the apostles Peter and Paul, we thus concede to those forcefully and magnanimously fighting these often mentioned pagans one year's remission of the sins for which they have made confession and received a penance as we are accustomed to grant those who go to the Lord's Sepulchre. To those who die in this fight we grant remission of all their sins, if they have received a penance.[34]

The letter is summarised in detail here to emphasise its unusual composition. It deviates markedly from the composition of contemporary crusading letters in encompassing several unrelated subjects, focusing on both the fight against the pagans and the state of affairs in the Scandinavian Churches. The many exhortations, which partly correspond with the problems mentioned in the papal letters issued in the same month to the Swedish Church, may reveal another reason why the pope had been hesitant to support the missionary plans in the first place. The curia does not seem convinced that the princes and peoples of the Scandinavian countries had shown sufficient allegiance and obedience to the Roman Church and its local representatives, hardly surprisingly in light of the reported irregularities in the young Swedish Church and the Danish king's initial support for the anti-pope and the rift between the Danish king and archbishop during the schism.

By including a description of the pagan attacks on the Christians in the region, the pope emphasised that the war against them was defensive, thus justifying the use of force as a defensive measure to protect the Church. But in his exhortation to the addressees he stated that the purpose of the war was not only defence, but also the expansion of the Christian faith through the conversion of the infidels: 'to defend the truth of the Christian faith bravely and to expand the Christian faith forcefully …'[35] By combining the ideas of *defensio* and *propagatio* of the faith[36] he came close to proclaiming a missionary war. This of course ran counter to the principle long held in the Church that conversion of non-Christians must be voluntary.[37] When, as mentioned above, on 5th July 1175 he approved Alberto de Morra's draft for the letter to the Order of Santiago and issued it as *Benedictus Deus*, he again in effect allowed enforced conversion by exhorting the Order to fight not only to protect the Christians, but also to bring about the conversion of the Saracens.[38]

The letter to the Scandinavian princes differed from Alexander's crusade bulls for the Holy Land – *Quantum predecessores* of July 1165,[39] *In quantis pressuris* of June 1166,[40] *Inter omnia* of July 1169,[41] and *Cor nostrum* of January 1181[42] – not only in its composition, but also with regard to the indulgences and privileges granted, terminology, and the papal involvement in the organization of the campaigns.

The indulgence granted to crusaders for participation in the crusades in aid of Jerusalem was consistently a plenary one. The bulls of 1166, 1169 and 1181 make a distinction between *'milites ad terminum,'* knights who went to the Holy Land not on crusade but as an act of service to defend the Holy Land,[43] receiving an indulgence dependent on their length of service, and crusaders who unfailingly receive full remission of sins. In contrast, the indulgence granted in *Non parum animus* of 1171 or 1172 to participants in the Baltic expeditions was only one year's remission of sin. This was, according to the letter, as quoted above, the same indulgence as that received by those going on pilgrimage to the Lord's Sepulchre in Jerusalem.[44] That the indulgence for pilgrimage to the Lord's Sepulchre was a year's remission of sin had been stipulated by Alexander already in 1163, when he granted noblemen who kept the terms of a settlement they had reached with the abbey of Cluny an indulgence of 'one year of that penance which you have received with contrite and humbly stricken heart just like those who go on pilgrimage to Jerusalem.'[45] By granting participants in the Baltic enterprise only one year's remission of sin, Alexander broke with the line taken by Eugenius III, who had issued a plenary indulgence to crusaders fighting in the Baltic.

Alexander's policy on the crusade in Spain may throw further light on these findings. In 1175, he issued *Memore pariter*, addressed to all Christians in Spain, authorizing a crusade against the Muslims. After having described the Muslim incursions he promised an indulgence to those who fought against these 'Saracens.' Those who died in battle would receive a full indulgence, whilst those who survived and had served for a year would receive an indulgence equivalent to that enjoyed by those who went on pilgrimage to the Lord's sepulchre,[46] in other words, a year. As is apparent, the indulgence for participation in the crusade on the Iberian Peninsula is very similar to that granted in *Non parum animus* for participation in the Baltic campaigns. Alexander's predecessor, Anastasius IV (1153–1154), had granted participants in Count Raimond Berengar IV's crusade against the Muslims a full crusade indulgence, using the same words as Eugenius III in his bull *Quantum praedecessores* of 1st December 1145 concerning a crusade to the Holy Land.[47] Anastasius had thereby placed crusades on the Iberian Peninsula on an equal footing with those in aid of the Holy Land, just as Eugenius had done. With *Memore pariter* of 1175 Alexander, however, reduced the spiritual rewards for participants in the crusade in Spain, just as he had done with the crusade in the Baltic region.

The extent of the indulgence was not the only difference between the bulls authorizing crusades to the Holy Land and that concerning the Baltic region. The letters for the Holy Land mention a series of privileges granted those who fought in defence of Jerusalem, such as papal protection of the fighters, their *familiae*, and their goods,[48] but none of these privileges were granted to participants in the Baltic enterprise. Likewise, whereas Anastasius had given crusaders in Spain the privilege of papal protection for them, their *familiae* and their goods, Alexander did not include these privileges in his bull of 1175. He thus reduced the temporal privileges enjoyed by participants in the campaigns in the Baltic and Spain. Another difference is that the bulls concerning the Holy Land refer to the crusades as *tam sanctus opus* and *tam sanctus iter* and to the participants as having taken the cross, while such 'crusade terminology' is not used in *Non parum animus* or, for that matter, in *Memore pariter*.

Yet another difference is found in the level of papal commitment in the recruitment of participants. As his position in the struggle against Emperor Frederick grew stronger, Alexander became more engaged in the organisation of the preaching and thus in the recruitment for the crusades to the Holy Land,[49] as is apparent in his appeals of 1169 and 1181. When on 29th July 1169 he sent out *Inter omnia*, he also issued a letter to Archbishop Henry of Rheims, ordering him to co-ordinate the recruitment for the crusade in France and giving him detailed instructions about the organisation of the efforts in aid of the Holy Land, although he did not grant him legatine powers.[50] On 16th January 1181, the same day as he sent *Cor nostrum* calling on all faithful to come to the aid of the Holy Land, he issued *Cum Orientalis terra* to all leading churchmen in the West, setting out guidelines for recruitment, exhorting the clergy to support the preachers sent out by the pope to promote the crusade and to ensure that the recruitment campaign met with success.[51] There is, however, no evidence that he attempted to ensure the success of the Baltic enterprise by involving the curia in the recruitment campaign through the issue of such guidelines.

In conclusion, Alexander did not follow Pope Eugenius III's policy on the Baltic crusades. Eugenius's bull, *Divini dispensatione* of April 1147, had set a precedent for the authorisation of a crusade against the pagans in the Baltic region. He had granted participants in the Baltic crusades a full indulgence and had endeavoured to secure papal representation by appointing a papal legate for the crusade. But it was only after repeated requests from the Danish Church – and perhaps quite reluctantly – that Alexander decided to support warfare against the pagans in the Baltic. He did not issue a full crusade indulgence and did not put the Baltic expeditions on an equal footing with the crusades in aid of the Holy Land. Furthermore, he does not appear to have attempted to achieve any papal control over the recruitment campaign for the Baltic expedition or the expedition itself. He appears, therefore, to have been creating a hierarchy of those campaigns which were conducted as penitential wars in the service of the Church, rewarding participation in crusades in aid of the Holy Land with plenary indulgences and temporal privileges not enjoyed by those who took part in campaigns fought elsewhere. This policy may be explained by a fear of repeating the events of the Second Crusade when the diversion of resources from the Holy Land to several theatres of war had had disastrous results. The kingdom of Jerusalem was still under pressure in the early 1170s as Saladin repeatedly attacked its territory,[52] but Alexander's calls for help in the East of 1165, 1166, and 1169 had met with little response. This may have made him keen to reserve what resources he could raise for that cause.

Alexander III thus clearly chose not to follow the line of his predecessor. In fact, the analysis of papal policy on the Baltic crusades between 1147 and 1254 has shown that in the twelfth and early thirteenth centuries the papal policy on the campaigns in the Baltic was discontinuous, varying considerably from pope to pope. It was, in fact, only from the pontificate of Honorius III (1216–1227) that the popes consistently recognised the Baltic crusades as being on a par with the crusades to the Holy Land. As to the impetus behind the extension of the crusade concept from the Holy Land to the Baltic, the idea of proclaiming a crusade in the Baltic as part of the Second Crusade in 1147 did not originate with Eugenius, but was the result of pressure – channelled through Bernard of Clairvaux – from German magnates.[53] Likewise, Alexander's perhaps somewhat reluctant support for the missionary campaign in the Eastern Baltic was the result of pressure from the Danish archbishop and his allies. Papal policy was thus driven by the local powers of the region, with the curia merely being reactive rather than initiating. Only from the pontificate of Gregory IX (1227–1241) onwards did the papacy take on a more active role.

NOTES

1   See for instance Kahl 1980; Lotter 1977; Hehl 1980; Constable 1953; Roscher 1969; Bombi 2001.

2   Riley-Smith 2002, pp. 87–88.

3   Letter of 11th April 1147 in PL 180, cols 1203–1204; undated letter of 1147 in PL 180, col. 1262; Riley-Smith 1987, p. 98; Hiestand 2001, p. 38.

4   Morris 1989, pp. 192–195; Skyum-Nielsen 1971, pp. 166–169.

5   Skyum-Nielsen 1971, pp. 180–181.

6   Letter [5th August 1164] in DD 1:2, no 153; letter [1164] in DD 1:2, no 157.

7   See letter [1160 x 1162] in DD 1:2, no 142; letters [1162 x 1176] in DD 1:2, nos 149–150; letter [1177 x 1180] in DD 1:3, no 73. For Peter of Celle's relations to Eskil, Pope Alexander III, Bernard of Clairvaux and the Cistercians, see Feiss 1987, pp. 1–17. See also Leclercq 1946, pp. 10–11.

8   Letter [before September 1171 x 1172] in DD 1:3, no 21; letter [1172 x 1174] in DD 1:3, no 34. It cannot be determined with any certainty whether Fulco ever visited his missionary field. See letter [1172 x 1174] in DD 1:3, no 34; letter [1171 x 1173] in DD 1:3, no 29. See Johansen 1951, pp. 90–94; Nyberg 1975, p. 12; Nyberg 1998, pp. 60–61, for discussions of Fulco's possible visit to the Eastern Baltic region. The plans were still in place in the late 1170s; see letter [1178 x 1180] in DD 1:3, no 81; letter [1179 x 1180] in DD 1:3, no 88.

9   St Bernard, *De consideratione* III:1 in PL 182, cols 757–760.

10   Christensen 1980, pp. 256–259; Andersson 1964, p. 396.

11   Valdemar undertook an expedition to Pomerania shortly after the canonisation of Canute in June 1170 and an expedition to Stettin in 1173. See Nyberg 1976, pp. 175–177. See also Skyum-Nielsen 1971, pp. 213ff.

12   Letter [5th August 1164] in DD 1:2, no 153; Andersson 1964, pp. 399ff.

13   Christensen 1980, p. 258.

14   St Bernard, *De consideratione* III:1 in PL 182, cols 757–760; Blanke 1928/1963, pp. 389–391.

15   Letter of 9th September [1171 x 1172] in DD 1:3, no 25. For the dating of this letter and others issued in September 1171 or 1172, see Weibull 1940, *passim*.

16   Letter of 17th September [1171 x 1172] in DD 1:3, no 28; letter of 9th September [1171 x 1172] in DD 1:3, no 26.

17   Letter of 11th September [1171 x 1172] in DD 1:3, no 27. Having survived only as a copy in Peter of Celle's letter-book, *Non parum animus* of 11th September lacks *intitulatio* and *inscriptio*, but the addressees were, according to the heading in the

letter-book, kings, princes and faithful in the Danish, Swedish, and Norwegian king-doms.

18 Skyum-Nielsen 1971, pp. 154–156.

19 Letter [1171 x 1173] in DD 1:3, no 29.

20 For a similar interpretation, see Weibull 1940, p. 94, and Johansen 1951, p. 91.

21 'Nonquam ergo uobis molestum debet esse, quod a uobis postulatur in auxilio propa-gandæ catholicæ fidei: quia et dei et domini nostri Iesu Christi laus inde augmentatur, meritum uestrum cumulatur, salus infideli populo acquiritur' in letter [before September 1171 x 1172] in DD 1:3, no 22.

22 Ullmann 1972, pp. 54, 66–67, 124–125; Noble 1995, pp. 582–583; Shepard 1995, p. 241.

23 *Instructio fidei catholicæ ab Alexandro III pontifice romano ad soldanum Iconii missa* in PL 207, cols 1069–1078; Kedar 1984, p. 93.

24 Letter of 5th July 1175 in *Bullarium Equestris Ordinis S. Iacobi de Spatha*, pp. 13–16; for Alberto de Morra's drafting of this bull, see Ferrari 1960, pp. 63ff, 117; Kedar 1984, p. 47. See also *The Rule of the Spanish Military Order of St. James, 1170–1493*, pp. 110, 146.

25 The letters concerning the mission are: letter of 17th September [1171 x 1172] in DD 1:3, no 28; letter of 9th September [1171 x 1172] in DD 1:3, no 26; letter of 11th September [1171 x 1172] in DD 1:3, no 27; letter of 9th September [1171 x 1172] in DD 1:3, no 25. The letters concerning the Swedish Church are: letter of 7th September [1171 x 1172] in DD 1:3, no 23; letter of 8th September [1171 x 1172] in DD 1: 3, no 24; letter of 11th September [1171 x 1172] in *Diplomatarium Suecanum* 1, no 56; letter of 10th September [1171 x 1172] in FMU 1, no 26; letter of 17th September [1171 x 1172] in *Diplomatarium Suecanum* 1, no 61. All nine letters were issued at Tusculum and bore the date but not the year of issue, but are assumed to have been issued in 1171 or 1172.

26 Falkenstein 1986, pp. 44–46.

27 Falkenstein 1986, pp. 51, 54–55.

28 Phillips 1996, pp. 7, 150–151, 188–189.

29 Letter [1171 x 1173] in DD 1:3, no 29.

30 Letter of 11th September [1171 x 1172] in PL 200, cols 861–862; letter of 29 September [1171 x 1172] in PL 200, col. 864; letter of 29th September [1171 x 1172] in PL 200, cols 864–865; letter of 29th September [1171 x 1172] in PL 200, col. 865.

31 'Non parum animus noster affligitur et amaritudine non modica et dolore torquetur, cum feritatem Estonum et aliorum paganorum illarum partium aduersus dei fideles et Christianæ fidei cultores grauius insurgere et immaniter debacchari audimus, et christiani nominis impugnare uirtutem' in letter of 11th September [1171 x 1172] in DD 1:3, no 27.

32 '... diuino cultui intendere, misericordiam et iustiam et iudicium diligere, a rapinis et iniquis operibus abstinere, deuota deo et accepta obsequia impendere, prædictæ sacrosanctæ Romanæ ecclesiæ, tanquam matri et magistræ uestræ, debitum honorem et reuerentiam exhibere, episcopis, sacerdotibus et aliis prælatis uestris humiliter obedire et eis decimas, primitias et oblationes et alias iustitias suas reddere et ipsos tanquam patres et pastores animarum uestrarum honarare modis omnibus studeatis et iura eorum defendere, manu tenere propensius et conseruare curetis...' in letter of 11th September [1171 x 1172] in DD 1:3, no 27.

33 '... armis cælestibus præmuniti et apostolicis exhortationibus confirmati ad defendam christianæ fidei ueritatem spiritu fortitudinis accingamini, taliter in brachio forti ad propagandam christiani nominis religionem intendentes...' in letter of 11th September [1171 x 1172] in DD 1:3, no 27.

34 'Nos enim eis, qui aduersus sæpe dictos paganos potenter et magnanimiter decertau-erint, de peccatis suis, de quibus confessi fuerint et poenitentiam acceperint, remis-sionem unius anni, confisi de misericorida dei, et meritis apostolorum Petri et Pauli, concedimus, sicut his qui sepulcrum dominicum uisitant concedere consueuimus. Illis autem, qui in conflictu illo decesserint, omnium suorum, si poenitentiam acceperint,

remissionem indulgemus peccatorum' in letter of 11th September [1171 x 1172] in DD 1:3, no 27.

35 '... taliter in brachio forti ad propagandam christiani nominis religionem intendentes...' in letter of 11th September [1171 x 1172] in DD 1:3, no 27.

36 Roscher 1969, p. 198.

37 Canonists declared that pagans should not be forced to accept baptism, a view put forward by Pope Gregory I (590–604), among others, and the canonist Ivo of Chartres and maintained throughout Christian history. See letter from Gregory I of 16 March 591 in *Regesta Pontificum Romanorum* 1, no 1104 (738); Ivo, *Decretum* I, no. 182 in PL 161, col. 106; Ivo, *Decretum* I, no. 285 in PL 161, col. 125; Muldoon 1979, p. 11.

38 Letter of 5th July 1175 in *Bullarium Equestris Ordinis S. Iacobi de Spatha*, pp. 13–16; Kedar 1984, p. 47.

39 This bull closely resembled Eugenius III's bull *Quantum praedecessores* of December 1145 and offered participants a similar indulgence. 'Nos autem, vestrorum quieti et ejusdem Ecclesiæ destitutioni paterna sollicitudine providentes, illis qui tam sanctum et neccessarium opus, et laborem devotionis intuitu suscipere et perficere decreverint, illam peccatorum remissionem quam præfati prædecessores nostri Urbanus et Eugenius Romani pontifices instituerunt, auctoritate nobis a Deo concessa, concedimus et confirmamus...', 'Peccatorum remissionem et absolutionem juxta eorumdem prædecessorum nostrorum institutionem omnipotentis Dei et beati Petri apostolorum principis, auctoritate nobis a Deo concessa, talem concedimus, ut qui tam sanctum iter devote incoeperit, et perfecerit, sive ibidem mortuus fuerit, de omnibus peccatis suis quibus corde contrito et humiliato confessionem susceperit absolutionem obtineat, et sempiternæ retributionis fructum ab omnium bonorum remuneratore obtineat' in letter of 14th July 1165 in PL 200, cols 384–386.

40 Although this bull contained some elements from *Quantum predecessores* of 1165, it contained several new passages, including an expanded indulgence formula. 'Preterea quicumque de uiris bellicosis et ad terre illius defensionem idoneis ad loca illa, que dominus et redemptor noster Iesus Christus corporali presencia sanctificauit, deuocionis amore accesserint et ibi duobus annis contra Sarracenos pro christiani nominis defensione pugnauerint, nos de misericordia Dei omnipotentis et beatorum apostolorum Petri et Pauli meritis confidentes eis omnium peccatorum suorum, de quibus corde contrito et humiliato confessionem susceperint, absolucionem facimus, nisi forte aliena bona rapuerint uel usuras extorserint aut furta commiserint, que omnia debent in integrum emendari. Si uero in facultatibus delinquentium non fuerint, que ea ualeant emendare, de commissis ueniam, prout diximus, nichilominus consequantur. Hi autem, qui illic per annum, sicut diximus, moram habuerint, de medietate iniuncte sibi penitencie peccatorum suorum indulgenciam et remissionem obtineant. ... Preterea omnibus dominicum sepulcrum pro instanti necessitate uisitare uolentibus tam in itinere morte preoccupatis quam usque illuc peruenientibus laborem itineris ad penitenciam, obedienciam et remissionem omnium peccatorum iniungimus, ut post huius carnis ergastula uitam eternam consequi mereantur' in letter of 29th June 1166 in *Papsturkunden für Templer und Johanniter*, no 53.

41 The indulgence formula here reads: 'Nos autem sollicitudine vestram favore apostolico prosequentes, illis qui pro divinitatis amore laborem hujus profectionis assumere, et quantum in se fuerit implere studuerint, de indultæ nobis a Domino auctoritatis officio, illam remissionem impositæ poenitentiae per sacerdotale ministerium facimus, quam felicis memoriæ Urbanus et Eugenius patres et antecessores nostri temporibus suis statuisse noscuntur, ut videlicet qui ad defensionem terræ idoneus, et ad hoc obsequium expeditus, suscepta poenitentia biennio ibi ad defensionem terræ permanserit, et sudorem certaminis ad præceptum regis et majorum terræ pro amore Christi portaverit, remissionem injunctæ poenitentiæ se lætetur adeptum, et cum contritione cordis et satisfactione oris profectionem istam satisfactionis loco ad suorum hanc indulgentiam peccatorum, nisi forte rapinæ vel furti, vel perceptæ usuræ reos esse constiterit, in quibus, si facultas adfuerit, non purgatur peccatum, nisi restituatur ablatum. Si vero facultas reddendi defuerit, prædicta satisfactio ad istorum quoque remissionem

sufficiat peccatorum. Qui vero per annum in hoc labore permanserit, exoneratum se de medietate satisfactionis impositæ auctoritate apostolica recognoscat. ... Præterea omnibus sepulcrum Dominicum pro instanti necessitate visitare volentibus, tam in itinere morte præoccupatis, quam usque illuc pervenientibus, laborem itineris ad poenitentiam, obedientiam et remissionem omnium peccatorum injungimus, ut post hujus certaminis ergastula vitam æternam consequi mereantur' in letter of 29th July 1169 in PL 200, cols 599–601.

42   The indulgence granted was: 'Præterea, quicunque de viris bellicosis et ad illius terræ defensionem idoneis, illa sancta loca fervore devotionis adierint, et ibi duobus annis contra Saracenos pro Christiani nominis defensione pugnaverint, de Jesu Christi pietate, et de beatorum Petri et Pauli apostolorum auctoritate confisi, eis omnium suorum, de quibus corde contrito, et humiliato confessionem susceperint, absolutionem facimus delictorum: nisi forte aliena bona rapuerint, vel usuras extorserint, aut commiserint furta, quæ omnia debent in integrum emendari. Si vero non est in facultatibus delin-quentium, unde valeant emendari, nihilominus consequentur veniam, prout diximus, de commissis. Hi autem, qui illic per annum, sicut diximus, moram habuerint, de medietate sibi injunctæ poenitentiæ indulgentiam et remissionem suorum obtineant peccatorum. Omnibus autem sepulcrum Domini pro instanti necessitate visitare volentibus, sive in itinere moriantur, sive ad istum locum perveniant, laborem itineris ad poenitentiam, et obedientiam, et remissionem omnium peccatorum injungimus, ut de vitæ præsentis ergastulo ad illam beatitudinem, Domino largiente, perveniant, quam nec oculus vidit, nec auris audivit, nec in cor hominis ascendit, quam repromisit Dominus diligentibus se' in letter of 16th January 1181 in PL 200, cols 1294–1296.

43   See Riley-Smith 1997, pp. 157–161, for a discussion of such *milites ad terminum* or 'para-crusaders'.

44   'Nos enim eis, qui aduersus sæpe dictos paganos potenter et magnanimiter decertau-erint, de peccatis suis, de quibus confessi fuerint et poenitentiam acceperint, remis-sionem unius anni, confisi de misericorida dei, et meritis apostolorum Petri et Pauli, concedimus, sicut his qui sepulchrum dominicum uisitant concedere consueuimus' in letter of 11th September [1171 x 1172] in DD 1:3, no 27. The indulgence formulae in the letters concerning the Holy Land of 1166, 1169 and 1181 also refer to *sepulchrum dominicum visitare*, but here it is consistently made clear that this refers to visits made on crusade, in reply to the papal call, by the addition of the phrase *sepulchrum Dominicum pro instanti necessitate uisitare*.

45   'Nos autem tam vobis quam successoribus aliis qui praedictae Clun. Ecclesiæ et his quae ad eam pertinent Ecclesiis atque personis ecclesiasticis continuam servaverint pacem, de misericordia Dei et beatorum Petri et Pauli apostolorum ejus meritis praesumentes, annum unum illius poenitentiae, quam corde contrito et compuncto humiliter recepistis, sicut et iis qui petunt Hierosolymam, relaxamus' in letter of 18th July 1163 in PL 200, col. 250; Paulus 1922–1923, vol. I, p. 166 and vol. II, p. 307.

46   'Nos [ergo], quicunque pugnando contra ipsos massamutos decesserint, eis omnium peccatorum suorum, de quibus penitentiam corde contricto [egerint], confisi de miseri-cordia redemptoris et beatorum apostolorum Petri et Pauli meritis, veniam indulgemus; his autem qui per annum contra predictos massamutos in propriis expensis pugnaverint, illam remissionem peccatorum suorum, de quibus confessi fuerint, facimus quam his qui sepulcrum dominicum visitant assequuntur' in letter of 23rd March 1175 in 'Tres bulas inéditas de Alejandro III', pp. 167–168.

47   Letter of 24th September [1153 x 1154] in *Papsturkunden in Spanien*, no 70.

48   *Quantum predecessors* in letter of 14th July 1165 in PL 200, cols 385D–386A; *In quantis pressuris* in letter of 29th June 1166 in *Papsturkunden für Templer und Jo-hanniter*, p. 253; *Inter omnia* in letter of 29th July 1169 in PL 200, col. 601B–C; *Cor nostrum* in letter of 16th January 1181 in PL 200, cols 1295D–1296A.

49   See Phillips 1996, pp. 150, 154, 246.

50   Letter of 29th July 1169 in PL 200, cols 601–602; Phillips 1996, p. 189.

51   Letter of 16th January 1181 in PL 200, cols 1296–1297.

52   Riley-Smith 1987, pp. 84, 104; Phillips 1996, p. 208.

254

53 Letter [after 13th March] 1147 in *S. Bernardi Opera*, vol. 8, no. 457; Riley-Smith 1987 p. 96.

BIBLIOGRAPHY

Sources

Bullarium Equestris Ordinis S. Iacobi de Spatha. A. Cordova & A. Rosales & J. Agurleta (ed.), Madrid 1719.

Diplomatarium Danicum. A. Afzelius et al. (ed.), Copenhagen 1938–.

Diplomatarium Suecanum. J. G. Liljegren et al. (ed.), Stockholm 1829–.

Papsturkunden für Templer und Johanniter. R. Hiestand (ed.), Göttingen 1972.

Papsturkunden in Spanien. Vorarbeiten zur Hispania Pontificia. I. Katalanien. P. Kehr (ed.), Berlin 1926.

Regesta Pontificum Romanorum. P. Jaffé (ed.), Leipzig 1885–1888 (2nd edition), 2 vols.

The Rule of the Spanish Military Order of St. James, 1170–1493. E. G. Blanco (ed.), Leiden 1971.

S. Bernardi Opera. J. Leclercq and H. Rochais (ed.), Rome 1957–1977, 8 vols.

'Tres bulas inéditas de Alejandro III'. F. Fita (ed.), *Boletín de la Real Academia de la Historia* XII, 1888, pp. 164–168.

Literature

I. Andersson 1964, 'Uppsala ärkestifts tillkomst. Till 800-årsjubileet av ärkebiskop Stefans invigning' *Historisk tidskrift* II:27, pp. 389–409.

F. Blanke 1928/1963, 'Die Entscheidungsjahre der Preussenmission (1206–1274)', in H. Beumann (ed.), *Heidenmission und Kreuzzugsgedanke in der deutschen Ostpolitik des Mittelalters*. Darmstadt, pp. 389–416.

B. Bombi 2001, *Innocenzo III e la 'praedicatio' ai pagani del nord Europa. Missione e crociata (1198–1216)*. Unpublished Ph.D. thesis, Università Cattolica del Sacro Cuore, Milan.

A. E. Christensen 1980, 'Eskil', in S. C. Bech (ed.), *Dansk biografisk leksikon* 4. Copenhagen, pp. 256–259.

G. Constable 1953, 'The Second Crusade as Seen by Contemporaries', *Traditio* IX, pp. 213–279.

L. Falkenstein 1986, 'Appellationen an den Papst und Delegationsgerichtsbarkeit am Beispiel Alexander III. und Heinrichs von Frankreich', *Zeitschrift für Kirchengeschichte* 97 (vierte Folge XXXV), pp. 36–65.

H. Feiss 1987, 'Introduction', in H. Feiss (ed.), *Peter of Celle. Selected Works*, Kalamazoo, pp. 1–40.

A. Ferrari 1960, 'Alberto de Morra, postulador de la orden de Santiago y su primer cronista', *Boletín de la Real Academia de la historia* CXLVI, pp. 63–139.

E.-D. Hehl 1980, *Kirche und Krieg im 12. Jahrhundert. Studien zu kanonischem Recht und politischer Wirklichkeit*. Stuttgart.

R. Hiestand 2001, 'The papacy and the Second Crusade', in J. Phillips & M. Hoch, *The Second Crusade. Scope and consequences*. Manchester, pp. 32–53.

P. Johansen 1951, *Nordische Mission, Revals Gründung und die Schwedensiedlung in Estland*. Stockholm.

H.-D. Kahl 1980, 'Wie kam es 1147 zum "Wendenkreuzzug"?', in K.-D. Grothusen & K. Zernack (ed.), *Europa Slavica – Europa Orientalis. Festschrift für Herbert Ludat zum 70. Geburtstag*. Berlin, pp. 286–296.

B. Z. Kedar 1984, *Crusade and Mission. European Approaches toward the Mulims*. Princeton.

J. Leclercq 1946, *La spiritualité de Pierre de Celle (1115–1183)*. Paris.

F. Lotter 1977, *Die Konzeption des Wendenkreuzzugs: Ideengeschichtliche, kirchenrechtliche und historish-politische Voraussetzungen der Missionierung von Elbe-und Ostseeslawen um die Mitte des 12. Jahrhunderts*. Sigmaringen.

C. Morris 1989, *The Papal Monarchy. The Western Church from 1050 to 1250*. Oxford.

J. Muldoon 1979, *Popes, Lawyers, and Infidels. The Church and the Non-Christian World 1250–1550*. Philadelphia.

T. F. X. Noble 1995, 'The papacy in the eighth and ninth centuries', in R. McKitterick (ed.): 1995: *The New Cambridge Medieval History. Volume II: c. 700–c. 900*. Cambridge, pp. 563–586.

T. Nyberg 1975, 'Eskil av Lund och Erik den helige', in *Historia och samhälle. Studier tillägnade Jerker Rosén*. Lund, pp. 5–21.

T. Nyberg 1976, 'Kreuzzug und Handel in der Ostsee zur dänischen Zeit Lübecks', in O. Ahlers & A. Graßmann & W. Neugebauer & W. Schadendorf (ed.), *Lübeck 1226. Reichsfreiheit und frühe Stadt*. Lübeck, pp. 173–206.

T. Nyberg 1998, 'The Danish Church and Mission in Estonia', *Nordeuropaforum* 1, pp. 49–72.

N. Paulus 1922–1923, *Geschichte des Ablasses im Mittelalter vom Ursprunge bis zur Mitte des 14. Jahrhunderts*. Paderborn.

J. Phillips 1996, *Defenders of the Holy Land. Relations between the Latin East and the West, 1119–1187*. Oxford.

J. Riley-Smith 1987, *The Crusades. A Short History*. London.

J. Riley-Smith 1997, *The First Crusaders, 1095–1131*. Cambridge.

J. Riley-Smith 2002, *What Were the Crusades?* 3rd edition. Basingstoke.

H. Roscher 1969, *Papst Innocenz III. und die Kreuzzüge*. Göttingen.

J. Shepard 1995, 'Slavs and Bulgars', in R. McKitterick (ed.), *The New Medieval Cambridge History. Volume II c. 700–c. 900*. Cambridge, pp. 228–248.

N. Skyum-Nielsen 1971, *Kvinde og Slave. Danmarkshistorie uden retouche*. Copenhagen.

W. Ullmann 1972, *A Short History of the Papacy in the Middle Ages*. London.

L. Weibull 1940, 'Påven Alexander III:s septemberbrev till Norden', *Scandia* XIII, pp. 90–98.

THOMAS LINDKVIST

Crusading Ideas in Late Medieval Sweden

S weden emerged later than Denmark and Norway as a Christian and European monarchy. Christianisation, the establishment of an ec- clesiastical organisation and the making of an incipient kingdom were cultural and political processes that took place later in what eventually became Sweden. Swedish kingship and political institutions were more fragile and forms of legitimisation of power were often less elaborated. This might be one of the explanations of why crusading activities and crusading ideas were less prominent in the political history of medieval Sweden than in Denmark for example.

No Swedish king participated in the crusades to the Holy Land. In the church of the Holy Nativity at Bethlehem there are representations of Saint Olaf of Norway and Saint Canute of Denmark, but not of Saint Eric of Sweden.

There was, however, a tradition of Swedish crusades connected with the integration of present Finland into the emerging kingdom of Sweden. Saint Eric, Earl (*jarl*) Birger Magnusson and Marshal Torgils Knutsson have been described as leaders of the three successive crusades from the mid-twelfth century to the end of the thirteenth century. The tradition of three successive crusades integrating the eastern part of the medi- eval Swedish realm is, however, mainly a construction of the national historiography of the nineteenth century. How Finland became a part of Sweden and the origins of the Swedish speaking population in its coastal regions is too complicated a historical process to be reduced to three expeditions.[1]

The crusade of Saint Eric in the 1150s has been much debated in the research and the historical authenticity of his expedition has been ques- tioned.[2] The earliest records of this expedition and the consequent sword mission among the Finns are the legend of Saint Eric the king and the legend of Saint Henry, the missionary bishop accompanying him, both written in the late thirteenth century. There are no contemporary sources. The two legends were composed when the new cathedral of Åbo (Turku) was being built and the diocese organised as a part of the Swedish ecclesiastical province of Uppsala. This was also the period when the Swedish crown gained firmer control in the eastern part of the realm, when construction of the castles at Åbo and Tavastehus (Hämeenlinna) started. The late thirteenth century was also a period when the Swedish crown, under the leadership of Marshal Torgils Knutsson, initiated an aggressive expansionist policy in the east. What was termed the third Swedish crusade in the historiography tradition of the nineteenth century started in 1293 and resulted in the building of the fortress of Viborg (Viipuri), the easternmost stronghold of the Swedish kingdom for many centuries. We know little of the actual historical circumstances concerning the crusading activities of Saint Eric, but in the late thirteenth century it was important to remember (or perhaps invent) this crusading activity, which legitimised the wars in the east.

Sweden controlled the northern shore of the Gulf of Finland from the late thirteenth century, for shorter periods Sweden had a military presence in the estuary of the River Neva (Landskrona) and at Keksholm (Käkisalmi) on the western shore of Lake Ladoga. The wars and conflicts between Sweden and Novgorod in this strategically important region came to a temporary end through the peace treaty at Nöteborg (Pähkinäsaari, Orekhov) in 1323, when a frontier was settled, although not always undisputed.[3]

When King Magnus Eriksson renewed an aggressive Swedish eastern policy with a war against Novgorod in 1348–1351 he consciously acted as a crusading king. The Danish historian John Lind has clarified the ideology and his role as a crusader king, as well as the impact Birgitta Birgersdotter, the future saint, Saint Bridget from Sweden had. She admonished Magnus Eriksson to carry out a crusade in some of her revelations. Later she vigorously attacked the king for his military failure. The king at least intended to act as a crusader. In his great testament of 1346 he made a crusader vow – the last of Swedes known to have made one – and allocated substantial resources to finance it.[4] The war was short and not successful and the expedition coincided with the arrival of the Black Death in Sweden. There was thus a Swedish tradition of crusades, mainly in order to Christianise the peoples who at least sometimes were considered and described as pagans in Carelia (Karjala) and Ingria (Inkeri), although the political and military aims often were directed against Novgorod. There were, however, few, if any explicit allusions to Saint Eric as a predecessor and prototype as a Swedish crusading king in the eastern parts of the Baltic region.

The border remained more or less unchanged but not entirely peaceful, although the wars were limited in time and space. In the Late Middle Ages, in the 1490s, a short, but fierce war took place. During these hostilities crusading ideas were invoked. The political scene in the east changed. Novgorod was in decline as a political power and was finally conquered and assimilated by the rising Grand Duchy of Moscow in 1471. Grand Prince Ivan III of Moscow prosecuted a more offensive policy against its western neighbours, Sweden and the Livonian Order.

A more severe military and political threat thus emerged in the east. Intensive fortification commenced. The castle at Viborg was strengthened and an outpost fortress, Olofsborg (Olavinlinna), was built in Savolax (Savo) in the 1470s, the first fortress in the medieval kingdom of Sweden built to resist attacks with firearms. It was claimed by the Russians that it was located on the wrong side of the border of the Nöteborg treaty of 1323, so that its construction aggravated the latent conflict between Sweden and Moscow.[5]

In the autumn of 1494 Muscovite troops crossed the border and ravaged and pillaged in Carelia. The political situation was precarious and complicated in Sweden. The king of the union, Hans, was not recognised in Sweden. The regent (*riksföreståndare*), Sten Sture, had ruled Sweden in all but name as a king since 1470. This was a period when the political system in Sweden could be characterised as an aristocratic republic.[6] There were, however, rival fractions within the Swedish aristocracy the main antagonists being the Regent and the Archbishop of Uppsala, Jacob Ulvsson. The conflict was complicated and intricate and it concerned among other things the privileges of the Church. A complicated affair concerning the estate of Hammersta south of Stockholm, confiscated by the Regent, aggravated the dispute. Sweden was, as at many times during the late Middle Ages, on the brink of civil war.

The Muscovite assault made collaboration between the Regent and the Archbishop necessary. The Russians besieged the fortress of Viborg. Late in the winter troops were sent from Sweden to the front in Finland. The Regent himself went to Finland in late autumn 1495 via the Åland islands with mainly German mercenaries. The Russian siege of Viborg failed, an attempt to storm the castle being in vain. In 1496 Russians ravaged widely in Finland, Carelia, Nyland (Uusimaa) and Ostrobothnia (Pohjanmaa). In the autumn negotiations commenced and ended with an armistice in 1497.[7] The result of the war was a status quo, except from a harassed countryside in Finland.

The war was short and not strategically important or decisive. On the Swedish side it was entirely defensive. In any case, crusading ideology was not absent, the crusading idea being much in evidence in the rhetoric concerning this war. The sources are the correspondence between the Bishop of Åbo (Turku), Magnus Stiernkors, and the Archbishop and between the Archbishop and the Regent, Sten Sture, another important source also being the Sture chronicle (*Sturekrönikan*), the last of the medieval Swedish rime chronicles, which ends a long tradition of history writing in medieval Sweden. The chronicle is probably based upon eyewitness account, since it is quite detailed on the war and was probably written shortly afterwards. As with all the Swedish chronicles the author is anonymous. It might be a collective or a work of compilation[8]

In the part describing the war, the tone is rather hostile when describing Sten Sture, portraying him as hesitant. He is criticised for being late in going to the Finnish front, etc. The message was that he was much more interested in the domestic power struggle than in defending the nation. The initiative in organising the defence of Finland in what was described as a Christian war against the schismatics is ascribed entirely to the Archbishop and the Bishop of Åbo.

Jacob Ulvsson became Archbishop in 1470. He had studied in Rostock and spent some years in the late 1460s at the papal curia in Rome,[9] shortly after the fall of Constantinople and when the Ottomans advanced on the Balkans and threatened the Greeks and the Christian kingdoms. Jacob was in Rome when the Turkish offensive against the Albanians caused great anxiety in Rome and the world of Western Christianity. The wars against the Turks were considered as crusades, but they had an entirely defensive purpose.[10]

Jacob exploited the crusade aspect during the Russian war. The influential Bishop of Strängnäs, Kort Rogge, who had also spent several years in Italy, also attached importance to the crusade ideology.[11] These clerics also stressed that the war was not only a crusade, but a national war as well, St Eric being used as a crusading and national symbol. During this war St Eric really had to play his role as a crusader king, highlighted as the king 'who first brought Christianity to Finland.' The defensive war had to protect Christianity, and Saint Eric was to be the patron of the Swedish military force. In the Sture chronicle there is a detailed description of how the banner (or *vexilium*) of Saint Eric was brought from Uppsala cathedral to Stockholm and Saint George's chapel and there solemnly handed over to the regent before his departure to Finland. The banner is said to always have been kept in the cathedral, but is only mentioned in this instance, there being no other references made to it in other sources. Evidently the banner was lost during the struggle in Carelia. Several admonitions from the Archbishop to the Regent to return the banner remained unanswered.[12] Three learned men were sent by the Archbishop with the Regent to the front in order to preach Christianity, thus further stressing the missionary and converting intention.[13]

Pope Alexander VI issued a bull confirming and legitimising this war as a crusade. The bull was issued in July 1496 and after frequent requests and demands by Hemming Gadh, provost of the cathedral of Linköping, and resident Swedish representative at the papal curia in Rome. The bull gave full remission to those who participated in the war and indulgence to those contributing money. The Russians were characterised as schismatic, following Hemming Gadh's application, and a threat to true Christian community in Finland. Gadh's activity in Rome was on behalf of the Archbishop, Jacob Ulvsson, but delay prevented the bull arriving in time. The war was over already.[14] A crusading bull against the schismatic Russians was in contradiction to the aims of the papacy of persuading the Russians to participate in a crusade against the Turks. This papal policy in fact caused a general decline in the interest in pursuing crusades in the Baltic Sea region.[15] A papal bull in favour of the Swedes also interfered in the conflict between the Regent, Sten Sture and Hans, formally the king of the union. King Hans was allied with Ivan III by a formal treaty in 1493, directed against Sten Sture, described as their common enemy.[16] This was perhaps the reason why the bull was kept for a long period by the archbishop of Lund before it was sent to Uppsala.[17] On the other hand Hemming Gadh had managed to persuade the pope to admonish Hans to abstain from hostile acts against the regent of Sweden during the Russian war.[18]

Saint Eric's career as a national saint began late. Unlike his Norwegian counterpart, Saint Olaf, he was a slow starter as a popular saint, his cult being limited for a long period. His cult was supported by his own dynasty, but the Erikian dynasty was not undisputed. The liturgy was mainly promoted in the diocese of Uppsala and his cult remained local and regional. Eric advanced as one of the patrons of the realm in the fourteenth century, and was mentioned in the royal oath, together with Virgin Mary, in the law of the realm, but the cult was not widespread, at least not outside the province of Uppland. Olav of Norway was the principal representation of the just king, even in Sweden. Olav was a popular saint not least in the northern and Finnish part of the medieval kingdom of Sweden.[19]

The great boost for the cult of Saint Eric came in the 1430s, this royal saint advancing as a national symbol during the Engelbrekt revolt against the King of the union, Eric of Pommerania.[20] He was put on the great seal of the realm that the council made in the absence of a recognised king. The council of the realm acted collectively as representative of the kingdom of Sweden. Eric was propagated as a national saint mainly by the cathedral of Uppsala, Jacob Ulvsson being very active. The archbishop ascribed the victory over the King of the union, Christian I, at the battle of Brunkeberg in 1471 to Saint Eric. The victor himself, Sten Sture, however, promoted Saint George, or in Swedish *Sankt Göran* as his patron. This saint fitted better with the general knightly ideals. Sten Sture sponsored the magnificent and famous sculpture of Saint George by Berndt Notke in the church of St Nicholas (nowadays *Storkyrkan)* in Stockholm, followed by minor sculptures in the parts of the realm he controlled.[21] The archbishop thus promoted Saint Eric not only as a national saint, but also as a counter to the Regent's Saint George. When Archbishop Jacob founded the tiny University of Uppsala in 1477, it was placed under the patronage of Saint Eric. There was a substantial increase in iconographic representations of Saint Eric from the 1430s in the entire realm. He was often portrayed as a young knight wearing his banner with the three crowns.[22] A national symbol was needed that represented not merely a just king, but a just Swedish king. A form of elite nationalism or proto-nationalism promoted by the council of the realm (*riksrådet*) and the archbishop of Uppsala emerged.[23] Saint Eric thus became a national saint late in his posthumous career and the tradition of his crusade to Finland was reinvented.

The war in the 1490s was regarded a national crusade. In parts of Europe the state-directed national crusade developed in the fifteenth century. The international crusades waned away after the defeats at Nicopolis in 1396 and Tannenberg in 1410. The wars ending the Reconquista on the Iberian peninsula were crusades, but they were also, and foremost, national wars. The Portuguese and Spanish expansion in North Africa could be regarded as national extensions of the crusades. As early as 1415 the capture of Ceuta in Morocco was considered to be a crusade. A national crusade was in the interest of the state, but not centrally initiated by the papacy.[24] Since crusades were constantly redefined and it is difficult to establish a definition that covers all wars in the Middle Ages that have been so characterised; even if the Swedish-Russian war in the 1490s lacks many, if not all, criteria of the earlier crusades it fits well into the line of crusade-like wars in late medieval Europe. It might be doubtful, mainly because of the lack of sources, whether Saint Eric as a historical person ever carried out a crusade in his lifetime. As a national saint he became finally a crusader king in the 1490s. The external Muscovian threat caused an internal crisis and the idea of crusade was mobilised, although the references to Saint Eric were in general mainly for domestic use.

NOTES

1 For the integration of Finland, see the discussion in Weibull 1940, Sjöstrand 1994 and Lindkvist 2001 with references. The medieval origins of the Swedish-speaking population are recently and interdisciplinarily discussed in Ivars & Huldén (ed.) 2002.
2 For the discussion about Saint Erik and his cult, see Lindkvist 1996 and Lindkvist 1999.
3 Gallén & Lind 1968–1991.
4 Lind 1991. On the war and King Magnus Eriksson's eastern politics, see also Nordberg 1995, pp. 85–106; DS Nr. 4069.
5 Gardberg 1993, pp. 108ff.
6 Schück 1984. Concerning Sten Sture as politician, see Palme 1968, pp. 156–239.
7 FMU Nr. 4734; cf. FMU Nr. 4731. Larsson 1997, pp. 355–362.
8 SMK, pp. 123–144, lines 3577–4198; Hagnell 1941, pp. 85ff, 104, 140f.
9 Kellerman 1935, pp. 18–31.
10 Kellerman 1935, pp. 166–168; Housley 1992, pp. 99–110.
11 Kellerman 1935, p. 76.
12 FMU Nrs. 4631, 4633, 4646, 4730; SMK, p. 126f, lines 3651–3692.
13 FMU Nr. 4631; Kellerman 1935, p. 220.
14 ST Nr. 548; FMU Nr. 4682.
15 Housley 1992, pp. 372f; cf. also Housley 1992, pp. 336f.
16 FMU Nr. 4521.
17 Styffe 1875, p. cxcv; Carlsson 1915: 41–43; cf. Christiansen 1980, p. 191.
18 HSH, pp. 18, 42.
19 Knuutila 1997; Lundegård 1997; Lindkvist 1999 with references.
20 Ahnlund 1954.
21 SMK, p. 82, lines 2386–2391; Kellerman 1935, p. 119; Svanberg 1993.
22 Thordeman 1954.
23 Larsson 1997, pp. 208–210; Reinholdsson 1998, pp. 51–64.
24 Housley 1992, pp. 285–321, 452ff.

BIBLIOGRAPHY

Sources

Diplomatarium Suecanum, vol. 5, ed. B. E. Hildebrand, Stockholm 1858–1865.
Finlands medeltidsurkunder, R. Hausen (ed.), vol. 5–6, Helsingfors 1928–1930.

Handlingar rörande Skandinaviens historia, 18. Stockholm 1833.
Svenska medeltidens rimkrönikor, vol. 3, G. E. Klemming (ed.), Stockholm 1867–88.
Sveriges traktater med främmande magter, O. S. Rydberg (ed.), 1, Stockholm 1877.

Literature

N. Ahnlund 1954, 'Den nationella och den folkliga Erikskulten', in B. Thordeman (ed.), *Erik den helige. Historia, kult, reliker*. Stockholm, pp. 109–154.

C. Carlsson 1915, *Hemming Gadh. En statsman och prelat från Sturetiden. Biografisk studie*. Uppsala.

E. Christensen 1980, *The Northern Crusades. The Baltic and the Catholic Frontier 1100–1525*. London.

J. Gallén & J. Lind 1968–1991, *Nöteborgsfreden och Finlands medeltida östgräns*, 1–2. Helsingfors.

C. J. Gardberg 1993, *Finlands medeltida borgar*. Helsingfors.

K. Hagnell 1941, *Sturekrönikan 1452–1496. Studier över en rimkrönikas tillkomst och sanningsvärde*. Lund.

N. Housley 1992, *The Later Crusades 1274–1580. From Lyons to Alcazar*. Oxford.

A.-M. Ivars & L. Huldén (ed.), 2002, *När kom svenskarna till Finland?* Helsingfors.

G. Kellerman 1935, *Jakob Ulvsson och den svenska kyrkan under äldre Sturetiden 1470–1497*. Stockholm.

J. Knuutila 1997, 'Sankt Olav i Finlands kyrkliga konst under medeltiden', in L. Rumar (ed.), *Helgonet i Nidaros. Olavskult och kristnande i Norden*. Stockholm, pp. 91–114.

L.-O. Larsson 1997, *Kalmarunionens tid. Från drottning Margareta till Kristian II*. Stockholm.

J. Lind 1991, 'Magnus Eriksson som birgittinsk konge i lyset af russiske kilder', in T. Nyberg (ed.) *Birgitta og hendes klostre i Norden*. Odense, pp. 103–128.

T. Lindkvist 1996, 'Med Sankt Erik konung mot hedningar och schismatiker. Korståg och korstågspolitik i svensk medeltida östpolitik', in M. Engman (ed.) *Väst möter öst. Norden och Ryssland genom historien*. Stockholm, pp. 13–33.

T. Lindkvist 1999, 'Erik den helige och det svenska kungadömets framväxt', in O. Skevik (ed.), *Kongemøte på Stiklestad. Foredrag fra seminar om kongedømmet i vikingetid och tidlig middelalder*. Verdal, pp. 119–134.

T. Lindkvist 2001, 'Die schwedischen Kreuzzüge nach Finnland in der Geschichtsschreibung', in F. Peterick & D. Putensen, (ed.) *Pro Finlandia 2001. Festschrift für Manfred Menger*. Reinbek, pp. 49–66.

I. Lundegård 1997, 'Kampen om den norrländska Olavskulten', in L. Rumar (ed.), *Helgonet i Nidaros. Olavskult och kristnande i Norden*. Stockholm, pp. 115–136.

M. Nordberg 1995, *I kung Magnus tid. Norden under Magnus Eriksson 1317–1374*. Stockholm.

S. U. Palme 1968, *Sten Sture den äldre*, second edition, Stockholm.

P. Reinholdsson 1998, *Uppror eller resningar? Samhällsorganisation och konflikt i senmedeltidens Sverige*. Uppsala.

H. Schück 1984, 'Sweden as an Aristocratic Republic', *Scandinavian Journal of History* 9, pp. 65–72.

P. O. Sjöstrand 1994, 'Den svenska tidigmedeltida statsbildningsprocessen och den östra rikshalvan', *Historisk tidskrift för Finland* 79, pp. 530–571.

C. G. Styffe 1875, *Bidrag till Skandinaviens historia ur utländska arkiver*, 4. Stockholm.

J. Svanberg 1993, *Sankt Göran och draken*. Stockholm.

B. Thordeman 1954, 'Erik den helige i medeltidens bildkonst', in B. Thordeman (ed.), *Erik den helige. Historia. kult reliker*. Stockholm, pp. 173–232.

C. Weibull 1940, 'När och hur Finland blev svenskt', *Scandia* 13, pp. 1–21.

JOHN H. LIND

Puzzling Approaches to the Crusading Movement in Recent Scandinavian Historiography

Danish Historians on Crusades and Source Editions as well as a Swedish Historian on Crusading in Finland[1]

As indicated in the title, this is not about medieval history writing, and to the extent it is about crusading ideology, it is not medieval but what we could call present-day 'ideology' on the crusades and the crusading movement, or, perhaps rather the absence of 'crusading ideology' in modern research, if such an expression is permitted.

With a background in Russian history, I have come to work with the history of the Scandinavian crusades with none of the research traditions or views on the subject that has been accumulated in Scandinavian research. Therefore, I do not initially share a set of beliefs, attitudes or approaches that other Scandinavian historians in this field have grown up with and may unwittingly have adopted, built upon or, as in recent years, rebelled against. Consequently, I may be in a better or at least different position to detect what – for want of better – I have in my title called *Puzzling Approaches*.

The approaches I am going to talk about may have their origin in ideological abstractions at various levels of generality, or may simply reflect a provincial narrowness among scholars, seeing Scandinavia or the individual Scandinavian countries as isolated islands, unaffected by what took place in the surrounding world. What they all have in common is what in my opinion amounts to a distorted view of what the Scandinavian crusades were.

Generally speaking, I think that the attitude with which Scandinavian historians have traditionally approached the crusades, not least the crusades in the Baltic region, has been influenced by the fact that they are mainly Protestants. This has imbued them with a certain scepticism towards everything linked to the Catholic Church in general and to the papacy in particular, distrusting explicit or official motives for various actions, looking instead for hidden motives. This especially applies to the crusades and I will start by quoting some recent Danish historians to make my point.

Danish Historians on the Crusades

The best-balanced approach is probably to be found in the account by Aksel E. Christensen in his part of the *History of Denmark*, 1977. Nevertheless, he claims that the main purpose of the Danish wars against the Slavic Wends in the period of Valdemar I the Great changed from being defence of the Danish shores to 'conquests alleged to be mission and crusades.'[2] Consequently, in his view the 'Wendish crusades' were not crusades at all.

Christensen's colleague and in many respects antithesis at Copenhagen University, Niels Skyum-Nielsen, was much more outspoken. In his provocative and stimulating work, *Woman and Slave. A History of Denmark without Deception*, he saw the Wendish Crusades of 1159–1169 as 'raids of revenge and plunder' first disguised 'under the cross as religious sign, as long as that was possible, then with the Cross as political sign.'[3] A raid by Valdemar I to Finland, which the king, in Skyum-Nielsen's reading of the source, undertook in approximately 1170 in support of his father-in-law, was characterised as, 'crusade and plunder, mixed wonderfully with commercial and family interests.'[4] Obviously Skyum-Nielsen in neither case accepts that these attacks were in any real sense crusades.

In the most recent general history of Denmark, the author of the volume covering the period 1050–1250, Ole Fenger, makes two statements concerning Danish crusades worth commenting on.

First, he compares the Danish crusades against the Wends with the violent expansion of the Christian faith to the Saxons and Slavs by Charlemagne: 'Then [in the period of Charlemagne], the means were made holy by the good purpose, which cannot be said about the later Danish raids of piracy to the lands of the Slavs.'[5] Admittedly, this is not a very elegant translation, but it is literal and it is puzzling. Apart from the fact that the concept of crusades or 'to go to war under the sign of the Cross' was not yet thought of in the ninth century, it is difficult to comprehend where exactly the difference lies. Of course Saxons were Christianised as result of Charlemagne's Saxon wars, but so were the Slavs against whom the Danish raids were directed in the twelfth century.

Another point of view in Fenger's account to which I want to draw attention is this. In talking about the crusades to Estonia and Livonia, Fenger describes how 'they were gradually turned into imperialistic ventures guided by secular interests' and he continues, by contrast, to characterise the crusades to the Holy Land as 'real' crusades. Therefore, describing how Archbishop Absalon's brother, Esbern Snare, persuaded a number of aristocrats to go to the Holy Land in a famous speech, after the news of Jerusalem's fall had just reached the very aristocratic and presumably drunk Christmas-party assembled in Odense in 1187, Fenger stresses that 'there were Danes who did choose the *real thing*, the crusade to the Holy Land' (*italics, JHL*).[6]

This distinction between considering crusades to the Holy Land to be *genuine* crusades and those in the Baltic region by implication to be *fake* seems to be made almost automatically by Danish and Scandinavian historians. Furthermore, it seems to be a distinction made without any preceding reflection upon how crusades to the Holy Land actually differed from Crusades in the Baltic apart from geography. It is, however, easy to demonstrate that the motives for going on crusade to the Holy Land were just as mixed as they were for those who went on crusades in the Baltic. There was the same combination of greed and ulterior motives that we can find in the Baltic Crusades. Just think about the rush among leaders of the First Crusade to carve out principalities for themselves long before the conquest of Jerusalem, or the subsequent hesitation among some of them to participate in that final stage of the crusade. On the other hand, although sources are sparse concerning the Baltic crusades, there can be no doubt that those two noble laymen, Asmundus and Godmundus, who were recorded sometime in the twelfth century in the Memorial List of Lund Cathedral's Chapter, the *Liber Daticus Lundensis,* as killed among the Wends 'under the sign of the Holy Cross', were genuine crusaders who died in the expectation of receiving the otherworldly goods promised to crusaders.[7]

Surprisingly, or perhaps not, the scholar most negative in regard to the Danish crusades in the Baltic was the church historian Hal Koch. His characterisation of the crusades as a 'fantastic, outrageous spectacle' starting shortly before 1100 indicates his general attitude to the crusading phenomenon. As Koch sees it,

> Denmark did not at first catch up [with the movement], although Danes were eager to depict the wars with the Wends as crusades. Such an interpretation of the Danish raids across the Baltic Sea is, however, rather too generous. A large proportion of the Wends was long since Christian. Besides, the Danish efforts were by no means aimed at converting anybody to Christianity but only at ravaging and plundering.[8]

Not least in this case the negative attitude towards the crusades to the Holy Land in particular may be attributed to Koch's outspoken Protestant outlook.

Editing Sources and Crusades

Koch was also one of the initiators of a research tradition which came to dominate the scholarly debate on the Danish High Middle Ages in the twentieth century, the question of the relationship between the two institutions of Kingdom and Church or *Regnum et Sacerdotium.*

In recent years there has been a tendency to view Danish historiography as insular or introvert, indifferent to outside incentives from international scholarship. Our present project, *Denmark and the Crusades,* out of which this seminar has grown, was to a certain extent established as part of such criticism of older generations of historians. But it is not quite true, and the dominance the discussion of the balance of power between *Regnum et Sacerdotium* assumed in Danish historiography was the result of such an external stimulus. In Germany they had such a discussion; consequently

Denmark got one. Therefore, a student studying history in the 1960s, soon got the impression that, if he wanted to qualify himself, he had to pronounce and substantiate a view on the relationship between *Regnum et Sacerdotium.*[9]

When the *Denmark and the Crusades* project began, a convenient way of getting a general view of the relevant sources in order to establish which documents to dismiss and which to reserve for closer scrutiny was to read the summaries of documents edited in the *Diplomatarium Danicum.*

The *Diplomatarium Danicum* corpus and its companion of Danish translations, *Danmarks Riges Breve*, is undoubtedly a major achievement by Danish historical science in the twentieth century. Although mistakes in such a gigantic project are, of course, unavoidable, the user expects that the summaries give a fair impression of what any given document is about. An important group of documents concerning information on the Scandinavian crusades are the so-called September Letters from 1171 or 1172, sent by Pope Alexander III to recipients in Scandinavia. They have only been preserved as a corpus thanks to the fact that Peter of Celle, then Abbot in Saint-Remi in Rheims and a close friend of Archbishop Eskil, was in close collaboration with Eskil on the subject and therefore received copies of these and other letters concerning Scandinavia.[10]

Having read the summary of one of these letters, however, I became very surprised later to discover the actual contents of the letter. The letter in question is dated 11th September and is addressed to kings, princes and other Christian believers in the realms of the Danes, Norwegians, Sveonians and Gothonians.

According to the editorial summary, Pope Alexander III first:

> admonishes kings, princes and other Christians in Denmark, Norway and Sweden, to show the church due respect and comply with commands issued by the ecclesiastical authorities, pay them tithes, give donations and defend their rights,

before going on:

> and defend them against attacks from Estonians and other pagans. Finally the Pope grants one year's indulgence to anyone who joins in the fight against pagans similar to the one the Pope grants to those who visit the Holy Sepulchre.[11]

Of course the latter part of the summary means that that the document was bound to be of interest in a study of the Baltic crusades in any case. The summary, however, suggests that the letter first of all has to be seen in context with the conflict between *Regnum et Sacerdotium* in the Scandinavian countries, whereas the fight against pagans was of secondary importance. However, when we read the letter itself we discover at once that this impression is completely untrue:

> The Pope starts his letter by expressing how worried he is to hear that the wild Estonians and other pagans in those regions threaten those who believe

in the Christian faith. Therefore he praises the lord because the Scandinavian kings, princes and other Christians faithfully uphold their Christian faith and preserve the unity of the church by adhering to the Roman church, leader of all other churches and, consequently, the one that binds them together.

As leader of the churches, the Pope now urges the recipients of the letter to lay emphasis on their service to God, rule well by giving just verdicts, abstain from plunder, honour the church, humbly obey the bishops and priests, pay the tithes and in every respect preserve the rights of ecclesiastics '*so that they, armed with the heavenly weapons, ... can prepare valiantly to defend ... and expand the Christian faith and defeat the enemies.*' Therefore the Pope concedes to those who fight against the often-mentioned pagans one year's redemption of the sins they have confessed and for which they have agreed to do penance, in the same manner, etc.

Obviously this letter is not at all about *Regnum et Sacerdotium*. It is all about the fight against the 'wild Estonians and other pagans in those regions' and about organising a crusade against them. The section in middle of the letter, where the Pope talks about internal affairs in the Scandinavian societies, is included to guarantee that the secular rulers understand the necessity of peace and harmony at home so that they and their societies at large are able to concentrate on the fight abroad. The author of the summary seems, however, to have been so uninterested in the subject of crusades and the fight against pagans and so engrossed in the Danish scholarly tradition of his time that he automatically read the conflict between *Regnum et Sacerdotium* into the letter. Thereby he has, no doubt without wishing to do so, completely distorted the contents and purpose of the letter.

It is not difficult to find other instances that show the same lack of interest among the editors of the *Diplomatarium Danicum* in the Danish involvement abroad as a result of the crusading movement.[12] A letter issued between 12th and 16th September 1237 by the General Chapter of the Cistercian Order is one such instance. Having presumably received bad news about the situation in the Cistercian Abbacy in Kolbatz, the General Chapter directed a letter to the abbot of Herrisvad Monastery in Scania, ordering the abbot to go to Kolbatz fully authorised by the order to correct and reform the abbacy there, accompanied by another Cistercian abbot, presumably of his own choice.[13]

The Cistercian monastery in Kolbatz was a Danish foundation of the early 1170s,[14] after the Danes, upon the conquest and incorporation of Rügen in 1168, had turned their interests further east towards the western part of Pomerania. The 1237-letter is in itself evidence of the fact that the Kolbatz Abbacy was then still seen to be linked to Denmark by the Cistercian Order.[15] The inclusion of this letter in the *Diplomatarium Danicum,* could, of course, be seen as a negation of my claim that the editors were uninterested in the Danish involvement abroad. But this is not so. The reason for including the document is not that it concerns the Kolbatz Monastery but the fact that it is addressed to the abbot of the Danish monastery at Herrisvad in Scania. This is made quite clear by the fact that only two weeks after the General Chapter had issued its letter, Pope Gregory IX on 3rd October 1237 issued a bull to the Kolbatz Abbacy receiving it and its possessions under his protection: 'monasterium de Colbas Caminensis diocesis ... sub beati Petri et nostra protectione suscipimus.'[16] It would seem that this bull invalidates the letter from the Cistercian General Chapter. In *Diplomatarium Danicum,* however, there is no clue to the existence of this bull. Therefore, unless a scholar happens to have seen a reference to this source elsewhere, he will invariably misinterpret the impact of the letter from the General Chapter. This letter would seem to confirm continued Danish influence in Pomerania at this time, while the papal bull indicates that this influence was declining or already non-existent. And precisely this, continuation or rejection of Danish influence in the region, could very well be what both letters are about.[17]

In contrast to this lack of interest among the editors in recording Danish political or institutional involvement abroad, there seems to have been no end to their interest in recording the personal involvement of individual Danes abroad, whether or not that had any relevance for Danish history at large. For instance, while not including a reference to Pope Gregory's bull, the editors have chosen to include a reference to a document issued by the Bishop of Minden to the monastery in Nenndorf, simply because one 'Iohannes Danus' is mentioned among the witnesses.[18] Much the same can be said about the inclusion of a number of documents with no conceivable relevance for Danish history issued by Queen Ingeborg of France or documents in which she is mentioned, simply because she was Danish-born.[19]

This is also indicative of a fairly parochial attitude among the editors of the *Diplomatarium*, which in other cases can have serious consequences for our understanding of Danish involvement in those regions of the Baltic targeted by the crusades, and also the relative importance this involvement had. A case in point is the papal bull issued by Honorius III, 15th June 1218. The text itself has been published *in extenso*.[20] Having read the summary, according to which the pope urges the Danish archbishop and his suffragans to support the Prussian Bishop Christian's missionary work among the heathen Prussians in various ways, the reader must inevitably think that Denmark and the Danish Archbishop Andreas was at the time Honorius's most trusted partner in executing papal crusading policy in the Baltic region. This is of course hardly so, which the reader will discover as soon as he actually starts reading the letter itself, since it is in fact addressed, not to the Danish archbishop, but to 'Archbishop Sigfridus of Mainz and his Suffragans.' Only after the text itself do the editors of Honorius's register add that a similar letter was sent to 'the Archbishop of Lund and his suffragans' ['In eundem modum scriptum est Lundensi archiepiscopo et suffraganeis eius']. This slight misrepresentation in the summary might after all not be considered such a serious error on the part of the editors. A seasoned reader of papal bulls will, however, suspect that the letter was not just sent to Mainz and Lund, as the editor, perhaps unwittingly, lets the reader believe. And this is where, I think, the parochial attitude on the part of the editors assumes some importance. Obviously it has not been thought important for a correct interpretation and evaluation of the impact of the papal letter to mention the number and range of its recipients. To find out exactly to whom this letter was sent the user of the *Diplomatarium* must turn to some of the other major source editions. There, sure enough, he will find that the list of recipients was fairly large, as the same letter was sent to no less than eight archbishoprics with their suffragans in addition to one exempt bishopric, scattered over most of Northern and Central Europe:

> In eundem modum scriptum est Magdeburgensi archiepiscopo et suffraganeis eius, archiepiscopo Coloniensi et suffraganeis eius, Salezburgensi et suffraganeis eius, Gnesnensi et suffraganeis eius, Lundensi et suffraganeis eius, episcopo Caminensi, Bremensi et suffraganeis eius, und Trevirensi et suffraganeis eius.[21]

Consequently, the Danish archbishop had by no means been singled out by the pope to play any particularly important role in connection with the Prussian mission. There is, however, one important point in the list that the incomplete rendition in the *Diplomatarium* has deprived its reader of.[22] This concerns the position in the list of the bishopric of Kammin. Both Magdeburg and Gniezno had in recent times endeavoured to incorporate Kammin into their provinces. As a result, the pope had put the bishopric of Kammin under his direct protection. This had been solemnly confirmed in 1188, that is, soon after the Danes had taken control of the region in 1185. Still some historians have claimed that two successive bishops invested after the Danish take-over, Sigfrid (1186–1191) and Sigwin (1191–1219), were Danes, indicative of a strong Danish influence in the region. This view has been disputed by Jürgen Petersohn, however.[23] The fact that the papal administration has placed Kammin immediately after Lund in the list of recipients could indicate that the pope saw a close link between the Danish archbishopric and the bishopric of Kammin. The succession of recipients in the list therefore suggests that these two successive bishops of Kammin both could have been installed from Lund and could indeed be Danes.

Thomas Lindkvist on Crusades in and out of Finland

The historians mentioned so far are either not present at our seminar or are already dead, so what has so far been said may perhaps not generate spirited discussion. Also, I have so far only commented on problems concerning Danish historiography and the Danish crusades, whereas, in the title I have promised to talk about Scandinavian historiography at large. Therefore I have chosen to finish the article by taking as my point of departure an interview given a few years ago by a historian who is both present and, I am happy to say, very much alive.

The historian in question is none other than my good friend and predecessor on the rostrum, Thomas Lindkvist. As a docent for many years at the Swedish-language university, Åbo Akademi, Lindkvist has like myself had a past in Finland and like me he has, of course, often been concerned with crusades in or out of Finland.

In no other Scandinavian country has the concept of crusades played such a great role as in Finland, where an essential period of its medieval history, roughly speaking from 1150 to let us say 1350, is simply called the *Period of the Crusades*. This period has even been subdivided into the period of the so-called First Crusade, the years around the middle of the twelfth century, the Second Crusade, the period around the middle of the thirteenth century, and the Third Crusade, the period from the end of the thirteenth century. This way of dividing Finnish history into periods is, of course, as Thomas Lindkvist has also often pointed out, fairly modern, originating with Erik Gustav Geijer.

Finland or rather Finns have mainly been victims of the crusades. This role as victims has often been strongly stressed by a certain national-romantic historiography, born out of the *Fennoman* movement of the nineteenth century. On the other hand, it would undoubtedly be true to say that the present state of Finland owes both its existence as a separate independent political and cultural entity and the fact that it is a western society to the crusades. Therefore a more recent, differently weighted, but still slightly nationalistic school of thought, as well as public opinion at large, has acquired a fairly positive view on the Period of the Crusades. This has, in particular, been the case in periods when the main concern of Finns has been the relationship with their eastern neighbour. Occasionally scholars of this school have even gone to extremes in dodging or even ne-gating source information in order to present the incorporation of Finland into Sweden as a peaceful process, guided by a shared interest in defending western values against Russians or Russian-allied Carelians.[24]

I now proceed to the interview in question with Lindkvist, which ap-peared in the official newsbulletin of Åbo Akademi, *Meddelanden från Åbo Akademi* in April 1998, and must be said to have had an almost of-ficial, programmatic intent. It was entitled 'The Crusades to Finland were no Ecclesiastical Enterprises.'[25]

In the interview Lindkvist makes many statements concerning the proc-ess of Christianisation in Finland and the process of Finland becoming part of the nascent Swedish state formation, to which I would readily subscribe. For instance, that archaeological finds show that Christianity was present in Finland long before the Period of the Crusades.[26] This, however, does not mean that Finns in general were Christians before the crusades.

The title of the interview invites comment. The source of the so-called First Swedish Crusade, the Life of Eric, claims that King Eric was accompanied by a bishop on his expedition to Finland, normally dated to the 1150s. This must at least have made the expedition into a semi-ecclesiastical enterprise. Admittedly, Lindkvist does not – and quite rightly – consider this source, dated to the late thirteenth century, to be contemporary. Furthermore, as we shall see, he seems to think that it was only at that time, during the so-called Third Crusade, that a crusading ideology appeared in Sweden. It was therefore only then that a need to present earlier military expeditions as crusades arose. Accordingly, it was then that an expedition Eric Jedvardsson might have led in the twelfth century was turned into a crusade. Here it must, however, be pointed out that since, independent of the Life of Eric, Russian chronicles, just like the Life, portray Swedish expeditions in both 1142 and 1240 as joint princely-episcopal enterprises,[27] the participation of a bishop in Saint Eric's expedition is not necessarily a product of crusading fervour in the late thirteenth century.

But let me start my selection of quotes from the interview with this:

> The so-called crusades were not about Finnish versus Swedish. The events in Finland during the Early Middle Ages ... will not be seen as an attempt from the Swedish side to take over Finland; rather, it concerns a gradual change in society. The view that Sweden conquered Finland step by step is a fabrication of the nineteenth century.[28]

The fact is, however, that Finland[29] did become part of Sweden during the crusading period. It did not become part of Novgorod, although there are hints in medieval sources that this could have been an alternative; and it was certainly more or less a step by step process, although, perhaps, less distinctly so than the notion of three crusades suggests.

Furthermore, the expression Lindkvist uses here to evade using words like 'crusade' or 'conquest' seems to me to strike a slightly apologetic note. I would like to dwell on this for a moment. However, let me first tender another quote. In talking about Birger Magnusson's so-called Second Crusade to Finland, described in Eric's Chronicle, Lindkvist stresses, 'It was not a crusade although it is described as such in the Chronicle.'[30] Keeping this in mind I shall now return to my former quotation from the interview: '*events in Finland* during the Early Middle Ages will not be seen as an attempt from the Swedish side to take over Finland, rather it concerns a gradual change in society' (*italics*, JHL).

'Events in Finland' (Händelserna i Finland) is a formula I have seen used before in a historiographic debate. A debate, however, that concerned a much later period, namely the period of the 'events in 1918' (Händelserna i 1918), that is, the traumatic and vengeful civil war that broke out in Finland after the socialists or *Reds* had taken power in the southern part of Finland in January 1918 which, after the *White* victory, ended in a massacre of defeated *Reds*. Following the White victory this was called a *War of Liberation*, both by the victors, historians and a large proportion of the public. Once the political situation had changed radically after the Second World War, left-wing historians particularly started to use the label *Class War* for these 'events', before the more neutral *Civil War* came into more general use. But to some, especially authors of schoolbooks, the question had by now become so sensitive that, instead of choosing a term that might distress some of the pupils or their parents, they settled for the anaemic 'events in 1918'.[31]

It appears that something very similar has happened to Lindkvist in his treatment of the period 1150–1350. He does not consider it suitable to use a word like crusade about what happened, although it is described as such in the sources, and he does not want to talk about conquest either, although Finland did end up being integrated into the Swedish State: therefore, 'events in Finland.'

It is, however, not this phenomenon that prompted me to finish my reflections on 'puzzling' approaches to the crusades with Lindkvist's interview, but two other claims Lindkvist made. Claims which, I think, reflect his general view on what the moving factors in history are, especially at this stage of medieval history, and which seem to show how this general view, ideology if you like, has sometimes been able to replace actual sources in the reconstruction of what happened – or even negate information in actual sources.

Speaking about the so-called First Crusade, Lindkvist said:

> It is quite possible that a Swedish king directed an expedition to the region of Åbo [Turku] towards the middle of the twelfth century, but the purpose was definitely not to expand Christianity. Nothing in *contemporary sources* indicates that Christianisation of Finland happened by the use of violence (*italics*, JHL).[32]

Lindkvist continues,

> those campaigns that did occur – the one by Saint Eric was probably one of many – were rather *plundering raids* (*italics*, JHL).[33]

This, I think, raises the interesting question of what is mentioned in *contemporary* sources and what is not. Where does Lindkvist find evidence in contemporary sources to substantiate the view that the one, perhaps, two raids we find mentioned in the sources, together with those hypothetical raids he speaks of,[34] were for plunder? Since I doubt very much that there is such a source, I think that this is a case where Lindkvist's general theory on early statehood and the process of state formation has taken over the role of sources, a theory he elaborated in *Predatory Incursions, Royal Taxation and the Formation of a Feudal State in Sweden, 1000–1300* some years ago.[35]

Concerning the accompanying allegation that 'nothing in contemporary sources indicates that christianisation of Finland happened by the use of violence,' I would like to point out the often-quoted bull *Gravis Admodum*, one of the so-called September Letters, mentioned above. This letter was issued by Pope Alexander III on 9th September 1171 or 1172 and addressed to the Archbishop of Uppsala, and his suffragans together with Earl Guttorm. No doubt this is a contemporary source, and whatever interpretation we apply to the text and whoever we identify as the actors, two facts seem certain: 1) the Swedish involvement in Finland has, according to this contemporary source, nothing to do with plunder; and 2) the Finns did not adopt Christianity voluntarily but, if nothing more, then at least under threat of violence from the Swedes. These are the pertinent sections in the letter:

A serious complaint has been submitted to the Apostolic See to the effect that the Finns, whenever an enemy army threatens them, promise to observe the Christian faith wishing to receive priests that can guide them in the Christian faith. But when the army retreats they deny the faith, scorn the priests and persecute them severely. Therefore... in future, beware of their duplicity and falseness so that they cannot, if they land in an emergency, obtain help and security from you unless they surrender their fortresses to you, if they have any, or otherwise provide security, so that they are not able to retract or deceive you but are forced without fail to adhere to and observe the Christian creed.[36]

The account the Pope here gives of the false Finns had become almost a *topos* by the 1170s in Christian descriptions from the crusading period of the difficulties Christian missionaries as well as Christian crusaders experienced in their attempts to convert pagan peoples. Perhaps the earliest example of this in the Baltic Region is to be found in the *Chronicle on the Polish Dukes and Princes*, composed before 1118 by an anonymous Gallic author, known as *Gallus Anonymus*. In describing the efforts by the Polish Duke Boleslav III to Christianise (and subjugate) the 'Prussians, Pomeranians and other Slavs further to the west,' Gallus Anonymus described how these peoples accept baptism when they are under pressure but reject the faith when they have recovered strength.[37] In this case the constant adherence by the newly converted pagans clearly depends on the permanent presence of a Christian army. According to Alexander's letter the situation in Finland is the same. Only the presence of a Swedish army, safely entrenched in the Finnish strongholds,[38] can ensure the permanent adherence of the Finns to the Christian Faith. Therefore the use of force by the Swedes is at least foreseen by the Pope. Here it should be remembered that the Pope wrote this letter along with a number of letters to the region, of which one from 11th September, already mentioned above, explicitly urged the recipients, among whom were also the recipients of the *Gravis Admodum* bull, to preach a crusade against the Estonians and *other pagans in the region*. The *Gravis Admodum* bull must thus be seen as part of a co-ordinated crusading effort in the region.

This aspect of the letter, the threat of violence from the Swedes against the Finns, has often been ignored, because Alexander's letter at the same time, it seems, introduces a third party, an 'enemy army.' Alexander claims that it is in fact the appearance of this enemy army that forces the Finns to overcome their disinclination to adopt Christianity, so as to receive help from the Christian Swedes. In a manner of speaking, it is this enemy army that takes over the role of the actual crusading army. By introducing this enemy force, the Pope – or his Swedish informants – manages to minimise the force the Swedish Christians have to use in order to Christianise the Finns.

Who this enemy army represents is not specified, but speculations on that point have preoccupied Finnish scholars much more than the fact that the Swedes according to the letter were urged to establish themselves in Finland by military means, which, incidentally, they did. Most often the enemies mentioned in the bull have been identified as Russians, i.e., Novgorodians, while the Swedes and Finns have been seen as allies.

This was the unqualified view taken by one of the two most prominent Finnish medievalists of the recent past, Kauko Pirinen.[39] In making this identification, Pirinen seems to have been more influenced by a wish to link Finland with Sweden and the West than by actual sources. Thus the view that Novgorodians precisely at this time should have threatened the Finns – or Swedish power in Finland – is highly unlikely. First of all, there are no indications in the sources of Novgorodian activity or interests so far west before the attack on Turku in 1318.[40] At that time, however, the situation was entirely different. Sweden had long since conquered Tavastia, had moved into Carelia and was now threatening the Carelian Isthmus with its important trade links. By striking at Turku, Novgorod hit at the Swedish administrative centre in Sweden's *Eastern Lands*. Altogether it was only in the 1220–1230s that Novgorod systematically turned its attention towards parts of what is present-day Finland, and then the target was Tavastia. Secondly, in the 1160–1170s, Novgorod was hardly able to conduct an aggressive policy in west, fully occupied as it was defending its valuable possessions in Northeast Russia against the Central Russian principalities.[41] This conflict soon turned into a battle for the very existence of Novgorod as an independent state, culminating in 1170 with the famous battle and victory over the Suzdalians and a large coalition of Russian princes before the walls of Novgorod,[42] a victory that later took on legendary proportions because of the alleged miraculous intervention of the *Icon of God's Mother of the Sign*. Furthermore, during the ten years that precede this battle and over the next five years Novgorod exchanged its prince no less than ten times and was for a period without a prince. This means that Novgorod hardly ever in that period possessed an army capable of raiding far from its borders.[43]

Accordingly, it seems that Russians in this interpretation of the *Gravis Admodum* bull are able to appear as *deus ex machina* on 'the once a threat, always a threat' -principle, so that the Russian threat can be called upon as the cause of an event, whether or not they were in fact able to present such a threat at the time.

Pirinen's contemporary and colleague, Jarl Gallén, was less outspoken in his interpretation, stating simply that 'the Finns had become Christians under threat from the East, but returned to paganism when Swedish help was no longer needed.'[44] That allows for a much more plausible scenario than the assumption of a Russian threat – that is, if the enemy threat was real at all and not simply the product of Swedish propaganda in Rome finding its way into the papal letter. Apart from the implied resistance from the Finns in *Gravis Admodum,* the earliest information we have on resistance to Christianity and the Swedes during the Swedish expansion into present-day Finland concerns the Finns' immediate neighbours to the east, the Tavastians. Incursions by them into a newly Christianised Finland could induce those Finns who were genuinely converted to ask for Swedish help, while Finns less firmly converted would tend to dissociate themselves from the Swedes and Christianity at the first opportunity, and, perhaps, even ally themselves with the alleged 'enemy'. That would be a scenario not unlike the one implied by Gregory IX in his bull of 9th December 1237, urging the Swedish archbishop and his suffragans to preach a crusade against Tavastian apostates who had rebelled against the labours of the Swedish bishops and their predecessors and, induced by nearby enemies of the cross, reverted to their old errors.[45] Be that as it may. The use of force by the Swedes in keeping the Finns loyal to Christianity is undeniably implied in the contemporary *Gravis Admodum* bull. In this connection, it has, of course, to be stressed that the Swedish expansion into Finland did not lead to a subsequent ethnic suppression like that which happened south of the Gulf of Finland, where a type of apartheid society arose and the population became divided into a privileged minority, consisting of Germans (Deutsche) and a suppressed majority which, regardless of its ethnicity, was simply referred to as 'Un-Germans' (*Undeutsche*).

Some of the points Lindkvist raised in the interview in 1998 were anticipated in an earlier article, published in 1992, entitled 'When Finland Became Swedish. On the Swedish Need of Crusades against Finland.'[46] There he gives a more comprehensive presentation of his position, again clearly guided by his general view on early state formation. He claims that it was only towards the end of the thirteenth century that a more developed feudal state of European type came into existence in Sweden. Only from this time is the levy system (*ledung*) recorded, allowing the king to dispose of men and ships. Presumably neither Saint Eric nor Earl Birger had the possibility of levying a fleet. And while expeditions around 1200, according to Lindkvist, were basically late Viking raids, an expedition towards the east carried out by Earl Birger could probably only have consisted of aristocrats from Östergötland with their personal retinues. But by the end of the thirteenth century Swedish society had experienced such fundamental, organisational and political changes that an expansionary policy in the east became possible. The Swedish state now needed the concept of crusading in order to justify the war against Novgorod (i.e., the so-called Third Crusade of Torgils Knutsson), and only now was there was a need in Sweden to present earlier military expeditions as crusades.

We have already seen how this general theory of the development of Swedish society and the late appearance of a crusading ideology seems to have influenced Lindkvist's view of Saint Eric's crusade. In the same way this theory, rather than actual sources, also seems to have to determined the view Lindkvist applied to the so-called Second Crusade to Tavastia in the 1992 article. Here he has lined up with a long tradition within Finnish historiography, maintaining that the expedition was organised by the primate of the Finns, Bishop Thomas, rather than Swedish secular authorities in the person of the earl or Birger Magnusson.[47] According to Lindkvist the ecclesiastic organisation in Finland was loose until the end of the twelfth century, but at the beginning of the thirteenth century it took on a firmer shape under Bishop Thomas. At that time the ecclesiastical organisation in Finland was more firmly established than Swedish secular rule.[48] Therefore, if a military expedition[49] really took place in 1238 (or 1239), it was rather the bishop (i.e., Bishop Thomas, JHL) than the [Swedish] earl who was the inspirational force and organiser.[50] The fact that Eric's Chronicle attributes the role as leader of the expedition to Birger Magnusson, Lindkvist seems to see as a result of the same 'legitimising bias,' which I referred to above. This 'bias' the authors of both Life of Eric and Eric's Chronicle, writing at the end of the thirteenth and the beginning of the fourteenth centuries, applied to their respective works as result of the assumed need to project the rising crusading ideology back in time.[51] The campaign in 1238/1239 was, like Saint Eric's campaign in the 1150s, thus turned into a Swedish crusade only in the early fourteenth century.

While the postulated late adoption of a crusading ideology in Sweden collides with Pope Alexander III's September Letters, in time closely linked to the First Crusade,[52] Lindkvist's view on the Second Crusade similarly collides with the actual wording of Gregorius IX's crusading bull of 9th December 1237, which is, after all, a principal contemporary source for this expedition. Here the Pope explicitly urges not the Finnish bishop but the Archbishop of Uppsala and his suffragans (among whom the Finnish bishop, of course, is included) to preach a crusade against the Tavastians, after they had oppressed the '*Regnum Sweorum*.' Furthermore, the Pope explicitly asserts that he has written the bull in response to information he has received not from the Finnish bishop, but from the Swedish Archbishop.[53]

As to Birger Magnusson's role in the expedition: even if we do accept as a hypothesis that the author of Eric's Chronicle, because of later ideological manipulations, could have falsely attributed the leadership of a Crusade to Tavastia in 1238/1239 to Birger Magnusson, the same can hardly apply to the fact that Russian sources name Birger as leader of the subsequent 1240 expedition to the Neva. In this expedition he is, by the way, accompanied by a number of Swedish bishops, not just one. Even if the Finnish bishop did participate in this campaign, a supposition not supported by any source, he must have been accompanied by at least one bishop from mainland Sweden. With this in mind, we have no reason not to accept the designation of Birger in Eric's Chronicle as leader of the expedition to Tavastia as correct.[54]

It is tempting, in conclusion, to turn Lindkvist's argument on its head, by claiming that it is difficult in medieval sources to find support for the view that the Swedish conquest of Finland and the conversion of the Finns to Christianity was peaceful. The need for describing the incorporation of Finland as non-violent had not yet arisen when the sources were produced. That happened much later, when it was felt necessary to represent Swedes and Finns as staunch allies standing firmly in defence of joint western values against the dangers from an eastern neighbour. At that time a need was felt to project this view back to earlier periods, so that Swedes and Finns could be presented as allies when Finland was conquered and the Finns converted to Christianity.

But while present-day historians may recoil from describing the Swedish conquest of Finland and the conversion of the Finns as violent, a medieval historian like the author of Eric's Chronicle had no such scruples. This is how as a contemporary of the Third Crusade he described the conversion of the Tavastians during the Second Crusade: those who surrendered and accepted baptism kept their estates and lives; those who did not were killed.[55] It is always dangerous to disregard data we find in the sources simply because they do not fit in with a general theory we have developed or adhere to. Such general theories are more often than not the result of present-day notions or ideologies. They have their allotted time before they are invariably replaced by others. In contrast, data in sources lives a safer life.

NOTES

1 The reader will undoubtedly notice that there is a certain polemic twist to this paper. What the reader will miss is the atmosphere of conviviality in which the seminar took place and which characterised the exchanges between the two main antagonists as well as the ensuing discussion in general.

2 'Men udover kystforsvar mod plyndring må hovedformålet snart være blevet erobringer under påberåbelse af mission og korstog.' See Christensen 1977, p. 334.

3 'Det skete under korset som religiøst mærke, så længe det var muligt, derpå med korset som politisk tegn'; Skyum-Nielsen 1971, p. 151. For aspects of this, see Lind 2000, pp. 93–99.

4 'Det var kors- og byttetogt, handels- og slægtsinteresser blandet vidunderligt sammen,' Skyum-Nielsen 1971, p. 184. The fact that this postulated raid is the result of a misunderstanding on Skyum-Nielsen's part and never really took place is irrelevant in this context; cf. Lind 1992b, pp. 256–261.

5 'Dengang blev midlerne gjort hellige af det gode formål, hvad man ikke kunne påstå om de følgende danske pirattogter til slavernes lande'; Fenger 1989, p. 232. Consequently, when it comes to the Danish activities in the Baltic Fenger only speaks of crusades in connection with the expeditions to Estonia and Finland; Fenger 1989, p. 238.

6 'Den kristne mission i det østlige Østersøområde antog mere og mere karakter af en konkurrerende tysk og dansk imperialisme, båret af verdslige interesser. Også derfor skal det ikke forties, at der var danske, der valgte den ægte vare, korstoget til Det hellige Land for at befri de hellige steder "fra hedningernes smuds"'; Fenger 1989, pp. 239–240.

7 Their names were entered under 4th August by a hand dated to the twelfth century, 'Asmundus et Godmundus, illustres laici, apud Slavos sub signo sancte crucis occisi sunt'; *Lunde domkapitels gavebøger*, p. 196.

8 'Korstogenes fantastiske og forargelige skuespil begyndte kort før 1100. I første omgang kom Danmark ikke med. Man var ganske vist heroppe ivrig for at betragte venderkampene som "korstog", men en sådan fortolkning af de danske togter over Østersøen er lovlig velvillig. En stor del af de vendere, man bekæmpede, var for længst kristnede, og desuden gik de danske bestræbelser ingenlunde ud på at omvende nogen til kristendommen, men på at røve og plyndre'; Koch 1963, p. 340.

9 This research tradition culminated with Breengaard 1982.

10 On these letters, see Weibull 1940, pp. 90–98.

11 'Pave Alexander 3. opfordrer konger, fyrster og andre kristne i Danmark, Norge og Sverige til at vise kirken skyldig ærbødighed, til at rette sig efter de gejstlige myndigheders befalinger, til at yde dem tiende og offergaver og til at værne deres rettigheder og forsvare dem mod esternes og andre hedninges angreb og tilstår alle, der går i kamp mod hedningene, et års syndsforladelse i lighed med den, paven giver dem, der besøger den hellige grav.' *DD* I:3, no. 27. The volume was edited by C. A. Christensen, H. Nielsen and L. Weibull.

12 A similar case as regards the summaries can be found in *DD* I:5, no.164, dated 1219–1231, where, according to the summary, 'King Valdemar the Young proclaims and confirms that Niels Countson in the presence of King Valdemar II Sejr has conferred two villages on Esrom Monastery.' Here the editor thought it more relevant to mention the economic transaction, than the fact that Niels wanted to go on crusade to the Holy Land and therefore had to turn some of his estates into cash, which actually caused the transaction ['Niels with the byname Count's son who, expecting his reward in the eternal life, is about to set out on a *peregrinatio* to Jerusalem'].

13 *DD* I:6, no. 242.

14 The date varies slightly in the sources and literature; the Annals from Kolbatz itself, however, are dated 1174.

15 This can, of course, be explained by the fact that it was a daughter house, presumably of the Esrom Cistercians.

16 *Pommersches Urkundenbuch* 1, no. 344.

17 That this is indeed so seems to be indicated by an earlier letter from the General Chapter, dated 13–16 September 1228 (cf. *DD* I:6, no. 83), authorizing the abbot of Ås Monastery in Halland to inform the abbot of Kolbatz of the penalty he had incurred by not having appeared (in Denmark?) for the two preceding years. Possibly the non-appearance of the Kolbatz abbot may be linked to the disintegration of Danish power in Wenden after 1223. It was probably also a consequence of this disintegration that the Premonstratensian Abbot of Tomarp Monastery in Scania had been deprived of the paternity over the Premonstratensian monastery at Grobe on Usedom in 1230, a decision he tried to have revoked in 1234; cf. *DD* I:6, no. 181.

18 *DD* I:6: no. 87.

19 See for instance *DD* I:4, no.168; *DD* I:6, no. 239; *DD* I:7: no.10, 18. An extreme example is provided by *DD* I:4: nos. 139–140, both dated 29th May 1208. Of these only Doc. no. 140 concerns Queen Ingeborg: Pope Innocent III instructs his Legate, Cardinal Deacon Guala, to try to put an end to the case of witchcraft brought by King Philip against the queen. If this has little relevance for Danish history, Doc. no. 139 has none, simply mentioning that the Legate is in France to preach a crusade. The almost complete inclusion of the Ingeborg documents raises the question of why documents concerning other Danish princesses married into foreign dynasties were not likewise included.

20 *DD* I:5, no. 142. In this case the editor was Skyum-Nielsen.

21 See for instance *Preussisches Urkundenbuch* I:1, no. 29.

22 The same incomplete list of recipients can be suspected with regard to several other documents; cf. e.g. *DD* I:5, nos. 29, 193.

23 Petersohn 1979, p. 445 n. 42.

24 Finland's internationally best known scholar of crusading historiography, G. A. Donner, provides a clear example of this in Donner 1930, pp. 73–86.

25 Lindkvist & Erlin 1998.

26 The archaeological record has recently been assembled by P. Purhonen in a recent dissertation, Purhonen 1998 (English summary, pp. 184–197); the conclusions Purhonen draws from this record are, however, not always convincing.

27 *NIL*, pp. 26, 77.

28 'De s.k. korstågen handlade inte om finskt mot svenskt. Händelserna i Finland under tidig medeltid då kyrkan och statsmakten växer fram skall inte ses som ett försök att från svensk sida överta Finland, det handlar snarast om en gradvis omvandling av samhället. Uppfattningen att Sverige successivt erövrade Finland är en konstruktion som skapades under 1800-talet'; Lindkvist & Erlin 1998.

29 Finland is here to be understood as the regions and peoples of Finland (Proper), Tavastia, (western) Carelia together with regions to the north of these. But whenever I or the sources quoted in the paper, referring to the Middle Ages, talk about Finland or Finns it is of course Finland (Proper) and Finns (Proper) that is meant.

30 'Det handlar alltså inte om ett korståg trots att det beskrivs som ett sådant i krönikan'; Lindkvist & Erlin 1998.

31 Nyberg 1996, p. 92.

32 'Det är mycket möjligt att en svensk kung riktat en expedition mot Åbotrakten vid mitten av 1100-talet, men syftet har definitivt inte varit att utbreda kristendomen. Det finns ingenting i det samtida källmaterialet som tyder nå att kristnandet av Finland skulle ha skett med våld'; Lindkvist & Erlin 1998.

33 'De kampanjer som förekom – Erik den heliges var troligtvis ett av många – torde snarast haft karaktären av plundringståg'; Lindkvist & Erlin 1998. Lindkvist expressed in 1992 a similar view: 'Det finns i och för sig inget egendomligt i att en svensk maktägande person företog ett krigståg under 1100-talet; men då torde det närmast ha varit fråga om ett plundrings- eller tribut-krävningsföretag.' Lindkvist 1992, p. 564.

34 It should be said that I do not disagree with Lindkvist that there were probably more raids than those actually mentioned in the sources. For instance, the 'other one' than the so-called First Crusade is only mentioned by coincidence in the Novgorod Chronicle in 1142, because the Swedish fleet happened to encounter a Novgorodian merchant fleet. Of course we cannot be sure that the Swedish fleet was heading for Finland. As mentioned above, it was led by a king/prince (*kniaz'*) and a bishop.

35 This is the title of the English summary of Lindkvist 1990. Lindkvist's theory on the dominant role of plunder has proved quite influential in recent times, permeating some of the works by P. O. Sjöstrand. For instance, he sees the campaign by Birger Magnusson and a number of Swedish bishops to the Neva as result of a 'catholic and *plunder-economic* impulse' (*italics*, JHL), rather than as a crusade ('Snarare är det fråga om en katolsk och plundringsekonomisk impuls, som kom att kanaliseras mot den handelsmässiga nyckelpunkten Nevan'); see also Sjöstrand 1994, p. 566.

36 'Gravis admodum et difficilis est ad apostolicam sedem querela perlata, quod Phinni semper, imminente sibi exercitu inimicorum, fidem servare christianam promittunt et prædicatores et eruditores christianæ legis desiderantes requirunt, et recedente exercitu fidem abnegant, prædicatores contemnunt et graviter persequuntur. Unde .. universitatem vestram monemus atque mandamus, quatinus a fallaciis et fraudibus eorum ita prudenter et discrete de cetero caveatis, quod, si ingruerit necessitas, ad auxilium et defensionem vestram non possint recurrere, nisi munitiones, si quas habent, vobis tenendas assignent, aut alias, adeo sufficientem cautionem exhibeant et securitatem, quod a modo nullatenus pedes retrahere, aut vestram prudentiam valeant circumvenire; sed christianæ fidei documenta cogantur tenere firmiter et servare'; cf. *ST* I, no. 46.

37 Cf. Gallus Anonymus, p. 48.

38 Vanhalinna seems to have been one such stronghold that may have changed hands in the period between 1150 and 1200; see Luoto 1984, esp. pp. 151f. The importance of possessing strongholds in newly conquered and converted regions is also emphasised by the author of *Eric's Chronicle* in his description of both the Second and Third Crusades. Among the few additional pieces of information he offers regarding the Second Crusade was that Birger Magnusson on securing the conquest began to build a fortress: 'The crisne bygdo ther eth feste / ok satto ther i vine ok neste / Thz hwss heyter taffwesta borg,' *Erikskrönikan*, p. 9.

39 'Suomi ei siis ollut ruotsalaisten voittomaa, vaan suomalaisten ja ruotsalaisen välillä oli liittosuhde. Sen ehtoihin kuului kristillisen lähetystyön salliminen ja kristinuskon vastaanottaminen. Vihollisia ei mainita nimeltä, mutta ilmeisesti tarkoitetaan venäläisiä ja ehkä heidän liittolaisiaan karjalaisia'; cf. Pirinen 1991, p. 47. Sjöstrand seems to be convinced that the enemy was Novgorod ('högst förmodligen Novgorod'); Sjöstrand 1994, p. 561.

40 For this, see also Gallén 1954, pp. 147–153.

41 In 1169 the Novgorod chronicles relate that one Danslav Lazutinich went to Zavolochie, in Northeast Russia, with an army or *druzhina* consisting of 400 men to collect tax. Prince Andrei of Vladimir is then reported to have sent an army of no less than 7000 men from Suzdal to intercept them. See *N1L*, p. 33. This event is also referred to in a contemporary birch bark letter (no. 724) found in 1990; see Ianin & Zalizniak 2000, pp. 22–25.

42 *NIL*, p. 37.

43 Only after Iaroslav Volodimirovich became prince in the 1180s did Novgorod again experience some degree of political stability.

44 In the pope's letter 'få vi veta att finnarna blivit kristna under intrycket av fientligt hot österifrån, men att de återgå till hedendomen så snart de icke mera behövde svensk hjälp.' See Gallén 1998, p. 35.

45 'Nam, sicut transmisse ad nos vestre littere continebant, illorum qui Tauesti dicuntur nacio. que olim multo labore ac studio uestro et predecessorum uestrorum ad fidem catholicam conuersa extitit, nunc procurantibus inimicis crucis prope positis ad antiqui erroris reuersa'; *FMUI* I, pp. 29–30.

46 Lindkvist 1992, pp. 561–571.

47 On this tradition, see Lind 1992a, pp. 304–316, and Lind 2001, pp. 159–164.

48 This way of viewing the Finnish Church as separate from the Swedish State clearly links Lindkvist to a Finnish scholarly tradition. Contrast his compatriot and predecessor as 'Swedish' specialist in the crusades to Finland, W. M. Carlgren. Talking about Bishop Thomas, Carlgren saw the office as bishop in Finland both as the most important and hazardous office in the Swedish state administration ('biskopsposten i Finland vid denna tid måste ha varit en av den dåtida primitiva svenska statsförvaltningens viktigaste och mest utsatta'); Carlgren 1951, p. 260.

49 Lindkvist uses the Swedish 'krigståg' rather than 'korståg' (crusade) here, despite the assumed ecclesiastical origin of the expedition.

50 'I Finland fanns fram till slutet av 1100-talet en löslig kyrklig organisation. Det finska stiftet hade länge karaktär av missionsstift. Det var först i början av 1200-talet som en fastare kyrklig organisation tillkom under *biskop Thomas*. Det var en kyrklig organisation som var förhållandevis väl etablerad innan en världslig statsmakt skaffade sig fotfästen i det nuvarande Finland... Om krigståget mot tavasterna verkligen skedde 1238 (eller 1239), var det troligen mer biskopen än jarlen som var inspiratör och organisatör. Kyrkan födde det medeltida statssamhället i Finland'; Lindkvist 1992, p. 569.

51 'I denna politik fanns ett behov att såväl dagspolitiskt som historiskt motivera en "Drang nach Osten". Det var då [in the 1290–1320s] som man hade behov av korståg, att motivera krigen mot Novgorod som korståg och att framställa diverse gamla militära aktiviteter i öster som sådana företag. Det finns en legitimerande tendens i såväl Erikslegenden som Erikskrönikan'; Lindkvist 1992, p. 571.

52 Although we know little about how calls from the popes to Sweden regarding Swedish participation in crusades to the Holy Land, we do know that such calls were made and presumably acted upon much earlier than the end of thirteenth century, e.g., the bull from Innocent III to Archbishop Valerius of April-May 1213; cf. *ST* I: no. 62. We also know that Innocent III informed Valerius in another letter dated February 1217 that Archbishop Andreas of Lund was authorised to redeem those [in Sweden] who had already pledged to take the cross but were now unable to fulfil this pledge; cf. *DD* I:5 no. 112.

53 *FMU* I, pp. 29–30.

54 Lind 1991, pp. 269–295.

55 'Hwa them wille til handa gaa / ok cristin warda ok doop wntfa / honom lotho the gotz ok liiff / ok friid at liffua alt vtan kiiff / Huilkin hedin ey ville swa / honom lotho the dödin ouergaa'; *Erikskrönikan*, p. 9.

BIBLIOGRAPHY

Sources

DD *Diplomatarium Danicum* I:3–7, København 1957–1979.

Erikskrönikan enligt cod. Holm. D2. Rolf Pipping (ed.), Uppsala 1921.

FMU *Finlands medeltidsurkunder* I, Helsingfors 1910.

Gallus Anonymus, *Gallus Anonymus Chronik und Taten der Herzöge und Fürsten von Polen: Polens Anfänge = Slavische Geschichtsschreiber* 10. Graz 1978.

Lunde domkapitels gavebøger, 1884–1889, *Lunde domkapitels gavebøger.* C. Weeke (ed.), København, reprint 1973.

N1L *Novgorodskaia pervaia letopis' starshego i mladshego izvodov*, Moskva1950.

Pommersches Urkundenbuch 1. Stettin 1868–1877.

Preussisches Urkundenbuch I:1. Königsberg 1882.

ST *Sverges Traktater* I, Stockholm 1877.

Literature

C. Breengaard 1982, *Muren om Israels hus. Regnum og sacerdotium i Danmark 1050–1170.* København.

W. M. Carlgren 1951, 'Om Finlands relationer till Sverige och påvedömet 1216–1237', *(Swedish) Historisk tidskrift* 1950, pp. 247–284.

A. E. Christensen 1977, *Danmarks historie* 1. København.

G. A. Donner 1930, 'Om missionsmetoderna vid tavasternas kristning', reprinted in *Kring korstågen till Finland – ett urval uppsatser tillägnat Jarl Gallén på hans sextioårsdag den 23 maj 1968.* Helsingfors, pp. 73–86.

O. Fenger 1989, *Kirker rejses allevegne 1050–1250. Gyldendal og Politikens Danmarks historie* 4. København.

J. Gallén 1954, 'Åbo förstörelse 1198', reprinted in *Kring korstågen till Finland – ett urval uppsatser tillägnat Jarl Gallén på hans sextioårsdag den 23 maj 1968.* Helsingfors, pp. 147–153.

J. Gallén 1998, *Finland i medeltidens Europa. Valda uppsatser.* Helsingfors.

V. L. Ianin & A. A. Zalizniak 2000, *Novgorodskie gramoty na bereste (iz raskopok 1990–1996).* Moskva.

H. Koch 1963, *Politikens Danmarkshistorie* 3. København.

J. Lind 1991, 'Early Russian-Swedish Rivalry. The Battle on the Neva in 1240 and Birger Magnusson's Second Crusade to Tavastia', *Scandinavian Journal of History* 16, pp. 269–295.

J. Lind 1992a, 'Bishop Thomas in Recent Historiography. Views and Sources', in K. Julku (ed.), *Suomen varhaishistoria.* Oulu, pp. 304–316.

J. Lind 1992b, 'De russiske ægteskaber. Dynasti- og alliancepolitik i 1130'ernes danske borgerkrig', *(Danish) Historisk Tidsskrift* 92, pp. 256–261.

J. Lind 2000, 'Var Valdemarstidens venderkorstog "topmålet af hykleri"?' in C. S. Jensen (ed.), *Venderne og Danmark. Et tværfagligt seminar 2 december 1999 Syddansk Universitet.* Odense, pp. 93–99.

J. Lind 2001, 'The Order of the Sword-Brothers and Finland. Sources and traditions', in Z. H. Nowak (ed.), *Ordines militares – Colloquia Torunensia Historica.* Torun, pp. 159–164.

T. Lindkvist 1990, *Plundring, skatter och den feodala statens framväxt. Organisatoriska tendenser i Sverige under övergången från vikingatid till tidig medeltid, = Opuscula Historica Upsaliensia* 1. Uppsala.

T. Lindkvist 1992, 'När blev Finland svenskt. Om svenska behov av korståg mot Finland', *Finsk Tidskrift* 10, pp. 561–571.

T. Lindkvist & N. Erlin 1998, 'Korstågen til Finland var inga kyrkliga företag', Interview with Thomas Lindkvist in *Meddelanden från Åbo Akademi* 7 (24.4.1998), pp. 16–17. [http://www.abo.fi/meddelanden/forskning/1998_07korstag.sht].

J. Luoto 1984, *Liedon vanhanlinnan mäkilinna.* Helsinki.

F. Nyberg 1996, *Vändpunkter i Finlands historia.* Borgå.

J. Petersohn 1979, *Der südliche Ostseeraum im kirchlich-politischen Kräftespiel des Reichs, Polens und Dänemarks vom 10. bis 13. Jahrhundert.* Köln – Wien.

K. Pirinen 1991, *Suomen kirkon historia* 1: *Keskiaika ja uskonpuhdistuksen aika*. Porvoo.

P. Purhonen 1998, *Kristinuskon saapumisesta Suomeen*. Helsinki (English summary: On arrival of Christianity in Finland. A Study in the archaeology of religion, pp. 184–197).

P. O. Sjöstrand 1994, 'Den svenska tidigmedeltida statsbildningsprocessen och den östra rikshalvan', *Historisk tidskrift för Finland* 79, pp. 530–573.

N. Skyum-Nielsen 1971, *Kvinde og Slave, Danmarkshistorie uden retouche* 3. København.

L. Weibull 1940, 'Påven Alexander III:s septemberbrev till Norden', *Scandia* 13, pp. 90–98.

MARI ISOAHO

The Warrior in God's Favour

The Image of Alexander Nevskiy as a Hero Confronting the Western Crusaders

Alexander Nevskiy is a much-disputed figure, who for Russians has for centuries represented a warrior ideal defending their country and religion. It has been a commonplace of Russian historiography to present Alexander as a hero who resisted the Western crusade movement to the lands of Russia.[1] This image is mostly based on his hagiography, 'the Life of Alexander Nevskiy', one of the most popular medieval military legends in Russia. It is a source that creates a coherent, well-known and, in all its harmony and perfection, an icon-like image, by which people's impressions of Alexander have been influenced.

Alexander's Life is assumed to have been written in Vladimir in the 1280s, a couple of decades after his death.[2] The original manuscript of the Life has not survived, but due to its great popularity it was frequently copied, and was also included in many Russian chronicles.[3] The very fact that Alexander's Life has survived in such different forms, which date from various times and differ slightly from each other, makes it possible to examine the birth and development of his image. The aim of this chapter is to point out some important factors that one has to observe in using 'the Life of Alexander Nevskiy' as a source for historical studies and concerning his status as a hero confronting the Western crusading fervour.

As the object of this study is the image of Alexander Nevskiy in medieval historiography, it is necessary to define what the meaning of the term 'image' used here is. One may say that the language and mind of medieval man was that of pictorial images, where also religion became blended into a cohesive system of symbols, colours, and meanings. The boundaries of faith and images became confused to some extent as the salvation of a human was largely dependent on the visual system of symbols.[4] The religious world was symbolised through allegories which for their part were signified by numerous saints with their special characteristics, and the entire substance of the life of the mind sought to find an outlet in visual, pictorial form. The visualisation of the medieval mind was through pictures, miniature paintings, Gothic statues and, in the East, by icons, offering pictorial representation of image-allegories. However, in this chapter the interest is not the pictorial images expressed through art, but rather the images of the mind, although these images referred to the same system of symbols which can be expressed through art in physical form. These images functioned as mental aids in controlling the chaotic world of the mind.

In the terminology of the historical image research an image is commonly understood as a concept which is created in one's mind when all the information received about a certain topic becomes part of one's general concept of the world. In addition to knowledge, an image includes opinions, attitudes, and beliefs.[5] An image differs from an attitude in that it usually survives a long time, changes slowly, and is often simple.[6] These characteristics fit well with the concept many researchers have of the nature of descriptions of the medieval saints. The collective demands of the hagiographies are based on the undercurrents of the slowly changing world-view through which the term 'image' used in historical image research is also defined. The image offered by a saint's Life is at the same time a simplified model of reality.[7]

The interest in images in medieval hagiographies derives from the question of what these texts are actually about. It has been said that these descriptions not only tell us about the values of their writers, individual men of the Church, but convey the collective knowledge of the history, world-view, and values of the entire society. The writer of the saint's Life, whose memory reaches back over generations, can thus be considered anonymous. Stories about saints do not so much describe independent individuals, but more correctly concepts of higher ideals and holiness, morals, and the values of pious people. Being so, images of saints can be considered as part of the collective consciousness, the world-view of the period. The view of the collective nature of hagiographic description has usually been accepted without reservation.[8] Thomas J. Heffernan emphasises the significance of hagiographies for studies of the mind of the medieval man. According to him, these biographies describe exactly what Braudel has characterised by the term *longue durée*. Although the storyline of the hagiographies is patterned, it does express the interaction between its writer and the society which is its audience. Because the saints' Lives are written for cultic purposes, they repeat social norms recognised as correct and promote social cohesion.[9]

In reading hagiographies, one also has to remember that the reality during Middle Ages was different from what we understand to be reality today, because it was harmonic, hierarchical, and determined. Because reality was determined, a language of symbolic representation which was in agreement with commonly accepted norms was used to describe it. This is what constitutes clichés. This is also the reason why saints' Lives described using these clichés are often so stereotypical and impersonal, and explains why they are such appropriate objects for the study of images. While saints' Lives in their own way describe the needs of society, it is important to keep in mind that the norms of hagiography changed over time, as did those of society.[10]

The traditional approach of the critical study of history has been to determine how much real and reliable factual information is included in the text. For a long time the critical study of history considered the hagiographical source material as useless because of its manipulative and factually unreliable nature. Only in the second half of the twentieth century did researchers again become interested in hagiographical material. These days, one does not look for factual information in the saint's lives, but strives to study the principles of medieval literature and the way of thinking of the people of the past.[11]

'The Life of Alexander Nevskiy' has had an important position in representing the tensions between the East and the West. Historians have used the Life of Alexander as one of the most important sources in describing the political situation between the East and the West in the thirteenth century, other source materials being very few. However, like images in general, the image of Alexander Nevskiy in his Life has changed in the course of time, so that it has reflected contemporary ideals. The problem has usually been to use the Life as if there were only one source about Alexander's life, thus overlooking the fact that there are several different medieval versions of his hagiography.[12]

Concepts characteristic of different periods can be observed in the various medieval editions of Alexander's Life stemming from different times and places. Interesting questions are what kind of acts and what aspects have been emphasised in Alexander's deeds. What kind of image of him do these different editions transmit? This article does not intend to survey the whole of the development of Alexander's image in the various medieval redactions of his Life, but merely to give a brief account of some crucial points in this development.[13]

First Image – The Aristocratic Warrior Ideal

Recently, some historians have cast doubt on the significance of the battles fought by Alexander, the one against the Swedes by the river Neva in 1240 and that against the Germans at Lake Peipus in 1242.[14] Inevitably this makes one wonder whether the large-scale Western Crusade movement ever took place in northern Russia during Alexander's reign. According to the new views, the battles in question, which were previously considered to be so fateful and in which the 'aggression of the Catholic Church' was quelled, are more accurately characterised as border skirmishes typical of the period, whose significance did not particularly differ from other battles fought in the border regions of Russian lands.[15]

The composition of the Life is greatly in debt to other medieval literature, such as the princely descriptions of the chronicles and war stories. Its writer was an educated man, who was able to present his hero as an ideal fighting warrior king, fully comparable with biblical and antique warrior kings, who were in the special favour of God or the gods, like Alexander the Great or the Roman Emperor Vespasian.[16] The dualism in the nature of 'the Life of Alexander Nevskiy', combining an earthly war story with the hagiography of an ideal Christian ruler, is its most striking feature. The title in itself, in full, the Story of the Life and Bravery of the Pious and Orthodox Great Prince Alexander (*Povesti o zhitii i o khrabrosti blagovernago i velikago knyazya Oleksandra*)[17] reveals that the narrative is a combination of two literary genres; a war tale, *povest'*, and hagiography, *zhitie*. The Life had an enormous influence on medieval Russian conceptions of bravery and the image of the ideal ruler is described as one elaborate part of it.

'The life of Alexander Nevskiy' is composed of series of different events which together form the story of Alexander's life from his birth to his death. The most celebrated events of the hagiography are the battle descriptions, through which the image of Alexander as a skilful war hero and the suppressor of the Western Crusade movement has been conveyed. Alexander's victory over the Swedes at the River Neva in 1240 is one of the most important acts described in his Life, and has significantly shaped his image as a defender of Russia against the western threat. Apart from the passage in the older version of the Novgorod I Chronicle, there are hardly any sources on the Battle of the Neva other than Alexander's Life, at least not ones which could be considered contemporary descriptions. No Swedish source mentions this event, and the other Russian chronicles pay no attention to it, unless they have borrowed events from the Life later in order to supplement their narrative.[18] There is, therefore, some reason to examine what the battle description given in the hagiography is actually composed of and what kinds of rhetoric, or as Heffernan puts it, what ritualised acts the writer of the Life has used.

The preparation for the battle of the Neva reflected the typical formula of medieval war literature, where events preceding the battle are described in a very formulaic fashion so that going to war was a long series of clichéd events, in which a more powerful, envious king of a neighbouring country intends to conquer the lands of the hero. The hero is thus forced to a test of strength which he turns to his own advantage. This is exactly how the best-known war classics of the time described their heroes entering the battle. This model for going to war is most clearly visible in three medieval literary examples which this article discusses next.

The Life tells us about the Roman[19] king from the 'Land of Midnight' who, on hearing about Alexander's reputation, boasted that he would conquer Alexander's country. He sent a messenger to Alexander and said: 'If you can, resist me. I am already here conquering your land.'[20] An equivalent boast is found in the Old Testament, where the king of Assyria, Sennacherib, sends his messenger to brag about the size of his power and orders the King of Judah, Hezekiah, to submit to his power unconditionally.[21] In the Life, Alexander's reaction to this threat was to get angry and go to Church.[22] Hezekiah, for his part, 'rent his clothes, and covered himself with sackcloth, and went into the house of the Lord.'[23]

The third similarity in the plot was a speech encouraging the troops. Both chiefs make stirring speeches to their men when the enemy was threatening,[24] which faithfully follows the rhetorical advice of Greek and Roman historiography. It was probably Thucydides who invented the genre of war orations, which was then adopted by later historians and became more and more rhetorical in character. Polybios had already examined the exhortations (*parakleiseis*) of generals to their armies, especially the speech delivered immediately before the battle. Both Arrian and Quintus Curtius Rufus reported how Alexander the Great addressed his men before the battles of Issos and Gaugamela, and there is every reason to believe that the battle exhortations belong entirely to the conventions of historiographical rhetoric, since there are no traces of such speeches in reality. The genre of battle exhortations presents a continuation of the ancient historiographic tradition, which was eagerly imitated by later medieval authors of chronicles.[25]

To make a more specific and clearer comparison between the war of Alexander and that of the king of Judah, the writer ascribes the miracle that had saved Hezekiah to Alexander:

> There happened a miracle that reminds us of the one which took place in olden times, during the reign of King Hezekiah, when Jerusalem was attacked by Sennacherib, King of Assyria. Suddenly there appeared an angel of Lord, who killed one hundred and eighty-five thousand Assyrian warriors, and when the next morning came their bodies were found there. The same occurred after Alexander's victory when he defeated the king: numerous enemy soldiers who had been killed by the angel of the Lord were found on the other shore of the River Izhora,[26] which Alexander's regiments had not reached.[27]

The boasting that took place between Hezekiah and Sennacherib is to be found also elsewhere in medieval war literature. The boasting of an envious king is a central theme in the so-called 'Alexander Romance', which relates the life of Alexander the Great and which was extremely popular in Europe during the Middle Ages. Alexander the Great had the first place *ex officio* in the war stories of that period.[28] Following Pseudo-Callisthenes's Alexander Romance, the Slavic translation called *Aleksandriya* was among the earliest remains of the secular literature in medieval Russia as well.[29] In the Russian *Aleksandriya*, Darius, the King of Persia, sent his messenger to Alexander, bragged about his own power, and belittled Alexander's status. Showing off led to a war in which Alexander defeated Darius.[30] This brief reference to one of *Aleksandriya's* main themes leads us to another medieval story. Closely related to the matter of Alexander was a Byzantine story of Digenes Akrites, whose epic story emerges in the tenth century, largely following the model which emphasised the chivalric ideals also symbolised by Alexander the Great.[31]

The Tale of Digenes Akrites has survived in six Greek manuscripts, dated from the fourteenth to the seventeenth century.[32] In addition to these, there are also three Russian manuscripts, which date to the seventeenth and eighteenth centuries.[33] The Greek texts, especially the fourteenth–fifteenth century *Grottaferrata* manuscript, has usually been seen as closest to the original story. However, there are several scholars who believe that the Russian version of the Tale (*Deyanie prezhnykh vremen chelovek*, or in brief *Devgenievo deyanie*) reflects the archaic features of the original story better.[34]

288

In the Greek *Grottaferrata* version of the tale, the Roman king Basil hears rumours about the fame of the frontier hero called Digenes and invites Digenes to meet him to see this with his own eyes. Digenes refuses to go and writes to the king that if he wishes to see his worthless servant he should ride down to the Euphrates. The king then arrives at the river where he meets Digenes who entertains the king with an exhibition of strength. The king is quite impressed by what he sees and he restores to Digenes all the possessions which had been confiscated from his grandfather and then confirms his authority over the border lands. The king and Digenes then separate on the most warm and friendly terms.[35]

In the Russian version of the Tale, Digenes has changed his name into more Russian form, Devgeni. The Tale of Devgeni describes the meeting of the hero and the great king in a very different way. Here we are confronted with the bragging theme again. The Tale includes an episode in which Devgeni receives a message from a certain Tsar Vasili:

> Famous Devgeni! I would very much like to see you. Come to visit my domain since your bravery and fortitude is known everywhere in the world. And I also love you with all my heart and would like to see you in the flowering of your youth.[36]

At first it seems that the attitude of Tsar Vasili is the same as King Basil's in the Byzantine *Grottaferrata* version of the Tale, but as the story goes on, it becomes evident that the Tsar's mind was poisoned with envy against Devgeni. Tsar Vasili's sweet words did not blind Devgeni, who took it more as a challenge to battle instead.[37] This is exactly what happened between the Roman king from the Land of Midnight and Alexander Nevskiy.[38] Devgeni answered the great king proudly like Alexander the Macedonian in *Aleksandriya* and accepted the challenge. Now the plot of the Tale of Devgeni unfolds nearly identically way to Alexander Nevskiy's Life. King Vasili arrives at the Euphrates with his army where he camped and set up his large tent.[39] Similarly, 'the Life of Alexander Nevskiy' relates that the battleground was located along a river; the king arrived 'at the Neva in his insanity.'[40]

The description of the enemy camp is also interesting. The Tale of Devgeni reports how Vasili set up in his camp an enormous tent, the roof of which was coloured red and decorated with gold.[41] This luxurious tent symbolised most clearly the wealth and power of the Tsar. The tent-theme continues in the Life, in which the great golden tent of the Swedish enemy was finally pulled down. This was accomplished by one of the brave men of Alexander Nevskiy, Savva, who 'charged a big, golden-crowned tent and cut its pole. When the tent fell, Alexander's regiments were very much encouraged,'[42] naturally enough, the collapse of the tent symbolised the loss of power and defeat of the great king. It was also part of the tendencies of war literature to mention that Alexander Nevskiy started the battle as a defender, being out-numbered in manpower.[43]

A Finnish scholar, Vilho Mansikka, made a detailed survey of the composition of 'the Life of Alexander Nevskiy' in 1913, specifying the origins of the literary formulas of the hagiography.[44] N. Serebryanskiy has also sought the literary origins of the formulas of 'the Life of Alexander Nevskiy.'[45] It is thus somewhat surprising to see how little effect this has had among the historians who want to seek the real events in these literary depictions. Several attempts have been made to reconstruct what actually happened in the battle of Neva in 1240, but as long as Alexander's Life is the only source for that event, these reconstructions are doomed to fail.[46]

Although V. D. Kuz'mina has strongly argued about the origin of the Russian Tale, which she dates to the eleventh or twelfth century,[47] it is a somewhat disputed question whether the Tale of Devgeni was actually known in medieval Russia as early as that, because there are no surviving manuscripts from that period. Francis J. Thompson has been critical of the early dates of the early Russian medieval literary sources, because most of the remaining manuscripts survived only as later copies.[48] However, 'the Life of Alexander Nevskiy' strongly indicates, that the model for going to war in the above-mentioned war tales was familiar to its writer. The literary models of the Life have been passed to northern Russia from Galich, the most south-westerly parts of medieval Russia, where the characteristics of the war literature were also strongly apparent in Galich's Princely Chronicle of the thirteenth century.[49]

It is easy to see, that the ritualised acts the writer of the Life used confirm a very earthly ideal of a warrior. The rhetoric borrowed from the war descriptions made Alexander Nevskiy parallel to the pan-European knighthood ideal of the medieval period. This functioned through analogies borrowed from literature.[50] The idealised heroic image of Alexander Nevskiy was supported by drawing a parallel between his name and that of Alexander the Great, one of the ideal warriors best known to medieval people. In Alexander's case, *Nomen est omen*. Comparing Alexander Nevskiy at the ideal level with this Hellenistic period world conqueror made it possible to realise Alexander Nevskiy's mortal figure as a war hero. Without a ready model, the image of Alexander as an ideal warrior would have been incomplete. Through this analogy, Alexander Nevskiy was put on the map of the multidimensional medieval existence.[51]

The writer of the Life of Alexander was clearly familiar with the requirements the true knight had to fulfil, because the Life repeats metaphors well-known in Europe expressing the honour of war. There is even one account of the awesome reputation of Alexander which follows exactly the same pattern that Joinville used when describing the reputation of Richard the Lionheart among the Saracen children in the Holy Land.[52] Consequently, the warrior description of Alexander Nevskiy corresponds to a large extent with the ideology that the whole of Christian Europe expected from its feudal aristocracy. This makes the historical value of the Neva description seem obvious; it must not be considered as an eyewitness account of the battle in which Swedish crusaders were beaten. The description of another great battle of Alexander, the Battle on the Ice in 1242, also has dynastic claims in its background.[53]

The Change in the Image

To emphasise features dealing with copying and editing of the medieval manuscripts, one can compare the medieval writer to the icon painter. There was a custom in Russia that several masters may have worked on a single icon while it was being painted. Even after an icon was ready, it was prepared and painted with colours and styles considered ideal during each period. The icons were not provided with signatures because they were not exhibits of their makers' skills, but symbolised different aspects of divinity on earth. Similar considerations also applied to the medieval writings which served the same function, the manifestation of divinity on earth, which was preserved by the copiers of each period according to its norms and ideals.[54] Neither did a literate medieval Russian make a significant distinction between the creating, copying, editing, and translating of the text. For this reason, it was entirely permissible for the copiers to modify their texts by using the norms prevailing in the literature. Thus the medieval source cannot provide information about concepts and the language of the period when it was created, but about the norms and language of the period of the copyist.[55] From the critical point of view, this fact has the utmost importance because it is the views of different periods reflected in editions of 'the Life of Alexander Nevskiy' which makes it possible to study the change and development in the image of the ideal hero. One can examine concepts that are characteristic of different periods using editions written at different times, how these concepts have modified the saintly image of Alexander Nevskiy, and what their effect was, especially in depicting him as a crusading military hero.

The period also changed the literary style of the hagiography. Much happened in literature during the fourteenth century. Cultural bounds with Bulgaria, Serbia and Byzantium from the middle of the century gained in strength and a great deal of literature was translated into Russian, including an increasing number of biblical texts and, at the end of the century, a new literary style developed in the Balkans that allowed more personal feelings to appear. This style became established above all in Moscow and coincided with a new 'national movement' – as often cited in Russian patriotic historical writings – expressing the new self-confidence and trust in the future of Russia under the leadership of Moscow.[56] The status of Moscow was highlighted in the Kulikovo Cycle stories of the famous Battle of Kulikovo in 1380, led by victorious Great Prince of Moscow, Dmitry Donskoy. Its tales elevated the battle into the most important single event of the epoch and proclaimed loudly that the future glory of Russia was laid on the valiant shoulders of the great princes of Moscow. The cycle is divided into four tales: the Short and the Expanded Chronicle Accounts, *Zadonschina* (meaning literally 'The Tale of Events Beyond the Don'), the Tale of the Destruction of Mamai (*Skazanie o Mamaevom poboische*), and the Story of the Life and Death of the Russian Tsar, the Great Prince Dmitry Ivanovich (*Slovo o zhitii i o prestavlenii velikogo knyazya Dmitriya Ivanovicha, tsarya russkago*). These individual pieces are extremely difficult to date, since the surviving manuscripts are from the end of the fifteenth century at the earliest, apart from a short chronicle entry included in the 1408 chronicle edition.

The earliest short account of the Battle of Kulikovo is found in the chronicles that used the edition of 1408 as their basis, such as the Trinity, Simeon and Rogozhkiy Chronicles.[57] The description of the battle in these is concise, mentioning the main features of Dmitry Ivanovich's victory: how the pagan descendants of the Ishmaelites, the Tatars, gathered their troops against the Christians, how the treacherous Khan Mamai had shown his anger towards Dmitry and vowed to capture all of the Russian lands, and how Dmitry, on hearing of this, hurried into battle in order to protect the land, its holy churches and the Orthodox faith. It also notes that Mamai and the Tatars were beaten in the bitter struggle because God had amassed his invisible forces against them.[58] A great Russian host of 200,000 men was blessed by Bishop Gerasim at Kolomna, from where the troops left for battle on 20th August, placing their faith in God and the Immaculate Mother of God and calling upon the Holy Cross to assist them. Dmitry then arrived at the River Don, where he received a letter from 'the honourable *Igumen* Sergey, a devout old man' who sent his blessing. Dmitry prayed for God's providence, just as God had blessed Moses, thereby acting according to the example of Alexander Nevskiy as recounted in his Life. Early on the morning of 8th December the troops took their places on the battlefield, at which Dmitry again prayed and made a speech to his troops. The Russian and Tatar armies then confronted each other and a fierce battle was fought which lasted for three hours.[59] At the ninth hour of the day[60] the heavenly troops arrived to assist the Russians. A host of angels was seen in the heavens, accompanied by the holy martyrs St George and St Demetrios and the Russian martyr princes Boris and Gleb as well as the leader of the heavenly host, the Archangel Michael.[61]

The Tale of the Destruction of Mamai introduced themes of its own into the narrative, by which its author demonstrated his fondness for the notion of the important eschatological role of Orthodox Russia in its holy war against Islam. The Tale of the Destruction of Mamai is also by far the most interesting part of the Kulikovo Cycle as far as any comparison of its content with that of 'the Life of Alexander Nevskiy' is concerned. The support of the clergy and the endorsement of the Orthodox Church enjoyed by Prince Dmitry had already been brought up in the Expanded Chronicle Account, but the Tale of the Conquest of Mamai further highlights the message of a war conducted by the Orthodox Church against the 'heathen' Muslims. Dmitry's relationship with the pious monk Sergey is depicted in more detail when he enters the Monastery of the Holy Trinity to meet him and receive his blessing. Sergey blessed Prince Dmitry and his army with holy water, and made the sign of the cross on Dmitry's forehead. The *militia christi* idea is fully revealed in Dmitry's request to have two monks from the monastery, the famous warrior-monks Alexander Peresvet and Andrey Oslyab, among his troops. Sergey fulfils this request, and arms his fighting monks with heavenly weapons, crosses embroidered on their robes. He then gives his blessing to Dmitry and his troops, who are soon going to confront a pagan enemy and fight on behalf of Orthodox Christianity.[62]

Before the battle the great prince consulted with his closest military advisors, his 'brothers', Vladimir Andreyevich and the sons of Olgerd. The Lithuanian brothers stepped out and made a speech, an inspiring battle exhortation in the spirit of Alexander Nevskiy:

> If you want to have an unshakeable host, tell your men to cross the Don with not a single thought of return. Don't give a thought for the formidable power of the enemy, because God lies not in power, but in truth! Prince Yaroslav beat Svyatopolk after having crossed the river, and your forefather the Great Prince Alexander beat the king after crossing the River Neva, and you must follow their example. If we beat the enemy, we will all be saved, but if we fall, we will confront a mutual fate in death, all of us from princes to common men. So you, my Lord the great prince, should forget death and speak words of courage, so that your troops will be encouraged and we will see what a manly host of heroes they consist of.[63]

The valiant Russian troops pray that Dmitry will win the battle, just as the Emperor Constantine once did, and just as David conquered the forces of Amalek. Not only is Alexander Nevskiy exalted as one of the heroic paragons for Dmitry, but also his namesake Alexander the Great. The Lithuanian brothers are delighted at the sight of the glorious Russian troops, and they acknowledge this:

> Never before in our lifetime or after us will there be such a brave army. It is equal to the troops of Alexander of Macedonia and is comparable in its manliness to the men of Gideon, both of whom God armed with his strength.[64]

Following the model presented in the Life of Alexander, Dmitry raised his hands towards heaven and burst into tears, crying:

> Dear Lord, You who love the people! Because of the prayers of the holy martyrs Boris and Gleb, help me as you helped Moses against the troops of Amalek and my forefather, the Great Prince Alexander, against the Roman king, who wanted to ravage his lands...[65]

After the battle, Dmitry's men hail him:

> Rejoice O Prince, the equal of the ancient Yaroslav, the new Alexander, conqueror of the enemy![66]

The Tales of the Kulikovo hence developed the crusading spirit, depicting how an Orthodox prince confronted the cursed infidels, the 'pagan' Muslims, Alexander Nevskiy being one of the most important models of the prince fighting on God's side.

Not only was the model of Alexander's heroic fight used in the tales written in the new more elaborated literary style, but the Life of Alexander itself also went through a major development during the sixteenth century. Through the development of the Euthymian style, the new editions of

Alexander's Life partially broke away from the old models as the narrative became more intriguing. On the initiative of Metropolitan Macarius, the new redactions of the Life were written for the purpose of canonisation of Alexander in the middle of the sixteenth century. Altogether 39 new miracle-working saints were officially canonised by the councils of 1547 and 1549. This sudden sharpening of the attitude of the Russian Church towards its holy saints and their cults was a direct outcome of the emergence of the tsars in Moscow. Once the great prince of Moscow was elevated to the rank of tsar, ruler of a Christian empire, the Church of Russia was also elevated to first position in the ranks of Orthodox Christian Churches, and the glory and fame of a Church was manifested in its saints. The saints exhibited the spiritual beauty of the Church and helped it to achieve and maintain its important position as an intermediary in communicating the prayers of the people to God.[67]

Hence Metropolitan Macarius organized a huge literary project of collecting the lives of Russian saints into large compilations. The style of Macarius's literature circle has been described as in the 'imperial manner', which is characterised by lively narration, grandness, and imperial use of vocabulary, as well as literary effects such as lines written for a person to recite, which helped to create the feeling of suspense.[68] The image of Alexander Nevskiy appears for this reason to have become more vivid in the sixteenth-century redactions of his Life. A significant feature is that these redactions explain the significant occurrences of Russian history through Alexander's acts.

As the young Tsar Ivan IV was crowned and guided by Josephite clerics,[69] no doubt high hopes were held of a ruler who was expected to carry the weight of his God-ordained office in harmony with Christian ideology. It is obvious that the conquest of Kazan had an enormous influence on the whole ideology of the tsar and emperor, as this made the sons of Ishmael one essential target at the ideological level. This also worked out well in 'the Life of Alexander Nevskiy.'

The year 1547 was a turning point in the cult of Alexander. Once he was officially canonised as a miracle-worker for the whole of Russia, he became one of the saints whose existence testified the primary position of the Russian Church among the Orthodox Churches. This also placed new expectations on his hagiography. Several new editions of the Life were written, the first of which, the *Slovo Pokhval'noe*, was incorporated into the Moscow editions of Makariy's Great Menology, so that the Life included in the *Uspenskiy* edition of the Great Menology in 1550 had a sizeable list of the miraculous acts of healing that had been witnessed at the relics of the new miracle-worker.[70] The *Slovo Pokhval'noe* also established the image of St Alexander as the heavenly protector of the great prince of Moscow, an aspect that was derived from the miracle of the heavenly assistance afforded to his descendant Dmitry Donskoy at the Battle of Kulikovo.[71] The ancestors of Tsar Ivan were venerated in Moscow as an important imperial lineage descending from the Second Constantine, Prince Vladimir of Kiev, who baptised the people of the Russian lands. The reasons for the official canonisation of Prince Alexander can no doubt be traced to Ivan's personal involvement with the expansion of his Orthodox realm into the territory of the eastern Muslim tribes of Kazan as much as with official veneration of the position of the great Moscow princes by stressing their holy origins.

In Iona Dumin's redaction, written at the end of the sixteenth century, the political supremacy of Moscow over other principalities of Russia is legitimised by condemning the republican political system of Novgorod as morally questionable, and by demonstrating through Alexander's acts how the centralised political system is the best alternative from the citizen's point of view.[72] The sixteenth-century editions transmit the image of Alexander Nevskiy as a person who sacrifices himself for his country by emphasising the cruelty of the Tatar conquerors.[73]

Thus, as the historical narrative of Alexander Nevskiy developed during the Middle Ages, its features became an integral part of the representation of the myth of a heroic defender. Even though the original First Edition of the Life was well preserved and survived in several sixteenth-century manuscripts, it was inevitably the image projected by the new editions that spread in the popular consciousness and remained alive and fresh, making it easy to adopt and to absorb into wider concepts of history, religion and world order. It was on these medieval foundations that the popular image of Alexander as the ideal prince, defending his people, Russia and Orthodox faith, was based. Historians making use of the huge resource of medieval history contained in the chronicles discovered Prince Alexander Yaroslavich in the pages of the sixteenth century chronicles of Moscow which preserved the official history of the era of the culmination of the Ryurikovichi myths of the imperial destiny of the tsars.

The flexibility of the image of the ideal prince was great. The core idea was the warrior who defends the right cause. As this cause in the sixteenth century appeared to be the fighting against the Muslims, the redactions of that time showed Alexander producing miracles as he participated alongside Dmitry Donskoy and Ivan IV in the most important battles against the Tatars.[74]

As Alexander Nevskiy was developed through the Medieval Age as the one of the heavenly defenders of the Moscovite state, its image was well guarded during later generations. As Peter the Great transferred the cultic centre of Alexander Nevskiy from the city of Vladimir to his new capital, St Petersburg, the image of Alexander was also changed to fit Peter's new state ideology better. The ideological reworking in the image of the heavenly protector of Russia continued during nineteenth century romanticism, when the Orthodox tradition of the Russian past became one important feature strengthening the Russian national movement. This was the time when influential historians like Nikolai Karamzin offered a polished image of a devout great prince, using the great sixteenth century chronicles and the Book of Degrees as their main sources.[75] As 'the Life of Alexander Nevskiy' offered this self-sacrificial image of a prince with epic simplicity, it was also easy to use during the Second World War as patriotic ideal. This search for a moral example in defending Russia has been preserved in modern Russia, which is once again eagerly exalting the memory of Alexander. Karamzin's History of the Russian State was published during the rule of Nikolai I, the time of national awakening and the genesis of the Russian idea. Referring to this idea is not strange, even for modern researchers. The basic facts of the Russian idea can be expressed through Alexander Nevskiy, including high morals, loyalty to the fatherland and faith in national salvation.[76]

The study of the development of the image of Alexander Nevskiy in his hagiographical redactions is quite revealing in many ways. It not only tells us how the image of Alexander changed with time, but also how the historians interpret history by using this image. The Russian historians have mainly acted like the ancient copyists of chronicles, having rewritten history again and again according to the requirements of their own era. In this writing process the coherent and emotional image of Alexander Nevskiy in the great era of the rise of Moscow has in all its harmony hit on something that still appeals to the feelings of Russians. The key to understanding Alexander's great role in Russian history is essentially what his hagiography presented, a historical idea of a warrior king in God's favour. The medieval scholars and clerics, the chroniclers and hagiographers understood and valued that idea and used it to legitimise the deeds of their contemporary rulers. They could not seek the authority of Alexander's Life to express the new ideas and political order without changing something of the original description. They could not, nor did they want to change the basic essence of the ideal ruler, but they changed the settings; the political situation and religious tension. Doing so, they created a living history, in which the deeds and the spirit of the ancestors were followed by the descendants. And what is even more important, by doing so, the descendants in their own way simultaneously created the spirit of their ancestors, often matching their own ideas of just war, meeting the claims of the Crusades.

NOTES

1 See, for example, Begunov 1995, p. 163; Pashuto 1968; Shaskol'skii 1978, pp. 147–196; Ramm 1959, pp. 159–179.
2 Begunov 1965, p. 61; Begunov 1979, p. 60; Fennell & Stokes 1974, p. 108.
3 One of the earliest texts of Alexander's Life is in the Laurentian Chronicle, a manuscript containing the beginning of the Life, which dates to the 1370s. Alexander's Life also has an important position in the Pskovian chronicles, as well as the later Novgorodian chronicles.
4 The world of images of the religious art of the Middle Ages from the twelfth century to the end of the fourteenth century has been brilliantly analysed by Camille 1989.
5 Alenius 1996, pp. 11–12.
6 Fält 1982, p. 10; Fält 1997, pp. 62–63.
7 Cf. Fält 1997, p. 63.
8 Delehaye 1921, p. 438; Gurevich 1988/1990, pp. 49–50; Granger & Ripperger 1987, p. 10.
9 Heffernan 1988, pp. 17–18.
10 See Heffernan 1988, pp. 19–22.
11 Heffernan 1988, pp. 17, 54.

12 The Life of Alexander Nevskiy has been preserved in several copies with different dates and has also been included in several chronicles since the fourteenth century. Consequently there are several versions, and scholars have attempted to categorise these into different redactions. However, there are considerable school differences in labelling and classifying the redactions. For instance, Begunov has counted the redactions of Alexander Nevskiy's Life between the thirteenth century and the eighteenth century as more than twenty, whereas Okhotnikova reports the number of redactions as only nine. Begunov 1995, p. 170; Okhotnikova 1987, p. 355.

13 I will discuss the image of Alexander Nevskiy in medieval hagiographical redactions and chronicles fully in my forthcoming doctoral dissertation *Warrior and Saint: the Image of Aleksandr Nevskiy in Medieval Russia*. On the image of Alexander Nevskiy, see my previous articles: Mäki-Petäys 2002 a, pp. 45–69; Mäki-Petäys 2002 b, pp. 99–115.

14 Lind 1991, pp. 269–295; Fennell 1983, pp. 105–106, 120–121; Korpela 1996, pp. 211–212.

15 See especially Fennell 1983, pp. 103–106.

16 The second edition of the Life gives Alexander the Macedonian as an example for Alexander Nevskiy. The Roman emperor Vespasian is depicted from the earliest version onwards as the paragon of bravery and military glory. Vespasian was the hero of Josephus in his widely-known history, the History of the Jewish wars. The second redaction of the Life of Alexander Nevskiy was printed in Mansikka 1913.

17 *Povesti o zhitiii*, p. 187.

18 The oldest version of the Novgorod I Chronicle does not contain the Life of Alexander, but the later chronicles of Novgorod interpolated the passages of the Life in their narration throughout their yearly chronicle accounts. The same applies to many other chronicles. The Laurentian Chronicle of the end of the fourteenth century gives the Life only in the year of Alexander's death, 1263. See *Novgorodskaya pervaya letopis' starshego i mladshejo izvodov*, pp. 77–84, 289–313, and *Lavrent'evskaya letopis'*, pp. 204–206.

19 The term 'Roman' refers here to the Roman Catholic king of Sweden.

20 «Аще тожеши противитися мне, то се есмь уже эде, пленяя землю твою.» *Povesti o zhitii*, p. 188.

21 IV Rg. 18, Vulgate.

22 See *Povesti o zhitii*, p. 188.

23 IV Rg. 19:1, Vulgate.

24 *Povesti o zhitii*, p. 188; compare with II Par. 32:6–8, Vulgate.

25 Hansen 1993, pp. 161–180. See also Bliese 1989, pp. 201-225.

26 The Izhora is one of the tributaries of the Neva.

27 *Povesti o zhitii*, p. 190.

28 Cary 1956/1967.

29 The legend of Alexander the Great was incorporated in Russian chronographies from the middle of the thirteenth century at the latest. Tvorogof 1987, pp. 35–37.

30 *Aleksandriya*, pp. 249–257.

31 Moenning 1993; Mavrogordato 1956/1999, p. 13.

32 Mavrogordato 1956/1999, pp. 82–84.

33 A fourth manuscript, dated to the fifteenth or sixteenth century, was destroyed in the great fire of Moscow in 1812. Kuz'mina 1962, p. 4.

34 Most Western scholars do not see the claims of archaism in the Russian Tale of Devgeni as justified. See, for example, Mavrogordato 1956/1999, pp. 25–26. It is however apparent that the numerous Soviet scholars have not been without justification for their claims. H. F. Graham wrote an excellent article in 1968 illustrating the awkward divide between the Soviet and Western scholars. Graham 1968, pp. 51–91. Since the Belgian scholar Henry Grégoire first suggested a more archaic origin for the Russian Tale than any of the known Greek versions, many Russian and Soviet scholars have concurred. This includes V. D. Kuz'mina, who is a leading Russian expert in this

field, and who has done a painstaking study on the redactions and the development of the Russian Tale of Devgeni. Grégoire 1942; Kuz'mina 1962. See also Speranskiy 1922; Syrkina 1960; Shevchenko 1979–1980/1982; Chernysheva 1989.

35 *Grottaferrata*, pp. 971–1089.

36 «Девгении славны, велие желание имам видетися с тобою. А ныне не ленись продитись к моему царству, зане дерзость и храбрость твоя прослыла по всеи вселеннеи. И любовь вниде в мя велия: видети хощу юность твою.» *Deyanie prezhnykh*, p. 154.

37 *Deyanie prezhnykh*, pp. 154–155.

38 See *Povesti o zhitii*, p. 188.

39 *Deyanie prezhnykh*, p. 155.

40 *Povesti o zhitii*, p. 188.

41 *Deyanie prezhnykh*, p. 155.

42 *Povesti o zhitii*, p. 190.

43 *Povesti o zhitii*, p. 188.

44 See Mansikka 1913.

45 Serebryanskiy 1915, pp. 175–221.

46 One of the latest attempts to reconstruct the happenings of the battle of the Neva was A. V. Shishov's, which completely failed to avoid the pitfalls created by the literary formulas of the story. See Shishov 1995, pp. 31–36.

47 Kuz'mina 1962, pp. 90–109.

48 Thomson 1999.

49 Likhachev 1947.

50 Mäki-Petäys 1999, pp. 22–27; Mäki-Petäys 2000, pp. 22–27.

51 Mäki-Petäys 1999.

52 *Povesti o zhitii*, p. 192; Joinville, *Chronicle of the Crusade of St. Lewis*, p. 155. Obviously this reference to the awesome reputation of Alexander follows the Galichian princely Chronicle which reports the reputation of the name of Roman Mstislavich, the father of the Galichian prince Daniil. *Ipat'evskaya letopis'*, p. 187.

53 More details of both the descriptions of the Battle of the Neva and the Battle on the Ice will be analysed in my forthcoming doctoral thesis.

54 Uspenskiy 1987, p. 58.

55 Uspenskiy 1987, pp. 56–57.

56 Likhatchev 1981, pp. 5–8.

57 There has been some debate about whether the short chronicle tale is the first account, or whether it is just a shortened version of the expanded chronicle tale. Most scholars are now convinced of the early date of the short version. Salmina 1981, p. 549. See also Danilevskiy 2000, pp. 271–272.

58 *Simeonovskaya letopis'*, pp. 129–130.

59 *Letopisnaya povest' o kulikovskoj bitve*, pp. 114–124.

60 Approximately two o'clock in the afternoon.

61 *Letopisnaya povest' o kulikovskoj bitve*, p. 128.

62 *Skazanie o Mamaevom poboishche*, p. 146.

63 *Skazanie o Mamaevom poboishche*, p. 162.

64 *Skazanie o Mamaevom poboishche*, pp. 164–166.

65 *Skazanie o Mamaevom poboishche*, pp. 168–170.

66 *Skazanie o Mamaevom poboishche*, p. 182.

67 Golubinskiy 1903, pp. 92–93.

68 Crummey 1987, p. 200.

69 Metropolitan Macarius himself was an ardent Josephite, a sect which formed the overwhelming majority of the Russian church leaders in his time. It was named after Joseph of Volokolamsk, a monastic reformer, who, unlike his contemporary, Nil Sorskiy, did not see any harm in monasteries possessing property and carrying out administrative duties, provided that the community respected the traditions of cenobitic monasticism in all their purity. In the last years of the reign of Ivan III, Joseph

had also devoted himself to a struggle against heresy, which was to be an important issue for the Josephite monks and clerics. Crummey 1987, pp. 125–131.

70 Droblenkova 1988, pp. 126-133. See also Miller 1979, pp. 268-276; Dmitrieva 1993, p. 211.

71 *Slovo Pokhval'noe*, p.27.

72 *Spisok redaktsii Iony Dumina*, pp. 77–96.

73 The cruelty of the Mongol conquerors and the attitude of sacrificing oneself for one's people are expressed in a way which is not present in the first edition of the Life of Alexander. The image that changed in the sixteenth century is presented particularly clearly in Vasili-Varlaam's redaction. *Spisok redaktsii Vasili-Varlaama*, pp. 42–43.

74 *Spisok redaktsii Iony Dumina*, pp. 103–104, 114–115.

75 See Karamzin 1842–1844/1988.

76 Begunov 1995, p. 169.

BIBLIOGRAPHY

Sources

'Aleksandriya', in *'Izbornik'. Sbornik proizvedeniy literarury drevney Rusi*. Moskva 1969.

'Deyanie prezhnykh vremen khrabryh chelovek', in V. D. Kuz'mina (ed.), *Devgenievo deyanie (Deyanie prezhnikh vremen khrabrykh chelovek)*. Moskva 1962, pp. 143–184.

'Grottaferrata', in J. Mavrogordato (ed.), *Digenes Akrites*. Oxford 1999 (1959).

Joinville, *Chronicle of the Crusade of St. Lewis*. F. Marzials (trans.), 1965 (1908).

'Ipat'evskaya letopis'', in *Polnoe sobranie russkikh letopisey. Tom 2*. Sank Peterburg 1843.

'Lavrent'evskaya letopis'', in *Polnoe sobranie russkikh letopisey, Tom 1*, Sankt Peterburg 1846.

'Letopisnaya povest' o kulikovskoy bitve', in *Pamyatniki literatury drevney Rusi, XIV–seredina XV veka*. Moskva 1981, pp. 112–131.

Novgorodskaya pervaya letopis' starshego i mladshejo izvodov. Moskva 1950.

'Povesti o zhitiii o khrabrosti blagovernago i velikago knyazya Oleksandra', in Yu. K. Begunov, *Pamyatnik russkoy literatury XIII veka 'Slovo o pogibeli Russkoy zemli'*. Moskva 1961, pp. 187–194.

'Simeonovskaya letopis'', in *Polnoe sobranie russkikh letopisey, Tom 18*. Sankt Peterburg 1913, pp. 132–189.

'Skazanie o Mamaevom poboishche', in *Pamyatniki literatury drevney Rusi, XIV–seredina XV veka*. Moskva 1981.

'Spisok "Vladimirskoy redaktsii" zhitiya, izvlechennyy iz Makar'evskikh Miney-Chet'ikh, po uspenskomu spisku, Moskovskoy sinodal'noy biblioteki', in V. Mansikka, *Zhitie Aleksandra Nevskogo. Razbor redaktsii i tekst'*. Sankt Peterburg 1913, pp. 15–31.

'Spisok redaktsii Iony Dumina po rukopisi Moskovskoy Tipografskoy biblioteki, No 346', in V. Mansikka, *Zhitie Aleksandra Nevskogo. Razbor redaktsii i tektst'*. Sankt Peterburg 1913, pp. 49–124.

'Spisok redaktsii Vasili-Varlaama po rukopisi Imp. Publichnoy biblioteki, Drevnekhranilishcha Pogodina, No 648', in V. Mansikka, *Zhitie Aleksandra Nevskogo. Razbor redaktsii i tektst'*. Sankt Peterburg 1913, pp. 33–48.

Literature

K. Alenius 1996, *Ahkeruus, edistys, ylimielisyys: Virolaisten Suomi-kuva kansallisen heräämisen ajasta tsaarinvallan päättymiseen (n. 1850–1917)*. Jyväskylä.

Yu. K. Begunov 1965, *Pamyatnik russkoy literatury XIII veka 'Slovo o pogibeli Russkoy zemli'*. Moskva.

Yu. K. Begunov 1979, 'Zhitie Aleksandra Nevskogo v sbornike iz sobraniya N. P. Likhacheva', *Trudy otdeli drevnerusskoy literatury* 30, pp. 60–72.

Yu. K. Begunov 1995, 'Zhitie Aleksandra Nevskogo v russkoy literature XII–XVIII vekov', in Yu. K. Begunov & A. N. Kirpichnikov (ed.), *Knyaz' Aleksandr Nevskiy i ego epokha*. Sankt Peterburg, pp. 163–171.

J. R. E. Bliese 1989, 'Rhetoric and Morale: A Study of Battle Orations from the Central Middle Ages', *Journal of Medieval History* 15, pp. 201–226.

M. Camille 1989, *The Gothic Idol: Ideology and Image-Making in Medieval Art*. Cambridge.

G. Cary 1956/1967, *The Medieval Alexander*. Cambridge.

T. Chernysheva 1989, 'Kompozitsiya "Digenisa Akrita" i "Devgenievo deyanie"', *Trudy otdela dreverusskoy literatury* 42.

R. O. Crummey 1987, *The Formation of Muscovy 1304–1613*. London.

I. N. Danilevskiy 2000, *Russkie zemli glazami sovremennikov i potomkov (XII–XIV vv.), kurs lektsiy*. Moskva.

H. Delehaye 1921, *Les passios des martyrs et les genres litteraires*. Brüssels.

R. P. Dmitrieva 1993, 'Agiograficheskaya shkola mitropolita Makariya (na materiale nekotorykh zhitiy)', in *Trudy otdela drevnerusskoy literatury* 48.

N. F. Droblenkova 1988, 'Velikie Minei Chetii', in *Slovar' knizhnikov i knizhnosti drevney Rusi. Vyp. 2 (vtoraya polovina XIV–XVI v.) Chast' 1*. Leningrad.

J. Fennell 1983, *The Crisis of medieval Russia 1200–1304*. London.

J. Fennell & A. Stokes 1974, *Early Russian Literature*. London.

O. K. Fält 1982, *Eksotismista realismiin: Perinteinen Japanin-kuva Suomessa 1930-luvun murroksessa*. Rovaniemi.

O. K. Fält 1997, 'Global History, Cultural Encounters, and Images', in S. Tønneson & J. Koponen & N. Steensgaard & T. Svensson (ed.), *Between National Histories and Global History*. Helsingfors, pp. 59–70.

E. Golubinskiy 1903, *Istoriya kanonizatsii svyatykh' v' russkoy tserkvi*. Moskva.

H. F. Graham 1968, 'The Tale of Devgeni', *Byzantinoslavica: International Journal of Byzantine Studies* 29, pp. 51–91.

R. Granger & H. Ripperger 1987, *The Golden Legend of Jacobus de Voragine*. New Hampshire.

H. Grégoire 1942, *Digenes Akritas*. New York.

A. Gurevich 1988/1990, *Medieval Popular Culture: Problems of Belief and Perception*. Cambridge.

M. G. Hansen 1993, 'The battle exhortation in ancient historiography. Fact or fiction?' *Historia. Zeitschrift für alte Geschichte*. Band XLII, Heft 2, pp. 161–180.

T. J. Heffernan 1988, *Sacred Biography: Saints and their Biographers in the Middle Ages*. New York.

N. M. Karamzin 1843–1844/1988, *Istoriya gosudarstva rossiyskago*. Reprintnoe vosproizvedenie izdaniya 1842–1844 godov. Moskva.

J. Korpela 1996, *Kiovan Rusj. Keskiajan eurooppalainen suurvalta*. Hämeenlinna.

V. D. Kuz'mina 1962, *Devgenievo deyanie (Deyanie prezhnikh vremen khrabrykh chelovek)*. Moskva.

J. H. Lind 1991, 'Early Russian-Swedish Rivalry: The Battle on the Neva in 1240 and Birger Magnusson's Second Crusade to Tavastia', *Scandinavian Journal of History* 16:4, pp. 269–295.

D. S. Likhachev 1947, 'Galichkaya literaturnaya traditsiya v zhitiy Aleksandra Nevskogo', *Trudy otdely dreverusskogo literatury* 5, pp. 36–56.

D. S. Likhachev 1981, 'Literatura vremeni natsional'nogo pod'ema', in *Pamyatniki drevnerusskoy literatury, XIV–seredina XV veka*. Moskva, pp. 5–26.

V. Mansikka 1913, *Zhitie Aleksanrdra Nevskogo, razbor redaktsiy i tekst'*. Sankt Peterburg.

J. Mavrogordato 1956/1999, *Digenes Akrites*. Oxford.

D. B. Miller 1979, 'The Velikie Minei Chetii and the Stepennaja Kniga of Metropolitan Makarii and the Origins of Russian National Consciousness', in *Forzungen zur Osteuropäischen Geschichte*, Band 26. Berlin.

U. Moenning 1993, 'Digenes = Alexander? The Relationship between Digenes Akrites and the Byzantine Alexander Romance in their Different Versions', in R. Beaton & D. Ricks (ed.), *Digenes Akrites. New Approaches to Byzantine Heroic Poetry*. Cambridge.

M. Mäki-Petäys 1999, 'Nomen est omen: Esimerkkejä Aleksanteri Nevskin py-himyselämäkerran kiclikuvista', *Faravid* 22 23, pp. 163–180.

M. Mäki-Petäys 2000, 'Border Heroism in the Life of Alexander Nevskiy', *Etnichna istoriya narodiv Evropi: Zbirnik naukovih prats'*, 5, pp. 22–27.

M. Mäki-Petäys 2002 a, 'Warrior and saint. The changing image of Alexander Nevsky as an aspect of Russian imperial identity', in C. J. Chulos & J. Remy (ed.) *Imperial and national identities in Pre-revolutionary, Soviet, and Post-Soviet Russia*. Helsinki, pp. 45–69.

M. Mäki-Petäys 2002 b, 'On the applicability of image research to the study of medieval hagiographies', in K. Alenius & O. K. Fält & S. Jalagin (ed.) *Looking at the other. Historical study of images in theory and practise*. Oulu, pp. 99–115.

V. I. Okhotnikova 1987, 'Povest' o zhitiy Aleksandra Nevskogo', in D. S. Likhachev (ed.), *Slovar' knizhnikov i knizhnosti drevney Rusi, vyp. 1 (XI–pervaya polovina XIV v.)*. Leningrad.

V. T. Pashuto 1968, *Vneshnaya politika drevney Rusi*. Moskva.

B. Y. Ramm 1959, *Papstvo i Rus' v X–XV vekakh*. Moskva.

M. A. Salmina 1981, 'Letopisnaya povest' o Kulikovskoy bitve', in *Pamyatniki literatury drevney Rusi, XIV–seredina XV veka*. Moskva, pp. 549–552.

N. Serebryanskiy 1915, *Drevne-russkiya knyazheskiya zhitiya*. Moskva.

I. P. Shaskol'skii 1978, *Bor'ba Rusi protiv krestonosnoi agressii na beregakh Baltiki v XII–XIII vv*. Leningrad.

I. Shevchenko 1979–1980/1982, 'Constantinople Viewed from the Eastern Provinces in the Middle Byzantine Period', in *Ideology, Letters and Culture in the Byzantine World*, London. Originally in *Harvard Ukrainian Studies* III/IV, part 2.

A. V. Shishov 1995, 'Polkovodcheskoe iskusstvo knyaz'ya Aleksandra Yaroslavicha v Nevskoy bitve', in Y. K. Begunov & A. N. Kirpichnikov (ed.), *Knyaz' Aleksandr Nevskiy i ego epokha*. Sankt Peterburg, pp. 31–37.

M. Speranskiy 1922, *Devgenievo deyanie*. Petrograd.

A. Y. Syrkina 1960, *Digenis Akrit*. Moskva.

F. J. Thomson 1999, *The Reception of Byzantine Culture in Medieval Russia*, Ashgate.

O. V. Tvorogof 1987, 'Aleksandiya Khronograficheskaya', in D. S. Likhachev (ed.), *Slovar' knizhnikov i knizhnosti drevney Rusi. Vyp. 1 (XI–pervaya polovina XIV v.)*. Leningrad.

B. A. Uspenskiy 1987, *Istoriya russkogo literaturnogo yazyka (XI–XVII vv.)*. München.

ANTTI RUOTSALA

The Crusaders and the Mongols
The Case of the First Crusade of Louis IX (1248–1254)

It is well known that the thirteenth-century imperial Mongols were mostly enemies of Western Christendom. Twice the crusade was preached against them. First it was authorised by Pope Gregory IX during the Mongol invasion of Europe in 1241, and later by Pope Alexander IV in 1260 when the Mongols were again oppressing Europe and especially, by occupying Syria, the Latin colonies in the Holy Land.[1]

However, in addition to conflicts, there were also opportunities for peaceful relationships or even co-operation between these two parties. This was particularly the case during the Western crusades against the Muslims. In the following I shall present an example concerning the seventh crusade, i.e., the first crusade (1248–1254) of Louis IX.

The French King Louis IX started his unlucky crusade to Northern Africa in June 1248. At first the royal squadron landed in Cyprus in September that year. When the king was making preparations for his attack on Egypt, two Nestorian envoys named Da'ud and Markos sent by Eljigidei[2] – the commander of Mongol-Persian army – arrived at Nicosia on the 20th December 1248. They carried Eljigidei's letter to the king, written in the name of Great Khan Güyük, the grandson of Chinggis Khan. The letter was in Persian, but the king had it translated de verbo ad verbum into Latin.[3]

The letter from Eljigidei expressed great sympathy with Christianity and reported the good state of the Christians in the Mongol Empire. Eljigidei announced that he had been sent by Güyük to protect the Christians as well as to rebuild their churches, and that he prayed God for the success of the Christian forces against those 'who despise the Cross.'[4]

The letter differed radically from the previous Mongol ultimatums to the popes and rulers of the Christian West. Furthermore, during the negotiations the Nestorian envoys confirmed, among other things, that the name of pope was honoured by the Mongols. In fact, Eljigidei had long been a Christian, and Great Khan Güyük had been baptised. His mother was the daughter of Prester John, the legendary mighty Christian ruler of the farthest East and the potential ally of the Christians. Both Güyük and Eljigidei intended to help the Christians to free Jerusalem.

Finally, as Eljigidei was planning to lay siege to Baghdad the following spring, he hoped that the Franks would carry out a simultaneous attack on Egypt, thus preventing the Sultan from coming to the aid of the Caliph of Baghdad.[5]

All this seems to have aroused enthusiasm among the crusaders, and they no doubt, as they were later to discover, got too optimistic an impression of the importance of Christianity among the Mongols. This impression had also resulted from the letter of the Armenian Constable Smbat (Sempad) to King Henry of Cyprus dated 7th February 1248. Smbat was the brother of He'tum I, King of Lesser Armenia. His letter commented on the great number of Christians in the Mongol Empire and described the great favour shown to Christians and their faith by the Mongol sovereigns.[6] From the chronicle of Matthew Paris it is known that the information on these hopeful events in Cyprus soon travelled from Paris to England.[7]

The exaggerated Christian tone in Eljigidei's letter shows that religion was the major channel of communication between these two parties. Most messages have actually been sent with the help of religion in the so-called premodern societies – including both the medieval European and the traditional Mongol culture.[8] However, the crusaders had no doubt wondered whether the Mongols were really their Christian brothers. The devastating Mongol invasion of Europe (1241–1242) was still fresh in mind. Furthermore, the cunning or, rather, treacherous nature of the Mongols was also very well known. Could it be a question of the schemes of the Mongols as well as fabrications of their Nestorian envoys? Were those envoys only spies?[9]

An unsolved question is the role of the Eastern Christians in this manoeuvre. There were plenty of Nestorians in high positions at the Mongol administration, particularly the Nestorian-oriented Uighurs. Some of the Mongol aristocracy was also practising Nestorianism, along with other religions.[10] Moreover, at that time the Armenians were endeavouring to create a Frankish-Armenian-Mongolian coalition against the Muslims.[11]

In any case, the nomadic Mongols were an explosive new force which had suddenly irrupted into the world already divided by the Christians and Muslims for 600 years. Understandably, many cultures and groups in connection with them tried to guide the Mongol expansion in the appropriate direction from their point of view as well as to convert these 'barbarians' to their own religion. Now the Latin Christians seemed to have the advantage over all other parties, especially the Muslims. This opened entirely new missionary as well as military horizons.

In January 1249 Louis IX sent a seven-man embassy to the Mongols led by the Dominican Andrew of Longjumeau.[12] Eudes of Châteauroux, the papal legate in Cyprus and the Latin Near East and an intimate of Louis, surely played a very important role in creating the king's policy towards the Mongols during the crusade. Eudes wrote the letters to the embassy for example.[13] The leader of the embassy, Andrew had been one of the papal envoys to the Mongols sent by the Council of Lyons in 1245. This experienced man had worked as an interpreter in Cyprus during the negotiations. The king obviously waited long for the undertaking because the embassy's presents to the Mongols included fragments of the True Cross as well as a splendid tent-chapel. Probably the intention of the crusaders was at first only to explore the aims of the Mongols, to strengthen the position of Christianity among them, as well as both converting them and uniting them to the Roman Church.[14]

The envoys travelled through Persia via Eljigidei's encampment to the Mongol capital Khara Khorum in Mongolia. They did not, however, encounter the Great Khan Güyük who had died a year before, but instead his widow and first wife Oghul Khaimish. The embassy had to return with regrettable news to Palestine in April 1251. The widow sent Louis an arrogant letter written most likely in order to heighten her prestige in the campaign of succession among the branches of the family of Chinggis Khan. She acknowledged the embassy as if it were actually bringing the formal submission of the Christian West. She demanded that Louis pay tax (gold and silver) to the Mongols henceforth, otherwise the king would be destroyed. The letter surely lessened the king's enthusiasm for the speedy conversion of the Mongols as well as his hope of a coalition with them.[15]

However, a mutual effort to create a coalition against the Muslims lay behind these contacts. In particular, Eljigidei seems to have wanted this, and was also the initiator of these efforts. The Mongols had already consolidated their position in Persia and Asia Minor, and were now striving for the Abbasid Caliphate of Baghdad, which they conquered in 1258. For the Mongols, at the moment, it was also reasonable to keep the Muslim regions of their Empire safe from the invasion of the crusading army. The aims of the Mongols were no doubt very promising from the crusaders' viewpoint. This possibility of a coalition and co-operation between the crusaders and the Mongols changed, however, into the breakdown of their relations within a year.

If realised, the coalition against the Muslims might have had significant consequences. However, it was never realised. Why? In my opinion the reasons should be sought not only by analysing the changing political as well as military alignments – which of course are very important – but also the religious-ideological viewpoints of both parties.

First, the Mongols at that time were primarily shamanists and supporters of their old folk religion – as were their aristocracy. Since they were neither Christians nor Muslims, and tried to stay outside of these two worlds, there was no real opportunity for religious-ideological brotherhood or even dialogue. Moreover, the Mongols used sedentary peoples in their army as well, and had a habit of setting Eastern Christians such as the Armenians and Georgians against the Muslims.[16] I consider that with Louis and his crusading army the Mongols simply exploited this previous experience. The Mongol Empire was still rapidly expanding and the Mongols thought expressly of conquest.

Furthermore, the letter of Eljigidei shows interestingly one fundamental principle of the Mongols which was conspicuously in contradiction with the crusading ideology. He announced to the crusaders that the Great Khan had forbidden the crusaders to favour some special sect of Christianity.

The Latins, Greeks, Armenians, Nestorians, Jacobites and all worshippers of the Cross were one in the eyes of God and the Mongol Emperor. This same attitude was also expected of the French King.[17] The Mongols seemed to have been very well aware of the religious intolerance of the crusaders, whereas in the Mongol Empire all religions – including the Muslim religion and all the pagan practices – were under special protection guaranteed by the Mongol law, the jasagh. Any kind of activity against religions or religious sects was forbidden, and was usually punished with death. Privileges were given to all religions and they were accepted even-handedly.[18]

Another matter is that the Mongols threatened all nations outside their empire with their continuous striving for world domination. The Mongols thought that they carried out their expansion as the chosen people of the Sky-god or the Eternal Heaven, Tenggeri, the Great Khan being His representative on earth.[19]

The Mongols also regarded themselves as superior to other peoples – especially those peasants and townsfolk tied to one place and enslaved by their masters. Settling down signified weakness and decadence. This ethnocentric attitude was further stirred by the hegemonic position of the Mongols in the world. Equal communication with the other party was basically impossible from their point of view.[20]

The events during the first crusade of Louis IX prefigured the forthcoming ones. Later, from the second half of the thirteenth century to the beginning of the fourteenth, when the era of the great crusades was already over, the Western and Mongol attempts at mutual coalition centred round the Islam-oriented Ilkhans of Persia for many years. The Mamluks of Egypt were the common enemy. There was very minor and sporadic co-operation in the Palestine. However, on the whole the efforts remained negligible this time as well.[21] Jean Richard has argued that the crusaders felt mistrust towards the Mongol diplomatic contacts in the 1260s partly because of the bad experiences Louis had during his first crusade.[22]

Some outstanding scholars, including René Grousset, Denis Sinor, and Gian Andri Bezzola have, in one way or another, said that in these cases the crusaders missed their 'golden opportunity' in neglecting to ally themselves with the Mongols.[23] In my view, the opportunity did not really exist. From the crusaders' standpoint it was wise to be principally neutral in the conflict between the Mongols and the Mamluks. The Mongols were also threatening the Latin colonies in the Holy Land. Furthermore, co-operation with them against the Muslims of Egypt would have provoked the Muslim population under the dominion of the crusaders into resistance.

Besides, there were serious religious-ideological obstacles between the crusaders and the Mongols. An association with the pagan Mongols would certainly have been disapproved of by the Roman Church – and not only because the nomadic forces from the Golden Horde were repeatedly attacking Eastern Europe. Regarding the first crusade of Louis IX, let us remember that the papal legate Eudes of Châteauroux was among his crusading forces. Furthermore, it has been assumed that Louis could probably not have been able to persuade the princes of Eastern Europe to join his crusade because of the unsettled conditions created by the Maangol invasion. Some Christian rulers in Scandinavia, e.g., the king of Norway, Haakon, also used the invasion of pagan tribes in Baltic, including the Mongols, as an excuse for not joining Louis's crusade. Of course, these were also good grounds for avoiding a very onerous as well as expensive operation.[24]

In sum, if the crusaders had undertaken open and extensive military co-operation with the Mongols, it would surely have been much more problematic than simply manipulating them to attack the Muslims.

Be that as it may, in examining the crusades it is perhaps worth noting that there were often more than two opposing sides. Both the crusaders and the Muslims themselves were often very divided,[25] but there could also be other, 'outside' parties who tried to benefit from the situation and to guide both the crusaders and possibly also their adversaries into an appropriate direction from their point of view. Of course, the crusaders also tried to benefit from these often very complicated political and religious-ideological alignments. Sometimes the crusaders may have been only a piece in a great mosaic.

NOTES

1 For the crusade of 1241, see Jackson 1991, passim; Strakosch-Grassmann 1893, pp. 112–113, 129–139. For the crusade of 1260, see Jackson 1980, pp. 509–510; Richard 1969, pp. 51–52. See also Purcell 1975, pp. 67–69, 88–91.

2 The English transliteration of Mongolian and other oriental languages follows the practice in Franke & Twitchett (ed.) 1994.

3 Eudes de Châteauroux, p. 625.

4 '... contemnentibus crucem', Eudes de Châteauroux, p. 625.

5 The original version of Eljigidei's letter has disappeared, but its translations made in Cyprus have been preserved. The Latin translation was incorporated into Eudes's report to Pope Innocent IV (1243–1254) dated 31st March 1249; Eudes de Châteauroux, pp. 625–626. It is also included in the Speculum historiale of Vincent of Beauvais; Vincentius Bellovacensis, p. 1316. The French version of the letter is in the Chronica majora of Matthew Paris; Matthaeus Parisiensis VI, pp. 163–165. For the envoys' statements, see Eudes de Châteauroux, pp. 626–627; Jean de Joinville, p. 282; Vincentius Bellovacensis, pp. 1316, 1317. Both the chronicle of the French historian William of Nangis (d. 1300) and the letter of Jean Sarrasin, chamberlain to Louis IX, are other primary sources; Guillelmus de Nangis, pp. 358–367; Jean Sarrasin, pp. 569–571. For studies concerning the events in Cyprus, see e.g., Bezzola 1974, pp. 150–156; Richard 1983, pp. 493–496; Ruotsala 2001, pp. 44–46,65–66; Schmieder 1994, pp. 80–83.

6 Smbat's letter was quoted by Eudes of Châteauroux and later by Vincent of Beauvais, Eudes de Châteauroux, p. 626; Vincentius Bellovacensis, pp. 1316–1317. On Smbat's letter, see especially Richard 1986, pp. 683–696; see also Bezzola 1974, pp. 152–154.

7 Matthaeus Parisiensis V, p. 80. See also Bezzola 1974, p. 161.

8 Cf. Crone 1989/1994, pp. 78–80; Ruotsala 2001, pp. 78–79.

9 The Mongol treachery was frequently reiterated in the Western literature of those days. For instance, see the statements of the Franciscan John of Plano Carpini in his travel account Historia Mongalorum (1247/1248): 'Iracundi sunt hominibus

aliis multum et indignantis nature, et etiam aliis hominibus sunt mendaces, et fere nulla veritas invenitur in eis. In principio quidem sunt blandi, sed ultimo pungunt ut scorpio', Iohannes de Plano Carpini, p. 247, passim. See also Bezzola 1974, pp. 96, 144, 147. Plano Carpini was the main papal envoy of the Council of Lyons to the Mongols in 1245. Both Louis IX and Eudes of Châteauroux were surely aware of his work – possibly they had read it. On the other hand, there have been doubts about the Nestorian envoys being impostors. The famous Orientalist Paul Pelliot made it clear, however, that it was a question of a true embassy; Pelliot 1931–1932, pp. 13–37. See also Bezzola 1974, p. 150.

10 The Turkic, Nestorian Uighurs, from whom the Mongols adopted both their skill of writing and their writing system, were the first non-nomadic civilisation subjugated by the Mongols. Because the Uighurs were able to write Mongolian in their own writing system, they achieved a privileged position in the imperial administration. Nestorianism came, however, to Mongol society primarily through the exogamy of the Mongol aristocrats, because their wives originated mainly from the Nestorian upper classes of their nomadic neighbours; Allsen 1987, pp. 67–68; Jagchid & Hyer 1979, pp. 188–191.

11 See Der Nersessian 1962, pp. 652–653; Saunders 1971, pp. 79–80. This Armenian tendency can still be seen in La Flor des Estoires de la Terre d'Orient written by the prince and monk Het´um of Gorigos, the nephew of Het´um I, King of Lesser Armenia. This book, an account of the Mongols, was presented to Pope Clement V in Poitiers in 1307; see Jackson 1980, pp. 484–486; Schmieder 1994, pp. 114–117.

12 No report remains of the journey of Andrew's embassy, and information on its experiences is very scant, see Eudes de Châteauroux, p. 627; Jean de Joinville, pp. 282–288; Vincentius Bellovacensis, pp. 1317–1318. A summary of the King's letter to the Mongols is included in Eudes de Châteauroux, p. 627. See also Bezzola 1974, pp. 156–157, 163–164; Pelliot 1931–1932, pp. 38–84.

13 See Bezzola 1974, pp. 150–152, 154–157; Ruotsala 2001, pp. 64–66. About Eudes' letters; Eudes de Châteauroux, p. 627; Vincentius Bellovacensis, pp. 1317–1318.

14 The Roman Church, of course, also had a desire to get in contact with the Mongols and convert them to the True Faith. However, at the same time it obviously tried to organise an anti-Mongolian bloc under the leadership of Pope Innocent IV by negotiation with the religious leaders of Eastern Churches; see Bezzola 1974, pp. 112–113; Szczésniak 1956, p. 16.

15 See Jean de Joinville, pp. 287–288. John of Joinville commented on the letter's influence on the king in his biography of Saint Louis completed in 1309: 'His Majesty, I can assure you, bitterly regretted that he had ever sent his envoys to the great King of the Tartars'; op. cit., p. 288. It is impossible that Andrew of Longjumeau, the experienced traveller, envoy, and master of oriental languages, would have made those mistakes in etiquette as some previous Western envoys who had badly angered the Mongol sovereigns, like the Dominican Ascelin, the papal envoy of the Council of Lyons to the Mongols in 1245–1248; see Simon de Saint-Quentin, pp. 95–107. Probably because of the failure of the first effort, the later envoy of the king to the Mongols in 1253–1255, the Franciscan William of Rubruck, had only unofficial status, and was merely concerned with missionary work.

16 See Boase 1978, pp. 25–26; Ratchnevsky 1983, p. 153. This appears in the observations of John of Plano Carpini; Iohannes de Plano Carpini, pp. 292, 296, 301.

17 '& in litteris suis Rex terrae augeatur magnificentia sua. Ita praecipue quod in lege Dei non sit differentia inter Latinum, & Graegum & Armenicum, Nestorinum & Jacobinum, & omnes qui adorant crucem. Omnes enim sunt unum apud nos. Et sic petimus ut Rex magnificus non dividat inter ipsos, sed sit ejus pietas & clementia super omnes Christianos'; Eudes de Châteauroux, pp. 625–626. Cf. Vincentius Bellovacensis, p. 1316.

18 The Mongol attitude towards the various religions was by no means the same as the modern Western European religious tolerance originating from the Enlightenment. From the Mongol viewpoint the world was full of supernormal powers, and it would

have been foolish to insult them. The Mongol administration also knew how important it was for the moods of the empire's population, especially its spiritual well-being, that everybody could freely practise their own religion; see Allsen 1987, pp. 121–122; Ratchnevsky 1983, pp. 162, 173–174, 179–180.

19 See de Racheviltz 1973, pp. 23–25; Ratchnevsky 1983, pp. 141–142; Ruotsala 2001, pp. 103, 108–109.

20 See Jagchid & Hyer 1979, p. 147; Ratchnevsky 1983, pp. 152, 157; Ruotsala 2001, pp. 58, 91, 132–133. For the nomadic point of view in general, see Khazanov 1983/1984, pp. 198–199.

21 See Boyle 1976, pp. 27–40; Richard 1969, pp. 51–57; Schmieder 1994, pp. 89–91, 108–109. The Mongol intentions are apparent in the letters of the Ilkhans Hülegü (1262), Arghun (1289), and Öljeitü (1305) for instance; Haenisch 1949, pp. 220, 229–230; Meyvaert 1980, pp. 252–259.

22 Richard 1983, pp. 511–512.

23 See Jackson 1980, pp. 481–482, including footnotes. In the following I will enlarge on and modify the standpoints of Peter Jackson and J. J. Saunders; cf. Jackson 1980, pp. 482–483, 511–512; Saunders 1971, pp. 108, 114–115.

24 For the attitudes in Eastern Europe and Scandinavia, see Jordan 1979, p. 33; Richard 1983, pp. 184–185.

25 For the situation during the first crusade of Louis IX, see Strayer 1962, pp. 497–498, 505–506.

BIBLIOGRAPHY

Sources

Eudes de Châteauroux, 'Odonis episcopi Tusculani epistola ad Innocentium papam IV', in L. d'Achéry (ed.), *Spicilegium sive collectio veterum aliquot scriptorum qui in Galliae bibliothecis delituerant*. Editio altera, tomus III. Parisiis 1723, pp. 624–628.

Guillelmus de Nangis, 'Gesta sanctae memoriae Ludovici regis Franciae', in *RHG,* Vol. XX. Paris 1860, pp. 309–462.

E. Haenisch 1949, 'Zu den Briefen der mongolischen Il-Khane Argun und Öljeitü an den König Philipp den Schönen von Frankreich (1289 u. 1305)', *Oriens* 2, pp. 216–235.

Jean de Joinville, 'The Life of Saint Louis', in Joinville & Villehardouin, *Chronicles of the Crusaders*. Translated with an Introduction by M. R. B. Shaw. Harmondsworth 1980 (1963), pp. 161–353.

Jean Sarrasin, 'Les mesaiges que li Tartarinz envoierent au roi de France', in *Continuation de Guillaume de Tyr de 1229 a 1261*, in *RHC*, vol. II. Paris 1859, pp. 569–571.

Iohannes de Plano Carpini, 'Historia Mongalorum', edizione critica del testo latino a cura di E. Menestò, in Giovanni di Pian di Carpine, *Storia dei Mongoli*. Biblioteca del 'Centro per il collegamento degli studi medievali e umanistici nell'Università di Perugia' 1. Spoleto 1989, pp. 225–333.

Matthaeus Parisiensis, *Chronica majora*, vol. V, VI. H. R. Luard (ed.) Rerum Britannicarum medii aevi Scriptores, Rolls Series 57: 5–6. London 1880–1882.

Simon de Saint-Quentin, *Histoire des Tartares*. J. Richard (ed.), Documents relatifs a l'Histoire des Croisades publiés par l'Académie des Inscriptions et Belles-Lettres, VIII. Paris 1965.

P. Meyvaert 1980, 'An Unknown Letter of Hulagu, Il-Khan of Persia, to King Louis IX of France', *Viator* 11, pp. 245–259.

Vincentius Bellovacensis, *Speculum historiale*. Photomechanischer Nachdruck der Akademischen Druck- und Verlagsanstalt, Graz 1965, (1624).

Literature

T. T. Allsen 1987, *Mongol Imperialism. The Policies of the Grand Qan Möngke in China, Russia, and the Islamic Lands, 1251–1259*. Berkeley–Los Angeles–London.

G. A. Bezzola 1974, *Die Mongolen in abendländischer Sicht [1220–1270]. Ein Beitrag zur Frage der Völkerbegegnungen*. Bern–München.

T. S. R. Boase 1978, 'The History of the Kingdom', in T. S. R. Boase (ed.), *The Cilician Kingdom of Armenia*. Edinburgh–London, pp. 1–33.

J. A. Boyle 1976, 'The Il-Khans of Persia and the Princes of Europe', *Central Asiatic Journal* 20, pp. 25–40.

P. Crone 1989/1994, *Pre-industrial Societies*, Oxford UK–Cambridge USA.

S. Der Nersessian 1962, 'The Kingdom of Cilician Armenia', in R. L. Wolff & H. W. Hazard (ed.), *A History of the Crusades*. Vol. II, *The Later Crusades 1189–1311*. Philadelphia, pp. 630–659.

H. Franke & D. Twitchett (ed.) 1994, *The Cambridge History of China. Alien regimes and border states, 907–1368*. Vol. 6. Cambridge–New York–Oakleigh.

P. Jackson 1980, 'The Crisis in the Holy Land in 1260', *The English Historical Review* 95, pp. 481–513.

P. Jackson 1991, 'The Crusade Against the Mongols (1241)', *The Journal of Ecclesiastical History* 42, pp. 1–18.

S. Jagchid & P. Hyer 1979, *Mongolia's Culture and Society*. Boulder, Colorado.

W. C. Jordan 1979, *Louis IX and the Challenge of the Crusade. A Study in Rulership*. Princeton.

A. M. Khazanov 1983/1984, *Nomads and the Outside World*. Translated by J. Crookenden, with a Foreword by E. Gellner. Cambridge Studies in Social Anthropology 44. Cambridge.

P. Pelliot 1931–1932, 'Les Mongols et la Papauté. Chapitre II (suite)', *Revue de l'Orient chrétien* 28, pp. 3–84.

M. Purcell 1975, *Papal Crusading Policy. The Chief Instruments of Papal Crusading Policy and Crusade to the Holy Land from the fall of Acre 1244 to the final loss of Jerusalem 1291*. Studies in the History of Christian Thought, vol. XI. Leiden.

I. de Rachewiltz 1973, 'Some Remarks on the Ideological Foundations of Chingis Khan's Empire', *The Australian National University Department of Far Eastern History, Papers on Far Eastern History* 7, pp. 21–36.

P. Ratchnevsky 1983, *Činggis-Khan. Sein Leben und Wirken*, Münchener ostasiatische Studien, Band 32. Wiesbaden.

J. Richard 1969, 'The Mongols and the Franks', *Journal of Asian History* 3, pp. 45–57.

J. Richard 1983, *Saint Louis. Roi d`une France féodale, soutien de la Terra sainte*. Paris.

J. Richard 1986, 'La lettre du Connétable Smbat et les rapports entre Chrétiens et Mongols au milieu du XIIIème siècle', in D. Kouymjian (ed.), *Armenian Studies in memoriam Haig Berbérian*. Lisbon, pp. 683–696.

A. Ruotsala 2001, *Europeans and Mongols in the Middle of the Thirteenth Century: Encountering the Other*. Annales Academiae Scientiarum Fennicae; ser. Humaniora, tom. 314. Helsinki.

J. J. Saunders 1971, *The History of the Mongol Conquests*. London.

F. Schmieder 1994, *Europa und die Fremden. Die Mongolen im Urteil des Abendlandes vom 13. bis in das 15. Jahrhundert*, Beiträge zur Geschichte und Quellenkunde des Mittelalters, Band 16. Sigmaringen.

G. Strakosch-Grassmann 1893, *Der Einfall der Mongolen in Mitteleuropa in den Jahren 1241 und 1242*. Innsbruck.

J. R. Strayer 1962, 'The Crusades of Louis IX', in R. L. Wolff & H. W. Hazard (ed.) *A History of the Crusades*, vol. II, *The Later Crusades 1189–1311*. Philadelphia, pp. 487–518.

B. Szczésniak 1956, 'The Mission of Giovanni de Plano Carpini and Benedict the Pole of Vratislavia to Halicz', *The Journal of Ecclesiastical History* 7, pp. 12–20.

Index of Persons

311

Index of Place names